Programming the Web: An Introduction

Barrie Sosinsky
Valda Hilley

InformationTechnology

Mc Graw Hill **Technology Education**

Boston   Burr Ridge, IL   Dubuque, IA   Madison, WI   New York   San Francisco   St. Louis
Bangkok   Bogotá   Caracas   Kuala Lumpur   Lisbon   London   Madrid   Mexico City
Milan   Montreal   New Delhi   Santiago   Seoul   Singapore   Sydney   Taipei   Toronto

PROGRAMMING THE WEB: AN INTRODUCTION
Published by McGraw-Hill Technology Education, a business unit of The McGraw-Hill
Companies, Inc., 1221 Avenue of the Americas, New York, NY, 10020. Copyright © 2004 by The
McGraw-Hill Companies, Inc. All rights reserved. No part of this publication may be reproduced
or distributed in any form or by any means, or stored in a database or retrieval system, without
the prior written consent of The McGraw-Hill Companies, Inc., including, but not limited to, in
any network or other electronic storage or transmission, or broadcast for distance learning.

Some ancillaries, including electronic and print components, may not be available to customers
outside the United States.

This book is printed on acid-free paper.

1 2 3 4 5 6 7 8 9 0 DOC/DOC 0 9 8 7 6 5 4 3

ISBN   0-07-286605-5

Editor in chief: *Bob Woodbury*
Publisher: *Brandon Nordin*
Senior sponsoring editor: *Donald J. Hull*
Developmental editor: *Lisa Chin-Johnson*
Marketing manager: *Andy Bernier*
Media producer: *Greg Bates*
Senior project manager: *Jean Lou Hess*
Production supervisor: *Gina Hangos*
Lead designer: *Pam Verros*
Supplement producer: *Lynn M. Bluhm*
Senior digital content specialist: *Brian Nacik*
Cover design: *Pam Verros*
Interior design: *Pam Verros*
Typeface: *10/12 New Baskerville*
Compositor: *Black Dot Group*
Printer: *R. R. Donnelley*

Library of Congress Control Number: 2003114503

www.mhhe.com

McGraw-Hill Technology Education

At McGraw-Hill Technology Education, we publish instructional materials for the technology education market, in particular computer instruction in post–secondary education—from introductory courses in traditional four-year universities to continuing education and proprietary schools. McGraw-Hill Technology Education presents a broad range of innovative products—texts, lab manuals, study guides, testing materials, and technology-based training and assessment tools.

We realize that technology has created and will continue to create new mediums for professors and students to use in managing resources and communicating information to one another. McGraw-Hill Technology Education provides the most flexible and complete teaching and learning tools available as well as offers solutions to the changing world of teaching and learning. McGraw-Hill Technology Education is dedicated to providing the tools for today's instructors and students, which will enable them to successfully navigate the world of Information Technology.

- McGraw-Hill/Osborne—This division of The McGraw-Hill Companies is known for its best-selling Internet titles, Harley Hahn's *Internet & Web Yellow Pages*, and the *Internet Complete Reference*. For more information, visit Osborne at **www.osborne.com.**

- Digital Solutions—Whether you want to teach a class online or just post your "bricks-n-mortar" class syllabus, McGraw-Hill Technical Education is committed to publishing digital solutions. Taking your course online doesn't have to be a solitary adventure, nor does it have to be a difficult one. We offer several solutions that will allow you to enjoy all the benefits of having your course material online.

- Packaging Options—For more information about our discount options, contact your McGraw-Hill Sales representative at 1-800-338-3987 or visit our Web site at **www.mhhe.com/it**.

McGraw-Hill Technology Education is dedicated to providing the tools for today's instructors and students.

Preface

Overview

Programming the Web: An Introduction, a part of McGraw-Hill's Web Developer Series, is designed for the first course in a Web programming curriculum. It presents a technical introduction to the technologies and languages used to program the Web. The scope of the book will provide a foundation to meet the prerequisites for the more in-depth courses on particular languages that make up the Web programming curriculum.

Programming the Web: An Introduction differs from similar works in that it dedicates two chapters to teaching fundamental programming skills that are used in the majority of the languages covered. It also will go into enough detail on HTML, XML, Java, JavaScript, ASP, and Perl/CGI so that students have the exposure they need to be successful in the more in-depth courses later in the curriculum.

Author's Notes

The book is organized into five parts following a logical progression of the technologies and topics related to Web programming. Part One introduces and explains basic Web browser technologies such as HTML, XML, and CSS. Part Two deals with computer programming fundamentals and the application of programming languages to enhance the functionality of Web pages. Part Three presents programming constructs and syntax specific to JavaScript and VBScript, which are used to write programs to make Web pages dynamic and interactive. This section is designed to get readers recognizing, writing, and analyzing scripts. Part Four builds on everything readers have learned to this point by showing them how to put the knowledge to practical use. In this section, readers will trail through the building of Web pages implementing DHTML and using industry standard tools, Dreamweaver and FrontPage. Part Five shows the readers how to extend their Web pages by writing programs that interact with Web servers.

Following this order should instill confidence in the readers' ability to recognize, use, and analyze the basic technologies in Web programming. The level and scope of material is such that it gives readers enough exposure through explanations and examples to enable them to build, troubleshoot, and improve.

Part One

Part One covers the basic Web browser technologies.

Chapter 1. Internet Fundamentals

This chapter will help readers draw the relationship between the Web, a browser, and the technologies that sit behind it.

Chapter 2. Building a Web Page with HTML

This is an introduction to get readers recognizing and writing HTML. This chapter will build a foundation for making HTML documents accessible on a wide range of browsers.

Chapter 3. XML and XHTML

This chapter is an introduction to XML technologies. It presents the principles and use of XML (Extensible Markup Language) beginning with the concepts of tagging and markup, then moving on to a few advanced topics such as validation and presentation.

Chapter 4. Markup Transformations

This chapter introduces Cascading Style Sheets (CSS) as a simple mechanism for adding style (e.g., fonts, colors, spacing) to Web documents. The chapter begins with a quick introduction to CSS to acquaint readers with the reasoning behind CSS, what it is, and how it works.

Part Two

Part Two provides the programming fundamentals needed to work with the languages in the rest of the book.

Chapter 5. Web Programming: A Programmer's Perspective

This chapter discusses programming techniques and issues as they relate to the Internet and Web. It begins with a general introduction to the discipline of computer science to prepare the readers for learning to use the various programming languages introduced in this book and lead them through general techniques and important programming concepts, such as algorithms, data types, and data structures.

Chapter 6. Object Programming

To use an object-oriented language, students need to understand the underlying concepts before attempting to write code. This chapter helps readers to understand what an object is, what a class is, the relationship between objects and classes, and how objects use messages to communicate. The chapter begins by describing the concepts behind object-oriented programming and progress to show readers how to translate the concepts into code. The chapter contains some source code designed to give the readers exposure and to help them associate it with the concepts and terminology presented in the chapter.

Part Three

Part Three gets the readers recognizing, writing, and analyzing scripts.

Chapter 7. Client-Side Scripting with JavaScript

In this chapter, readers learn to create Web-based applications that run completely within a Web browser using JavaScript.

Chapter 8. Client-Side Scripting with VBScript

Readers learn to use or create VBScript variables, arithmetic and logical operators, built-in and custom functions, and conditional statements and loops, as well as understand variant subtypes. It's presented here because it is considered the preferred scripting language for Active Server Pages (ASP).

Part Four

Part Four extends the Web page with server-side programming.

Chapter 9. Understanding Dynamic HTML

Dynamic HTML is a combination of technologies: HTML or XML, JavaScript, DOM, and CSS. All of these technologies have been discussed in the earlier chapters. In this chapter, readers trail the process of creating Web pages that use DHTML.

Chapter 10. Beginning Active Server Pages

Chapter 11. Introduction to Java Applet Programming

Part Five

Part Five brings together the technologies and techniques from the first four parts and gets readers working with the technologies.

Chapter 12. CGI with Perl

The chapter leads readers through a quick primer on CGI in order to implement CGI scripting using Perl.

Chapter 13. Dynamic Action with Macromedia Dreamweaver MX

In this chapter, the readers will apply key object-oriented programming fundamentals presented in Chapter 6 and the Java programming language explained in this chapter. Readers learn to write small server-side applications (servlets).

Chapter 14. Creating Dynamic Web Pages with FrontPage

Appendix A: Creating a Virtual Directory

STUDENT CD

The accompanying Student CD contains all the code examples found throughout the chapters and exercises in the text, which is also available on the book's Web site.

Instructor's Resource Kit

The Instructor's Resource Kit is a CD-ROM containing the Instructor's Manual in MS Word, a Test Bank in both MS Word format and Computerized Brownstone test-generating software, and PowerPoint presentation slides.

Instructor's Manual

- Chapter learning objectives
- Overview of chapter
- Teaching tips and strategies
- Lecture notes
- Solutions to all QuickCheck Questions, Review Questions, and Exercises

Test Bank

The Test Bank, using Diploma Network Testing Software by Brownstone, contains 1,000 questions that are identified by the level of difficulty, which is clearly indicated for each question.

There are 100 questions per chapter. The Test Bank consists of 60 Multiple Choice and 40 True/False questions per chapter.

PowerPoint Presentation Slides

PowerPoint presentation slides are available as a lecture presentation program developed in Microsoft PowerPoint. These slides are developed to correspond to related text material and are available for every chapter to enhance class presentations of the text material.

Custom Web Site

http://www.mhhe.com/webdev/sosinsky

The course Web site includes a Student Center and an Instructor Center. For the Student Center, there are code examples from the text, answers to QuickCheck questions from the text, and additional multiple question exercises for every chapter. The Instructor Center has all the materials from the Instructor's Resource Kit and any or all updates, all of which are available for downloading.

Digital Solutions for Instructors and Students

PageOut

PageOut is our Course Web Site Development Center that offers a syllabus page, URL, Custom Web Site content, online quizzes, gradebook, discussion board, and an area for student Web pages. For more information, visit the PageOut Web site at www.pageout.net.

Acknowledgments

Our thanks to the McGraw-Hill team: Lisa Chin-Johnson, Dan Silverburg, and all the editors and production staff who worked so hard to get this book into shape, and to the academic reviewers and professional programmers who reviewed each chapter and offered many suggestions that made this a better textbook.

The McGraw-Hill staff offers their sincere appreciation and special thanks to Professor Ahmed Mesbah of the University of Toledo for his tireless help, important insights, diligence, patience, and valuable encouragement throughout the entire process.

Brief Contents

Contents

Internet Fundamentals

OBJECTIVES

1. Appreciate the scope of the Internet's impact on our everyday life.

2. Learn about the different components that make the Internet work.

3. Understand how standards, services, and protocols allow disparate hardware and software to work together.

4. Have a basic understanding of Internet architecture and addressing.

5. Be able to understand how the World Wide Web, Web browsers, and Web servers work.

INTRODUCTION

The **Internet** had its origins in American research and defense work of the 1970s and 1980s. The rise of the Internet in the 1990s once the system was released into the public domain will come to be seen as one of the great technological and sociological achievements of the modern era. In time it may have as profound an effect on civilization as the telephone had on communications, and perhaps may even rival the impact Guttenberg's 1450s invention of the moveable type printing press had on literacy. The Internet is still too young to fully gauge its impact. In 2003 it is estimated that more than 500 million people out of the 7 billion people living on this planet have access to the Internet worldwide, about 7 percent. The numbers are growing at an astonishing clip as entire countries' social systems are converted from paper to Web access.

When you are connected to the Internet, you are accessing the world's

*   Largest post office.
*   Greatest library.
*   Biggest store.

1

- Most powerful data transmission network.
- The preferred method for computers of one type to talk with computers of any other type.

In the very near future, you will be able to add to this list

- The world's largest classroom (or greatest university) through remote learning capabilities.
- The world's most powerful newspaper, magazine, TV, and radio carrier.
- The main portal (or view port) to your government, health care, and most service organizations.
- The transmission network of choice (indeed!) for nearly all applications written to use networked services.

It's easy to use superlatives when talking about the Internet, but it is very hard to determine where the technology is going to take us. In an era when homes, refrigerators, cars, and even perhaps your own personal physical self will be addressable over the Internet, the possibilities are truly astonishing.

For all of these capabilities, there is the never-ending requirement for trained programmers to create and improve the applications of tomorrow. In the 21st century, perhaps only biotechnology offers as bright a future as computer programming for the Web does.

Our goal in this chapter isn't to present you with the glorious (albeit brief) history of the Internet. Here you will learn about some of the fundamental principles required to make the Internet work, how the Internet and Internet applications are structured, and the role of programmers in developing new applications and maintaining existing ones. This chapter should give you some insight into how your programs must work in order to succeed, and why different programming languages or development systems are used in different areas of Internet technology.

Infrastructure

The Internet is just what its name implies—a network of networks; or to be more precise, a wide area network, or WAN. Nobody actually owns the Internet, although there are companies that own parts of it. Two government agencies, the Defense Advanced Research Projects Agency (DARPA) and the National Science Foundation (NSF), funded the creation of the original Internet network for research and military use. There were two motivations for the work. First, they wanted to establish a network that could allow computers of all types to talk with one another, as well as a means to connect from a terminal (or, as it turns out, a personal computer) to the various types of connected computers that projects relied on. The second motivation was to create a network that could survive a nuclear attack by being highly redundant.

The person most associated with conceptualizing the Internet's infrastructure and playing a pivotal role in its funding was DARPA's Director J. C. R. Licklider, who funded the initial work in 1963–64 and directed the group at Bolt, Beranek, and Newman in Cambridge, Massachusetts, that did the initial experiments in time sharing and networking. Prior to the fund DARPA gave out to universities, there wasn't a single university in the United States that even offered a Ph.D. in computer science.

The solution to both of these needs was to create a distributed network architecture that provided redundant pathways from one computer to another. A fabric topology was adopted, which is often referred to as the "Web." When one transmission point or pathway fails, data is routed to other paths—thus providing fault tolerance in case of system failures. Your brain uses a similar approach, a so-called neural network to create redundant and multiple pathways for the electrical transmission of information.

In order to make data redundant, the system uses what are called packets, bite-size chunks of data with headers that describe what the data belongs to, who's sending it, and who is the intended receiver. These packets are sent as a stream and will be rebroadcast by the source unless a signal is received from the recipient that the package was received. The recipient assembles the data from the collection of packets using the information they contain, and by validating the packets using error-checking algorithms. By adopting a packet-based approach, the Internet is able to successfully send large data files using a transmission medium that is intermittent and variable. Packets that don't arrive are retransmitted, perhaps traveling a different path, until the entire message can be assembled by the host. The "cloud" architecture of the Internet is illustrated in Figure 1.1.

The Internet can be broken down into the following fundamental parts:

- **Routers and switches. Routers,** such as the ones sold by Cisco (among others) are special-purpose computers that direct traffic in the form of data packets to their intended recipient. When one route is blocked or busy, routers choose another path using routing tables (both static and dynamic tables) and intelligent algorithms, thus ensuring that data traffic on the Internet is fault tolerant. You'll also find hubs or switches, bridges, and gateways on the Internet. *Hubs* or *switches* connect nodes without any routing or data translation abilities. *Bridges* are used to link different local area networks, or LANs, together. *Gateways* are a special type of bridge that also can do data translation—for example, turn a PC file into a Macintosh file.

- **Cabling backbone.** The fiber optic networks called *backbones* that carry much of the Internet traffic under our city streets or across the oceans

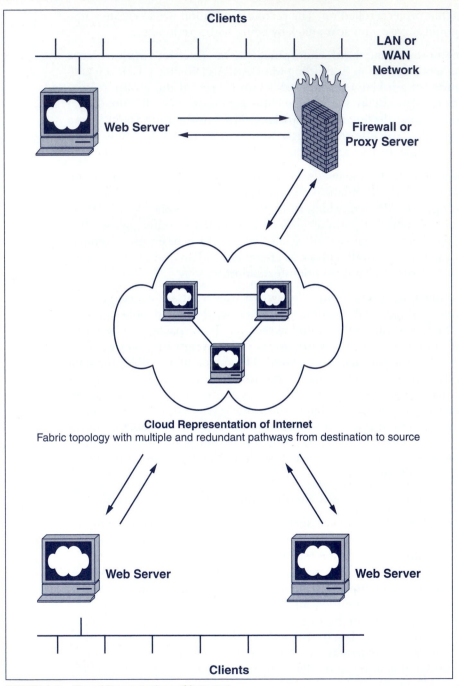

FIGURE 1.1   Cloud Presentation of Internet

The Internet uses a packet-switched fabric-type architecture that is highly redundant and fault tolerant. The multiple paths available from origin to destination make a specific path impossible to describe, so often the Internet infrastructure is portrayed as a "cloud."

and the satellites that circle our planet all contribute to the transmission of Internet traffic and are all owned by government agencies or large corporations.

A next generation version of the Internet backbone called *Internet2* (http://www.internet2.edu/) also has been funded and is in limited usage. It will link over 100 universities with a 2.4-gigabits-per-second network that is capable of, among other things, being able to transmit full-motion streaming video. Many people believe that the Internet2 will serve as the replacement for the current Internet.

- **Last mile connection.** The last mile connections are typically owned by phone and telecommunications companies, with hookups offered by *Internet service providers,* or ISPs (hosts). ISPs are companies that sell a monthly connection and related services to customers. AOL, MSN, Earthlink, and AT&T Worldnet are examples of service providers.

- **Name servers**. Several companies and government agencies own and operate the **name servers** that translate the Internet address (which for IPv4 are in the octet form ###.###.###.###) into friendly names like AOL.com or CNN.com, and vice versa. For example, CNN's Web site's address is 64.36.16.84. Each three-number set allows numbers up to 256. When you register a domain on the World Wide Web, you in a sense are renting an ownership interest in the Internet using a **registrar** that works with the InterNIC (a company that owns the registration database for .COM, .ORG, .NET, and others), which owns and administers the name servers. You are assigned an IP address, as well as a network type (A, B, C, or D), which determines how many nodes can be accommodated by your domain.

QuickCheck Questions

1. What happens when a router fails?
2. Who owns the Internet?

The Role of Standards

It's best to think of the Internet in terms of a set of standards or agreed-upon conventions. Those standards govern how nodes (points) on the Internet are addressed, what the data stream over the wires must look like, and how applications should behave in order to communicate with other applications. These standards are codified by working groups (most often international in scope) who accept proposals, examine their implications often by issuing requests for comments (RFCs) to which any interested party can respond, and draft and disseminate standards for people to follow in their work on the Internet. This sort of "peer" review process arises from the Internet's roots as a research tool for universities and the defense establishment.

The best known standards organizations are

1. The Internet Society (www.isoc.org), a nonprofit group that works on broad Internet use issues.

2. The Internet Engineering Task Force (IETF; www.ietf.org), which determines how different protocols or agreements are structured.

3. The World Wide Web Consortium (W3C; www.w3c.org), which develops the standards for Web applications and is based at MIT.

The principle behind a standards-based approach is to try and make disparate hardware, operating systems, and applications work together. Fundamental aspects of Internet behavior are nearly universally adopted. Thus, for example, all **browsers** (programs that can read HTML markup **tags** and compose a page based on the content) can read a simple text file with standard HTML tags like HEAD, BODY, and so forth. However, later submissions such as particular kinds of animation tags or certain kinds of Cascaded Style Sheets (a set of styles used in Web documents that were proposed by Microsoft) are always adopted by one browser or another. So what you see in Microsoft Internet Explorer won't necessarily be the same as what you see in Netscape Navigator.

All vendors observe what may be called the "Principle of Graceful Degradation." If a browser doesn't understand a particular tag or can't display the results of some external applet (small program or module), then the browser ignores that data or instruction and composes the page without it. At least that's how it's supposed to work, but, alas, browsers do crash sometimes from these incompatibilities.

Often there are specifications for what to do when a browser can't display something. When a browser is text based (as many of the early browsers on cell phones are now, and many of the early browsers on the Internet were), the ALT tag instructs the browser to display an alternative text instead of the graphics file that is referenced. We'll get further into this topic in the next chapter, but the important point to remember from this discussion is that you have to test your programs and code against different browsers to see that the functions you need are supported. It's an unfortunate fact, but many Web sites optimize for a particular browser or offer alternate sites. This practice is slowly going away as Microsoft Internet Explorer's market dominance is forcing other browser manufacturers to follow suit with features that that browser supports.

Services and Protocols

As already mentioned, the Internet uses a **packet-switching** architecture—and for good reason. If you are sending data over a connection that you can't count on being reliable, you need to send smaller chunks of data and have a means for determining that all of the data arrived correctly at the target from the source. When you send data traffic across the Internet, a **protocol** (or

Tech Tip

Web Resources
A good place to start out reading more about the Web and its development is the three sites mentioned here. In addition, you will find a list of resources that describe the history of the Internet at http://www.isoc.org/internet/history/.

Tech Tip

Web Resources
Remember when programming for the Internet that you should always test your Web sites and programs for their actions in at least Internet Explorer and Netscape Navigator. It's even prudent to test how your features will appear in previous versions of the browser. Don't assume everyone is running the latest and greatest browser. If your audience is using other browsers (like HotJava, for example), make sure you test on those as well.

agreed specification) called the **Transmission Control Protocol/Internet Protocol (TCP/IP)** is used. The Transmission Control Protocol (TCP) part forms the data into bite-size chunks called **packets** and the Internet Protocol (IP) part routes them to their intended address.

TCP specifies how large the packets should be (typically less than 1,500 characters), adds addressing information to the packet's header, and encapsulates the data in an envelope, along with the instructions necessary to have those packets be reassembled into the original data that was sent. Headers include sender and destination addresses, the Time-To-Live (TTL) that determines how long the packet should be kept, date and time of creation, and other factors. You see this kind of information in the headers of your email when they are displayed.

Error checking in the form of a checksum is included in each packet to determine if the packet arrived intact at its destination. It's assumed that some percentage of packets are going to be dropped or may be corrupted upon arrival, so the intended recipient will send a message back to the initiating source that a packet is missing; and when all the packets are assembled, the target will send a received signal to the source.

The software that receives and translates TCP/IP signals and commands is called a **socket,** or a TCP/IP stack. Sockets have a feature called **ports,** which are a specified numbered "channel" that a data transfer of a specific type may use to communicate. Ports are registered in a central database so that they may be widely used, leading to the so-called standard for each protocol called a "well known port." For HTTP that port is 80, and a full specification of a URL using only IP nomenclature (not friendly DNS names) often includes the port number as the last element (e.g., http://132.94.62.15:80). Port numbers can be reassigned or hidden. For example, Microsoft's Internet Security and Acceleration Server (ISA), which is a combination firewall and caching server, uses the 8080 port for its traffic, and does the appropriate translations and mappings.

Tech Tip

Well Known Ports
For a complete and current listing of well known port assignments, go to http://www.iana.org/assignments/port-numbers.

QuickCheck Questions

3. What is a packet?
4. What role does a socket play?

In many operating systems, TCP/IP is added as a network component and operates as a system service, but for high-performance network-attached filers, TCP/IP stacks are embedded in a custom silicon chip called an ASIC for faster performance. The Windows version of the socket is called Winsock, while for the Macintosh it is MacTCP.

The TCP/IP traffic flows from your computer through your network card for a LAN, cable modem, or DSL (Direct Subscriber Lines). Your network card's driver is the software that interfaces between the computer and the network. For modem (phone) connections, the two software protocols that are used to translate the Internet's TCP/IP protocol are the Point-to-Point (PPP) and the Serial Line Internet Protocol (SLIP). Whenever possible you should use the latest versions of this software for better performance. By the way, you can connect to the Internet without using TCP/IP, PPP, and SLIP, but you won't be able to use the World Wide Web if you do so.

While for many people the World Wide Web is the Internet, there are many services that run on the Internet. One of the oldest tools on the Internet is the Telnet service. Telnet lets your computer emulate a terminal and connect to and control another remote computer. When you use Telnet (which is a text-only service), you get a real feeling for what it was like to use the Internet to connect to hosts prior to the days when the Web existed. The service often offers not only commands but text-based menus. Other services you will encounter are the **File Transfer Protocol (FTP),** which is widely used; Gopher; WAIS; Archie; UseNet news services; a variety of mail services such as the Simple Mail Transfer Protocol (SMTP), Post Office Protocol (POP), and IMAP; in addition to HTML. HTML is the means used to describe Web pages to browsers.

You will find a variety of forms of HTML, of which SHTML (a secure version) sends encrypted traffic over the net to secure servers. You know when you are using SHTML because you see an address shtml:// appear in your browser's address bar, and a lock icon in the status bar. Each of these services and protocols is assigned a specific port with which it can communicate to and from a Web server.

Internet Architecture

The original architecture of the Internet was called the **client/server** model—something also called a two-tiered architecture. A server is the computer that runs an application (like a Web server) and stores and processes data, while the client requests the services of the server, receives data, and displays it. In its most common form, a PC or terminal serves the role of a client, and a more powerful computer plays the role of a server.

Web Servers

Application servers that serve up resources based on HTTP requests and transfers are called hosts or Web servers. Most of the time Web servers serve up Web pages that are displayed in a browser. The most widely deployed Web server is APACHE, an open-source product that is programmed by the general community and managed by a committee. Versions of APACHE are available for all platforms. APACHE is actually a play on words, derived from "a patch-y server." The Web server that probably is responsible for the most traffic on the Web is Microsoft's Internet Information Server or IIS. There are many different Web servers on the market today including Sun's iPlanet Web server (derived from Netscape's Enterprise server), Zeus, and others that are purely Web servers. However, any application can add an HTTP stack and serve up Web pages, so you will find Web servers embedded in applications like FileMaker Pro and Oracle.

Web servers do more than just handle HTTP requests; they also send requests to run scripts such as Perl or Common Gateway Interface (CGI) scripts to the applications that can handle them. These program calls run applets that perform a variety of tasks such as database record retrieval, forms processing and posting, and animation. For example, many of the add-in components that are native in Microsoft's FrontPage application require that the request programs (FrontPage services) be loaded on the server. Web servers also provide address handling, security, and a variety of system configurations such as bandwidth throttling (controlling the amount of bandwidth available to a client or application), path selection, and so forth.

Keep in mind that the notion of client and server is turned on its head when UNIX X-servers are discussed. In X-architecture, the PC or terminal is the server, while the application running on the X-server is the client.

This simple Internet architectural model has over time been significantly modified in a number of ways. Since the processing demands of many users' client systems could overwhelm even the most powerful server, programmers have the option of structuring programs so that they use either server-side or client-side processing—or more often a combination of the two. When you add components to your browser—ActiveX components, Java applets (that use a client's Java Virtual Machine), Flash components, and so forth—you are enabling client-side processing. The addition of server components such as CGI scripts, Perl, and other programs enables server-side processing.

Multi-Tiered Architectures

While a two-tiered architecture serves well for many Internet applications, particularly ones with small transactions, it is poorly suited to multi-step processes where an interruption in the connection could put the entire data transaction in jeopardy. Consider what happens in a travel reservation system such as Travelocity.com or Expedia.com when you request a flight. You are in the process of paying for the flight when your connection dies. In a two-tier system, the transaction would be voided (since it wasn't completed), and the heavy-duty Oracle, DB2, or SQL Server database that underpins the system would be forced to ROLLBACK the transaction to the system's previous state in order to release the seats for sale to someone else. ROLLBACK is a SQL command that throws away any unfinished transaction(s) and returns your database to a previous state. To make this system more resilient and efficient (and not lose the sale), application developers have adopted a three-tier architecture with the following layers:

- Presentation layer. The Presentation layer takes the role of the client, requesting services and data, displaying results, and accepting input from the user.

- Business Logic layer. In this layer are transaction or messaging servers (often called "middleware") that store the transaction and its state and maintain and apply rules that establish the validity of the transaction.
- Data layer. The Data layer contains the application servers that READ and WRITE the data to storage.

The three-tiered architecture is illustrated in Figure 1.2.

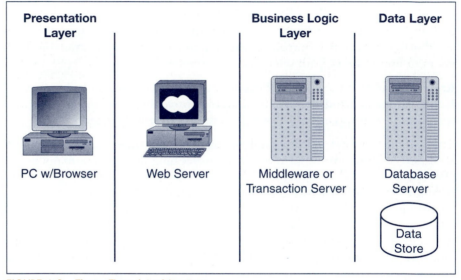

FIGURE 1.2   Three-Tiered Architecture
A three-tiered architecture allows transactions to be better processed when a connection is intermittent or transient.

In really large systems, the three-tiered model can be extended into an *n*-tiered system with multiple middle layers. Often programmers find themselves writing software for one of these layers or another. Examples of applications that run in each of these layers are a browser on a client for the Presentation layer, IBM or Microsoft Transaction Server for the Business Logic layer, and an enterprise database like Oracle as the backend Data layer.

Returning to our example of a flight purchase, when you initiate the reservation, the transaction is stored on a messaging or transaction server. Should you lose your connection, the transaction is secure. When the connection is regained, you are logged back into the transaction server, where you pick up your partially completed transaction and proceed. Essentially the *n*-tiered model eliminates the need for the client to directly access the server with a reliable or persistent connection.

QuickCheck Questions

5. How can you tell that you are using a secure HTML transfer protocol?

6. Why would a three-tiered architecture be useful to a messaging application?

Addressing

The Internet relies on a highly specified system for naming nodes, collections of nodes (domains), resources, and the means of accessing those resources. All of these addressing requirements are tightly specified by the standards bodies mentioned earlier in this chapter, and are published as part of a highly public vetting process. The IP (Internet) protocol is responsible for how nodes are addressed and a variety of security and data integrity services; so as we transition from IPv4 to IPv6, new capabilities are added. The TCP (Transmission Control Protocol) specifies how packets are formed and assembled, and how addresses are included into transmission. To begin with though, let's make the connection on how addresses are translated into friendly names, and how addresses are doled out. The net result of all of this is that resources on the Web are uniquely defined, identified, and accessible.

Domain Naming Services

The Internet Protocol version 4 specifies that Internet addresses are in the octet form ###.###.###.###, where each ### or octet can run from 0 to 255 (2^8). Thus www.cnn.com is 64.236.16.116, www.yahoo.com is 64.58.76.179, www.ebay.com is 216.33.156.119, and so forth. What an amazing chore it would be if we actually had to remember these numbers, as the numbers are essentially meaningless. So in order to use friendly names, the Internet uses a system called the **Domain Name System,** or **DNS.** With DNS, powerful *name servers* (called root servers) run a database that maps addresses to friendly names. Each domain extension such as .COM (commercial), .EDU (education), .GOV (government), .ORG (organization), .CA (Canada), .UK (United Kingdom), .BIZ, .NAME, and even .TV (for the Pacific island nation of Tuvalu) has its own name servers.

If users had to query the root name server every time they needed to translate a friendly name, the Internet would only be able to handle a small fraction of the traffic it does now. To improve DNS performance, DNS servers are placed throughout the Internet, at ISPs, for example, and on local area networks and recent requests and their responses are cached (that is, stored for later use). If your local DNS server doesn't have the answer, then it passes the request on up the line. Caching, as it turns out, is a common technique for enhancing Internet performance. You'll find cached Internet files on your computer (for Windows the cache is located by default at `C:\Documents and Settings\ <Profilename>\Local Settings\Temporary Internet Files`), on your local Internet access point (proxy server, firewall, or gateway), and even at your ISP. Large sites such as CNN.com use caching services like Akamai to replicate their data throughout the world.

While each address or node on the Internet is unique, the DNS friendly name system is organized into a hierarchical structure. When you register a domain with a registrar such as Register.com, say WebProgrammer.com, that domain is assigned an IP address. If you create additional addresses within your domain they would be named WebProgrammer.com/service, WebProgrammer.com/support, WebProgrammer.com/accounting, and so on. These second-level domain names can refer to real servers or computers, with or without a unique IP address, or they can be virtual subdomains. As you descend the hierarchy, you create addresses such as WebProgramming.com/accounting/receivables. In some instances you will see addresses of the type accounting.WebProgrammer.com that are mapped to the same subdomain.

To be really precise, the IP address that is assigned to a computer or system isn't actually associated with the computer itself. The address is assigned to the network interface, which in most instances is a network interface card (NIC) or a networking chip on your computer's motherboard. The essential distinction becomes important in computers that are multi-homed such as proxy servers, firewalls, gateways, and routers. A firewall may have two (dual-homed) or more network interfaces. One interface communicates with your internal LAN, while the other interface communicates with the outside world (usually the Internet). Both interfaces have very different addresses, and both may be running different protocols, in essence providing protocol isolation that makes it hard for hackers to penetrate inside your network.

Uniform Resource Locators

Not only is each numeric address on the Internet unique, but every document, file, or resource referenced on the Internet has a unique address referred to as the **uniform resource locator** or **URL.** A URL starts with the protocol that is used to connect to that Internet service, followed by the domain name, server (optional), and the path to the resource, finally followed by the name of the resource. Resources can be files, CGI (Common Gateway Interface) programs, Java applets (also programs), graphic files, and other things. A well-formed URL and its components are shown in Figure 1.3.

Consider the following URLs:

* http://www.nytimes.com/pages/world/index.html. This URL uses the **HyperText Transfer Protocol (HTTP)** to view information in the domain NYTIMES.COM on the COM name server. In the WORLD subfolder within the PAGES folder, the resource referenced is the INDEX.HTML file. This is an example of a static Web page, and the file INDEX.HTML (or HTM for Windows) is the default page for that folder. Static Web pages are pages that always contain the same data, while dynamic Web

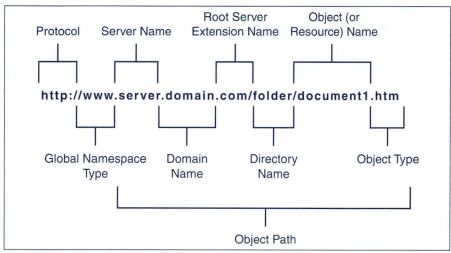

FIGURE 1.3   The Parts of a Well-Formed URL

pages are pages that change based on the user, client, or data submitted. If you enter http://www.nytimes.com, you are taken automatically to the INDEX.HTML page in the top-level folder. Keep in mind that folders could also be servers and may not necessarily refer to a hierarchy of directories in a real file system. Thus, the location of .../pages/world/... might be on one server, while /pages/national... might be on another server.

- http://www.here-now.org/archives.asp. This URL uses the HyperText Transfer Protocol to view information in the domain HERE-NOW.ORG of the ORG name server to reach a page called ARCHIVES. The suffix .ASP refers to an Active Server Page, which is a page composed on the fly using Microsoft's dynamic page specification. ASP and other dynamic page generation programming technologies are described in much more detail later in this book. Dynamic pages are used to query databases for current data or customized data and display that data on a browser or Web page.

- ftp://ftp.microsoft.com/. This URL uses the File Transfer Protocol to reference Microsoft's FTP site. FTP is a faster data transfer protocol used for file transfer. It references a hierarchical display of folders and files. Many FTP sites are viewable in part or as a whole as a GUEST with no password required. However, most FTP sites require logins in order to access specific areas.

- barries@business.earthlink.net. You probably recognize this as an email address. The first part, BARRIES, is the username, and after the "at" symbol comes the server name (BUSINESS), followed by the domain EARTHLINK.NET. More commonly, the server is omitted and you see an address that looks like barries@earthlink.net.

Network Types

IP addresses are assigned on the basis of the size of the enterprise and its purpose. These network sizes are described as Class A, Class B, or Class C. There are Class D and Class E networks, but they aren't assigned externally to organizations on the Internet.

The IPv4 numbering scheme is a 32-bit address, and the different classes break down as follows:

* Class A: nnn.###.###.###
* Class B: nnn.nnn.###.###
* Class C: nnn.nnn.nnn.###,

where nnn are fixed numbers and ### are variable numbers in the range of 0 to 255. Since the first three numbers are always assigned, you can tell which class the network is by the value of the first numbers. Class A networks are found in the range 0 to 127; Class B within 128 and 191; and Class C are found between 192 and 223. More importantly, the capacity of a Class A network is 16 million addresses, that of a Class B network is over 65,000 addresses, and Class C has 256 addresses (although only 255 are assignable).

Really large networks such as AOL, MSN, AT&T Worldnet, CompuServe; large companies such as IBM and Microsoft; and hosting services and telecommunication giants such as Earthlink and AT&T are assigned Class A addresses.

DHCP

If you examine IPv4 addresses, you will notice that there are one billion possible *static IP addresses* that can be assigned. The highest number possible is 999,999,999,999, while the lowest number is 000,000,000,000. One billion addresses seemed like an unimaginably large number to the researchers who first developed the Internet, but in an age when even toasters may be on the Internet along with all of China, getting a static IP address for your computer from an ISP is getting increasingly difficult and expensive. And, of course, there are many addresses that are reserved for special uses and aren't available for assignment.

To get around the problem of limited fixed addresses a system of internal routing was created using what started out as a HOSTS file. The routing server has a static IP address (typically), and the administrator assigns temporary or dynamic IP addresses from a reserved pool of available addresses by entering them as records (lines) in a `HOSTS` text file along with their friendly name to clients. You can still find the `HOSTS` file in use in UNIX systems, and it's even squirreled away inside Windows' system folder (`C:\WINDOWS\SYSTEM32\DRIVERS\ETC`). The `HOSTS` file stores the friendly name of a computer and its internal IP address taken from a range of addresses that are "private" addresses and can never be assigned on the Internet by convention. You add, delete, and modify records in the `HOSTS` file by editing its text as new computers are brought online and others are retired. As you can imagine, once a network grows beyond a certain size, managing the `HOSTS` file becomes a terrific bother.

A system known as the **Dynamic Host Configuration Protocol,** or **DHCP,** automates what the `HOSTS` file did manually. DHCP is a network broadcast service that will automatically assign dynamic IP addresses from a pool and manage how long those addresses can be used (the length of the leases). When your computer connects to a network that uses DHCP, it issues a DHCPDISCOVER broadcast to find a DHCP server. DHCP server(s) will then issue a DHCPOFFER packet with an available IP address and the IP address of the server. Your computer will select an appropriate DHCP server and send back a DHCPREQUEST packet. Finally, a DHCPPACK packet confirms the address and establishes the lease. If you connect to your ISP by modem and have "Automatically Obtain an IP Address" selected (a dynamic IP address), you'll probably see a new IP address every time you log onto your service. For network-assigned addresses, your lease might run a few days, a few weeks, or a few months depending upon what your network administrator sets.

The World Wide Web

Most of us are familiar with the **World Wide Web (WWW)** and have worked with it in our daily work. The Web is a relatively new part of the Internet that offers a means of identifying and accessing data anywhere. A **hypertext** link can point to a binary file, a document, a graphics file, a location in a document, and almost any object that a computer program or file system can describe in any location. The World Wide Web's hypertext address space "virtualizes" location so that you don't need to be aware of where the information actually is stored, only how to reference its location.

The founders of the World Wide Web hoped that, as the Web was generally adopted, it would come to play a role in the way people lived and worked. Although most visualized that it would provide access to data, few would have guessed that the Web could store the state of transactions both online and locally (for example, as cookies), and that that state information could be used to tailor the interaction of the Web for a user in very powerful ways.

A Brief History of the Web

To many people the World Wide Web, or just simply "the Web," is synonymous with the Internet. While the Internet has its roots in the 1970s when the work on packet-switching networks was being done, the Web as an invention is really only a dozen years old. That doesn't mean that the idea of a World Wide Web wasn't conceptualized earlier on. In the 1960s Ted Nelson first discussed the concept of links, hypertext, and hyperspace, and described how links could be made to resources leading to a new kind of educational or referential resource where the reader need not perform a sequential read in order to use the material effectively. Nelson further made the analogy to how the human mind works and learns, and to a new concept—electronic books. Nelson's contribution is more fully described at http://www.iath.virginia.edu/elab/hfl0155.html.

Nelson's work was highly regarded and launched several efforts to create a hypertext system with a global namespace. One such effort (of many) was started at the University of Minnesota and named Gopher.

Most people credit the British researcher Tim Berners-Lee with the creation of the World Wide Web. Berners-Lee, who is now the 3Com Founders Professor at the Laboratory for Computer Science (LCS) at the Massachusetts Institute of Technology (MIT), also chairs the World Wide Web Consortium, a steering committee for the development of the Web. Berners-Lee was a physics researcher in 1989 at the CERN European Particle Physical Laboratory when he proposed a global hypertext address space where information could be referenced by what was originally called a "Universal Document Identifier" (from which the URL is derived), and the information could be fetched using his and his coworkers' HyperText Transfer Protocol.

The Internet has more services than just simply the Web, but the Web has become far and away the most important part of the Internet. The vast majority of the programming jobs you will find that are Internet-related are jobs that program applications or services for the Web.

Browsers

Berners-Lee went on in 1990 to create a program called WorlDwidEweb, which was a graphical (point and click) hypertext editor for the NeXT UNIX workstation. He then wrote a Web server and released both into the public

Tech Tip

Web Resources
Tim Berners-Lee's home page at www.w3.org/People/Berners-Lee/ is a good source of reference links to Web resources.

domain in the summer of 1991. Also released at that point was the specification for UDIs, HyperText Markup Language (HTML), and HyperText Transfer Protocol (HTTP), which was put on the first server (info.cern.ch) to promote its adoption. The aforementioned server is no longer online, but CERN's address is http://public.web.cern.ch/public/, with information about the Web found at http://public.web.cern.ch/public/about/achievements/www/www.html. An account of his work also may be found in his book *Weaving the Web,* by Tim Berners-Lee with Mark Fischetti (Harper San Francisco; hardback: ISBN: 0062515861).

The World Wide Web really took off when the next generation of browsers such as Erwise, Cello, Viola, and Mosaic began to appear and capture the general public's imagination. The early browsers provided hypertext links to documents, some basic page composition (headings, lists, and text formatting, for example), but no images. Mosaic, developed at the University of Illinois's supercomputer center (www.ncsa.uiuc.edu) by Marc Andressen in 1993, added images and more page composition features and is generally regarded as having started the race to develop the dominant Web browser.

There were a number of commercial Web browsers under development in 1994 when Jim Clark (one of the original founders of Silicon Graphics workstations) joined with Andressen to form Mosaic Communications. By 1995 Mosaic had changed its name to Netscape and its Mozilla logo to the current Netscape stars logo, and released Netscape 1.1, followed by 1.2 for Windows 95. Netscape popularized the World Wide Web beyond the rarefied halls of science by adding many of the HTML extensions that made page composition more powerful and Web pages more attractive that we take for granted today. It would be difficult to underestimate the impact of Netscape; by the summer of 1995, the company owned more than 80 percent of the entire browser market. Netscape Navigator 2 in March 1996 was the second seminal product introduced by Netscape and added frames, Java, JavaScript, and the plug-ins extensible component architecture, while Navigator 3, introduced in August 1996, added background colors in tables, additional formatting options, frame borders, spacers, ARCHIVES, and APPLET elements.

In 1995 Microsoft entered the Web browser market by introducing Internet Explorer as part of its Plus package and began a two-year marketing and technology battle in what would come to be called in the trade press the "Browser Wars." By 1997 Microsoft had bundled Internet Explorer in the Windows operating system for free, and by 1998 had become the dominant browser and market leader in terms of client usage. Navigator was a commercial product requiring a paid license, which placed Netscape at a disadvantage. This battle was in large part responsible for the antitrust action filed against Microsoft by 18 states and the District of Columbia during the Clinton administration that has recently been settled by an agreement with Microsoft and the Justice Department to make it easier for other vendors to become the default application and for OEMs (original equipment manufacturers) to modify the Windows desktop.

In Figure 1.4a, we have shown the home page for the http://www.cnn.com/ site. You may use the **View | Source** option of Internet Explorer's menu to see the source code that was received and rendered by the browser. Figure 1.4b

FIGURE 1.4A   Internet Explorer Rendering of CNN.com's Web Site
a. Graphical display of CNN.com's home page.

shows a partial listing of the source code. Observe and compare the graphical display of the Web page (Figure 1.4a) with the source code (Figure 1.4b). You will see that most of the source code is HTML, but many other external capabilities are also called.

Browsers have become multifunctional, incorporating mail programs, graphics rendering, file format translation, data and code interpreters (XML, for exam-

FIGURE 1.4B Internet Explorer Rendering of CNN.com's Web Site
b. Underlying source code view of CNN.com's Web site. What you see is that most of the code is HTML, but many other external capabilities are called, such as Java applets.

ple), and more. Given that browsers are also extensible, Netscape first and then Microsoft have built a whole suite of products around their browser. Today there is the distinct possibility that operating systems will play a supporting role to browsers, a possibility that Microsoft was forced to defend against in the marketplace by their development of Internet Explorer and that browser's strong attachment to the Windows operating system. On Windows, HTML is one of the formats in which you can save Microsoft Office files. The Active Desktop on Windows also lets you have ActiveX components on your desktop that will actively display stock tickers, the weather, and Web pages without your browser running.

Microsoft has the dominant position in the marketplace in Windows and a majority usage on the Macintosh, and does not compete in the UNIX and Linux marketplace. Netscape Navigator is in second place based on its majority usage on UNIX systems and a sizable percentage of Macintosh users.

QuickCheck Questions

12. Who was credited with popularizing the concept of hypertext?

13. Why are browsers so important?

Portable Languages

Another very important development in the history of the Web has involved the development of portable languages to support multiplatform programming. This is best exemplified by Sun's introduction of its Java programming language in 1991 and the JavaScript development scripting language. Java was the result of a development effort aimed at creating a language that could work with all kinds of small portable devices. It was adapted to the Web, where its ability to create programs you could "write once, run anywhere" was seen to be an important advantage in an environment meant to support multiple and disparate operating systems. With Java you install a core instruction kernel for a particular operating system called a Java Virtual Machine or JVM. Any Java applet or program that runs on that platform calls the services of the JVM and will not operate if it doesn't find those services.

The "Green Project," as it was initially called, developed as a demonstration on an interactive, hand-held device controller with an animated touch screen the called *7, or "Star Seven." The name arises from the feature on the Sun phone system that lets you answer your phone from any extension. Sun tried to apply this technology to TV set-top boxes and built a demo called First-Person—but this type of interactive TV was about 12 years early to market. So Sun set about looking for other areas where Java could be used, and the Internet was a natural choice. A detailed history of the development of Java may be found at http://java.sun.com/features/1998/05/birthday.html.

Sun's team built WebRunner, a Mosaic clone, a browser that came to be called HotJava, which is still bundled with the Solaris operating system, and was able to demonstrate some impressive multimedia technologies. Sun released Java into the public domain in 1995, and eventually the capabilities of Java caught the attention of Netscape, who included it in Navigator in 1995. Eventually the entire industry licensed the Java Virtual Machine, including IBM, Apple, and Microsoft. Java has spawned not only a scripting language, but the Java Development Kit (JDK), the JavaBeans distributed application architecture, thousands of servlets, tens of thousands of applets, Java Foundation Classes (an object model), the JavaOS for Business, and, most importantly, a generation of very capable Java-based applications that are now the standard method for programming cross-platform multi-OS applications.

Microsoft has always had a love/hate relationship with Java, primarily because the company saw it as a threat to their core operating system business. After all, why program applications for Windows when you can create applications for browsers and have these applications run everywhere? But Microsoft was in a quandary. They needed Java to fit into network and enterprise-computing environments, but they also had in-house technologies that they wanted to promote. For example, Microsoft's Visual Basic has five million programmers, and the company wanted those programmers to be able to create Internet applications. Microsoft also has a different object model called the Common Object Model, or COM. Microsoft has promoted COM as a programming model, and components written with the COM model are called ActiveX components. Microsoft first extended COM across the network as DCOM, or Distributed COM, and more recently to their initiative for the development of Web services.

The net (so to speak) result of all of this is that Microsoft created extensions of Java to support their technologies, making it difficult for many Java applets to run properly on the Windows platform. Sun, who licenses Java, accused Microsoft of violating the Java license. After litigation, Microsoft was found in violation of their Java license and forced to pay a fine. But the final result seems to be that Microsoft is moving away from Java. In the next big step, Web services, a portable programming language, is seen to play a pivotal role. Microsoft's Web services program is dubbed .NET (pronounced "Dot Net"), and for the programming framework that Microsoft has built, they have introduced a new language called C# (pronounced "See Sharp") that builds on the work of Java.

HTML: The Language of the Web

The HyperText Markup Language, or HTML, is the method used to specify page composition on the Web. At least, that is the way HTML started out. As you will see in the next chapter, and subsequent chapters, HTML has picked up tags that let you do much, much more with your pages than just simple formatting and page layout. HTML uses a subset of SGML, the Standardized General Markup Language. We won't talk much about SGML in this book, although not only is HTML based on it, but XML (eXtensible Markup Language) is as well. XML, as you will find out later in Chapter 3, is becoming important for database Web transactions and for data and document transfers. SGML is an international standard markup "language" that lets you define in a text file different parts of a document.

I put the word "language" in quotes because if you ask any hard-core programmers, they will let you know in no uncertain terms that HTML isn't really a programming language. And in a sense they are right. When you think of a well-specified programming language, you think in terms of using different logic functions, defining variables of different data types, error checking, and other features that aren't really part of HTML (or SGML or

XML for that matter). HTML contains a set of instructions on how to compose a page. You can see the underlying HTML code by selecting the View Source command in Internet Explorer or its equivalent in other browsers. The Source view is what you would see in an HTML editor or in a Web site composition tool, and represents the code or instructions necessary to compose the Web page.

If you browse an HTML document, you will find a variety of tags using the following syntax:

```
<OpeningTag>...stuff...</ClosingTag>
```

Sometimes it's hard to find the closing tag because it's a long way away from the opening tag: for example, the `<BODY>...</BODY>` tags. Also, although it's good programming practice to use both opening and closing tags, not all tags require their ending tag. An example would be the `<BR>` or Break tag. However, since XHTML demands well-formed tags (both opening and closing pairs in the right precedence or sequence), we always write code that conforms to this practice.

In practical terms, HTML's files (which take an HTM extension for PC files and usually take an HTML extension for Macintosh files) are a lot like the Adobe Page Description Language or PDL files that the Acrobat Reader reads. Both are readable text files; that is, you can open either file type using the Windows Notepad, Macintosh TextEdit, or UNIX Text Editor (or vi, the Visual Editor). Underlying PDL is the Postscript graphics programming language, which is a very complete graphics manipulation environment, while HTML relies on other programming languages to code specific functionality.

HTML became important because it was chosen as the method used to display pages in a class of software applications that came to be called browsers that run on client systems. The applications on which pages are served up to browsers on clients are now referred to as Web servers. You can have large powerful computers running as Web servers, or have a personal Web server on your own desktop such as Microsoft Personal Web Services that allows a much smaller degree of connectivity in peer-to-peer computing networks.

HTML has been continually expanded and extended over time, adding things such as Cascading Style Sheets, or CSS. In addition to different specifications of the standard, you will see technologies like Dynamic HTML or DHTML used for animation effect or changing a Web page on the fly and eXtensible Markup Language, or XML, which is used for document-based data transfers. DHTML is a collection of technologies that can use the Document Object Model, or DOM, CSS, along with client-side scripting languages to animate objects on a Web page. You'll learn about these technologies further in chapters to come.

Tech Tip

Parsers

The part of a browser that "reads" HTML is called a *parser*. The parser is responsible for recognizing tags, checking for the tags' elements, and implementing the instructions. Parsers have rules that determine which tags to implement first and in what order (called *precedence*). Each succeeding version of your browser improves on the previous version's parser, both adding functionality as well as optimizing performance. Not only do some browsers have HTML parsers, but they might include other parsers such as XML parsers as well.

QuickCheck Questions

14. What happens if you don't use a closing HTML tag to match the opening tag?

15. How do you view the underlying HTML in a browser?

The Web Browser: Your Window on the Web

Web browsers work by reading a text file containing markup instructions. While you can open any text file in a browser, only files with the file extension HTML or HTM that have been associated with a browser application will automatically be opened. Your browser uses the instructions contained in the tags to compose a page and display that page inside a browser window. Not only does a browser read the HTML file to display the text it contains, it also

- Formats the text.
- Adds heading, lists, and tables and links to resources or objects located elsewhere.
- Displays images (which are downloaded files), most commonly in the form of JPEG or GIF image files that reference a URL in another location.
- Runs scripts or small programs written in JavaScript, VBScript, Pearl, CGI, and a variety of other scripting languages (which are described in subsequent chapters in this book).
- Calls small programs that have been added to the browser's plug-in architecture (often called helper applets). An example of a helper applet would be when your browser uses the Adobe Acrobat Reader plug-in to open a PDF file.
- Calls external programs used to provide additional capabilities. External program calls can display an independent object in a browser frame such as a 3-D interactive visualization of a car with its component parts; or let you hear or listen to a video and audio stream in Real Audio, Quick-Time, Windows Media Player, or a host of other programs.

All of these actions are instructions based on the HTML tags and the information that is embedded inside them.

An HTML file doesn't contain the images, scripts, or programs defined in the appropriate tags. When a resource is required, your browser makes a request for the object at its URL (uniform resource locator), most often using the HyperText Transfer Protocol (HTTP). To optimize network performance, first your browser's local cache is checked for the object, then your local server, and then your ISP's server; finally, the request goes out to the actual location of the site to do the data transfer. Caching is where you dedicate a portion of either your memory or disk space to recently downloaded information.

It is a very powerful method for boosting performance because your browser fetches the data from RAM or disk with none of the latency or lag time associated with downloading that information from the Internet.

Many browsers support other protocols besides HTTP. The second most common transfer protocol supported by browsers is the File Transfer Protocol, or FTP. FTP is a much more efficient method for uploading and downloading files than HTTP; and although browsers can perform FTP transfers, they aren't quite as fast as the FTP transfer utilities that you can find. To get a look at an FTP site in your browser, go to ftp://ftp.sun.com/ to view Sun's FTP site (shown in Figure 1.5). FTP sites often provide read-only or limited access to their sites as a guest (no password) until you log in as a specific user.

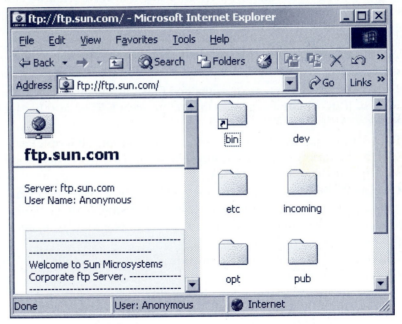

FIGURE 1.5　An FTP Site

Browsers also often display and use FTP sites. Here is Sun's site displayed in Internet Explorer.

Browsers essentially paint your screen in an order that is optimized to put the fastest, easiest-displayed information on your screen first. Other information that must be fetched is rendered later. If you have ever watched a browser display a page on a very slow computer, you can readily assess how a browser goes about its business. First, elements that the browser can render without outside resources are painted on the screen: borders, frames, and text. Then as resources such as images start to become available, they are painted one after another. So small image files like GIF representations of buttons in a toolbar might paint in first; larger images like photographs would appear next; and if there is something that requires calculations, is large, or is accessed over a slow connection, that appears last.

To improve browser rendering speed, Web site developers spend a lot of time optimizing their pages, reducing file sizes and the number of colors (color levels), or using special tricks like interlaced GIF files. An interlaced GIF (Graphic Image File) file is a bit-mapped (paint type) file that is described in successive chunks. GIF files are built up one pass at a time as additional lines are drawn, appearing to become better resolved over time. This technique and file format, first developed by America Online, gives the viewer the opportunity to see a low-resolution image that gives them the idea of the content, and thus speeds up the decision to move onto another page.

Sometimes resources are not always available: you lose your connection, you are forbidden access, and so on. Many browsers display standard error messages, but unfortunately don't often describe them in English. From Internet Explorer 5 on, more friendly messages are displayed. Table 1.1 gives a few of the more common browser errors.

TABLE 1.1 Common Browser Errors

Error Number	Title	Meaning
400	Bad Request	The server cannot parse the URL you entered. Check that you have used all of the appropriate symbols and letters.
401	Unauthorized	You do not have privileges to view that URL.
403	Forbidden (or Connection refused by host)	This resource is not available to you; you may not have the appropriate username, have entered your password incorrectly, or some other reason.
403.9	Access Forbidden. Too Many Users Connected	Web servers allow site managers to limit the number of users that can connect to a particular page, folder, or their site.
404	Not Found (or File not found)	The Web site is live, but the page can't be located. Check your URL carefully. Sometimes you can circumvent this problem by removing the last level and moving up a folder in the URL's path (e.g., changing http://www.sosinsky-group.com/reports/storage.htm to http://www.sosinsky-group.com/reports.
409	Proxy Authentication Required	There is a problem with your connection through the proxy server or firewall. Check your client software for the correct proxy address and port number.
500	Internal Error	There is a server problem.

Continued

TABLE 1.1 Common Browser Errors (continued)

Error Number	Title	Meaning
503	Service Unavailable	The Web site can't be contacted. This can mean that the site's Web server has stopped responding, your connection is down, or a variety of other problems.
	Bad file request	Your browser may not support this file type.
	Computer connection timed out	A slow or dropped connection may generate this message. Try again later.
	Server Does Not Have a DNS Entry; Failed DNS lookup; or DNS entry not found	The DNS service cannot match your URL to a valid friendly Internet address. Check the URL, try the page again, or try later.
	File contains no data	The site exists, but your page doesn't. Sometimes this occurs when a site is being refreshed or is under construction. Try the URL again.
	Helper application not found, or Viewer not found	The browser can't associate the file with an applet.
	Host unavailable	Server may be down; try later.
	Network connection was refused by host; or Too many connections; Try again later	There are probably too many connected users at the moment.
	No virtual host specified	Occurs when you submit a form (typically in Internet Explorer). You should refresh the page in order to determine if the form was submitted.
	Unable to locate host	The server may be down or you may have lost your connection. Try refreshing the page and checking your URL for typos.
	Invalid Page Fault in Kernel132.DLL	Found on Netscape when system resources aren't available, you are using out-of-date video drivers, or have a corrupt swap/paging file. Try closing your applications and restarting.

Summary

The Internet is a network of networks tied together by a common set of services and protocols. The two key ideas that give the Internet its capabilities to both be resilient and have global reach are that it is built with a packet-switching fabric architecture and that it can support a global namespace that uniquely identifies resources for use be they on your computer or halfway around the world. Development on the Internet has used a standards-based approach so that its protocols like TCP/IP and HTTP (for example) are now de facto standards for all computer operating systems, and most applications. In time the bulk of the networked computer programs written will be written to work over the Internet.

The most influential part of the Internet is the World Wide Web. The World Wide Web uses servers running the HTTP protocol to provide resources so that a class of applications called browsers can display pages and documents on your local computer. Browsers are now powerful software suites, with extensible plug-in architectures that allow the addition of powerful small programs called applets or helpers that can perform almost any computer function imaginable. The need to communicate with different kinds of computers makes browsers a unique application to use. To further support cross-platform computing, the industry has developed a number of "portable" languages such as Java and C# that can be written once and run on many platforms using an interpreter on that platform.

We are entering an era where Web services will play an increasingly important role in providing application functionality. So Web programming may be seen to be one of the brightest and most critical disciplines in all of computer science.

browser
client/server
Domain Name System (DNS)
Dynamic Host Configuration Protocol (DHCP)
File Transfer Protocol (FTP)
hypertext
HyperText Transfer Protocol (HTTP)

Internet
name server
packet
packet switching
port
protocol
registrar
router

socket
tags
Transmission Control Protocol/Internet Protocol (TCP/IP)
uniform resource locator (URL)
World Wide Web (WWW)

1. What happens when a packet is lost and does not arrive at its intended destination on the Internet?
2. What function does the HTTP protocol serve?
3. What purpose does a socket serve?
4. How do routers work, and what service do they provide?
5. Describe how friendly names are obtained from IP addresses.
6. Why is caching so important, and where is caching used on your computer as well as on the Internet?
7. What advantages does a three-tiered architecture have for a high transaction system such as an Internet reservation system?
8. Why was Java such a programming sensation when it was first introduced?
9. What is a URL?
10. What kinds of Web services do you think would be particularly valuable to programmers?

Lab Exercises

1. Your company wishes to publish an online news magazine on the Web. Describe the process required to register a domain, create content, and upload that content so that it is available to outside people to view.

2. Find some examples of Web sites that look different in Microsoft Internet Explorer and in Netscape Navigator (or some other pair of browsers). What do you think accounts for the differences that you see?

3. Take a screenshot of the CNN Web site. Identify all of the different elements on the screen that you can.

Building a Web Page with HTML

OBJECTIVES

1. To understand how HTML is used to create pages on the World Wide Web.

2. To learn the basic tags, and how they are used.

3. To appreciate how attributes can modify tags for more powerful control of your content.

4. To use different kinds of hyperlinks to create an interactive medium.

5. To explore the use of images, tables, frames, and other elements that help make the Web a visual medium.

INTRODUCTION

HTML, or the **HyperText Markup Language,** is, as you saw in the previous chapter, the underlying set of instructions that makes it possible for a browser to render a Web page. HTML can be powerfully extended to include many other constructs, many of which are defined within the currently accepted HTML standard and universally adopted, while other extensions (often newer ones) are not always used by one vendor or another. HTML also allows further extension to run scripts, provide calls to external programs, and work with dynamic data and multimedia extensions to HTML (such as Active Server Pages and Java Server Pages, Dynamic HTML, Flash, and so forth). But a simple text document is the foundation for it all.

To access and display HTML documents, you must use a browser program. The two most common browsers are Microsoft's Internet Explorer or Netscape Navigator. There have been several versions of both of these programs, and each (along with the other browsers out there) adds support for features as they go along. A feature that works in Microsoft Internet Explorer 6.x therefore might not work in version 5.x or earlier; worse still, that same feature might not work in another browser. Still, most browsers implement the basic HTML you will learn in this chapter the same way, so what you learn in this chapter will nearly always apply.

A browser program allows you to see the results of your work, so that you can verify that your Web pages look the way they are supposed to and that the links lead to the pages they are supposed to. Until you actually put your page on the Internet for public viewing, you can work locally on your own machine while your page is under construction and you are testing it. In this chapter we will write basic HTML and check the display in a browser. While many HTML editors can shield you from actually learning (or more importantly remembering) HTML when you build Web pages, knowing HTML is a major aid when things go wrong, when you want to insert a special feature, or when you need to optimize your pages to make them load faster.

Building a Web Page

In order to write an HTML document, you need a text editor that can save your work in **ASCII** (pronounced "ask-key") text format. ASCII is an encoding method for characters that translates numbers, symbols, and letters into a digital format. Basic text editors such as Notepad in Windows or Simple text in Macintosh will work fine.

Any word processing application such as WordPerfect, WordPad, or Word will also do, as long as you remember to save your results in *TEXT* only. The resulting **TEXT file** should have a .TXT, not a .DOC extension, and should display Notepad's icon on the PC or a Text icon on the Macintosh. Better yet, Microsoft Office and many other modern programs let you save a file out as an HTML document, thus providing the conversion to an ASCII text format; however, Microsoft Office applications also add a log of extra code to the HTML files that they create—so stick to a text editor when creating sample code. While a .TXT document can be opened and browsed correctly by a browser, an .HTM or .HTML (on a PC) or an .HTML (on the Mac) file will automatically open correctly when you double-click on it.

To start, let's do a simple page and then analyze the parts.

Creating Your First Web Page

In order to create an HTML document that your browser can recognize, you need to declare that this is an HTML document by embedding all text and tags within the `<html>` starting tag and the `</html>` closing tag. To be brief, from now on we'll refer to tag couples using the following syntax: `<tag> . . . </tag>`, where the ellipsis indicates that some "stuff" goes there.

When you put the `<html> ... </html>` tags into your file, you are telling the application that reads this file when to start its HTML *parser* and when to stop running the parser. A **parser** is a program, set of routines, and modules that interpret the markup and can pass instructions to an application on how to handle the file. Other applications besides browsers can read HTML files, and this is the method used to tell applications that HTML markup follows. Similarly, other markup languages such as XML specify themselves so that a browser like Internet Explorer 5 or later with an XML parser can read and interpret it. A browser without an XML **interpreter** (such as Netscape Navigator) would simply ignore the XML tags and show them as text on a Web page.

Beyond the `<html> ... </html>` tags, there are a number of tags meant to define different parts of a document: `<head> ... </head>`, for headers; `<title> ... </title>`, for title text; `<body> ... </body>`, for simple text or body text; `<p> ... <p/>`, for paragraph delineation; and so forth. Let's look at a simple document that illustrates some of these tags before we go into depth on each kind of tag.

1. Open a new blank text file in your text editor.

2. Type in the following information exactly as written:

```
<!- MyFirst.htm ->
<html>
<head>
<title>My first HTML document</title>
</head>
<body>
<h2>First attempt at HTML</h2>
This is my first attempt at writing HTML. Doesn't it
   look <I>great</I>? This is easier than I thought!
<!-Just don't ask how I did it ->
<p>
<hr/>
Written by:
<cite>(insert your name here)</cite>
<br>&copy;2003</br>
<!- The above is an example of the break or line break
   tag. ->
For more information, contact us at:<br></br>
<a href="http://www.mycompany.com">My Company Inc.</a>
</body>
</html>
```

3. Save the document as MyFirst.htm in ASCII format.

4. Launch your Web browser.

5. Open the document you just created in your browser. It should look like Figure 2.1.

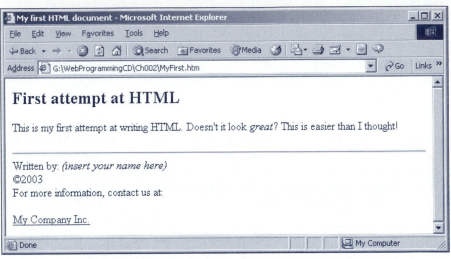

FIGURE 2.1   My First HTML Document

If your browser screen doesn't look like Figure 2.1, go back to the HTML instructions you created in the text editor program and make sure it exactly matches the code above. Save any changes and then return to your browser. Refresh the screen and see if the page is accurately depicted.

HTML has the ability to include special symbols in its output. These symbols include accented letters and many common symbols. To enter a special symbol, you would use the ampersand symbol followed by the number sign and the number of that symbol from a standard table of HTML character assignments. Thus, `&#147` and `&#148` are the curly quotes symbols " and "; and `&#216` would show the O slash character, Ø. An alternative specification for the O slash symbol is `&oslash`.

This simple example serves to demonstrate several basic elements of HTML, which are examined more fully in the following sections.

Formatting Text with Tags

You may have noticed how much typing you had to do in order to produce your HTML document, yet only a small amount of the information actually appears in the browser window. This is because the information that's bracketed by the less than (<) and greater than (>) symbols does not appear. All the data in between these symbols are the instructions to the browser on how to display or treat the content of your document. These instructions are known as **tags.**

The first word in a tag, after the opening less than (<) symbol, is its name. The tag name describes its function. For example, look at the first few lines of tags you typed. The first tag, `<html>`, indicates to the browser that this document is written in HTML. The next tag, `<head>`, includes information about the document that is not displayed in the Web page. The third tag, `<title>`, indicates the title of the document (note that this title, *My first HTML document*, appears in the title bar of the browser window in Figure 2.1).

Sometimes an abbreviation is used for the tag name instead of the formal name. For example, look at the `<h2>` tag on the seventh line of your HTML document. The `h` in this tag stands for heading. There are six different heading tags, `<h1>` through `<h6>`, in descending font size, from largest to smallest. The `<h2>` tag tells the browser to display "First attempt at HTML" in the second-largest heading size.

Look again at the title line and note that the title tag is repeated at the end of the document title with a forward slash (/). Many HTML tags are written in pairs like this with an opening, or start, tag and a closing, or end, tag. The end tag is differentiated from the start tag by this forward slash placement after the less than symbol (<). These start and end tags typically define the parameters of a particular area of your document. This area begins at the point where the start tag is placed in the source document and continues until the end tag is inserted.

There are also single HTML tags that don't require a closing tag. These tags are formatted slightly differently by inserting the forward slash (/) between the tag name and the greater than symbol (>). An example of this type of single tag is the `<hr/>` tag in the first HTML document (on the tenth line, just above the "written by"). This tag inserts a horizontal rule in the document. The reason that the `<hr>` tag can be written as either `<hr> ... </hr>` or `<hr/>` is that the tag indicates a line is to be drawn, and a line doesn't have "stuff" that goes into it.

In addition to actual single tags, there are also several tags where the insertion of the closing tag is optional. An example of this type of tag is the paragraph tag `<p>` (line 10) in your first document, which omits the optional closing tag (`</p>`). For these tags, the browser realizes that the row ends where the next one starts. It is a best practice, however, to always *include the closing tag* for the sake of clarity and to make sure your document is well formatted and will conform to XHTML standards.

Additional information within tags indicates special **attributes** that further define or modify a tag's actions. These attributes are inserted within the brackets of the start tag and always use an equal sign (=) to set a value for the attribute. This value is set within quotes. As a demonstration of this, add an attribute to the `<hr/>` line by adding `width="300"` after the `hr` in the tag, so that the new line looks like this: `<hr width="300"/>`. Save your changes and refresh your browser page. The new result should appear as in Figure 2.2.

Tech Tip

Well-Formed HTML
You may be able to get away without closing a tag, but you might pay for it later. Other variants of HTML, such as XML, are less forgiving and require closing tags in situations where HTML doesn't. An XML parser will reject a poorly formatted HTML document and won't run properly.

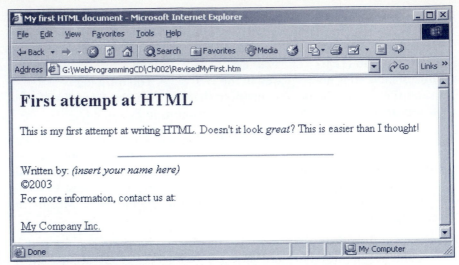

FIGURE 2.2   Revised MyFirst.htm Document as Rendered in Internet Explorer

Head and Body Elements

The two basic structures of HTML are the head and body elements. The `<head>` tag defines the head parameters. The head section contains information that isn't displayed in the browser but can be used by search engines to identify and classify the page—such as keywords. The basic purpose of the `head`, however, is to contain the title of the document. As mentioned before, the title should not be confused with the heading. The title is displayed in the title bar of the window displaying the Web page and not in the document itself.

In the first document that you completed, the following lines of HTML demonstrated this function:

```
<head>
<title>My first HTML document</title>
</head>
```

As you can see, the opening and closing `<head>` tags enclose the opening and closing `<title>` tags, which themselves surround the title text.

The title of a Web page is important as it is used to reference the page, for example, in a search engine or if you bookmark it. If no title is specified, the browser displays the filename in the title bar. Although the title can be very long, only that part of it that can fit in the title bar is displayed.

The opening and closing `<body>` tags set the parameters of the body section. Between these two tags is where most of your content goes—text, headlines, graphics, and so forth. Notice that when you view your first document (Figure 2.1), everything that appears in the browser is contained within the `<body>` tags.

Before going further, let's create a basic template for future exercises.

1. Open your text editor and type the following:

```
<html>
<head>
</head>
<body>
</body>
</html>
```

2. Save this document as `BasicFormat.htm` in ASCII format. (Use no spaces in the filename.)

Establishing Hypertext Links

One of the unique elements of Web pages is their ability to provide links to other pages. This is accomplished by means of **hyperlinks**—links are the original "hyper" in HyperText. Hyperlinks in an HTML document allow you to access and display other HTML documents on your own or others' servers by clicking on the associated word or phrase. They provide a one-click path to other HTML documents anywhere in the world so users can easily navigate to another page. These links can be established in a variety of formats, including multimedia, HTML, XHMTL, or XML. The ability to link Web pages from your own site or others' is one of the most efficient (and recognizable) aspects of the Web. No other medium allows you to so easily access another source or reference without physically obtaining the resource or document, finding the page, and finally accessing it.

In order to create a hyperlink, you enclose the linked text with opening and closing `<a>` tags (the a stands for *anchor*, which is explained in the next section). Within these tags, the `href` attribute contains the address of the page to be linked to the current one. An attribute is a property or modifier of a tag. By default, linked text appears as underlined blue text in a browser (many browsers let you change the color). This serves to separate it from nonlinked text and make it easy for users to find links on a Web page. In the first document you created (Figure 2.1), My Company Inc. is linked. In a real-world scenario, clicking this link would take you to another page that provided information about the company, and should you return to the original link, you will find that many browsers show the link in another color.

Tech Tip

Go to the Source
If at any time you want to view the source code for any document in a browser, simply click **View** and then click **Source**. This is a very good technique for learning HTML, as the source code for any page on the Web can be examined in this way. When you find a page that looks well done or includes an aspect you want to learn, you can study the inner workings of it by employing this procedure.

QuickCheck Questions

1. What is the difference between HTML and HTTP?
2. What tag is absolutely required for an HTML document, and what does that tag do?
3. What does the word hypertext mean?

Defining Relative and Absolute Anchors

To create a hyperlink to another document, you need to know the document's address so you can provide an anchor for it on your page. As you learned in the previous chapter, every document or location you access on the Internet has its own unique address, or uniform resource locator (URL). Every Web page's URL appears in the address bar of your browser. For example, a typical URL might be http://www.mycompany.com/sales/products/price_list.html. An *anchor* is a type of tag (`<a>`) that defines the source and the destination of the hyperlink. By surrounding text with anchor tags, a link to another document is established. The attribute of an anchor is its address to the connecting link, called the `href` attribute. Typing the statement `<a href=www.google.com>` creates a link to the Google search engine on your Web page.

Anything within the `<a>` tags can be linked, including images as well as text and various other files. We'll have more to say about working with images in the "Adding Graphic Elements" section of this chapter.

Links can either be *absolute* or *relative*. Absolute links provide the full Web address (URL) including the document's name, the pathname, the domain name of the server that hosts the file, and the protocol. By the way, URLs can be local, as in \\servername\directory\file.ext, as they would be if you made a Web page available offline, or were creating Web pages from files locally.

Relative links on the other hand are less well defined but are useful because the browser assumes when you link a filename that the link will use the same protocol and that the destination file is located on the same server and in the same directory as the current HTML document.

Links to pages on your own Web site, whether on the same or different page, are called *internal links*. These links do not require an **absolute anchor**. Remember, if it is not defined, the browser assumes the protocol, server, and domain name of the link are the same as those of the current page. Links that have a destination file to another Web site other than your own are called external links. These links must be absolute, that is, contain the protocol, domain name, and filename.

Let's add a hyperlink to the document we've been working on:

1. Open the `BasicFormat.htm` file you created earlier in your text editor.

2. In between the opening and closing body tags, insert a new line of text by typing the following line of text:

   `Look before you leap but...`

3. Enclose this line of text with opening and closing anchor tags `<a> ... </a>`.

4. Next, add a link by inserting an `href` attribute after the opening anchor tag and setting its value like this: **href="page2.html"**. (Note that this is a **relative anchor**.)

5. Check to make sure the HTML code you've entered looks like this:

```
<html>
<head>
</head>
<a href="page2.html"> Look before you leap but...</a>
<body>
</body>
</html>
```

6. Save this file as **page1.htm**.

7. Change the attribute value of the link to **page1.html.**

8. Change the link text to **he who hesitates is lost**.

9. Save this file as **page2.htm**.

10. Open the first file (page1.htm) in a browser. The page is shown in Figure 2.3 with the link displayed.

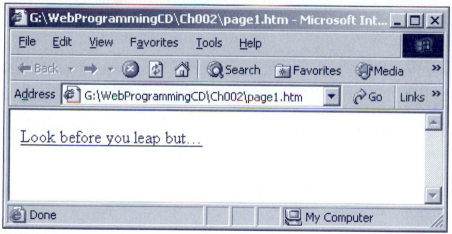

FIGURE 2.3   The Page with the Link Displayed

11. Click the link. Now the linked page shown in Figure 2.4 is displayed.

Ordered and Unordered Lists

Several different types of lists are supported by HTML. One type is an **ordered list,** which sequentially numbers each item in a list. Ordered lists duplicate a style in word processor that is typically called a numbered list. Another type of list is an **unordered list,** which places bullets instead of numbers in front of each listed item. For this reason, another name for an unordered list is a bulleted list.

The tag for an ordered list is <ol>. The entire list is enclosed within opening and closing <ol> tags. Additionally, each item on the list is preceded by a

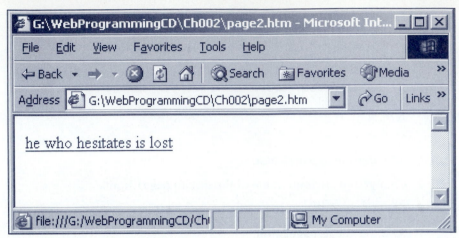

FIGURE 2.4   The Link on the First Page Leads to the Second Page

<li/> tag. This <li/> tag can assign attributes that format the numbering style used and define what the first number in the list will be.

Let's create an ordered list to see how this works:

1. Open the `BasicFormat.htm` file.

2. Create a new line after the starting <head> tag and type the text **Favorite Trumpet Players**.

3. Enclose this text between opening and closing (<title> and </title>) tags on the same line.

4. Create a new line between the starting and ending body tags and insert an opening ordered list tag <ol>

5. Add a closing ordered list tag </ol> on the next line.

6. Between the <ol> tags add an <li/> tag on a new line, and then type **Louis Armstrong** on the same line.

7. Add another <li/> tag on a new line underneath and type **Miles Davis**.

8. Repeat the same procedure with the following items, inserting each on a separate line (make sure the items are preceded by the <li/> tags): **Clifford Brown**, **Dizzy Gillespie**, **Chet Baker**.

9. Check to make sure that your HTML code is correct, and looks as follows:

```
<html>
<head>
<title>Favorite Trumpet Players</title>
```

```
</head>
<body>
<ol>
<li/> Louis Armstrong
<li/> Miles Davis
<li/> Clifford Brown
<li/> Dizzy Gillespie
<li/> Chet Baker
</ol>
</body>
</html>
```

10. Save this document as `orderedList.htm`.

11. Open a browser and open `orderedList.htm`. The final result should look like Figure 2.5.

FIGURE 2.5 An Ordered List
An ordered list sequentially numbers the items you enter.

Using the type attribute of the `<ol>` tag, you can change the style of the numbers for your list. To see an example of how this works, open the `orderedList.htm` file in your text editor and add the type attribute "a" to the first `<ol>` tag so that your new line looks like this: `<ol type="a">`. Save the file with a new name and open it in your browser. Your list should now be shown with the lowercase letters a through e instead of the numbers 1–5. Now try setting the type to "I" instead of "a"; each item should now have an uppercase Roman numeral next to it.

To create a bulleted or unordered list, you use the `<ul>` tag. To see how this works, replace the `<ol>` and `</ol>` tags in the `orderedList.htm` file with

`<ul>` and `</ul>` tags. Save this file as `UnorderedList.htm` and open it in a browser. A bullet instead of a number now precedes each item in the list.

You also can create what are called **definition lists** using the `<dl>` . . . `</dl>` tag. This tag creates a list that pairs the contents of the tag—a word or phrase—as a title with a description, or a longer explanation, and associates the two into a list where the subject is aligned left and the description is indented, the result of which is a listing that looks a lot like a glossary or dictionary.

Finally, you can nest these different lists, one inside another, so that you can create very effective listings such as a table of contents, indexes, phone and address books, and so on.

Applying Background Colors and Patterns

Most browsers display white or gray as the default **background** color of a Web page. Depending on your needs, however, different background colors can be used. The background color is determined by an attribute of the `<body>` tag, `bgcolor`. The value for this attribute can be expressed as either a color name or a hexadecimal color value. For example, typing `<body bgcolor="green">` will display a green background on your Web page. Most browsers recognize dozens of color names, from "burlywood" to "mistyrose" and "powderblue" to "navajowhite."

In our example, you can obtain the same result by replacing the word "green" with the hexadecimal number `#00FF00` (browsers require that the # sign be placed in front of a number to identify it as hexadecimal). Hexadecimal numbers are based on 16, rather than 10, as in the more familiar decimal system we use all the time. In a hexadecimal system, a single digit can represent any number from 1 to 16. This is accomplished by adding the letters A through F after 9. Thus, the number 10 in hexadecimal is A, 11 is B, 12 is C, and so forth. A six-digit hexadecimal number is used to represent a color value by making the first two digits equal the amount of red, the second two digits equal the amount of green, and the last two digits stand for the amount of blue. For example, red is `FF0000` and blue is `0000FF` (green we already know is `00FF00`). By combining these sets of values, a huge variety of colors (16.7 million for a 24-bit video board) can be produced and displayed.

Continuing on with our example, let's add a background color:

1. Open the file `BasicFormat.htm`.

2. Add a background color attribute by inserting `bgcolor="limegreen"` after the opening `<body>` tag, so that the line looks like this: `<body bgcolor="limegreen">`.

3. Save this file with a new name, like `bgcolorLimeGreen`.

4. Open the file in your browser. The background color of this page should now be lime green.

QuickCheck Questions

4. What is the general syntax of a hyperlink, and what do the parts indicate?
5. What is the difference between a relative and an absolute link?
6. What types of lists are supported by standard HTML tags?

Setting Text Fonts, Colors, and Styles

HTML was designed to convey information easily and rapidly, not as a complete word processing tool. The content is the paramount thing with HTML—not the layout or style. Consequently, you can't do fancy things like you do in a full word processing program. It is best to complete and spell check your text content in your standard word processing program, and then copy it separately into your HTML documents—or if you have a word processor that supports it such as Microsoft Word, save your document as an HTML file. If you have greater formatting needs for text, then refer to Chapter 4 for using style sheets. The formatting tags explained in this section are not fancy, but they are the easiest to learn and most widely used HTML formatting tools.

Changing Text Sizes and Fonts

Manipulating fonts and sizes involves using the font tag <font>, and its attributes `size` and `face`. The `size` attribute has values from 1 to 7, from smallest to largest. The default font size is 3. The `face` attribute contains the actual name of the typeface you wish to use.

To change font sizes in our example,

1. Open the `BasicFormat.htm` file you created.

2. Add the following text on a new line immediately after the first body tag.

   ```
   Despite numerous technical hurdles, sales have remained
   strong in major regions this fiscal year. As we head
   into the New Year, we are anticipating a net sales in-
   crease of 10% due to several new products. These prod-
   ucts have been through multiple trial stages and the
   outstanding results bode well for expanding market
   share. In addition, our new ad campaign, to which the
   company has committed an unprecedented amount of fund-
   ing, debuts in the spring.
   You can make up your own text content if you wish; this
   text is provided for reference. Make sure, however,
   that your own content is at least as long as our exam-
   ple.
   ```

3. Add opening and closing font tags <font> and </font> at the beginning and end of every sentence of text you typed.

Tech Tip

It's a Wrap
If you can't see the entire text, use the **Word wrap** tool; in Notepad, this option is in the **Format** menu.

4. Add a `size` attribute to the opening font tags `<font>`.

5. Assign a value of **1** to the first size attribute, **2** to the second size attribute, and so forth.

6. Check that the new code you've added to the table tag looks like the following:

```
<font size="1">Despite numerous technical hurdles, sales
have remained strong in major regions this fiscal year.
</font><font size="2">As we head into the New Year, we
are anticipating a net sales increase of 10% due to sev-
eral new products. </font><font size="3">These products
have been through multiple trial stages and the out-
standing results bode well for expanding market share.
</font><font size="4">In addition, our new ad campaign,
to which the company has committed an unprecedented
amount of funding, debuts in the spring. </font>
```

7. Save this file with the name `fontsize.htm`.

8. Open this new file in your browser. It should look like Figure 2.6.

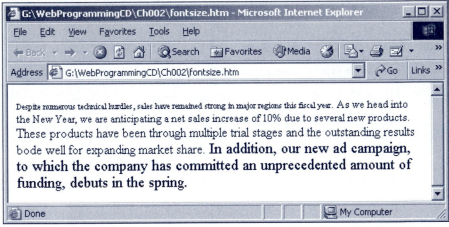

FIGURE 2.6   The Font Size Attribute Changes the Font Size of Your Displayed Text

You can customize fonts by using the `face` attribute and using the `font name` as the value. Fonts provide personality and style to your Web page; however, keep in mind that if the visitor to your page does not have your fonts installed on his or her computer, the default font will be rendered.

Let's illustrate how you change the font face in our example:

1. Open the `fontsize.htm` file you created in the last exercise.

2. Add a `face` attribute in addition to the `size` attribute.

3. Assign a value of **Springfield, Extra Bold** to the first `face` attribute; assign **Arial** to the second `face` attribute; **Verdana** to the third; and **Times New Roman** to the fourth.

4. Check to make sure the added code looks like the following:

```
<font size="1" face="Springfield, Extra Bold">Despite
numerous technical hurdles, sales have remained strong
in major regions this fiscal year. </font><font
size="2" face="Arial">As we head into the New Year, we
are anticipating a net sales increase of 10% due to sev-
eral new products. </font><font size="3" face="Verdana
">These products have been through multiple trial
stages and the outstanding results bode well for expand-
ing market share. </font><font size="4" face="Times
New Roman ">In addition, our new ad campaign, to which
the company has committed an unprecedented amount of
funding, debuts in the spring. </font>
```

5. Save this file with the name `fontsizeface.htm`.

6. Open this new file in your browser. It should look like Figure 2.7.

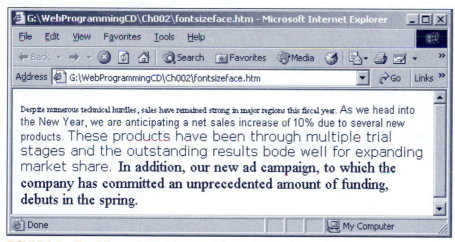

FIGURE 2.7   The Effect of the `size` and `face` Attributes on Text

Changing the text color is useful to attract the visitor's attention; however, if it is overused, the reader may be completely distracted or put off. It is also important that the text color chosen display clearly and not disappear or clash when combined with other colors or graphics on the page.

To change text color:

1. Open the `fontsizeface.htm` file you created in the last exercise.

2. Add `color` attributes in the font tags.

3. Assign the attribute value **red** in the first sentence of text.

4. In the next three sentences, assign the following color values: **mediumvioletred**, **royalblue**, and **saddlebrown**.

5. Check that the new code you've added to the table tag looks like the following:

```
<font size="1" face="Springfield, Extra Bold" color=
"red">Despite numerous technical hurdles, sales have
remained strong in major regions this fiscal year.
</font><font size="2" face="Arial" color=
"mediumvioletred">As we head into the New Year, we are
anticipating a net sales increase of 10% due to several
new products. </font><font size="3" face="Verdana"
color="royalblue">These products have been through
multiple trial stages and the outstanding results bode
well for expanding market share. </font><font size="4"
face="Times New Roman" color="saddlebrown">In addition,
our new ad campaign, to which the company has committed
an unprecedented amount of funding, debuts in the
spring. </font>
```

6. Save this file with the name `fontsizefacecolor.htm`.

7. Open this new file in your browser. It should look like Figure 2.8.

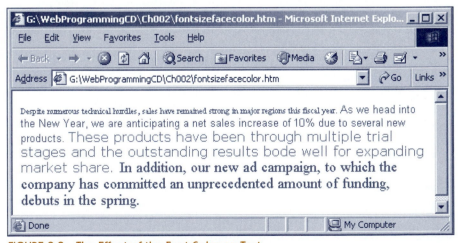

FIGURE 2.8   The Effect of the Font Color on Text

Creating a Default Text Style Using Base Font Attributes

It is a good idea to have all the pages on your Web site maintain a particular visual theme so that visitors get a coherent impression. You can create a default text by replacing the font tags `<font>` and `</font>` with a single base font tag `<basefont/>`. Insert the desired attributes, for example, size, font, and/or color, in between the `basefont` name and the forward slash. Unless indicated otherwise, all text will then conform to this style.

One nice effect for making text or a paragraph stand out on the page is through the use of callouts or block quotes. The HTML tag for block quotes is `<blockquote>`...`</blockquote>`. Any text enclosed within this tag is indented on both sides in some browsers and italicized in others.

Adding Graphic Elements

Besides texts and links, one of the most common contents of Web pages is graphic elements. Images can make your Web page design far more interesting and informative than just plain text. This section of the chapter explains the process of adding and handling graphic elements.

There are three types of bitmapped or painted image types that all browsers recognize: GIF, JPEG, and PNG. Each of these types can produce small file sizes that enable faster downloads.

- The **GIF (Graphic Interchange Format)** is the most common image type. GIF images are compressed in such a way that the file is much smaller, yet no image information is lost. Because of this type of compression, the GIF is very good for line drawings and large areas of solid colors. However, GIF files are not suitable for photographs or any other graphic with a large amount of colors because they only display up to 256 colors. One type of GIF file, called **Interlaced GIF** (developed by America Online) displays a low-resolution image that is filled in over time, thus enabling you to get a sense of what the image frame contains more quickly.

- The **JPEG (Joint Photographic Experts Group)** image type (.JPG on a PC, .JPEG on a Macintosh), unlike GIF, is very good for photographs and other color-intensive files because it supports up to 16.7 million colors and can be compressed at various levels. The downside of this format, however, is that in order to do this, a certain amount of information is lost when JPEG files are compressed.

- The **PNG (Portable Network Graphics)** is the most recent of the Web images types. Like the JPEG format, it supports up to 16.7 million colors, but it has an advantage in that it does not lose information like JPEG does when it is compressed.

Note that **BMP (bit-mapped images)** will only be seen on Internet Explorer browsers and are not recommended as a general image file for inclusion in Web pages.

If the image you're working with is not in one of the above formats, you'll have to convert the file before inserting it. There are multiple graphics programs that enable you to do this, and many of them such as Paint Shop Pro, Graphics Converter, and LView Pro are available as shareware on the Internet. Full-feature image editing programs such as Adobe Photoshop, and even Word, come with graphics conversion filters.

You'll notice on many Web pages that drawings or vector graphics are displayed. These objects, of which the Adobe **SVG (Scaleable Vector Graphic)** file format is an example, aren't part of the basic HTML specification but are displayed as the result of add-in or plug-in browser components. SVG is used to show Postscript-style graphics like charts and graphs that can be manipulated on a Web page. There are many vector formats available, meant to serve all manners of purposes ranging from 3-D visualization to gaming effects, and more.

Vector graphics are drawing programs that use mathematical expressions to create shapes. You can apply properties like fills and bounding lines to these shapes. The most important property of vector graphics is that these drawings scale perfectly to any size. Raster graphics, also called bit-mapped images, are composed of a mosaic of picture elements, or pixels, that create the appearance of an image. You see raster graphics in paint and photographic programs, and as the density of pixels increases, the image takes on a natural look. Raster graphics can be made smaller (usually at only proportional ratios) and maintain their quality, but when raster graphics are enlarged, the picture elements become more obvious—an effect called *pixilation*.

Embedded Images

The image tag `<img/>` is used to add an image to a Web page. The actual image used is defined by using the source attribute (`src`), which specifies the location of the image file to be used. As with a link to another page, the location of the image is set by typing its URL. If the image is on your local computer in the same directory as the Web page, the filename of the desired image is sufficient to identify it. But by defining its absolute URL, you can use any image anywhere on the Web. It is important to point out, however, that doing this means your computer has to contact the server that contains the graphic and this increases the amount of time it will take for the image to be downloaded. Additionally, if the server is not available, the desired image won't load at all. For these reasons, it is wise to save the desired graphic on your local machine whenever possible. This may not be an option if you are linking to a graphic that changes all the time, such as a weather map or a web-cam image.

To insert an **embedded image** into a Web page, use the following steps:

1. Open the file `BasicFormat.htm` in your text editor.
2. Create a new line within the body tags using the image tag `<img/>`.

3. Specify the location of the image by setting the source attribute (`src="industry_main.jpg"`) within the image tag.

   You can substitute any jpg file available on the machine you are working on; if you want to use an image accessed over a network, you must use an absolute anchor.

4. Make sure the new line you have written between the body tags looks like this:

   ```
   <img src="industry_main.jpg"/>
   ```

5. Save this file as `imageExample1.htm`.

6. Open the file in your browser. It should look like the one in Figure 2.9.

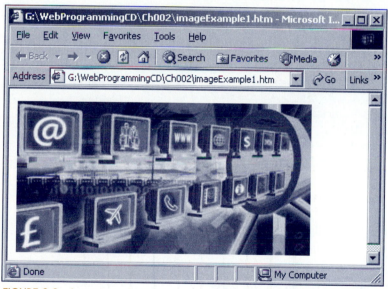

FIGURE 2.9   Inserting a Basic Image in a Web Page

Working with Image Attributes

The image tag `<img>` includes attributes that allow you to set the size of the image you are working with. These attributes are `width` and `height`. Let's demonstrate how `width` and `height` work in an example:

1. Open `BasicFormat.htm`.

2. Create a new line containing the image tag `<img/>` between the body tags.

3. Add the `width` and `height` attributes within the `<img/>` tag.

4. Set the width value to **600** (pixels) and set the height value to **250**.

5. Check to make sure the new image line you've added looks like this:

   ```
   <img src="industry_main.jpg" width="600" height="250"/>
   ```

   Image width and height values are set in pixels.

6. Save the file as `imageExample2.htm`. If you are using the Macintosh system, save the file as `imageExample2.html`.

7. Open this new file in your browser. The final result should look like Figure 2.10, with the allocated space for the image a wide rectangle.

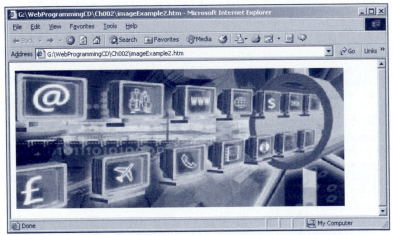

FIGURE 2.10 The `width` and `height` Attributes of the Image Tag Specify the Image's Size on the Web Page

The image tag also has an attribute that allows you to position the image where you want on the Web page.

Positioning Your Image on the Page

1. Open the `BasicFormat.htm` file you created.

2. Create a new line containing the image tag `<img/>` between the body tags.

3. Add the `align` attribute within the `<img/>` tag.

4. Set the `align` attribute to **right**.

5. Check to make sure the new image line you've added looks like this:

   ```
   <img src="industry_main.jpg" align="right"/>
   ```

6. Save this file as `imageExample3.htm`.

7. Open the file in a browser. The image should be aligned to the right of the Web page, as in Figure 2.11.

FIGURE 2.11   The Effect of the Position Attribute on an Image

Wrapping Text around an Image

Another action that can be accomplished using the `align` attribute is **text wrap,** that is, wrapping the text around an image, to make your page look more interesting:

1. Open the new file you created in the last exercise (`imageExample3.htm`) in your text editor.

2. Type a few lines of text after the image tag `<img/>`.

3. Within the image tag and after the `align` attribute, add the horizontal space `hspace` and vertical space `vspace` attributes.

4. Set the `hspace` value to **20** (in pixels) and the `vspace` value to **40**.

5. Check to make sure the image line looks like `<img src="industry_main.jpg" align="right" hspace="20" vspace="40"/>`.

6. Save this file with the name `wraparound.htm`.

   You will need this file for the next exercise, so save it to your desktop.

7. Open the `wraparound.htm` file in your browser. The result should look like the one in Figure 2.12.

Creating an Image Border

Yet another attribute allows you to create a border around your image:

1. Open the `wraparound.htm` file you created in the last exercise.

2. Add a `border` attribute at the end of the image tag inside the closing `/>`.

3. Set the value of the `border` to **25** (pixels).

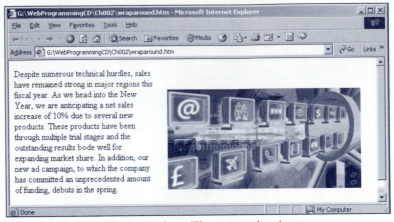

FIGURE 2.12   Text Can Be Made to Wrap around an Image

The width of the border is measured in pixels; setting the value to 5 creates a 5-pixel-wide border around the image.

4. Check that the new code you've added to the image line looks like `<img src="industry_main.jpg" align="right" hspace="20" vspace="40" border="25"/>`.

5. Save this file as `imageWithBorder.htm`.

6. Open the file you just created in your browser. It should look like Figure 2.13, with a black border around the image.

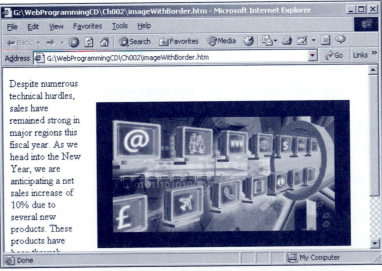

FIGURE 2.13   An Image with a 25-Pixel-Wide Border

Hyperlinked Images

By surrounding the image tag <img/> with anchor tags <a> . . . </a>, you link that image to another Web page or URL, and when users click on the image, they are sent to that page or the object is activated. This is a useful navigation tool—using images instead of text to direct a user through your site—and is the underlying technology behind all manner of useful constructs like **navigation toolbars,** clickable maps, and so forth.

Let's take a look at how to set up a clickable or linked image:

1. Open the file you created in the last exercise, imageWithBorder.htm.

2. Surround the image tags by adding opening and closing anchor tags <a> . . . <a/>.

3. Add an href attribute after the first anchor tag.

4. Assign a value of "**http://www.mcgraw-hill.com/utility/shop/industry.html**" to the href attribute where http://www.mcgraw-hill.com/utility/shop/industry.html is the full address of the Web page to link to.

5. Check that the new code you've added to the image tag line looks like the following:

```
<a href="http://www.mcgraw-hill.com/utility/shop/
   industry.html">
<img src="industry_main.jpg" align="right" hspace="20"
   vspace="40" border="25"/>
</a>
```

6. Save this file with the name ImageLink.htm.

7. Open this new file in your browser. It should look like Figure 2.13. Move your mouse over the image and check if the linked URL appears in your browser's status bar. Click the image. The linked Web page should open, as in Figure 2.14.

Animated Images

Animated GIF images contain multiple images that, when displayed one after another, give the appearance of animation. Only GIF images do this; JPEG images do not support animation. Free animated images can be found on the Web, but they must be downloaded and saved on your local machine before they can used.

Animated images can be used just about anywhere on a page that you would use a normal image (see Figure 2.15). Note that, when using animated images, however, they take a while to download and so should be used sparingly to avoid slowing down your Web page.

To create a page with an animated image, use the following steps:

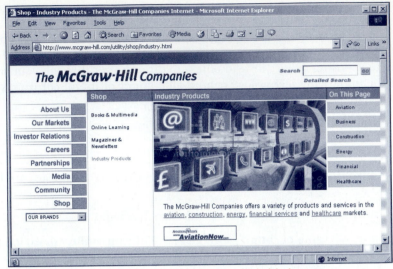

FIGURE 2.14   An Example of a Hyperlink or Clickable Image on a McGraw-Hill Web Page
Notice the hand cursor over the image and the reference to the URL in the status bar in the lower left corner.

1. Add a source attribute (`src`) to the image tag.

2. Assign a value of **.GIF** to the source attribute where `.GIF` is the filename of an animated image that is saved on your computer.

3. Save this file with an appropriate name.

4. Open this new file in your browser. The animated image should display in your browser.

Navigational Toolbars and Image Maps

An **image map** links many pages to one image. This is accomplished by assigning *hotspots* within the image that, when clicked, take you to the desired page. An image map has multiple hotspots, each of which takes the visitor to a different page, image, or file. A common use of this technique is to allow the user to select from a larger image a particular aspect of that image that he or she wants more information about. For example, a map of the entire United States may contain as hotspots individual states that, when clicked, take you to a detailed map of that area. There are two types of image maps: client-side and server-side image maps. A client-side image map is processed by your browser and doesn't require a CGI script to run. A server-side image map stores the image map on the server and uses an imagemap program on an NCSA HTTPd server or a bitimage on a CERN server to run using a CGI script.

A client-side image map can be developed using the <map> and <area> tags. Typically, we embed a series of <area> tags in a <map> tag to delineate the

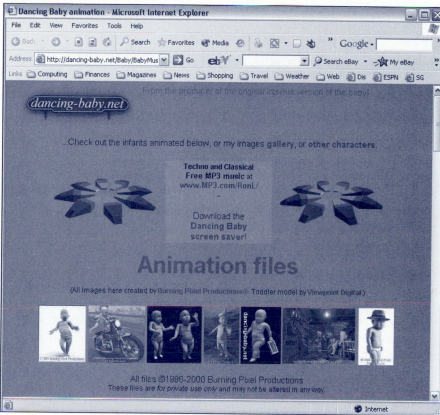

FIGURE 2.15   Animated Images

The home of the famous animated Internet Dancing Baby (http://dancing-baby.
net/Baby/BabyMus1.htm), star of screen and stage, is a phenomenon (albeit weird)
of our time and an example of how your animated images can make a difference.

area of the hotspots. We can use the `shape` and `coords` attributes of the
`<area>` tag to define areas of the hotspots. Finally, we can use the `href`
attribute to link a particular hotspot to a desired Web page. We will demonstrate the process with a simple example. Consider the image shown in Figure
2.16. We have outlined two rectangular areas in the image. We also have determined the XY coordinates of the northeast and southwest corners of the rectangular areas. The coordinates are in pixels, and these can be determined
easily by pasting the image on any image editor (such as Photoshop, Microsoft
Paint, or Paint Shop Pro). If you hover your mouse over the image, these software programs usually display the XY coordinates of the mouse pointer in the
status bar (at the bottom of the screen).

Creating the `<map>` is not an end by itself. Subsequently, we need to use the
map to display an image. This is usually accomplished by using the `usemap`

FIGURE 2.16   The XY Coordinates of Two Rectangular Hotspots in an Image

attribute of the $<$img$>$ tag. Suppose that when the user clicks on the left rectangular hotspot, we want the system to display the McGraw-Hill home page. On the other hand, if the user clicks on the right rectangular hotspot, we want the system to display the mcgrawhill_education.html page. The following code will accomplish these objectives:

```
<!– ImageMapExample.htm" –>
<html><head>
<map id="myMap01" name="myMap01">
<area shape="rect" coords="4,6,50,50"
   href="http://www.mcgraw-hill.com"/>
<area shape="rect" coords="53,6,200,45"
   href="http://www.mcgraw-hill.com/markets/mcgrawhill_
      education.html"/>
</map></head>
<body>
<img src="McGraw-Hill.jpg" usemap="#myMap01"/>
</body></html>
```

In the above code (`ImageMapExample.htm`), we have defined the hotspots in line numbers 3 through 6. In line number 8, we are displaying the McGraw-Hill.jpg using the `usemap` attribute. There are two other acceptable values of the `shape` attribute of an $<$area$>$ tag. These are `circle` and `poly` (for polygon). In the case of a circular area, you will need to specify the `coords` attribute as "x,y,r", where x and y are the XY coordinates of the center, and r is the radius. You may define a polygon as `shape="poly" coords= "x1,y1, x2,y2, . . . , xn,yn"`. In case you find it tedious to develop an image map, you may use software such as MapEdit, CutMap, or Mapthis to make the task more pleasant.

QuickCheck Questions

7. What image types are supported in HTML?

8. What image properties can you control using standard HTML tags?

9. What purpose does Interlaced GIF serve?

10. How is image animation created?

Enhancing the Web Page

As HTML developed, Web site builders required more and more tools to provide desktop layout and publishing features on their sites. Thus, features like frames and tables were added to HTML to make it easier to create attractive and informative pages. You can think of a **frame** as a Web page within a Web page; many frames are scrollable and can be independently formatted. Similarly, a table lets you create a regular grid into which you can place elements. Tables have turned out to be a very convenient way of designing attractive and easy-to-control page areas. In the sections that follow, we will look at these two useful features.

Organizing Information Using Frames

A simple Web page shows what is between the body tags and that's it, basically. By using frames, however, you can display multiple pages in the same browser window. Frames are also dynamic in the sense that users can scroll through them if the entire window cannot be seen within the established size parameters. They are commonly used in order to specify a fixed section of a page and a scrolling one (say a logo on the top and text you can scroll through below), or a fixed list of contents on the left and a scrollable information text on the right.

Multiple frames are contained within the `<frameset> ... </frameset>` tags. The `frameset` tags replace the `<body>` tags as containers from multiple frames.

Here's an example of how to create a **frameset** with the `cols` attribute:

1. Open the `BasicFormat.htm` file.

2. Replace the existing `<body>` tags with frameset tags `<frameset> ... </frameset>`.

3. Create two new `<frame/>` tags on new lines within the `<frameset>` tags.

4. Add the columns attribute `cols` to the opening `<frameset>` tag.

5. Set the value of the `cols` attribute to 50%, 50%; this creates two vertical frames of equal size on either half of the page.

Tech Tip

Comments and Hidden Text
It's good programming practice to provide information about the purpose of your code, as well as any special instructions, by embedding comments into your code. The HTML tag for comments is `<!- ... ->`. An example of a comment is shown in the code on the next page.

6. Make sure your page looks like this:

```
<!- Frames1.htm ->
<html><head></head>
<frameset cols="50%,50%">
   <!- These measurements are in pixels.
      Note that this is a comment and it will not
         appear on your Web page ->
   <frame/>
   <frame/>
</frameset>
</html>
```

7. Save this file with a new filename, such as `Frames1.htm`.

8. Open this file in your browser; it should look like Figure 2.17.

FIGURE 2.17   Two Frames with Equal COLS Attributes

Now let's illustrate the `rows` attribute:

1. Now go back to the source file and replace the `cols` attribute with a `rows` attribute.

2. Specify values of **25%**, **50%**, **25%** in the `rows` attribute.

3. Add another `<frame/>` tag on a new line within the `<frameset>` tags.

4. Make sure the changes you've made look like this:

```
<frameset rows="25%,50%,25%">
<frame/>
<frame/>
<frame/>
</frameset>
```

5. Save this file as `Frames2.htm`.

6. Open this new file in your browser; it should look like Figure 2.18.

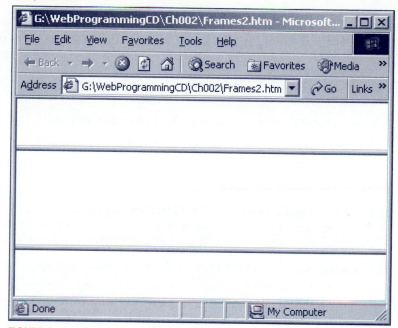

FIGURE 2.18   Three Frames with a 1:2:1 Ratio of Their rows Attributes

There are, in fact, seven attributes that frames can have:

- The src (source) attribute points to the source of the frame content, which can be an image, another page, a table of contents, and so forth.

- Each frame must have a unique name; giving a frame a name will not make that name appear in the browser window, but it does serve to identify the frame in your code and is used in some more advanced techniques, such as targeting, which is described below.

- As the name implies, the frameborder attribute allows you to specify the type of border (or lack thereof) your frames have.

- The marginwidth attribute specifies the width of the left and right margins of the frame, which display in a browser as white space around the frame's content.

- The marginheight attribute specifies the top and bottom margins of the frame.

- The scrolling attribute determines whether a frame has a scroll bar. The values for this attribute are Yes, No, or Auto (which means scroll bars appear automatically if the frame content exceeds the size).

- The noresize (that is, no resizing of frames allowed) attribute prevents users from changing the size of the frame, for example, if it will block your organization's logo or some other information you want to keep visible.

Since you've just learned how to create a frame, let's fill that frame with some content:

1. Open the `Frames1.htm file` using Notepad.

2. On the lines after the `<frameset>` tag, add the `name` attributes to each of the `<frame>` tags, **west** for the first and **east** for the second.

3. Add the `src` attributes to each of the `<frame>` tags, **west.htm** and **east.htm**.

4. Check that the `<frame>` tag lines look like the following:

   ```
   <frame name="west" src="west.htm"/>
   <frame name="east" src="east.htm"/>
   ```

5. Save this file with the name `Frames3.htm`.

6. Now create and save two small HTML files named `west.htm` and `east.htm`. Enter certain simple texts in the `<body>` tags of each of them (such as "This is the west frame" and "This is the east frame").

7. Open this new file in your browser. It should look like Figure 2.19.

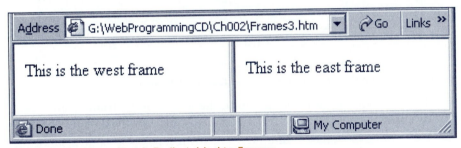

FIGURE 2.19   Name Text Is Easily Added to Frames

Targeting Frames

It is common to use two frames in a page: the one on the left is normally narrow and displays various links to other Web pages, while the one on the right displays the content of what is clicked on the left. Essentially, when the link on the left frame is clicked, the frame on the right loads the appropriate information. We implement this kind of linking using the `target` attribute of the `<a>` tag. In the `target` attribute, we can tell the browser in which frame it should display the linked document. We will illustrate this principle with a simple example using two side-by-side frames. Consider the following code (`TargetingFrames.htm`):

```
<!-TargetingFrames.htm ->
<html><head></head>
<frameset cols="50%,50%">
    <frame id="LeftFrame" name="LeftFrame" src="List.htm"/>
    <frame id="RightFrame" name="RightFrame"/>
<frameset>
</html>
```

Initially, when the browser opens the `TargetingFrames.htm` page, it will display the `List.htm`. The right frame will be empty because we have not assigned any value of the `src` attribute of the `<frame>` tag. To understand the application clearly, observe the contents of the `List.htm` as shown below:

```
<!-List.htm ->
<html><head></head><body>
<a href="Introduction.htm" target="RightFrame">Introduction
   </a><br/>
<a href="Fishing.htm" target="RightFrame">Fishing Products
   </a><br/>
<a href="Gardening.htm" target="RightFrame">Gardening
   Products</a><br/>
</body></html>
```

In the `List.htm` document, we have specified three `<a>` tags. Each of these `<a>` tags specifies a link to some other HTML document. We also have used `target="RightFrame"` in each of these tags. Thus, when the user clicks one of these links, the browser will display the appropriate document in the right frame. Figure 2.20 shows an instance of this application. In addition to the `TargetingFrames.htm` and `List.htm`, this application requires three other HTML documents: `Introduction.htm`, `Fishing.htm`, and `Gardening.htm`. To keep the application within bounds, we have used very simple pages for all of these documents. Now we present the listings of these HTML documents.

FIGURE 2.20   Linking between Frames Using the `target` Attribute

```
<!-Introduction.htm ->
<html><head></head><body>
We are the Hobbies'R us. We carry the finest fishing and
gardening products.
</body></html>


<!-Fishing.htm ->
<html><head></head><body>
We carry the following fishing products —
</body></html>
```

```
<!-Gardening.htm ->
<html><head></head><body>
Here are our gardening products —
</body></html>
```

Tables

Tables are used to present data and to position objects on a Web page. To display information, a standard table has elements such as rows and columns, cells, borders, headings, and captions. All these elements are defined by attribute tags placed within the basic table tags `<table> . . . </table>`. It's not always intuitive that a table was used for positioning on a page, especially when the table doesn't have visible borders, but tables are very widely used.

Creating a Basic Table

The data inside a table is represented in rows and columns. Table row tags `<tr>` mark the start of each new row. The spaces in each row and column that contain the table's data are called cells. `<td>` tags indicate each cell in a row. Let's illustrate how these are used by creating a basic table:

1. Open the `BasicFormat.htm` file.

2. Within the `<body>` tags, add opening and closing table tags `<table> . . . </table>`.

3. Within the `<table>` tags, add opening and closing table row tags `<tr> . . . </tr>` on a new line for each row. For this exercise, create three rows.

4. Within the table row tags, add opening and closing cell tags `<td> . . . </td>` for each cell in the row. For this exercise, create three cells in each row.

5. Compare the code you've created and make sure it looks like the following. Add the content in the example inside each cell tag.

```
<!- BasicTable.htm ->
<html><head></head><body>
<table>
  <tr>
    <td>1,387 tons</td>
    <td>435 tons </td>
    <td>829 tons </td>
  </tr>
  <tr>
```

```
      <td>3,116 tons </td>
      <td>1,023 tons </td>
      <td>1,957 tons </td>
   </tr>
   <tr>
      <td>1,874 tons </td>
      <td>894 tons </td>
      <td>982 tons </td>
   </tr>
</table>
</body></html>
```

6. Save this file with the name `BasicTable.htm`.

7. Open the `BasicTable.htm` file in a browser. It should appear as in Figure 2.21. Note how the data entered is arranged in rows and columns.

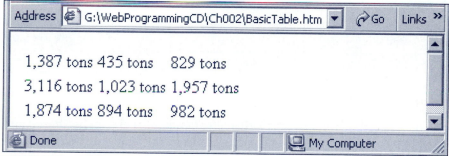

FIGURE 2.21   A Basic Table

Adding Borders

The other elements of a table can be added by specifying attributes of the various table tags. Once the data is entered in the cells, borders can be added to make the rows and columns clearer and easier to read. To include a border around a table, add the `border` attribute to the starting table tag.

Assigning a value to the `border` attribute also automatically creates a border between the individual cells. To specify how the borders around cells display, you use the `rules` attribute.

Let's illustrate a table border construction:

1. Open the `BasicTable.htm` file you created.

2. Add a `border` attribute to the `<table>` tag.

3. Assign a value of **3** (pixels) to the `border` attribute.

4. Check that the new code you've added to the `<table>` tag looks like the following:

`<table border="3">`

5. Save this file with the name `BorderTable.htm`.

6. Open this new file in your browser. It should look like Figure 2.22 with a border around the table.

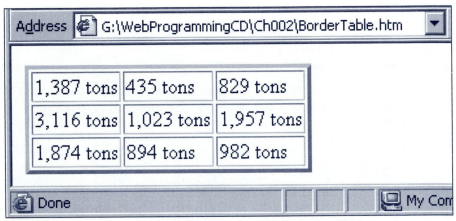

FIGURE 2.22   The `border` Attribute Adds a Border around the Table

Tables and Text Wrapping

The default setting for a table is with a left alignment. This can be altered and text can be wrapped around a table to give your page a more pleasing appearance. Here's an example:

1. Open the `BorderTable.htm` file you created.

2. Add an `align` attribute to the opening table tag.

3. Assign a value of **right** to the `align` attribute.

4. Create a new line containing text between the closing table tag `</table>` and the closing body tag `</body>`. Enter the following text:

Despite numerous technical hurdles, sales have remained strong in major regions this fiscal year. As we head into the New Year, we are anticipating a net sales increase of 10% due to several new products. These products have been through multiple trial stages and the outstanding results bode well for expanding market share. In addition, our new ad campaign, to which the company has committed an unprecedented amount of funding, debuts in the spring.

5. Check that the new code you've added to the table tag looks like the following:

```
<table border="3" align="right">
```

6. Save this file with the name `TextTable.htm`.

7. Open this new file in your browser. It should look like Figure 2.23 with the text wrapped around the right-aligned table.

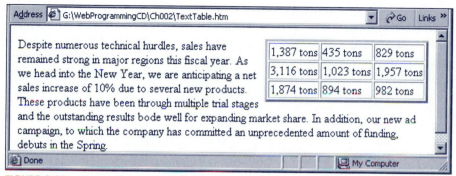

Despite numerous technical hurdles, sales have remained strong in major regions this fiscal year. As we head into the New Year, we are anticipating a net sales increase of 10% due to several new products. These products have been through multiple trial stages and the outstanding results bode well for expanding market share. In addition, our new ad campaign, to which the company has committed an unprecedented amount of funding, debuts in the Spring.

1,387 tons	435 tons	829 tons
3,116 tons	1,023 tons	1,957 tons
1,874 tons	894 tons	982 tons

FIGURE 2.23   Illustration of Text Wrapped around a Table and the `align` Attribute

Adding Headings

Tables require that each row and column have meaning. That meaning can be as simple as a grid address, say B23 or GG234, or more specific such as rows that represent years and columns that represent months. HTML supports special row and column headings to clarify the data you are presenting in your table.

Adding headings to a table requires the use of new table heading tags, as illustrated in the following example:

1. Open the `TextTable.htm` file you created.

2. Create a new row after the opening table tag `<table>` by typing opening and closing table row tags `<tr>` and `</tr>` on two new lines.

3. Add table opening and closing heading tags `<th>` and `</th>` on three new lines between the opening and closing table row tags.

4. Assign the content **West**, **East**, and **South** between the three table heading tags.

5. Check that the new code you've added to the `<table>` tag looks like the following:

```
<tr>
<th></th>
```

```
<th>West</th>
<th>East</th>
<th>South</th>
</tr>
```

6. Save this file as `HeadingsTable.htm`.

7. Open this new file in your browser. It should contain your column headings.

8. To add row headings, add opening and closing table heading tags `<th>` and `</th>` on a new line at the beginning of each row. Assign the content **Strawberries**, **Blackberries**, and **Raspberries** between the last three table heading tags `<th>`. Do not add content to the first row's table heading, which contains the column headings. Your code should look like the following:

```
<!- HeadingsTable.htm ->
<html><head></head><body>
<table border="3" align="right" >
  <tr>
    <th></th>
    <th>West</th>
    <th>East</th>
    <th>South</th>
  </tr>
  <tr>
    <th>Strawberries</th>
    <td>1,387 tons</td>
    <td>435 tons </td>
    <td>829 tons </td>
  </tr>
  <tr>
    <th>Blackberries</th>
    <td>3,116 tons </td>
    <td>1,023 tons </td>
    <td>1,957 tons </td>
  </tr>
  <tr>
    <th>Raspberries</th>
    <td>1,874 tons </td>
    <td>894 tons </tD>
    <td>982 tons </td>
  </tr>
</table>
```

Save the file with the same name.

9. Refresh your browser. It should look like Figure 2.24 with column and row headings.

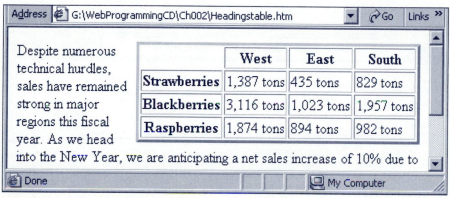

FIGURE 2.24 Table with Column and Row Headings
The addition of column and row headings makes a table's purpose clearer.

Rows That Span Columns

In order to label a whole section of a table, you may wish to add a row that spans several columns. This can be achieved by adding a column span attribute (`colspan`) to the table heading tags <th>, as illustrated in the following example:

1. Open the `HeadingsTable.htm` file you created in the last exercise.

2. Create a new row by adding opening and closing table row tags <tr> and </tr> immediately below the opening table tag.

3. On new lines between the table row tags, add two sets of opening and closing table heading tags <th> and </th>.

4. Leave the first table heading blank; add the heading text **Regions** between the second opening and closing table heading tags.

5. Add a colspan attribute to the opening table heading tag that contains the Regions heading text.

6. Assign a value of **3** (the number of columns you want the heading text to span) to the `colspan` attribute.

7. Check that the new code you've added to the table tag looks like the following:

```
<tr>
<th></th>
<th colspan="3">Regions</th>
</tr>
```

8. Save this file with the name `ColspanTable.htm`.

9. Open this new file in your browser. It should look like Figure 2.25.

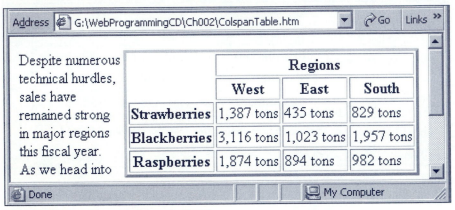

FIGURE 2.25 Table with Spanner Head

The column span, or `colspan`, attribute lets you create column heading groupings. A similar attribute, `rowspan`, lets you create a grouping of rows.

QuickCheck Questions

11. What is the difference between a frame and a table?

12. How do you create a table in HTML?

13. When would you use a table?

14. When would you use a frame?

Where You Go from Here

In this chapter, you have learned many of the most important HTML tags, but far from the majority of tags that have been created. You should have enough of an idea from your reading now to fill in many of the topics that we haven't covered in your further studies. Among the topics we didn't cover here are things like spacing, special symbol treatment, many additional font and paragraph tags, marquees, blinking and hidden text, alternative image (thumbnail) display, block quotes, banners, keyboard shortcuts, tab order for links, forms and form elements, inserting applets, and many additional layout features.

Space precludes a fuller treatment, but you will undoubtedly be exposed to these topics should you continue on learning more Web programming. Given how prevalent Web sites and content are, indeed it will be hard not to learn more about these topics regardless of what you decide to do in life.

In reality, it isn't really necessary that you become a wizard at HTML programming in order to build effective Web sites. Tools such as Microsoft Front-Page and Macromedia Dreamweaver shield you from having to know HTML. You create a page or set of pages, links, formatting, and so on in a graphical interface, point, click, and drag, and the program makes the underlying conversion to code. For the average Web designer (and there are millions of them now), programming in HTML means learning to program in the exceptions or extensions you need to achieve some special purpose. Still, a strong background in HTML "programming" will serve you well in all the other Web programming you do. It is the foundation stone that everything on the Web is built on.

Summary

HTML, the HyperText Markup Language, is a set of instructions or tags that define how content should be displayed in an application that parses HTML. Along with browsers, more and more applications can both read and write HTML files. An HTML file uses only ASCII characters, and it creates text-only files.

Tags are most typically found as pairs in the form `<tag>` . . . `</tag>`, where an opening tag encloses some "stuff" and the closing tag ends the action of the tag. The `<html>` turns on the HTML parser; while other tags delineate the `<header>` . . . `</header>`, where information about the document is stored but not displayed; the `<title>` . . . `</title>`, which controls the title of the browser or application window; and the `<body>` . . . `</body>`. There are many tags that control the layout of a page; others format text and add lists, tables, rules (lines), and so forth. HTML is an agreement, or specification, that changes over time, adding new features while maintaining old ones. The specifications for HTML contain literally hundreds of tags.

Most tags take attributes or modifications that help make the tag do more things. For example, the `<font>` tag can be modified with `color`, `size`, and other attributes that control the text contained within the opening and closing tags.

To make a Web page more visual, HTML can embed images (using the `<img src>` tag) and objects. In order to make information more readily available, HTML uses tags that create hyperlinks. The `<href>` tag can be applied to text, images, and objects. In order to make HTML more powerful, you can create absolute and relative hyperlinks that define a fixed URL or can reference a location that changes. HTML supports tables that contain data, clickable images, or image maps; navigation bars that can serve as branching or jumps to many other sites; and frames to show data derived from different Web documents.

absolute anchor
ASCII
attribute
background
BMP (bit-mapped images)
definition list
embedded image
frame
frameset
GIF (Graphic Interchange
Format)

hyperlink
HyperText Markup Language
image map
Interlaced GIF
interpreter
JPEG (Joint Photographic
Experts Group)
navigation toolbar
nested list
ordered list

palette
parser
PNG (Portable Network
Graphics)
relative anchor
SVG (Scaleable Vector Graphic)
tags
TEXT file
text wrap
unordered list

Review Questions

1. What does a browser need to display a Web page?
2. Describe ASCII.
3. Which tag(s) are required by a Web page?
4. Do all tags require opening and closing tags? What exceptions are there, and why do those tags work properly? How can omitting a closing tag cause you future difficulty?
5. How can you view the underlying source code for a Web page?
6. What tags would you need to create a table of contents down to three levels of heads?
7. What are image maps, where are they used, and how do you construct them?
8. What purpose do frames serve on a Web page?
9. Tables are most often used for a compact data display. What other purpose can they serve?
10. From what you've learned in this chapter, what major capabilities is HTML missing that require extensions?

Exercises

1. One common navigational construct creates a set of links that take you to different parts of your document. Create a list of letters in the alphabet at the top of the page and make each letter a link to a section title for that letter below. Create a client-side image map for a food pyramid, with each part of the pyramid referencing an external file.
2. Using an HTML dictionary, identify the tags found in the source code of CNN's home page, shown in Figure 1.4b.
   You can purchase third-party books that contain HTML tag listings and their explanations, but there are also several available online. Here's a sampling of online resources:
   http://www.w3.org/MarkUp/
   http://www.htmlhelp.com/
   http://www-math.uni-paderborn.de/dictionaries/Dictionaries/HTML-Dictionary/
   http://www.bensplanet.com/htmldic/index.asp

3. You have been given the task as a new Webmaster to create an online page version of this book for the world to admire and contemplate. Begin by creating the HTML code that recreates the first page in this chapter (Chapter 2).

4. In Microsoft Word and Excel, save a document and worksheet in HTML format. Open those documents and examine the source code. What do you notice about the HTML you see that is unique to these applications?

5. In Microsoft Word, use the table wizard to create a table with some sample data and some formatting. Save your document in HTML format, then open that table document in a text editor. Find the code associated with the table, select that code, and copy it to a new text file. Save that file as a second HTML document. Open your second document using your browser. Does the table in the browser look the same as in Word? Go back to your HTML table file and try removing or adding some table tags to create different looks. Describe how these changes are manifested in your browser.

6. Tables are often used to achieve positioning on a page. For example, you can use a table to create a display similar to one you might find in a newspaper. Create a page header and a three-column table, and add an image to a page. What advantages does a table have over a frame?

XML and XHTML

OBJECTIVES

1. To understand why XML is important and where it can be used.

2. To understand how XML differs from HTML and complements it.

3. To be able to construct and understand the syntax of XML documents.

4. To appreciate the use of DTDs and schema for validating XML data.

5. To gain an introduction to XHTML.

INTRODUCTION

XML, or the **eXtensible Markup Language,** is an important developing markup "language" that allows users, groups, organizations, companies, and whole industries to create standard collections of data that can be used locally, be transferred between users and computers, and provide a basis for a whole community to work with data. Since being able to share data universally with other people is the goal of the Internet, and the World Wide Web in particular, XML is becoming more and more important for a variety of uses such as dynamic data display and data interchange. In time, XML will perhaps become the most widely used native file format for productivity applications such as Microsoft Office.

The reason that XML is so useful is that most of the data description is based on tags that are defined for a specific purpose to suit your needs. An XML document or transaction is what you might get if you reduced a database or spreadsheet to a text-only document and included the descriptions of the data into that document. Since XML is self-describing, XML is also portable. With a well-formed XML document, one application doesn't need to know what the creator application was. Indeed, the receiving application doesn't even need to know what XML schema or template was used. Thus, one business can create a template for XML data, and another business can use that template to add data and very efficiently communicate with each other. Communications can include anything from data interchange to transactional data such as purchase orders or invoices.

The **metadata** (data describing other data) is already included in the XML data either as a separate file or as a set of tag declarations. The best way to conceptualize what XML and its tags represent is to think of XML as a meta-language applied to content. The word "meta" means encompassing or containing, and in this context, metadata is information that describes data. What you store in the Microsoft Active Directory, Novell's NDS (Novell Directory Services), or any LDAP (Lightweight Data Access Protocol) compliant directory service is metadata. XML is a language that lets you describe data.

In this chapter you are going to learn how XML data is described, where XML can be used, and why this language is so important that it was presented early on in this course. XML is a developing standard, and a relatively new one at that. Although much of XML is standardized, many more capabilities are being developed in the next couple of years. It's likely that there will be many more powerful features added to XML, but you can count on what you learn here still being valuable. The future of XML will likely be compatible with the past. Hopefully, there will also be easier ways to work with XML, and many more tools. Indeed, the next version of Microsoft Office will read and write XML.

While XML is an excellent means for describing data of all types (even binary files can be contained), XML is not a "presentation" or "layout" language as other interchange languages such as RTF (Rich Text Format), PostScript, and HTML are. XML offers only rudimentary capabilities. In order to use XML, you need to combine XML with HTML, either passing the XML through or combining the two together. That's what the developing standard of XHTML is supposed to offer. You also can combine XML with style sheets to achieve formatting. The two common formatting style sheets are XSLT and CSS, the eXtensible Style Sheets and Cascaded Style Sheets, respectively. CSS also can be applied to HTML, and is a developing standard that is supported by the major modern browsers. Using these two style sheets' capabilities it is possible to transform XML into all sorts of formatted documents or converted transactions. You will learn about these methods for transforming XML in the next chapter.

HTML vs. XML

Here's an example of how you might use HTML to describe a memo:

```
<!- Memo.htm ->
<html>
<head>062003 Memo23</head>
<title>Memo</title>
<h2>To: Accounting</h2>
<h2>From: Barrie Sosinsky</h2>
```

```
<h2>Date: 062004</h2>
<h2>Re: New Invoice Form</h2>
<br></br>
<p>Just a reminder that starting Monday we need to use the
  new invoice forms when purchasing outside items.</p>
<p>If you have any questions, give me a call.</p>
</html>
```

Now let's look at something similar using XML:

```
<!- Memo.xml ->
<?xml version="1.0" encoding="utf-8" ?>
<!- Here's an example of a comment. ->
<message>
   <filename>062003 Memo23</filename>
   <title>Memo</title>
   <to>Accounting</to>
   <from>Barrie Sosinsky</from>
   <date>062004</date>
   <subject>New Invoice Form</subject>
   <p>Just a reminder that starting Monday we need to use
      the new invoice forms when purchasing outside items.
      </p>
   <p>If you have any questions, give me a call.</p>
</message>
```

These two descriptions illustrate the fundamental difference between HTML and XML. At first glance HTML looks rather similar to XML, particularly because the document chosen is so recognizable. We've all sent memos like this, usually from a standard template. However, there are some important and subtle differences that make XML a very powerful method for data interchange.

Unlike HTML, XML rigidly enforces well-formed tags, also called **elements.** As you build your Web sites and construct HTML documents, in time you will want to incorporate XML data and applications into them. We'll get into some of the methods you might use a little later in this chapter and in the next one. (If you use sloppy HTML or poorly formed HTML, you will run into trouble with XML later on.)

Your recipient might not know HTML and see the `<h2>` tag. That tag shows up in several lines, but bears no relationship to the data it contains. You know, because you read in the previous chapter (hopefully), that `<h2>` is the second-level heading tag that describes a text formatting style. So, since tags like `<h2>` don't tell us much about the data, only how to format it, we embed additional information like To:, From:, Date:, and Re: to make the pieces of data more understandable.

In XML we use the tags `<to>`, `<from>`, `<date>`, and `<subject>`—not to mention `<message>`—to explain what the data means. Therefore, we don't have to waste time putting redundant information into the text. Chances are that your recipient knows what these tags mean.

But let's say that your document contained a number of items that aren't so widely known. Your company sells Widgets, and Widgets have certain properties such as an ID in the Widgets Directory, a color number assignment, and so on. You would use tags like `<widgetid>`, `<color#>`, and so forth. Your recipient still hasn't the foggiest idea what these tags mean, but here's the good part: in XML documents you declare what the tag is, what data it can contain, and, if you need to, information about how to make sense of the data. You could, for example, give them the ISBN number of the Widgets Directory, and they'd be all set.

HTML is hypertext, while XML is not. Hypertext requires the use of linkages (in addition to being a page description language). Without the necessary elements to link and to format a page, XML cannot be transformed as anything more than text or a diagram inside a browser or other XML **parser** (reading application).

You learned in the last chapter that the World Wide Web uses the HTML to display content in a browser, format that content, and provide instructions on how to lay out a page. As central as HTML is to the World Wide Web, some serious limitations have required its extension into many other areas. HTML, for example, doesn't handle calls to operating system or application APIs (application programming interfaces) well, has rudimentary multimedia capabilities, and doesn't have the capability to generate dynamic data based on user input. All of those capabilities are added to modern Web sites using extensions to HTML, which in turn call external programming or scripting languages, and use plug-ins and helper applications to fill in the blanks.

The omission of a dynamic data capability is of fundamental importance because as the Web has developed, many important capabilities rely on personalizing a viewer's browsing experience. Think of how much more difficult it would be to use Amazon.com, Travelocity.com, Expedia.com, eBay.com, or your online bank account if they didn't "remember" who you were and present you with your current shopping cart, your saved trip itinerary, or your history of deposits and withdrawals. Dynamic data doesn't necessarily mean that this information is stored for you (although it could be stored), but rather that the recipe for isolating this information is part of your profile, perhaps stored locally on your drive as a cookie (a small text-only preference file) or stored server side. Personalization also will lead to a time when vast user identification databases such as Microsoft Passport store information on literally hundreds of millions of users and provide the data required by numerous Web services to come—services that often take the form of programming modules with their own APIs.

So while HTML can present data, HTML doesn't describe what the data means, or how to use that data. HTML is focused on the look and feel or layout of the data, and really just serves the function of a container for any data it contains.

That's where XML (the eXtensible Markup Language) comes in. XML is a markup language that defines the content contained in a data file. Since XML was developed as a subset of SGML (as was HTML), people talk in terms of XML being a "document-oriented" "language." XML is "document oriented" in the sense that you can use XML to describe an invoice or collection of invoices, or any paper form you might choose. However, XML is used to describe any set of well-formed repeating data. And XML is a "language" in the sense that you declare a collection of tags and their meaning, and that collection is called a language (something that most programmers would find archaic). Thus, XML finds use as a new standard of data interchange, a format if you will.

QuickCheck Questions

1. What does a browser display on a page?
2. How is XML data displayed in your browser?
3. What purpose does dynamic data serve on the Web?
4. What is metadata?

At first glance, XML looks a lot like HTML in that the tags and the attributes of those tags are constructed very similarly to HTML. However, if you examine an XML document closely, what you will find is that while the tags in XML are well formed and precise, most tags aren't standard and can't be used in other XML uses. Not only is the data type in one XML document's `P.O. Number` field different from document to document, but there may be a `P.O. Number` in one invoice and not in another. And should two programmers define their tags with the names `P.O. Number` and `PO number`, those two tags would be incompatible. XML pays strict attention to the case of the text.

The point is that XML lets you define your own tags and use those tags for any purpose you require. There are strict rules on how tags need to be used in a document: tags must be well formed and be a matched pair (opening and closing), nesting and precedence are important, and other factors are important, but the tags you use can be made to suit your need. XML is self-describing, and using elements of XML you will tell or be told what the data means and how to use it. This ad hoc construction and the fact that XML looks a lot like HTML make XML very hard to describe, and very confusing to many people. So as you read on, consider that XML is in fact a distinct markup language, and one that has been integrated into HTML.

Tech Tip

XML vs. SGML
To get a further explanation of the differences between these two related markup languages, go to the W3C's site: http://www.w3c.org/TR/NOTE-sgml-xml-971215.

XML in the Real World

XML lets you build a data set the way you want. However, XML would be very inefficient if every document or data file it described was unique. You certainly can make each one unique, but that isn't why the technology is so useful and becoming so central. When you define an XML document and data set, perhaps you are using them only on your own system for your own use, a private definition. More likely, though, you might want to share your XML data with someone else, and so you send your data and its description along. Since XML is self-describing, your intended recipient could use that data. Should the recipient want to send you back new or altered data using the same data schema, then the two of you might agree on a common interchange form and you are on your way to a standard definition. When you substitute a large company for an individual, there are many recipients to that one source.

Let's consider a brief example. General Motors wants to streamline its procurement process with its thousands of suppliers, so it imposes a requirement that all invoices, statements, and purchase orders be in a very specific form, and contain very specific pieces of information formatted in a specific way. Being what is called a "channel hub" or "channel master," GM can impose these requirements, the net result of which is that its many suppliers are forced to adopt these requirements first on paper, and subsequently on computer-based forms. Channel masters are organizations that can impose their XML standard on others. This is the way many standard XML definitions arise. When a hub or master doesn't create a standard XML definition or language, you will find that there are industry working groups who will define a common scheme, indicating the kinds of documents that are standard for their industry, what each must contain, and in what order and form. Most of the important XML standards are from these working groups, and are often works in progress.

The Benefits of XML

Over the last 20 years, a technology called **EDI,** or **electronic data interchange,** has provided the framework for communicating between two computers bulk transactional data such as invoices or purchase orders (POs). GM, banks, and other large companies or organizations would then contract with a telecommunications provider to collect all of the invoices (and other documents) by modem or some other method, assemble all of the documents into a batch, and send that batch communication over a **VPN,** or **virtual private network.** Since VPN is a private transmission medium, it's secure—albeit much more costly than a distributed network like the Internet. Since the communication is text-only and batched, the process is efficient. However, the many companies participating in this network require special software, maybe different software for each company that they deal with, and the result is that EDI is both costly and complex.

Wouldn't it be nice if you could replace EDI with something that had the same benefits, but also offered

- Efficient transmission of text-based, self-describing data.
- Extensible technology based on your current and future data interchange needs.

- An open standard, so everyone can play.
- Software that is prevalent (a browser) and standard on everyone's desktop, and in which the viewing application can read and write data no matter what platform or computer you are using.
- A transmission medium that is both less costly and ubiquitous (the Internet).

That is exactly what XML is meant to do, and why XML will eventually make EDI obsolete. XML, like HTML, is a much simpler version of the SGML (Standard Markup Language) standard that was developed by the W3C (http://www.w3c.org) to make data interchange between disparate computers possible. However, XML is much, much easier to learn that SGML.

Among the uses for XML are

- As a container for data that you will use inside HTML files.
- As data that is stored separately from your HTML files.
- As an **interchange format.**
- As a way to store data in files or inside a database.

XML Application Deployment

XML is eventually going to replace EDI in all but a few instances. The very largest bulk transmissions will continue to be sent over VPNs for a long time to come. There are still communications such as military or commercial applications that require extreme security: those too will require VPNs. However, the allure of using the Internet for transactional data transmission and standardizing on widely available software makes XML far less expensive than VPN, and makes it possible for many more businesses and individuals to use these methods.

You are going to find that the next versions of major productivity applications like Microsoft Office (Office.NET), FileMaker Pro, and a host of other applications are going to let you save all of your files in an XML format. Once that happens, XML will become a central technology that all programmers will need to work with. You can expect to see XML as a standard feature in word processors, spreadsheets, and databases, as well as support in special high-transaction business servers such as Microsoft's BizTalk server.

Just like HTML, XML needs the following applications to be useful:

1. An editor to create the text either manually in a text editor, using a special HTML editing program, or using a full-blown WYSIWYG (What You See Is What You Get) Web page/site creation program.

2. A browser or application that can open and view XML documents, composing them from all of the required elements and objects.

3. A parser, which is the logic engine that can read XML and figure out what code to execute when, matters of precedence, and so forth, and pass the appropriate instructions along for a browser or other application to use.

Tech Tip

EDI and XML
To read more about the differences and uses of XML and EDI, go to the XML-EDI group page at http://www.xmledi.com, where you will find the latest information about recent activities in both areas.

An editor can be as simple as Notepad, contain specialized tools such as XML Pro, or be as complex as a special application that lets you create and manage tags in a visual interface such as Spyglass or XML Spy. Some browsers display XML (such as Internet Explorer and Mozilla) and some do not, but there are also special applications that are meant to read XML and display it.

Even with all of these tools, XML documents still need a way to format their data; otherwise it would be very hard to actually read an XML document after it is parsed by a browser. To fill in this gap, XML can work in conjunction with Cascading Style Sheets, Level 2 (CSS2), as well as with XML Stylesheets (XSL), both of which offer developers a way of laying out their data.

QuickCheck Questions

5. Why is XML important?
6. Where will XML be used in the future?
7. What problem(s) does XML attempt to solve?
8. What's missing in XML that is needed for display purposes?

Basic XML Syntax

All tagged languages require a declaration about which language is being used. This tag is usually the first line in the document, but not always. When an application sees this tag, it interprets it as a call to open the XML parser. For HTML, as you saw in the previous chapter, the tag pair `<HTML>` . . . `</HTML>` provides the container for the parser to act on. Most people just use this simple form of the tag, but you also can add on attributes such as version numbers if that is necessary. When a browser (or any other application that can read HTML) opens a text file and sees the tag `<html>`, it knows to turn on its HTML parser and interpret the text according to the rules that that application stores. The `</html>` closing tag turns off the parser. Oftentimes the closing tag is omitted, although it is good practice in HTML to include the closing tag and mandatory in XHTML.

For XML the declarative tag is

```
<?xml version= "1.0"? attribute list)> . . . </xml>
```

XML documents don't always use a closing tag (just like HTML) for the `<?xml>` tag because these documents are constructed to contain only XML data. It's assumed that once all nested pairs of tags are accounted for, no additional data will be described. Notice that the tag looks a little different than the `<html>` tag. You need `<?xml>` to turn the parser on. Additional information may be included in the tag, such as the version number of XML used (at present that is 1.0 only), and any number of attributes. For example, it's common to include the encoding used in an XML document, particularly when you are going to use the data in different languages or countries.

Any application that can work with XML must have a parser, as indeed Internet Explorer does, and eventually most mainstream applications will. A parser is a logic engine that examines the contents of a file, checks that file's tags for correctness (proper syntax), and using the instructions that are contained in the tag displays or modifies the data in an appropriate way. Not all data is parsed, although that is the default action. Certain data such as binary data (an image file, for example) is passed through the parser untouched.

There are two elements that can be placed before the `<?xml>` tag: **comments** and preprocessor **directives.** Comments in XML take the form

```
<!-comment text here->
```

and use a double hyphen to surround the comment. (This is the same syntax used in HTML.) You don't need to use spaces between the double hyphens and the comment text. Comments can appear anywhere in an XML document, and indeed good comments about the document's purpose and construction are very valuable to those people that come after you (or even to you at some later date). XML ignores comments and a browser will not display them.

Keep in mind that unlike HTML, XML requires very strict adherence to its syntax rules. There aren't many rules, and you will find them easy to learn, but they must be observed. This simplicity means that even simple software can work with XML easily. Consider this simple XML document that describes a software bug database.

```
<!- Bug_Data.xml ->
<?xml version="1.0" encoding= "ISO-8859-1"?>
<bug_data>
  <date>1/25/04</date>
  <reported_by>Barrie Sosinsky</reported_by>
  <subject>
    <subject_text>Navigator 2.5 XML File Open Issue
      </subject_text>
    <subject_category>File Open</subject_category>
    <subject_priority>Moderate</subject_priority>
    <subject_status>Open</subject_status>
  </subject>
  <description>The XML data document TEST.XML doesn't open
    correctly in Netscape Navigator 2.5 on
    Solaris</description>
</bug_data>
```

Notice that when the parser is turned on, this XML document asks for version 1.0 as well as the ISO-8859-1 (Latin-1/Western European) character set. The

Tech Tip

Commenting Out Code
A very useful programming technique is to use comments to remove sections of your code to check for errors. If there is a part of your document that is causing problems, you can comment out the appropriate sections until you isolate the exact part of the code that is the issue.

next line after the `<?xml>` tag is the root tag, `<bug_data>`. A root tag contains all other tags within it. You can think of the root tag as a container, and its naming should indicate what the purpose of the XML data file is.

Elements can be a **parent element,** with any elements nested within it being **child elements.** Child elements can be parents to elements contained within them, thus describing a formal hierarchy. Thus, the four elements contained inside the `<subject>` element are its children: `<subject_text>`, `<subject_category>`, `<subject_priority>`, and `<subject_status>` are all child elements of `<subject>`, and they are subchild elements of `<bug_data>`.

A parser would examine these tags and perhaps map them as a node map (as is the case with XSLT parsers, as described in the next chapter), and if the construction is correct, the browser would display it. If a structure is flawed, the parser will post an error and not display the result. If you copy the code above into a text editor and create a file called Bug_Data.xml, when you open this file using Internet Explorer, it will be displayed as shown in Figure 3.1.

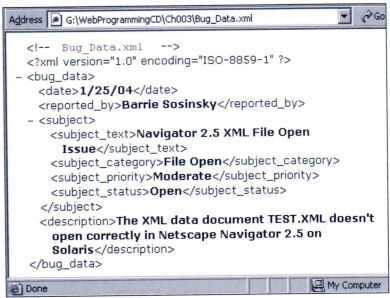

FIGURE 3.1   The Bug_Data.xml Data File Parsed and Displayed in Internet Explorer

Notice that all of the tags in XML are matched. In HTML you can have the following:

```
<p>Paragraph 1 . . .
<p>Paragraph 2 . . .</p>
<p>Paragraph 3 . . .</P>
```

and the HTML parser will correctly interpret the lone `<p>` tag. HTML is very forgiving. However, if you want to use your HTML with XML, or import it into XHTML, it is very important that you close all of your tags in HTML and that your HTML documents be similarly well formed, as is the case for Paragraph 2. HTML will also correctly interpret Paragraph 3, where the tag cases are different. However, XML tags are case sensitive and `<DESCRIPTION>` . . . `</Description>` will create a parsing error. This case sensitivity is a good reason to adopt a standard convention, such as all elements and value names are all uppercase symbols (most books' preference) or all lowercase symbols (what you will need to use if you use XHTML). Given the coming importance of XHTML, this book uses lowercase letters.

Consider the following two paragraphs:

```
<b><i>Paragraph 4. The number of this paragraph is 4, and
   4 is the number.</b></i>
<b><i>Paragraph 5. Paragraph 5 would follow Paragraph 4
   in all instances where you are working with base 6 numbers
   and above.</i></b>
```

HTML will correctly interpret both Paragraph 4 and Paragraph 5, and it will tolerate (some, not all) nesting errors. XML is much stricter and will only interpret Paragraph 5 correctly.

Once you assign special meaning in XML to characters like a double hyphen, :, &, <, >, ', and ", you need a mechanism to use that symbol in your text. XML assigns the symbols `&amp`, `&lt`, `&gt`, `&apos`, and `&quot` to take the place of these reserved characters in text. Another method you can use to display any character or character string as text is to declare it as character data using the `<![CDATA[...]]>` tag. Anything enclosed inside a CDATA tag will be passed through the parser as simple text. You can't nest CDATA sections within each other, and you don't need any special symbol representation inside a CDATA section. One useful application of CDATA tags is to enclose a Cascaded Style Sheet (CSS); CSS is discussed in the next chapter.

Elements, Attributes, and Values in XML Documents

Elements or tag pairs are the building blocks of XML. An element can be any allowed symbol or string, but it is best to make the element name meaningful. Elements can be modified by the use of *attributes*. An **attribute** is a description contained inside an element's opening tag that is assigned a single **value** that the tag can use as information for further use. Attributes are metadata for elements. All values need to be enclosed in quotation marks in order to be valid, and each value in a set of values needs to be separated by a comma. There is no restriction on the number of attributes an element may have, only on those attributes each having a unique name. Figure 3.2 shows the generalized syntax for element construction.

Tech Tip

Different Endings
Another difference that is not apparent without inspection is that XML inserts a line feed character after each line. Line feeds, AKA new line characters, tell a word processor to end a line and move to the next line without ending a paragraph. With formatting marks turned on, Microsoft Word displays a line feed character (Shift+Enter) as the "⏎" symbol. Different operating systems handle end of line symbols in different ways. In Windows applications, a new line might be the CR LF (carriage return, line feed) characters. The Macintosh uses only a CR symbol for a new line, while Unix applications store the LF character.

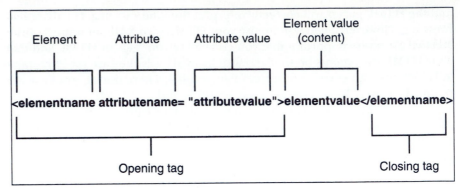

FIGURE 3.2　Elements of Element Construction

If you have multiple attributes, you might want to use a nested construction as show below:

```
<!- Books.xml ->
<books>
   <type physical_form="hardcover" >Coffee table size
      </type>
   <type physical_form="softcover" >Pocket book</type>
   <type physical_form= "magazine" >Tabloid</type>
   . . .
</books>
```

Any element that is normally empty can be written in shorthand in XML. An example of this is the following:

```
<image src="SomeImage.gif"/>
```

In this example, the <image> tag is an empty tag because it does not contain any further subelement, nor does it contain any text (value). However, notice that an empty tag may contain many attributes though. In our example, the <image> tag contains an attribute named "src". You can close an empty tag simply by adding /> to the end.

While the use of attributes is common, an alternative to using attributes is to define additional elements. Consider the alternative construction to the codes shown above:

```
<!- AlternativeBooks.xml ->
<books>
   <type><physical_form>hardcover</physical_form>Coffee
      table size</type>
   <type><physical_form>softcover</physical_form>Pocket
      book</type>
   <type><physical_form>magazine</physical_form>Tabloid
      </type>
</books>
```

Although the construction is different, the information provided is identical. So which type of construction should you use? Although it's a matter of preference, my preference is to use attributes in HTML but to use elements as much as possible in XML. It isn't always possible to avoid attributes and show identical information, but it can be done in many, if not most, cases. By using elements in place of attributes, you

- Can accommodate multiple values.
- Make it easier to add additional information.
- Make it easier for a parser to navigate your code.
- Have a more easily understandable hierarchical structure.
- Allow the DTD and XML schemas to validate your data better.

So it's best to use attributes for information that won't be used by the reader. One place where you might want to use an attribute is when you have a unique identification number or code. In HTML you can use the `name` or `id` attribute for this purpose, and it is worth adopting that practice for XML. With a unique ID you can access individual pieces of information in XML much more quickly.

QuickCheck Questions

9. What turns on a parser in an XML document?
10. Do all elements need closing tags?
11. What is an attribute, and when should you use it?

Data Definition and Validation

Not only must XML documents be well formed (matched tags with the same letter case) in order to be displayed in a parser, it is important from the standpoint of data accuracy to validate the data they contain. **Validation** not only checks the "well-formedness" of a document, but it also checks to see that the data conforms to a standard definition for a document of that type. With validation, you can make any set of XML documents conform to a standard specification or class. Essentially what you are doing is applying a template to your data, and that allows XML to be used in any number of applications.

There are three types of validation techniques used:

- An internal **Document Type Definition,** or **DTD**.
- An **external** DTD, most often a stand-alone file.
- An XML **schema,** which is a developing standard of the W3C.

Internal DTDs

Originally most documents were internally self-describing. They contained all of the elements' descriptions, along with data type, order, and precedence.

You can still set up your XML documents in this way using the following construction, called an **internal** DTD:

```
<!- MemoWithDTD.xml ->
<?xml version="1.0"?>
<!DOCTYPE memo [
  <!ELEMENT memo (to,from,subject,description)>
  <!ELEMENT to (#PCDATA)>
  <!ELEMENT from (#PCDATA)>
  <!ELEMENT subject (#PCDATA)>
  <!ELEMENT description (#PCDATA)>
]>
<memo>
  <to>Accounting</to>
  <from>Barrie Sosinsky</from>
  <subject>Time's People of the Year</subject>
  <description>You are being watched!!</description>
</memo>
```

The tag `<!DOCTYPE root [...]>` delineates the DTD. In this internal DTD, you see the `memo` element is the parent of four child elements (`to,from, subject,description`). The data type (#PCDATA) is short for parsed character data. The `#PCDATA` entry always appears in parentheses, and it refers to all letters, numbers, symbols, and entities that aren't part of tag construction. The order and precedence of the elements described in the DTD must be maintained in the XML data set in order for the document to be valid.

External DTDs

In nearly all cases, a DTD is a published file to which the XML data document contains a pointer. In an organization containing many people, using a set of DTDs means that any change made to a DTD will be propagated to every XML document that uses that DTD. If you had a DTD describing a memo and your company was a legal firm, you might want to add a `<PRIVACY>` . . . `</PRIVACY>` tag that would always contain the following text: "This memo is privileged communications, yatta, yatta, yatta . . ." Now every time someone goes to print an email based on this DTD, that information will be included. Better yet, *any* XML document that was previously created and uses this DTD will pick it up.

If you opened an external DTD corresponding to the internal one you saw above, it would look like this:

```
<!- Memo_template.dtd ->
<!ELEMENT memo (to,from,subject,description)>
<!ELEMENT to (#PCDATA)>
<!ELEMENT from (#PCDATA)>
<!ELEMENT subject (#PCDATA)>
<!ELEMENT description (#PCDATA)>
```

You make a call to a DTD file in an XML file using the following syntax:

```
<!Doctype memo system "Memo_template.dtd">
```

For example, the Correspondence.xml document shown below is referring to the DTD specified in the Memo_template.dtd.

```
<!- Correspondence.xml ->
<?xml version="1.0" standalone="no"?>
<!DOCTYPE memo SYSTEM "Memo_template.dtd">
<memo>
   <to>Accounting</to>
   <from>Barrie Sosinsky</from>
   <subject>Time's People of the Year</subject>
   <description>You are being watched!!</description>
</memo>
```

If your elements have attributes, you would declare them using the `<!attlist name value>` tag. To refer to an external DTD in your XML document, you would use the reference shown in Figure 3.3.

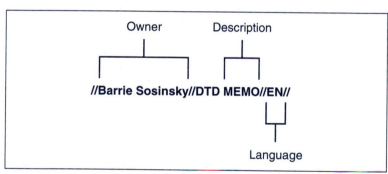

FIGURE 3.3   A Standard Name for an External DTD

To declare a personal external DTD, include the attribute `standalone="no"` as an attribute of the `<?xml>` tag, and reference that document from your XML file using the form `<!doctype root system "PATH/FILENAME.DTD">`. `system` refers to a personal DTD, and the path and filename must point to an absolute or relative URL where the DTD is located. To declare a public external DTD, use the following construction:

```
<?xml version= "1.0" standalone= "no"?>
<!-The above is a shortcut for a tag with no values->
<!doctype root public "PATH/FILENAME.DTD">
. . .
</root>
```

In the situation where there are an internal and an external DTD, the internal DTD overrides the external one.

Elements and Attributes in DTDs

You've seen how a DTD defines a simple element with one or more children in the previous sections. DTDs have their own formal way of describing various types of elements and attributes that are meant to impose a strong description on the data being handled. Table 3.1 describes some of the more common ELEMENT tag constructs.

TABLE 3.1   DTD Element and Attribute Constructs

To Define This	Use This Syntax	Notes
An empty element	`<!ELEMENT NAME EMPTY>`	You can have an empty element even if it takes an attribute with a value.
An element with a value	`<!ELEMENT NAME (value)>`	
An element with any value	`<!ELEMENT NAME ANY>`	Since ANY allows all combinations of text and characters, it does little to specify the contents of an element, and is only very rarely used.
An element with only text	`<!ELEMENT NAME (#PCDATA)>`	#PCDATA must be in parentheses and stands for parsed character data.
An element with only a single child	`<!ELEMENT NAME (childname)>`	Each instance of this element in every XML document must have one and only one child element or it is not valid.
An element with a sequence of child elements	`<!ELEMENT NAME (childname1, childname2,childname3, . . .)>`	Each instance of this element in every XML document that uses this DTD must have each of these child elements in the sequence listed or it is not valid.
An element with a choice of elements	`<!ELEMENT NAME ((childname1, childname2)|childname3)>`	This construct lets you choose from either supplying the combination of childname1 and childname2, OR childname3. The pipe symbol ("|") can be appended to this list to provide more choices.

Continued

TABLE 3.1   DTD Element and Attribute Constructs (continued)

To Define This	Use This Syntax	Notes
The number of units a value may have	`<!ELEMENT NAME (value1?, value2+,value3*)>`	The special symbols derived from the wildcard concept are ?, for zero or one unit; +, once at least or more; and *, as many times as you like including zero units.
An element with three or more values	`<!ELEMENT NAME (value1, value2,value3+)>`	
A simple attribute	`<!ATTLIST ATTRIBUTENAME value1>`	
An optional attribute	`<!ATLIST ATTRIBUTENAME value1 CDATA #IMPLIED>`	
A required attribute	`<!ATTLIST ATTRIBUTENAME (value1|value2) #REQUIRED>`	You can select either value.
A default value for the attribute	`<!ATTLIST ATTRIBUTENAME (value1|value2) "default" value2>`	Here value2 will be entered if no value is chosen.
Set a fixed value for an attribute	`<!ATTLIST ATTRIBUTENAME #FIXED value1>`	The `#FIXED` directive defines value1 as the default value that *must* be set.
An attribute with a unique and required value	`<!ATTLIST ATTRIBUTENAME ID #REQUIRED>`	The `ID` property is for a unique and nonrepeatable value in an XML document. If two or more of the same value is found, the XML document is not valid.
An attribute with a unique value	`<!ATTLIST ATTRIBUTENAME1 ATTRIBUTENAME2 IDREF #REQUIRED>`	The `IDREF` attribute property requires a value for ATTRIBUTENAME2 that matches a value found in ATTRIBUTENAME1. Use `IDREF`s with white-space-separated values to match any one of the list of values.
Restrict attributes to a valid XML name	`<!ATTLIST ATTRIBUTENAME1 ATTRIBUTE2 NMTOKEN #IMPLIED>`	Here `NMTOKEN` requires that the value of ATTRIBUTE2 be an XML name. An XML name is the word that identifies the content that follows. Use `NMTOKEN`s to supply a white-spaced-delimited list of valid names.

Entities

XML supports the concept of variables that are placeholders for text, something that is referred to as an **entity.** An entity reference is a reference to another entity. The different types of entities are shown in Figure 3.4. General entities load data into an XML document, while parameter entities reference data that is in the DTD. The internal and external categories refer to the placement of the entity into the DTD document or another external file. Finally, parsed entities are evaluated by the parser for their form while unparsed entities are simply passed through the parser as is. Parameter entities are always parsed.

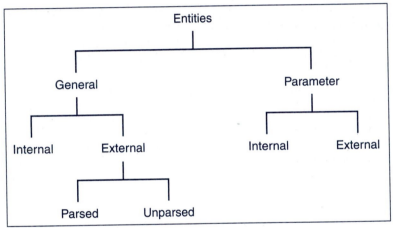

FIGURE 3.4   Entity Classes

You've already seen some internal general entities, the `&amp, &lt, &gt, &quot,` and `&apost` symbols are examples. An internal general entity is essentially declaring text that can be used in a DTD. The syntax for specifying entities in a DTD is as follows:

```
<!entity entityname value>
```

The value can be another entity, as long as there are no circular references. Consider the following example of an internal entity. In the DTD you would define

```
<!ENTITY BK "Programming the Web">
<!ENTITY AU "Barrie Sosinsky">
<!ENTITY PUB "McGraw-Hill">
```

Then in the XML file you could refer to these entities as follows:

```
<titles>&BK;&AU;&PUB</author>
```

This saves you a lot of time and gives you considerable flexibility. First, you don't need to remember the value(s) of each variable piece of content, and, second, you are free to make substitutions at any time and have your XML document pick them up.

To use the general entity in an XML document, you would insert the reference to it as `&ENTITYNAME`, where `ENTITYNAME` is either a word, a short definition, or, most often, an abbreviation. For larger, more complex entities, it may be convenient to store the data in a separate file. You would add the `standalone="no"` attribute to the XML document's `<?xml>` tag, and in the DTD refer to the external file using the following syntax:

```
<!entity entityname system "path/filename">
```

where the path/filename is a valid URL, and `system` means that you find the definition in another document. You also can substitute `PUBLIC ENTITYNAME` if the name is something that is a publicly listed entity in place of the URL. With those two entries in place, you can use the abbreviation `&ENTITYNAME` anywhere you need it in your XML file. External parameter entries are shortcuts you define that refer to one or more parts of the DTD.

All of the entities described so far are text, and in XML text is parsed or interpreted by the application that understands XML. However, XML data can include all sorts of content such as images, binary files, and other content that is unparsed or passed through. To use an entity for unparsed content, you would use the following entry in your DTD:

```
<!entity entityname system "path/filename" NDATA
   notationname>
```

where `path/filename` is a valid URL to the file with the unparsed content. The `NDATA notationname` refers to the `notation` element, which describes where you will find information about the file being referenced. Finally, you complete the information required for an unparsed entity by adding the following `notation` tag:

```
<!notation notationname system "file_information">
```

The reference to `file_information` can be a category that describes the content type, such as "movies/avi." To use the unparsed entity in your XML document, you would declare an attribute that references that entity in your DTD as follows:

```
<!attlist attributename entityname entity>
```

The italicized text is shown here to indicate the names of the attribute and the entity. The `entity` attribute is the final declaration required. To use the unparsed content in your XML document you would insert the entry

```
<attributename="value"/>
```

where `attribute` is the name of the attribute and `value` is the abbreviation you defined.

QuickCheck Questions

12. What does it mean that an XML document is well formed?

13. Name the three ways in which you can specify the data elements in an XML document.

14. What function do entities serve?

XML Schema

DTDs are constructed in a rather ad hoc fashion, and don't necessarily contain all of the tools for data typing that modern programming applications require. Therefore, the W3C has a standard called XML schema that will more completely formalize XML's data definition. The XML schema defines

- Elements and attributes.
- Element hierarchy (parent and child elements).
- The required number of elements.
- Element precedence.
- The required content of an element and the data type(s) of its attributes.
- Any default or fixed values, in addition to the variable data.

There are many additional reasons why you want to take the time and trouble to learn how to use XML schemas. XML schemas are tightly defined and extendable and contain more tools for data manipulation and data typing than a DTD does. XML schemas also are written in XML and, most importantly, support the concept of a namespace. **Namespaces** are a collection of related DTDs that represent a category description. You use a namespace as a means to identify a collection; it is the top-level name in the hierarchy and serves the purpose in a naming convention as the overall container for a particular type of XML document. Thus, specifying the particular namespace as part of a tag's definition frees a programmer from having to repetitively define every instance of any tag. We'll describe schemas and namespaces a little later in this chapter.

An XML schema document is a text file with an XSD file extension. XSD elements that contain text are described as simple types, and those with other elements are called complex types. Among the simple types are data types such as date, integer, and string that are built in, but you can define your own. Elements also can be named and reused throughout the schema, or they are anonymous and used only in the element with their defining elements.

One of the important reasons you might use a schema in place of a DTD to validate your XML data is in a DTD every element is a global element. In a schema you can have not only global elements, but local elements as well. That means that you can only use the element name once in a document. XML documents may reference an element more than once within the same document and with a DTD you can only have one definition for all references.

In a schema you can differentiate between global declarations, which appear at the top of the schema below the `xsd:schema` element. Schemas also let you define a locally declared element for a complex type definition that is used anywhere within the schema.

Here's an example of a call to a published schema:

```
<?xml version="1.0">
<xsd:schema xmlns:xsd="path/filename">
</xsd:schema>
```

You would save this as your XSD file.

The W3C has published a rather detailed tutorial on XML schema, which you can find at http://www.w3.org/TR/xmlschema-0/#POSchema, that is widely quoted. That tutorial offers an example of a more fully developed schema for a purchase order (PO.XSD) and the purchase order XML file. Figure 3.5 shows the XSD schema file that validates the XML data file shown in Figure 3.6 for a purchase order.

```
<xs:schema xmlns:xs="http://www.w3.org/2001/XMLSchema"
   targetNamespace="http://tempuri.org/po.xsd"
xmlns="http:tempuri.org/po.xsd" elementFormDefault=
   "qualified">
<xs:annotation>
   <xs:documentation xml:lang="en">
      Purchase order schema from Example.com.
      Copyright 2000 Example.com. All rights reserved.
   </xs:documentation>
</xs:annotation>

<xs:element name="purchaseOrder" type="
   PurchaseOrderType"/>

<xs:element name="comment" type="xs:string"/>

<xs:complexType name="PurchaseOrderType">
   <xs:sequence>
      <xs:element name="shipTo" type="USAddress"/>
      <xs:element name="billTo" type="USAddress"/>
      <xs:element ref="comment" minOccurs="0"/>
      <xs:element name="items" type="Items"/>
   </xs:sequence>
   <xs:attribute name="orderDate" type="xs:date"/>
</xs:complexType>

<xs:complexType name="USAddress">
   <xs:sequence>
```

FIGURE 3.5   An XSD Schema from Example.com.

Continued

```
                <xs:element name="name" type="xs:string"/>
                <xs:element name="street" type="xs:string"/>
                <xs:element name="city" type="xs:string"/>
                <xs:element name="state" type="xs:string"/>
                <xs:element name="zip" type="xs:decimal"/>
          </xs:sequence>
          <xs:attribute name="country" type="xs:NMTOKEN"
            fixed="US"/>
      </xs:complexType>

      <xs:complexType name="Items">
        <xs:sequence>
          <xs:element name="item" minOccurs="0" maxOccurs="
            unbounded">
            <xs:complexType>
              <xs:sequence>
                <xs:element name="productName" type="xs:
                  string"/>
                <xs:element name="quantity">
                  <xs:simpleType>
                    <xs:restriction base="xs:positiveInteger">
                      <xs:maxExclusive value="100"/>
                    </xs:restriction>
                  </xs:simpleType>
                </xs:element>
                <xs:element name="USPrice" type="xs:decimal"/>
                <xs:element ref="comment" minOccurs="0"/>
                <xs:element name="shipDate" type="xs:date"
                  minOccurs="0"/>
              </xs:sequence>
              <xs:attribute name="partNum" type="SKU"
                use="required"/>
            </xs:complexType>
          </xs:element>
        </xs:sequence>
    </xs:complexType>

      <!- Stock Keeping Unit, a code for identifying products ->
      <xs:simpleType name="SKU">
        <xs:restriction base="xs:string">
          <xs:pattern value="\d{3}-[A-Z]{2}"/>
        </xs:restriction>
      </xs:simpleType>

  </xs:schema>
```

FIGURE 3.5   An XSD Schema from Example.com.   (continued)

```
<?xml version="1.0"?>
<purchaseOrder xmlns="http://tempuri.org/po.xsd"
  orderDate="1999-10-20">
  <shipTo country="US">
    <name>Alice Smith</name>
    <street>123 Maple Street</street>
    <city>Mill Valley</city>
    <state>CA</state>
    <zip>90952</zip>
  </shipTo>
  <billTo country="US">
    <name>Robert Smith</name>
    <street>8 Oak Avenue</street>
    <city>Old Town</city>
    <state>PA</state>
    <zip>95819</zip>
  </billTo>
  <comment>Hurry, my lawn is going wild!</comment>
  <items>
    <item partNum="872-AA">
      <productName>Lawnmower</productName>
      <quantity>1</quantity>
      <USPrice>148.95</USPrice>
      <comment>Confirm this is electric</comment>
    </item>
    <item partNum="926-AA">
      <productName>Baby Monitor</productName>
      <quantity>1</quantity>
      <USPrice>39.98</USPrice>
      <shipDate>1999-05-21</shipDate>
    </item>
  </items>
</purchaseOrder>
```

FIGURE 3.6   The Purchase Order XML Data File

Namespaces

Namespaces are a collection of related elements that are identified by the namespace name. The value of a namespace is that you can refer to the namespace as part of a schema, and by using the namespace as part of a definition you can use elements with the same name that are unique because their values are referenced to a particular occurrence. Typically you encounter a namespace as part of a URL. The syntax for a namespace is shown in Figure 3.7.

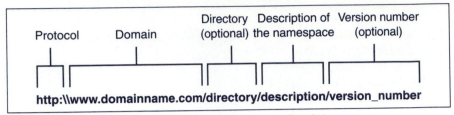

FIGURE 3.7   The Generalized Form of a URL with a Defined Namespace

To declare a namespace as the default namespace for an XML document, you would add the attribute `xmlns=` into the root tag of an XML document. If you only want that namespace to apply for part of your document, add the attribute to the element that contains all of the parts that are applicable. A namespace declared for a component element overrides a default namespace. The syntax for adding a namespace to an element is

```
<element elementname value xmlns:description="URL">
. . .
</element>
```

The description can be a name or abbreviation for the namespace. While the namespace applies, you can reference elements in that namespace within your XML document as PREFIX:ELEMENT or, in this case, DESCRIPTION: ELEMENTNAME. For a namespace containing information about the 50 U.S. states, you might see elements referred to as STATES:NAME, STATES:CAPI-TAL, and so forth. Attributes don't normally get defined as part of a namespace as they are usually already unique.

XML parsers evaluate all elements as if they were of the form PREFIX: ELEMENT. Declaration of the namespace is part of standard schema definition practice. However, in order to validate your XML document against a DTD, you will need to add the namespace prefix to each and every element in the form XMLS or XMLS:PREFIX. In the former case, you are referring to a default namespace, while in the latter case, you are indicating that the namespace only applies to part of your XML document. No wonder that the industry is moving away from DTD and to XML schemas as their validation engine.

You will find the W3C tutorial describing namespaces in more detail at http://www.w3.org/TR/REC-xml-names/.

QuickCheck Questions

15. Where would you find a schema?
16. How are namespaces referenced?
17. What does it mean to specify a data type?

The Document Object Model

The **Document Object Model,** or **DOM,** is an organizational scheme for describing the various objects used in HTML and XML documents. The purpose of this model is to provide a programmer with a method for creating, modifying, and navigating HTML and XML documents programmatically. The model is program language neutral. There are four parts to the DOM:

- Document object, which is the container object for data, components, and all processing instructions.
- Node object, which is the individual components.
- Nodelist object, which is the list of all nodes belonging to the same level.
- ParseError object, which is an object that stores the results of any processing, and in particular is used to log error conditions.

The DOM offers a tree view or node description of an XML document. Each of these objects has both properties and methods, and it's through the use of the DOM that it's possible to provide a description that allows programmers to reuse the work of others and to provide a standard means to process structured documents. We'll discuss the use of DOM in several of the chapters that follow.

Using XML Tools

Before leaving the topic of XML, it's worth mentioning that you can save yourself a lot of trouble by adopting a visual design tool in which you create your XML. We are going to talk about FrontPage and Dreamweaver in later chapters, and they perform this function for HTML. However, there are similar tools for XML, with considerable activity going on creating additional tools.

What an XML tool like XML Spy does for you is provide a way of creating XML syntax that is both easy to create, described visually, and checked for syntactical correctness. XML tools won't necessarily help you create tighter schemas, but they will prevent you from making silly errors that can be hard to spot. They also will speed up your work and provide many additional features such as documentation output.

To look at some of the many freeware XML tools available, go to http://www.garshol.priv.no/download/xmltools/name_ix.html. A Google listing of the popular commercial offerings is found at http://directory.google.com/Top/Computers/Data_Formats/Markup_Languages/XML/Tools/Editors/.

XHTML

XHTML is an extension of XML officially sanctioned by the W3C and is meant to replace HTML. The current standard is almost identical to HTML 4.01, but has the same strict requirements for well-formed tags and proper syntax that XML has. The advantage of working with well-formed markup code is that it will run browsers of various types; even the lightweight browsers that you might find on cell phones or PDAs are capable of processing the code without having to have the necessary functionality to make sense of errors. An XHTML page can be read by any device that can parse XML, while providing a means to write browser-independent documents.

XHTML Rules

The most important differences between HTML and XHTML are that in HTML

1. All tag names must be lowercase.

2. XHTML documents must be well formed and capable of being parsed by an XML parser.

3. All elements need to be correctly nested.

4. All elements must be closed, even empty elements.

We've covered these requirements early on in this chapter for HTML, so none of this should be new at this point.

XHTML also adds additional syntax rules for attributes:

1. They must be lowercase.

2. They must be in quotes.

3. Attribute minimization is not allowed.

4. You use the `id` attribute to replace the `name` attribute.

5. All DTD elements are required.

Let's take a brief look at these additional requirements. Instead of `<FONT SIZE=12>`, you would write `<font size="12">`, thus satisfying rules 1 and 2 above.

In order to satisfy the rule about attribute minimization, you would need to replace the following code:

```
<dl compact>
<input readonly>
<input checked>
<option selected>
```

with the following:

```
<dl compact="compact">
<input readonly="readonly">
<input checked="checked">
<option selected="selected">
```

To be syntactically correct, rule 4 requires that you would replace the link

```
<img src="image.jpg" name="image1" />
```

with

```
<img src=src="image.jpg" id="image1" />
```

The extra space before the "/>" characters is provided to give better compatibility with more browsers. The use of the `id` attribute applies to `a`, `applet`, `frame`, `iframe`, `img`, and `ma`.

Since the `lang` attribute is required for many tags in order to specify the language of the content the element contains, XHTML requires the use of the `xml:lang` attribute.

XHTML DTDs

In order to get the data-handling capabilities of XML in an XHTML document, it is required that you have a `DOCTYPE` declaration. The following is an example of a document template:

```
<!DOCTYPE Doctype reference here>
<- DOCTYPE isn't an XHTML element and doesn't get closed. ->
<html xmlns="http://www.w3.org/1999/xhtml">
<head>
<title>My title</title>
</head>
<body>
Text follows here
</body>
</html>
```

The first is the `<!DOCTYPE>` declaration you saw above. This DTD requires not only the `<!DOCTYPE . . .>` tag, but the `<head>` and `<body>` tags as well.

There are three different Document Type Definitions in use for XHTML:

* `Strict`, typically used with Cascading Style Sheet (see the next chapter for more on CSS).

```
<!DOCTYPE html
PUBLIC "-//W3C//DTD XHTML 1.0 Strict//EN"
"http://www.w3.org/TR/xhtml1/DTD/xhtml1-strict.dtd">
```

* `Transitional`, used when you need to work with browsers that don't support CSS.

```
<!DOCTYPE html
PUBLIC "-//W3C//DTD XHTML 1.0 Transitional//EN"
"http://www.w3.org/TR/xhtml1/DTD/xhtml1-transitional.dtd">
```

- Frameset, used when frames are used.

```
<!DOCTYPE html
PUBLIC "-//W3C//DTD XHTML 1.0 Frameset//EN"
"http://www.w3.org/TR/xhtml1/DTD/xhtml1-frameset.dtd">
```

Validation

Based on the rules you just learned, you can convert an HTML site to an XHTML site by adding a DTD and correcting any tags that require correcting. Depending upon how closely you followed these rules while composing your HTML pages, the amount of work required will vary. Over time, applications will add XHTML support, and your conversion job will become easier. There are tools such as HTML TIDY (see http://www.w3.org/People/Raggett/tidy/) that will convert HTML code for XHTML compliance.

Once you have converted your pages, you can use the W3C validation engine found at http://validator.w3.org/check/referer.

Summary

In this chapter you were introduced to the relatively new subject of XML, or the eXtensible Markup Language. Although XML looks similar to HTML, its use is vastly different. HTML describes content, while XML is a compact and well-formed means for describing data. XML will become an important interchange format for data between platforms and applications and for display on the Web.

XML's tags are mostly defined by the user for specific needs. Thus, the majority of the tags are named to describe the types of data contained in the document. XML requires strict adherence to syntax, and must be validated by a parser in order to be displayed. To help make XML data more accurate and more standardized, and to provide a template against which to construct the data, XML uses either internal element definitions, an external Document Type Definition or DTD file, or a schema. These definitions describe data types, strict orders of precedence, and other features that can't be described compactly within the XML data set.

XML is going to become increasingly important in future programming efforts, particularly on the Web, because when combined with technologies that can format XML data, they can serve as a means of populating a Web page. Transformation technologies discussed in the next chapter such as Cascaded Style Sheets, XSLT or XML style sheets, and XHTML provide the means to use XML data in almost any application that you might need it.

Key Terms

attribute
child element
comment
directive
Document Object Model (DOM)
Document Type Definition (DTD)
electronic data interchange (EDI)
element

entity
eXtensible Markup Language (XML)
external
interchange format
internal
metadata
namespace

parent element
parser
schema
validation
value
virtual private network (VPN)
XHTML

Review Questions

1. What are the fundamental differences between XML, XHTML, and HTML?
2. Where will you use XML and XHTML in the future?
3. How does XML compare to EDI?
4. What are an element, attribute, value, and entity?
5. What requirements are there that make an XML document "well formed"?
6. If you have a parsing error, describe one method for isolating that error and correcting it.
7. What purpose does a DTD serve, and how do strict, transitional, and frameset DTDs differ?
8. Why would you want to use an XML schema in place of a DTD?
9. Why are namespaces defined, and how are they used?
10. How do you programmatically manipulate an XML document?

Exercises

1. Define a DTD and an XML document for the Table of Contents of this book. Use only the first two chapters, but include all front matter and back matter.
2. Draw a node map for the elements described in your XML document in Exercise 1.
3. If you were going to represent common form elements such as radio buttons, check boxes, pick lists (selection box), required text fields, an image field, and an auto-entered text field as XML elements and attributes, how would you do so? Your instructor will provide a form from a Web page for you to work with. Reduce that form to different elements and attributes using the correct form.

Markup Transformations

4

OBJECTIVES

1. To learn how XSLT can modify XML and HTML.

2. To understand node maps and processing sequencing in XSL.

3. To see how CSS can format XML and HTML.

4. To learn how to construct styles and style sheets.

5. To prepare your HTML code so that it will be compatible with XHTML.

INTRODUCTION

With HTML you can control the page description of your Web pages; and with XML you can compactly and precisely describe data. Neither markup language has all of the elements you might like to have when programming a Web site. Specifically, HTML formatting can get messy and require considerable attention to detail in order to make your elements' format consistent with one another. XML, on the other hand, doesn't even consider how the data is going to look, only what the data is and how the data set is formed and validated.

In order to fill some of these gaps, several new technologies have been introduced. The W3C specification called XSL, or eXtensible Style Language, is meant to apply formatting to XML data. XSL has split into both the **XSLT** and **XSL-FO** specifications, where the "T" refers to the word **transformations** and the "FO" is for "formatting objects." Of the two, XSLT is in use and supported by the latest editions of the major browsers, although not always entirely consistently. XSLT is particularly useful because it not only provides some formatting capabilities, but an XSLT document can be written to map XML data transiting between applications, modify data, and a whole lot more.

The second topic in this chapter introduces Cascading Style Sheets (CSS), which are a mechanism for adding style (e.g., fonts, colors, spacing) to Web

> **Tech Tip**
>
> **The Home of the XSL**
> To get information on the current status of XSL as well as pointers to a number of resources, go to www.w3.org/Style/XSL/.

101

documents. If you've worked with styles or themes in a word processor, the concept of CSS won't seem very foreign to you. Essentially, you create named styles and a style sheet to support them. When you apply the style sheet to an XML or HTML document, your browser formats the content appropriately. Change the style sheet, and all of the changes appear the next time any document based on that style sheet is rendered in a browser. CSS has the support of recent versions of the leading browsers, and although the support is not entirely consistent, it is getting much better. Numerous productivity applications are adding CSS support to their repertoire.

Finally, this chapter ends with a brief introduction to XHTML, which as its name implies contains elements of both XML and HTML.

XSLT

XSLT transforms one XML data file into another XML data file so that the transformed data can be used in another application. An example of this might include the transformation of accounting information from one accounting application running on a mainframe to a spreadsheet or database running on your personal PC. XSLT is expressed as a text file with a set of markup tags that provide the necessary instructions for an XSLT processor to perform the conversion. You'll find XSLT processors embedded into standard productivity applications, and you can download one of several XSLT processors that are available. What the processor does is to scan the XML document and construct a node tree (a hierarchical representation), where each node in the tree is one element, attribute, or a piece of content such as text. A node tree is similar to the kind of mapping that a file system does to display content, such as you might see in the Microsoft Windows Explorer. The XSLT document provides the instructions to transform each of those nodes. You can think of an XSLT document as a set of templates, where each template identifies which node it acts upon, and the second part of the template describes the action that the XSLT processor should take.

Each XSLT document is required to contain a **root node** template that is applied to the root element of your XML document. A root template usually contains a set of instructions that are a mixture of both XSLT instructions for additional output or processing and some literal elements that are passed through into the resulting transformed XML document.

Consider the following XML document named BaseballTeams.xml:

```
<!- BaseballTeams.xml ->
<?xml version='1.0'?>
<baseball_teams>
  <team state= 'MA'>
    <team_name>Red Sox</team_name>
```

```
      <player>
        <number>24</number>
        <name>Manny Ramierez</name>
        <position>Right Field</position>
        <position>Designated Hitter</position>
      </player>
      <player>
        <number>45</number>
        <name>Pedro Martinez</name>
        <position>Starting Pitcher</position>
      </player>
      <player>
        <number>5</number>
        <name>Nomar Garciaparra</name>
        <position>Shortstop</position>
      </player>
      <!- More Player data ->
    </team>
    <!- Team and Player data ->
  </baseball_teams>
```

Essentially, the motivation of the above XML document is to store the information about many baseball teams. The root node is named `<baseball_teams>` and it will contain many `<team>` **elements.** Each `<team>` element will have an **attribute** named "state". Each team will also contain a `<team_name>` element and many `<player>` elements. A player will have a player number, name, and position.

Node Maps

The BaseballTeams.xml document will transform to the **node map** shown in Figure 4.1. Please note that we have shown only a part of the node map in this figure.

Once the node set is constructed for the XML document, the XSLT document is read and the instructions are processed. In XSLT terminology, the tagged set of instructions is called a **template**. Basically, the XSLT is a template-driven system. In the XSLT document, we need to provide one or more templates, and then we can use the `<apply-template>` element to specify when to use the template in a particular transformation process. We will provide a simple example of the `<template>` and `<apply-template>` elements in an XSLT document.

Suppose that we need to display the names of the teams in the BaseballTeams.xml document. First, we will develop the following XSLT file named Teams.xml:

```
1. <!- Teams.xsl ->
2. <?xml version="1.0"?>
```

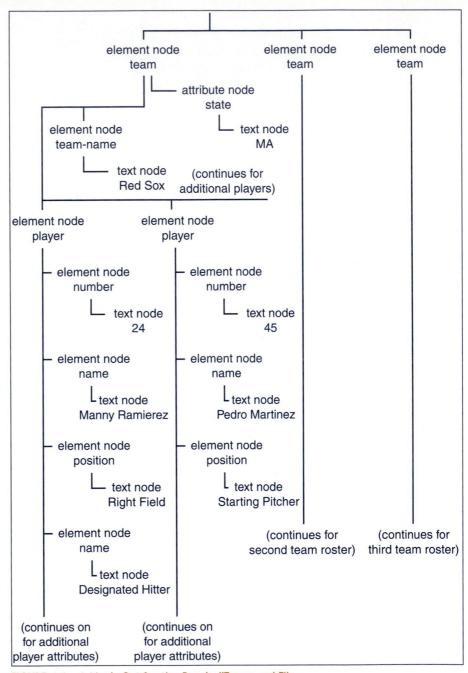

FIGURE 4.1   A Node Set for the BaseballTeams.xml File

```
 3. <xsl:stylesheet version="1.0"
        xmlns:xsl="http://www.w3.org/1999/XSL/Transform">
 4. <xsl:template match="/">
 5.    <xsl:apply-templates select="baseball_teams/team"/>
 6. </xsl:template>
 7. <xsl:template match="baseball_teams/team">
 8.    <xsl:value-of select="team_name" /><br/>
 9. </xsl:template>
10. </xsl:stylesheet>
```

The statement numbers are not necessary in an XSLT document. We have used the statement numbers for explanation purposes. There are two template definitions in the above code. The first definition starts at statement number 4, and the second definition starts at statement number 7. Each of these templates contains certain simple processing instructions (in line numbers 5 and 8, respectively). The first template is the root template, and the XSLT processor always starts with the root template. In line number 5, we are instructing the XSLT processor to apply the baseball_teams/team template for each team node of the node map. The processing instructions in the baseball_teams/team template, as defined in line numbers 7 through 9, use the `<xsl:value-of>` element to select the value of the team_name element. In Internet Explorer 6.0 (IE6), the selected value will be displayed on the browser.

Regardless of what templates you use, one template is always called the root node template. The call for the root node template is

```
<xsl:template match="/"> . . . </xsl:templates>
```

Preparation of the Teams.xsl document is not an end by itself. Subsequently, we will need to process the BaseballTeams.xml document using the instructions in the Teams.xsl. This can be accomplished by inserting the `<?xml-stylesheet>` statement in the BaseballTeams.xml document as shown below:

```
<!- BaseballTeams.xml ->
<?xml version='1.0'?>
<?xml-stylesheet type="text/xsl" href="Teams.xsl"?>
<baseball_teams>
  <team state= 'MA'>
    <team_name>Red Sox</team_name>
      <player>
        --- --- ---
      </player>
  </team>
  <!- Team and Player data ->
</baseball_teams>
```

Go ahead and insert the `<?xml-stylesheet type="text/xsl" href="Teams.xsl"?>` statement in the BaseballTeams.xml document and save it. Now open it in IE6. The system will display the names of the teams on the browser.

Processing Instructions

While a root node template is always applied, in order to call additional sub-templates you have to specifically name them. Their use is not automatic. Additionally, an XSLT style sheet may require multiple occurrences of the same node as only the first node of any particular node name is processed. To output HTML code, we can simply include the relevant HTML codes in appropriate templates. If necessary, we also can specify node selection criteria to include only certain desired node(s). We will illustrate these principles with an example. Suppose that we want to display the player number and player names of all players in a particular team (say, the Red Sox). The following XSLT document can be used to accomplish this objective:

```
<!- RedSox.xsl ->
<?xml version="1.0"?>
<xsl:stylesheet version="1.0"
   xmlns:xsl="http://www.w3.org/1999/XSL/Transform">

<!- The following template is the root template. A root
   template always matches the root "/". The XSLT processor
   will start with this template ->

<xsl:template match="/">
   <html><head><title>Current Roster</title></head>
   <body><h2>Red Sox Players</h2>
   <b>The current roster of the Red Sox Team
      includes:</b><hr/>
   <!- The above three lines of html codes do not involve
      any XSL processing instructions with any node. Thus
      the XSLT processor will simply copy these in the
      resulting document, which will be subsequently
      displayed on the browser.->

   <!- In the next instruction, we are asking the system to
      apply the player template only for the 'Red Sox' team.
```

```
    The system will apply the player template for each
    player of the team.  ->

<xsl:apply-templates
  select="baseball_teams/team[team_name='Red Sox']/
    player"/>
<hr/></body></html>
</xsl:template>

<!- In the following statement, we are defining the
    template for the player node. ->

<xsl:template match="player">
  <p>Player Number: <xsl:value-of select="number" />
    <br/>
  Name: <xsl:value-of select="name" /><br/></p>
</xsl:template>
</xsl:stylesheet>
```

If we insert the `<?xml-stylesheet type="text/xsl" href="RedSox.xsl"?>` in our BaseballTeams.xml and open it in Inernet Explorer 6.0, the system will display the screen as shown in Figure 4.2.

Expressions

To give XSL additional flexibility, you need to be able to apply templates to different parts of your XML document in order to customize your output. This is done using what is called a template rule. A template rule has three components:

1. The opening tag, which identifies the node to be acted on:
   `<xsl:template match="criteria">`.

2. The instruction in the center that describes the transformation to be performed on that node, such as:

   ```
   <xsl:apply-templates
     select="baseball_teams/team[team_name='Red Sox']/
       player"/>
   ```

3. And the final closing tag: `</xsl:template>`.

You can have as many templates as nodes, and the XSLT processor will match the node name to your criteria. If a match is not found, a built-in template is used by default.

XML often describes repetitive data that you want to act upon with a single command. The XSL batch command is

```
<xsl:for-each select="criteria"> . . . </xsl:for-each>
```

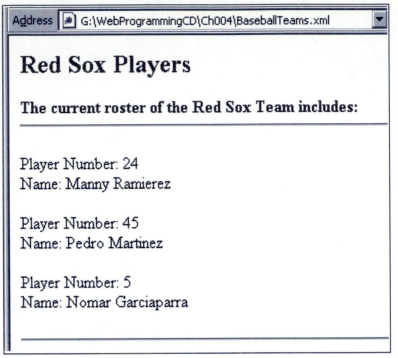

Address [ ] G:\WebProgrammingCD\Ch004\BaseballTeams.xml

Red Sox Players

The current roster of the Red Sox Team includes:

Player Number: 24
Name: Manny Ramierez

Player Number: 45
Name: Pedro Martinez

Player Number: 5
Name: Nomar Garciaparra

FIGURE 4.2   List of Red Sox Players

You might want to use this command to build a table, using the following construction:

```
<!-ForEachExample.xls ->
<?xml version="1.0"?>
<xsl:stylesheet version="1.0"
    xmlns:xsl="http://www.w3.org/1999/XSL/Transform">
<xsl:template match="/">
  <table border="1" bgcolor="white">
    <th>Number</th><th>Name</th>
    <xsl:for-each
      select="baseball_teams/team[team_name='Red Sox']/
        player">
    <tr><td><xsl:value-of select="number"/></td>
    <td><xsl:value-of select="name"/></td></tr>
    </xsl:for-each>
  </table>
</xsl:template>
</xsl:stylesheet>
```

The code above will run through the node map, evaluate each instance of a
player node of the Red Sox team, and build a set of table rows for the player

numbers and names. Anything that should be applied in the table should be included before the `for-each` instruction. Figure 4.3 shows the output when the BaseballTeams.xml is processed via the Internet Explorer 6.0 XSLT processor (MSXML4.0). Please note that we could have also used the `<apply-template>` command instead of using the `<for-each>` command.

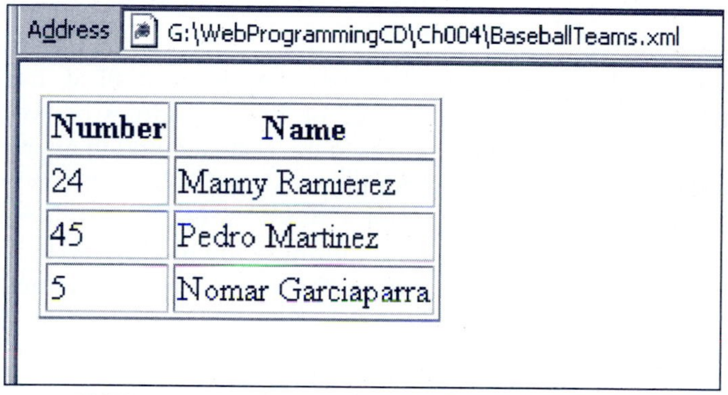

Number	Name
24	Manny Ramierez
45	Pedro Martinez
5	Nomar Garciaparra

FIGURE 4.3   Red Sox Players in Tabular Format

In addition to batch commands XPath has logic commands, an example of which is the `if` command:

```
<xsl:if test="condition">instructions</xsl:if>
```

The template above will process the instructions if the condition for the current node is true (or not). Even more useful and important from a programmer's perspective is the addition of branching with conditional logic, the equivalent of the IF...THEN...ELSE command. With branching you can create more flexible programs, modularize your code, and more easily update it. For XPath the syntax is as follows:

```
<xsl:choose>
  <xsl:when test1="condition">instructions1</xsl:when>
  <xsl:when test2="condition">instructions2</xsl:when>
  <xsl:when test3="condition">instructions3</xsl:when>
  --
<xsl:otherwise>instructions4</xsl:otherwise>
</xsl:choose>
```

This construction needs at least one `when` clause, but it can have as many `when` clauses as you wish. The XSLT processor evaluates `test1` and if the condition evaluates to `True` or `1`, it performs `instructions1` and goes to the next instruction after the closing tag `<xsl:choose>`. If `test1` is `False` or `0`, the processor goes to `test2` and tests that. The processor will continue testing until it finds a test whose condition it evaluates as `True`. If no branch test is `True`, then the processor performs the `instructions4` that follows the `<xsl:otherwise>` tag and exits the `<xsl:choose>` set.

Official Expressions

To view the official expressions for functions in XLS, go to the W3C's site at http://www.w3.org/TR/xpath#corelib.

You can see why this is so useful when you consider that all of these instructions can be calling entire programs or program modules based on conditions. This is exactly the kind of code used to create a menu in an event-driven program. Every so often the program is checking this branch (say every hundredth of a second); it looks for a mouse-down event and if it doesn't find it, the program exits the `xsl:choose` condition. When it does find it, it begins to evaluate which condition is true and performs the appropriate action based on that. For most HTML applications, you are not going to be building menus using XSLT, but the principle is the same.

Controlling Processing Order

Tech Tip

Early Exit
In any conditional branching structure, you should always evaluate the condition that will give you the fastest exit from the branch first. Put the most common choice first or, if you have a condition that takes a lot of time to evaluate, put that condition last.

Unless you specify otherwise, nodes get processed by XSL in their order in the XML data file. XPath contains functions that will allow you to change the order of processing. The simplest is the sort function. To sort nodes before further processing them with the appropriate templates, you use the `xsl:sort` command. The syntax for this command is as follows:

```
<xsl:sort select="condition" order="descending" data-
    type="text"/>
```

You use this command within the `xsl:apply-templates` or `xsl:for-each` elements and it should appear before instructions to process the nodes. While the `select` clause is required, `order` and `data-type` are optional. If you don't specify a descending sort, `xsl:sort` does a descending sort (Z to A, 9 to 0) by default. In instances where you are sorting numeric data, use the `data-type` "number."

XSL provides a means to add attributes to an element using the `<xsl:attribute>` command. This command is placed right after the opening tag for the element that it will describe.

```
<xsl:template match="position">
<xsl:attribute name="status">starter</xsl:attribute>
. . .
</xsl:template>
```

So the new attribute for a player's position is called `status` and is declared to be a `starter`. You could also point to the information (such as a file) to output the information that an attribute requires. The attribute clause allows you to add the attributes commonly found in many HTML tags so that your HTML output can be in standard form when the transformation is completed.

XSL applies the appropriate template to each node. In most cases you will use multiple templates, not one as you might with a word processor template. As you have seen, a template finds the node it is to operate on using a pattern match. Expressions are then used to specify a node set that is then processed. Using XPath syntax, a set of templates also may be specified by their location. Whereas a pattern will be matched to all patterns in an XML document, an expression is evaluated based on its context, often within the node in which it was used.

Sequencing the order in which nodes are processed is therefore a key issue. Often you want to process a node in relation to the node you are operating on, the current node. The current node is the one specified by the template being processed. If you used an `xsl:apply-template` command, the node or sequence of nodes it matches is the current node until the instruction is completed and the current node switches back.

Here are the ways you refer to various nodes based on your current position:

- **Current node.** You refer to the current node using the period character ("."). Thus, `<xsl:value-of select="."/>` would pull the value of the current node.

- **Parent node.** The **parent** of any node is referred to using two period symbols, as in `<xsl:value-of select=".."/>`. To find the attribute of a parent, you can use the `../@name` address. The `/@` symbol selects a node's attributes.

- **Sibling or niece nodes.** Refer to siblings or nieces (the child of a sibling) using `/sibling` or `/niece`.

- **Nephew nodes.** To select all of the nephew nodes, use the `/*/nephew` reference. The wildcard symbol (*) means "all."

- **Child node.** The **child** of any node is referred to directly within the element that it operates on as `child` or, alternatively, as `./child`.

- **Grandchild node.** A grandchild element would use a slash notation, as in `/grandchild`.

- **Descendant nodes.** The descendants are all of the nodes contained within the hierarchy of your current node. To refer to descendants, use the double forward slash symbol. For example, `<xsl:apply-templates select="//player"/>` would apply the instructions that follow to not only the player's name, but to the player's position and the player's number as well.

All of the above references are relative to your current node. However, from any place in your XML document processing, you can make a direct reference to a node using a path notation. Here are some direct references:

- **Root node**. To specify the root, type `/root`, which, for our example, would be `/baseball_teams`.
- **Second or sublevel**. To go down a level from the root, enter `/root/container`; for example, `/baseball_teams/team`.
- **Third level**. To go down two levels, use `/root/container/element`; for example, `/baseball_teams/team/team_name`.

Specifying a direct reference allows you to process nodes in any sequence you like, returning you to the current node after the instructions are processed.

Sometimes you want finer control over the location of a processing instruction. You can use an expression called a *predicate* that uses a Boolean test to select a subset node. For example, you might enter the following:

```
<xsl:apply-templates  select="baseball_teams/team[@state=
   'CA']/player"/>
```

In this example, any team node that has an attribute `state='CA'` would be selected. Another example might substitute `[status="starter"]` to test for whether the element has that attribute. To locate the last occurrence of `starter` in the `player_name` node, you might use the following expression: `[status="starter"][position()=last()]`. In addition to the equal sign, you can also use the following tests:

- **Comparison operators**. Among the common comparisons are `!=`, not equals; `&gt;`, greater than; `&gt;=`, greater than or equal to; `&lt;`, less than; and `&lt;=`, less than or equal to.
- **Position operator**. To test a position, use `position()=number` or `position=function()`, where `function` could be something like `first()+2`, or two characters in from the first one.

Node Operators

There are a whole set of operators that you can use to output derived data from your XML data using XSL, operators that sum the values of nodes, count the number of nodes, perform arithmetic, format, and so forth. The follow are examples of these types of functions:

- **Sum values**. Use the `sum()` function for this purpose. An example of this would be

```
   <xsl:value-of
select= "sum(/baseball_teams/team[@state='MA']/player/
   number)"/>
```

The above expression references the player number nodes of all teams that are from Massachusetts and sums their values. In our Baseball-Teams.xml example, this function returns the number 24 + 45 + 5, or 74.

- **Arithmetic**. Use `+` for addition; `-` for subtraction, `div` for division; `*` for multiplication; and `mod` for the modulus (remainder of division).

- **Rounding**. The functions `ceiling()`, `floor()`, and `round()` will round up, down, or to the closest integer.

- **Node count**. Use the `count()` function for this purpose; for example, the following statement will return the number 3:

```
<xsl:value-of select= "count(/baseball_teams/
    team[@state='MA']/player/number)"/>
```

- **Extracting values**. To extract part of a string, you use the `substring()` function. This function requires a start and stop position. Thus, the expression `<xsl:value-of select=substring("PLAYER_NAME", 3, 10)/>` would evaluate "dro Martin" when applied to the node with the value of "Pedro Martinez." You also can extract values based on the position of a match of a character in the string you are evaluating. The `substring-after(expression, c)` and `substring-before(string, c)` functions, where `c` is the character, mark the position from which you extract your substring.

- **Formatting**. To format a number, use the `format-number` function. The syntax for this function when expressing a percentage is `<xsl:value-of select="format-number(number value or expression evaluating to a number), '#0.0%')"/>`. The symbol # means that a number only appears when it is nonzero; 0 is the placeholder for a number that will always appear; and the period and percentage marks have their common meanings separating integer and decimals and indicating that the number is a percentage, respectively.

You can use the `translate()` function to control a string's capitalization. For example, `translate('Pedro', 'pedro')` would convert the XML data string into the mixed case output "String".

QuickCheck Questions

5. Why is node order important?
6. How can a template modify a node?
7. How should you construct a branch or loop to make it process faster?
8. What would you have to do to have a template act on the second position that Manny Ramierez plays?
9. How do you view a transformed XML document in your browser?

Cascading Style Sheets

Although you can format XML data using XSLT, and HTML tags can be formatted using attributes, using both of these techniques is tedious when repetitive formatting must be done. To provide HTML and XML data with a hierarchical style template or style sheet, Cascading Style Sheets, or **CSS**, were proposed primarily by Microsoft and adopted as a standard. Not everyone implements every aspect of CSS, but broad support in the leading browsers makes CSS a standard that will probably have widespread adoption.

What CSS does is to impose formatting to either an HTML or XML document based on the tag names in those documents. CSS is more widely used for HTML than it is for XML because not all browsers will read XML data directly. CSS is **hierarchical**, with one **style** added to the next. When CSS is applied to HTML, the styles it describes are added to those HTML tags, only changing the HTML formatting when there is a conflict between the two styles. With XML, no formatting is part of the data, so no conflicts arise.

CSS has gone through a couple of revisions called CSS1 and CSS2; support by browsers for some features and not others makes CSS a technique that must be used with some caution. You need to know when to apply certain features and not others, and you have to know what your audience will use to view your data.

Style Syntax

A style is composed of a **selector**, which identifies the element(s) to be formatted, and a description of the formatting, called a **declaration**. Declarations are further composed of a property, a colon, and the values to be applied. When a declaration specifies two or more properties, each of these properties is separated by a semicolon. Not every property has to be separated from the next by a semicolon. Certain properties that take multiple attributes such as `font` can be grouped together. Consider the following examples:

```
description{position:left;color:blue;font:bold italic 10pt
    Arial}
```

In the above example, `description` is the selector; `position`, `color`, and `font` are the declarations; and `left`, `blue`, and `bold italic 10 pt Arial` are their values. The latter declaration is equivalent to the following expansion: `font-weight bold italic;font-size 10 pt;font-family:Arial`.

In many instances, when you set a property like a font in CSS, the font stays set until another declaration changes it.

The general syntax for a style sheet is

```
selector {property:value}
```

Thus, an example of this would be

```
p {font-family: "times new roman"}
```

To use more than one property, each needs to be separated by a semicolon. You also can apply the same `property:value` to multiple selectors by grouping selectors, creating a list of selectors separated only by commas:

```
selector1,selector2, . . . {property:value1;value2; . . .}
```

In order to separate selectors into different classes, you would use the syntax

```
selector:class1 {property:value}
selector:class2 {property:value}
```

As an example, consider two paragraphs, one for body text and the other for emphasis:

```
p.body {text-style: normal}
p.emphasis {text-style: italic}
```

With these two definitions in your style sheet, your code would look like this:

```
<p body="body">
This paragraph will be in normal text.
</p>
<p class="emphasis">
This paragraph will be italicized.
</p>
```

You can use an `id` selector to apply a style to only one element. Any `id` attribute you use must be unique in the document in which it is applied. The following is an example of the syntax for the `id` selector:

```
p#id645 {text-style: left;color: blue}
```

The `id645` selector is applied in HTML as follows:

```
<p id="id645">This text will be left aligned and blue.</p>
```

Applying Styles

There are many different ways in which you can construct a selector so that the style is applied to the part of your HTML or XML document to which you need to apply it. Among the common ones are

- `*` . Apply the style to every element.
- `name(, name2, name3, . . .)`. Apply the style to the named element(s).
- `parent descendant`. Apply the style to all elements within the parent.
- `parent>child`. With this construction the style is applied to the child elements only.

- *name:first-child*. This applies the style to the first child element with the name `name`, as in `team_name:player_name`.
- *first+next*. This reference applies a style to the element directly after the first element.
- *name[attribute]*. Any named element that contains the named attribute will have this style assigned.
- *name[attribute=value]*. This construction assigns the style to any element where the named attribute matches the value indicated. Use the match phrase `[attribute~=value]` when one of the words in the attribute has the value specified. For programmer's purposes, a word is characters separated by delimiters, most often as it is here, with spaces (but sometimes with commas or tabs).
- `name:link`. Apply this style to an element that is an unvisited link. Use `name:visited` to style a visted link. The reference `name:active` is used for styling a link that is being activated (clicked on); `name:focus` references a link element that has been activated (tabbed into) but not yet selected; and `name:hover` will apply the style to a link covered by your pointer.

CSS supports what is called pseudo elements. You can apply styles to a single letter or to a first line in text. For example, to emphasize the first letter in a paragraph, you would use the following:

```
<!- first-letter.htm ->
<html><head>
<style type="text/css">
   div:first-letter
   {color: #ff0000; font-size:xx-large}
   /* This is a comment */
</style>
</head>
<body><div>
The first letter displayed in this line of text is extra
   extra large.
</div>
</body></html>
```

Please note the syntax for a comment in a style sheet, which is shown just above the closing style tag `</style>`.

When using pseudo styles, be aware that different browsers don't support all or some of these styles. For example, the emphasized first letter above requires Internet Explorer 5.5 or higher or versions of Netscape Navigator greater than 4.0.

CSS also supports what is called pseudo classes, which can modify all or part of a selector. The pseudo class is used as followed:

```
selector:pseudo-class {property: value}
```

or when used with a CSS, pseudo class would take the following form:

```
selector.class:pseudo-class {property: value}
```

Style Sheets

A **style sheet** is a collection of styles that apply to the elements in HTML or XML documents. These styles or rules are sometimes included within your document and are referred to as an internal style sheet; but most often these rules are stored in their own separate text document, given a .CSS extension, and referenced from within the HTML or XML document. Each type of style sheet has advantages.

External Style Sheets

There's a good reason why most style sheets are stored as external documents. When you have an external style sheet, it can serve as a template serving many HTML or XML documents. Since the formatting is applied when the data file is read, any change or improvement in an external style sheet will be instantly propagated to all documents that reference that style sheet.

To create a style sheet, do the following:

1. Open a text editor and create a new document.

2. Type a selector and the properties you wish to style: `selector{descriptor:value}`, as described previously.

3. Continue adding additional properties, and on additional lines more selectors as required.

4. Save the document and give it a .CSS file extension.

Style sheets have a very simple construction, and the only thing you really need to be careful about is saving the file with the right extension name and as a straight ASCII or text file.

Calling a Style Sheet

To call an external style sheet, you need to reference it from within your document. The style sheet is normally placed at the very start of your XML or HTML document as a declaration. For XML that declaration takes the following form:

```
<?xml-stylesheet type="text/css" HREF="PATH/FILENAME.CSS"?>
```

In an HTML document the syntax is as follows:

```
<link rel="stylesheet" type="text/css" HREF="PATH/FILENAME.CSS"/>
```

and you would place this tag within the head section of your HTML document.

If you want to put the processing instructions inside an XSLT document, you would use the syntax

```
<xsl:processing-instruction name="xml-stylesheet" >
type="text/css" HREF="PATH/FILENAME.CSS"?>
</xsl:processing-instruction>
```

and place this reference within the root template of your document.

In either case (in the XML or XSLT document), the result will be the same. You can have multiple style sheets, so your XML document may use this type of processing instruction elsewhere and any instruction to use a style sheet that is last takes precedence over those that came before it.

Internal Style Sheets

If your style sheet is internal, then all of your styles are self-contained. That has an advantage in terms of speed and reliability because you aren't relying on a network connection if that style sheet is somewhere else or something else that could go wrong.

With HTML you can add your style sheet directly in the head section of the document. For XSLT you should add any internal style sheets into the head section of the HTML code (most often in the root template).

To create an internal style sheet in XSLT, do the following:

1. In the root template, enter <style>.

2. On the next line, enter <![CDATA[, which passes the data through the XML **parser** as straight text (no processing).

3. Enter next <!-, which comments out the remaining part of the styles and suppresses their appearance inside a browser.

4. Then enter your list of selectors and descriptors as you would any style sheet.

5. Close out first the commenting with ->, the CDATA section with]]>, and finally the style tag with </style>.

If you want to put a reference to a style directly into the body of an HTML document, you can do so. In the style tag, you want to put in the attribute style="selector1:descriptor1; selector2:descriptor2; . . ." prior to where you want the style to apply.

You can apply an internal style sheet when you want a document to have a unique style. Here's an example of how an internal style sheet for a single document would look:

```
<head>
<style type="text/css">
hr {color: white}
p {margin-right: 50px}
body {background-image: url("path:/image.jpg")}
</style>
</head>
```

If you want to apply style sheets to elements within a page, you can use an inline style sheet:

```
<p style="color: sienna; margin-left: 20px">
This is a paragraph
</p>
```

The problem with inline style sheets is that they only apply to the one occurrence, and therefore don't leverage the main advantages of using style sheets.

QuickCheck Questions

10. What purpose does CSS serve?

11. What is meant by a style sheet and a style?

12. How does CSS compare with HTML?

13. How do you call a style sheet from within an XML or HTML document?

Formatting with CSS

The whole point of CSS is to make automating your HTML or XSL output easy. You create a CSS style sheet once, and anyone who uses that style sheet benefits from the work. Your organization benefits from the standardization. CSS has layout, paragraph, and character formatting.

Page and Paragraph Styles

Sizing an element can be controlled through a style using simple syntax. Use either `element_name(width:value)` or `element_name(height:value)`, where the value is either an absolute value (10pt) or a percentage of the parent.

When CSS is applied to an element, the output is an object with what is referred to as a bounding box. A bounding box is an invisible rectangular enclosure that completely surrounds an object. All graphical user interfaces display subsystems such as the Windows GDI (Graphical Display Interface) using this concept for drawing objects to the screen. Imagine a text box, if you will. The text box can appear either as a block occupying its own paragraph or inline and part of a line of text. To style a box as a block, you would use the *element_name*(display:block) style; while display(inline) puts the text inline. You also can use *element_name*(display:none) to *hide* an element. There are many other display properties, but not all are supported by the current crop of browsers.

You can format this box by applying various styles to it such as a border or margin, or adding additional internal space between the object inside the box and the border (called *padding*). The exact styles you can apply to an element are determined by the element type, and each style can take one or more different attributes, such as border color, border line width, border line type (dotted, dashed, solid, etc.), and so forth. Other modifications you can make to the bounding box include reducing its size and using the overflow property to determine where the excess content goes. You also can clip an element by showing only part of that element inside a rectangular bounding box using the clip:rect() property.

You may be familiar with the positioning commands in HTML. You can *position* objects using tag attributes such as left, right, and center. CSS supplies similar functionality. For example, the style *image_link*(display:right) would put that image to the right side of the page. In addition to top, bottom, and left, you also can provide both absolute and relative positioning in CSS. To specify an **absolute position,** use the *element_name*(position:absolute *side1:offset1;side2:offset2;* . . .). The side can be either left, right, top, or bottom; and the offset is the distance from that side expressed either in points (10pt), as a percentage of the parent, or as a relative value. To style a **relative position,** you would use the syntax *element_name*(position: relative *side1:offset1;side2:offset2,* . . .), where the variables (in italics) have the same meanings. Three-dimensional positioning using the z-index:x (x is the layer number) is also possible.

Text alignment is one of the important styles that is required for page layout. CSS has a set of them based on vertical alignment. Use vertical-align:value, where the value can be baseline, middle, sub, super, text-top, text-bottom, top, bottom, or a percentage of the height of the element in either a positive or up direction, or a negative or down direction.

Many other styles follow the syntax you've just seen for offset. Another example is the setting of border attributes. A *border* is a line surrounding an object and initially defined as the bounding box. There is a default style for all objects, and so borders have a default condition that also can be altered. To change a border's appearance use the *element_name*(*border1-side1:property1;* *border2-side2:property2;* . . .), where side can be -left, -right, -top, and -bottom, and property can be drawn from a list including thick, medium (default), thin, absolute (10pt or 4px), none, solid, dashed, dotted, solid double, inset, outset, ridge, and groove. If you don't specify a side, then the property applies to all sides of the border. You also can set border:color in a similar manner. You can abbreviate this syntax for many similar commands using border:trbl for top, right, bottom, and left; or margin:vh to set the margin for the top (vertical) or bottom (height) to the same value.

Here's a short list of some very similar styles that you can set in a CSS file:

- **Foreground and background effects**. Use
  `element_name(background:`*value*`)`, where *value* can be a color, transparent, or a pointer to an image file that you wish to use in the background using a standard URL reference. If you wish to tile an image, use `repeat` (for both), `repeat-x` (horizontally) or `repeat-y` (vertically), and `no-repeat` not to tile the image. For `foreground` substitute that keyword into the previous expression. Colors can be expressed in RGB by replacing a `color` name like `blue` or `red` with a value such as `#rrggbb` (maximum for each color is 255) or as a percentage of RGB expressed as `rgb(r%,g%,b%)`.

- **Margins**. The syntax is `element_name(margin1-side1:property1; margin2-side2:property2; . . .)`, where `-side` can be, `right`, `top`, and `bottom`; and the value can be either absolute units or percentages of the width of the parent element.

- **Padding**. Padding is extra space around the border. The syntax for the style is `element_name(padding1-side1:value1;padding2-side2: value2; . . .)`.

- **Text wrap**. The manner in which text flows around an image or object is called text wrap. The syntax of this command is `element_name(float:`*value*`)`, where *value* is `left` or `right`. To suppress text wrap, use `element_name(clear:`*value*`)`, and *value* can be either `left`, `right`, or `clear`.

- **Lists**. To set the style of a list, you would use `element_name(display:list-item;list-style:`*value*`)`. Several different list styles are available to you: `disc`, or bullet style; `circle`, for an open circle; `square`, for a solid square; `lower-alpha` and `upper-alpha`, for alphabetized lists; `lower-roman` and `upper-roman` for different Roman numeral lists; `decimal`, using standard Arabic numbers (integers, e.g., 1, 2, . . .); URL (`image.jpg` or `image.gif`); and `outside` or `inside` to display the list symbol to the left of the list or flush left.

- **Page breaks**. Use `page-break:`*value*`:always`, where *value* is either `before` or `after` to specify a page break. To remove a page break, use `page-break-after:auto` or `page-break::before:auto`.

As an example of applying a background color, you would use the following:

```
<!- BackgroundColor.htm ->
<html>
<head>
  <style type="text/css">
    body {background-color: blue}
    p {background-color:rgb(255,255,255)}
  </style>
</head>
<body><p>This is a paragraph, which has a white
  background. </p>
</body></html>
```

In the above code, the body's background is set to blue and the paragraph's background is set to white using an RGB value. You also can use hexadecimal values for color and set an opaque or transparent background.

Character Styles

If you are thinking that this is exactly the kind of thing you would use a graphical interface to code for you, you are right. Chances are that most of the work you do in CSS will be within applications specially set up to write this code for you. Having looked at page and paragraph attributes, let's briefly turn to character formatting. As it turns out, CSS is a much richer formatting language than HTML. Indeed, it has to be. Whereas you can format a lot of things in HTML, there is no formatting in XML—CSS must supply it all. The following are some of the more important CSS character styles:

- **Fonts**. To specify fonts by family, use `font-family:familyname`, where `familyname` might be Arial, Helvetica, Times Roman, and so forth. For Web applications you should specify two fonts, one for Windows such as Arial and another for the Macintosh such as Helvetica (an Arial equivalent). If you specify `serif`, `sans-serif`, `monospace`, `cursive`, and `fantasy`, browsers will elect to substitute default choices for you. To embed a font within a page (and make it available to users who don't have that font installed), use the `@font-face{font-family:fontname; src:URL(URL of font's location)}`.

- **Styling**. You can easily add bold or italic formatting to text. To bold text, use `font-weight:bold`. Other weight styles that are available to you are `bolder`, `lighter`, or a weighting factor in multiples of 100 between 100 and 900. For comparison purposes, 700 is considered bold, 900 is considered black, and 400 is book weight. You remove bolding by specifying `font-weight:normal`. To italicize characters, use `font-style:italic` (or, alternatively, `oblique`). To remove italics, use the style `font-style:normal`. To underline text, use `text-declaration:underline`, or substitute `line-through` for a strike-out text or `overline` for a line above the text. To remove any of the lining attributes, use `line-declaration:none`.

- **Text casing**. To set text case, use the `text-transform:value` style. The styles available are `capitalize`, `uppercase`, and `lowercase`. The `text-transform:none` style removes any of these transformations as well as any previous ones that might have been set.

- **Text color**. Color is also a style, and you can specify it using `color:value`. Values for color include common names, `#rrggbb` as an RGB value, and `rbg` where red, green, and blue are percentages.

- **Sizing**. To set sizing, use the `font-size:value` style. You can choose from `xx-small`, `x-small`, `small`, `medium`, `large`, `x-large`, and `xx-large` as absolute values, as well as entering the size of the text as 10pt or 10px. To make the font size either larger or smaller than is currently specified in your transformation, use the keywords `larger` or `smaller` or enter the percentage change (50%) relative to the current value.

- **Spacing**. The `line-height:value` style sets what page layout or word processors refer to as a paragraph's leading value. Leading is the amount of space before a line appears. The value gets multiplied by the font size to obtain a value for line height. Thus for 12-point text, a value of two gives 24 points of leading. The value also can be specified as a percentage, or by entering an absolute value in points or pixels.

  In addition to leading, you also can adjust kerning and tracking. Tracking is the adjustment of the word spacing, while kerning is the adjustment of letter spacing. You have fine control over these two adjustments down to individual spaces. Use `word-spacing:value` and `letter-spacing:value` for tracking and kerning, respectively.

- **Alignment**. Text alignment is done using `text-align:value`, where `left`, `right`, `center`, and `justify` are your options. Text alignment means the same thing in CSS that it means for paragraphs in word processors and page layout programs.

- **Background**. You can set the background for text just as you could set the background for the transformation as a whole. The style is `background:value`, where the value is a color name, a hex color, `transparent`, or a URL reference to an image file. You can set tiling options (`repeat`), whether the background scrolls or not (`scroll` or `fixed`), and position the background image at an absolute value from the top left corner of the page. See the background discussion earlier in this section for more details.

As you can see, CSS is a rich formatting language. We've barely scratched the surface here, but if you are interested in learning more, then you can go to CSS reference sources for more information. The World Wide Web Consortium hosts a section on its Web site devoted to CSS at http://www.w3.org/Style/CSS/.

> **Tech Tip**
>
> **Multiple Font Settings**
> CCS lets you specify multiple font values as a space delimited list, as follows:
> ```
> {font: bold italic
> 10pt/Arial;
> line-height:2;
> width:100}.
> ```

QuickCheck Questions

14. What are the significant differences between XHTML and HTML?

15. How can you control the processing order of a transformation?

16. What operators does XSLT support, and why are they used?

17. What important data types are missing from XML, and how are they dealt with by XSLT?

18. What functions does CSS offer that provide fine control over locating individual characters in a document?

19. Why is the word "cascaded" used in the name Cascaded Style Sheets?

20. What is a style sheet and how is it used?

21. How do styles get applied?

22. What will XHTML be used for?

23. What are the main differences between XHTML and XML?

Summary

Developing technologies are aimed at making HTML better at handling data and XML better as a source of data interchange. In this chapter, three different technologies were discussed: XSLT, or the eXtensible Style Language Transformations; CSS, or Cascaded Style Sheets; and XHTML or eXtended Hypertext Markup Language. What XSLT provides both HTML and XML is a method for altering both content and format based on a set of templates that can be applied. A template matches a location and provides an action to take at that location. XSLT is very flexible. It can create dynamic Web pages out of XML, format them, and pass them through to your browser. XSLT also can serve as the means for converting XML data output from one database into a data source that can be input into another different database, even one on another type of computer.

CSS is a means for applying formatting to XML and HTML. Using what are called styles, tags really, that reference a part of an XML or HTML document, CSS can provide page layout formatting, paragraph and character formatting, as well as word or string formatting. CSS is a much more powerful language for formatting XML or HTML than the tools that HTML provides you, and the regularity it can impose can be a major time savings for an organization. CSS is a developing topic, and not all browsers support it equally or well.

Key Terms

absolute position	node map	style sheet
attribute	parent	template
child	parser	transformation
CSS	relative position	XSL-FO
declaration	root node	XSLT
element	selector	
hierarchical	style	

Review Questions

1. Why does an XSL processor construct a node map prior to performing a transformation?
2. What is the one necessary node, how is it referenced, and what are its properties?
3. What are the major uses of XSLT?

1. Create a node map from the XML representation of this book's table of contents.
2. Use XSLT to convert your XML table of contents document into a standard HTML table.
3. Using the XML representation, use CSS to format that data into a table.

Web Programming:
A Programmer's Perspective

OBJECTIVES

1. To understand what a computer program is and how it works.

2. To get introduced to the basic principles of program design.

3. To understand the principles of object-based and object-oriented programming.

4. To learn the concepts of algorithms, variables, operators, branching and looping, functions, and data structures.

INTRODUCTION

Programming provides the instructions that tell a computer what to do. All the things that are done on computers today—from playing video games and music to displaying fancy graphics on Web pages to connecting buyers and sellers on an auction site—require a set of instructions to a machine.

There are many types of programming languages designed for various purposes. Some are general-purpose languages that can be used in almost any setting (such as BASIC and C++) and others are designed for database creation and customization (such as SQL). Our interests in this book are Web page programming languages such as HTML, JavaScript, Java, and VBScript. This chapter, however, does not deal with any specific language (although some examples are included from Java and HTML). Rather, it introduces general programming concepts and techniques that apply regardless of the language being used. The point is to establish a foundation for learning the various languages introduced later.

Programming Languages

Computers run on electricity. Why bring up this self-evident fact in the context of learning programming languages? The reason is that it is fundamental in the way a computer is given instructions. If you can think back to the simple science project many of us did or were shown in school, picture a wire running around a rectangular piece of cardboard. This project was a demonstration of an electrical circuit. A battery attached to the wire provided the current. A switch at one point could be turned on or off. When the switch was on, a small light connected to the wire went on. Turning the switch on meant touching the two ends of the wire so that electricity could travel all the way around the wire and create the circuit. This is what turned the light on.

This demonstration is analogous to how a computer works. The electricity from a battery or an outlet in the wall travels through a circuit on a silicon chip in the computer. The electrical current can either be on or off. "On" means the electricity is flowing through the circuit and "off" means the electrical current is stopped. Manipulating these on and off electrical states provides the computer with "instructions." If we digitize this information and call the "off" state zero (0) and the "on" state one (1), we have, in effect, created a way of communicating with the computer. This language of zeros and ones is called **machine language.** It is the only language a computer understands.

Now that there is a way to communicate with the computer, the problem becomes how to make this language usable to humans. As can be imagined, writing strings of zeros and ones is not the most intuitive way for humans to communicate. This is a problem not only in terms of having to tediously enter zeros and ones (not to mention the high likelihood of mistakes), but also because it becomes very difficult to know and trace back when mistakes occur. Debugging a program in machine language would be a nightmare.

Machine language, and those languages just above it, are known as **low-level languages.** This means they have to do with the internal workings of the computer. Humans who give instructions to the computers are known as **programmers.** The languages they work with are *programming languages,* which look more like English (though still far from the way we speak and write). Programming languages are standardized expressions that give instructions to computers. Programming languages are known as **high-level languages.** This means they use commands having to do with the problem being solved as opposed to the low level of communication of on and off that the computer understands. A programmer is not dealing with the nuts-and-bolts aspects of computer operation when he or she writes a program. Because programming languages are easier for programmers to write, understand, and work with, they are expressed at a higher level of logic than machine language.

Let's use an analogy to elaborate on this issue of high-level and low-level languages. Imagine an executive in a company with a very obedient, but very literal assistant. This assistant follows instructions to the letter, but has to be told *exactly* what to do or an error will result. The executive tells the assistant, "Get me coffee." The assistant will have no idea what to do. This assistant has to be told to

1. Walk to the cafeteria.

2. Go to the coffee machine.

3. Pick up a cup and hold it in one hand.

4. Pick up the coffee pot.

5. Pour the coffee into the cup until the cup is almost full.

6. Put the coffee pot back where it was.

7. Walk back to the executive's desk.

8. Place the cup of coffee on the desk.

Actually, we have simplified the instructions considerably—think about all the steps that really take place. Putting aside all variables such as what happens if there are no clean cups or the coffee pot is empty, the action of walking alone—placing one foot in front of the other—could require dozens of instructions, which take most babies about a year to get right. All of this may give you a greater appreciation of the power of a machine like the human brain.

The executive's statement, "Get me coffee," is analogous to a higher-level language. It would be inefficient for the executive to write a memo detailing all the steps necessary to complete the desired result. But the assistant can't do anything unless instructed in this way. It's the same situation for a programmer giving instructions to a computer. The problem is how to get a higher-level language that humans can work with into a form that the computer can understand. The solution is to use another program called a **translator** that takes the programming languages and converts them into machine code.

Translators come in two types: **interpreters** and **compilers.** Interpreters translate one line of code at a time. If there is a problem, they generate an error message right away. If not, the interpreter continues translating the next line until the end is reached. Each time the computer is shut off, however, the machine language conversion is lost. This means that in order to run a program using an interpreter as a translator, you have to have both the program and the interpreter. Since Web pages are viewed on all sorts of different computers with different browsers, Web programming languages such as VBScript and JavaScript use interpreters.

Compilers, on the other hand, translate an entire file of code all at once. The machine language instructions are stored in a separate file, usually called an executable file. When the computer is shut off, the translation remains present in this separate file.

The original file that is translated is the **source code** (which is written in a high-level language). Source code is a set of statements and instructions that programmers write when developing software. This source code is then translated into a lower-level **object code.** Object code is created by a compiler and is the machine language representation of the source code that a computer can understand. In reality, there are often a few steps between the source code and the object code, but for our purposes, this is enough to know.

QuickCheck Questions

1. How does a low-level language differ from a high-level language?
2. What is a compiler?
3. Explain the terms **source code** and **object code**. How are they developed?
4. What is the difference between an interpreter and a compiler?

Program Design

Although it may seem at first glance that what a programmer does is just sit down and write code, in order to write a successful program, first some planning must be done. The first step in this process is to clarify what the program is designed to do. Put another way, this process can be called defining the output. Unless you are writing the program only for yourself, this process usually involves speaking with either the client or whomever will actually be using the program to understand exactly what it is that this program will be designed to address. This output, or the goal of the program, must be specified as accurately as possible in advance (see Figure 5.1). You must know every Web page, audio/visual aspect, form, or printed report that your program produces.

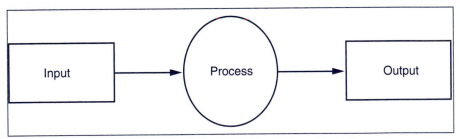

FIGURE 5.1   In Programming Input Is Processed to Produce Output

First, this will result in the program being more useful. For example, if your understanding as a programmer is that the code is primarily designed to introduce new product information on a Web site, and what is more of a priority is an easy interface for filling out request-for-information forms, the program will not be successful. It may work, but it will not be useful in terms of what the client wants. A corollary of this is that users will be happier and this will result in more work for you.

Second, forward planning saves time. Often, the debugging phase of a programmer's task takes longer than the original writing of the code. It is always easier to write the code correctly the first time than go back and change it later. Although at first this planning stage before jumping in and starting to write may seem like a waste, it can save hours of work on the back end. The more planning you do in advance, the faster you will finish the programming project.

Finally, planning avoids disappointment. If the client and users know in advance what a program can and cannot do, there will be a realistic expectation of the result of your work. Organizations and individuals often have misconceptions about what can be done, or what will be involved in getting the program to perform as expected. Plenty of advance discussion can expose these misconceptions up front and allow them to be clarified so that there isn't an issue later resulting from unfulfilled expectations.

Top-Down Design

Imagine, for a moment, that you have a project to do—not a computer project, but a real-world project, let's say replacing the windows of a house. This seems straightforward enough at first look; you need to get the windows and have them installed. Nothing could be simpler.

As you start the process of making the arrangements to have this done, however, you find out that someone you know can get you quality windows at a good price, but they don't do the installation. That's no problem because you also know someone who does all sorts of home construction, and they agree to do the installation of your windows. One thing this contractor mentions, however, is that they don't do painting. But this is fine too, because you know someone else that does painting. The other thing the contractor mentions is that since you have alarms on the current windows, you will need to have your alarm company in after the installation is complete to redo the alarm system with the new windows. As you see, the project is rapidly becoming more complex than originally thought, and you haven't even begun to consider what type of windows to pick out!

A project as involved as this requires organization. Take a look at Figure 5.2 as an example of a way to organize it in a form known as *top-down design*.

A real-world example like this, rather than a computer example, makes it easier to understand what is meant by a top-down design. As you can see, this type of organizational chart can be applied to many types of projects just as efficiently. The way to proceed is from the overall goal, that is, the top of the chart, down to the more detailed areas below. By the way, this example only shows the most superficial, general aspects; were we really to be carrying out this project, this chart would have to be more detailed and specific. But it serves to make the point even at this preliminary stage.

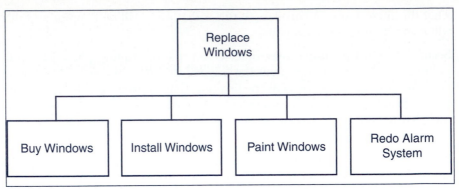

FIGURE 5.2   Top-Down Design

What a top-down design forces you to do is to continually keep in mind the overall goal of the project. Taking a large goal and then breaking it down into its component sections focuses your thinking. There are going to be dozens of details in this project and it's easy to get lost in them. By returning to the top of the chart while putting off the details as long as possible, you stand a much better chance of not forgetting something crucial. Working from the bottom-up leads to missing the forest for the trees.

Speaking of trees, if you look again at Figure 5.2, you will note that this design looks like an upside-down tree—imagine the top is the trunk and the categories spreading out below it are the branches. This tree structure is a common feature of many things having to do with computers (think of a folder directory in Microsoft Windows).

Now that we have the concept, let's turn to a real-world computer project. Suppose the project involves designing a company Web site. Let's do a top-down design. With a little thought, you can see that you can't just put "Web site" at the top. What is it that the client wants the Web site to do? Using the top-down model, you are immediately directed back to this important question. The project is already being broken down into component parts, thereby making the whole more manageable, while leading you to work closely with the client to avoid unpleasant results later, as discussed above.

What you realize is that you might need to make multiple designs like this to accomplish the various goals a client might have. Let's say the most important aspect of the Web site for the client is to increase the size of its database by collecting information about interested parties who visit. It becomes apparent that enabling visitors to register online should be one of the first things you consider when designing a program for this client.

Take a look at Figure 5.2 as an example of how you might begin to map this initial goal from the top down. One of the first things that might occur to you is that you need to create a form for visitors to fill out. This form needs to have an easy, intuitive interface so that people will complete it without throwing up their hands in frustration and going elsewhere. If they don't complete a field, you want to prompt them to do so. The form also must be comprehensive, meaning that it has fields for all the required information from each prospective customer.

Another thought that might occur to you is that the Web site will need to encourage visitors to register in some way. One obvious way to do this is to highlight the benefits of registration, which could be a free subscription to a relevant newsletter (for example) or up-to-date product information that wouldn't be available otherwise.

You have just started the process of designing your model, but you can see where this is going. Several drafts and multiple pages of tree structure will be necessary before you are ready to begin to write the actual program itself. When you do get to that stage, it will go much easier and quicker because you've done all the necessary preparation and thought it through beforehand. Your client will be happier and there will be less time needed to debug or redo the program.

Objects

Many languages used in Web programming are designed around the concept of objects. **Objects** are self-contained elements of a program that contain both the data and procedures to manipulate the data. Interaction with objects is only allowed in certain ways as they are designed to accomplish a specific task. A typical object in Web languages such as Java, C++, JavaScript, and VBScript is a string, which contains a series of characters (strings are defined later in this chapter).

An entire program may be made up of these independent routines known as objects. This is known as object-oriented programming (discussed in the next chapter), where different objects communicate with each other to perform tasks. This differs from more traditional *procedural* languages where data and procedures are separate. Theoretically, object-oriented programming makes programs easier to write and maintain.

There are several concepts that need to be understood in terms of objects:

- Also known as a procedure or behavior, a **method** is some process that is done with or to the object.
- A **property** is a value contained within the object that can be extracted.
- As the name implies, an **event** is a scenario that the object monitors and for which it takes a certain action when it occurs. For example, an event could be a user clicking a mouse button. Another example is the computer providing a notification that a certain time of day has been reached. The action or software routine that takes place as a function of the event is called an **event handler.**

Consider an object called a page that is found in the design of a Web site. The page object is a container object into which a program places other objects such as radio buttons, text, buttons, and so forth. One of the methods that the page object has is the page refresh. This method ignores what is in the local cache and calls for all of the objects shown on the page to be refreshed with current content and then redrawn. The method is referred to by name in program code that requires it, along with the object from which the refresh method is required. Refresh might be a method of other objects, and it certainly is a method of other members of the page class, so specific addressing is very important. A page has a number of methods that are built in, and you can certainly define and create your own.

Similarly, a page has numerous properties. Among its properties are height and width, background color, borders, and many others. As with methods, objects have a number of built-in properties; and you can define and create your own as required.

Finally, modern operating systems use an event-driven programming model. Numerous events are defined such as mouse up, mouse move, on object open, on object close, and so forth. Programmers use events as triggers to evaluate conditions and when appropriate act on those conditions to perform some action. Events aren't often created for objects, but do serve as containers for program code—either snippets (small code of one or two lines) or full programs with logic.

Algorithms

The essence of programming is solving problems—you take a problem in the real world (for example, how much have the average sales of snow blowers in Fargo, North Dakota, changed in the last 10 years) and write it in a language a computer can work with to come up with the answer. Before you can get to the stage where you are doing actual programming to solve problems, however, you must come up with a way to solve problems.

An **algorithm** is a sequence of steps or instructions given to a computer to accomplish a task or solve a problem. Some of the steps may repeat an indefinite number of times and some steps may require making a decision about whether to do two or more different things. An algorithm also can be a set of rules; for example, a search engine such as Google, Alta Vista, or Lycos uses an algorithm to find and order Web pages in response to a search command. It also can be a name for a small procedure that solves a recurrent problem, such as sorting data.

Defined simply, an algorithm is nothing more than a list of instructions on how to do something. An example might be the directions to your house you give to a friend: make a left out of your driveway, turn right at the next block, continue on the same road for 10 blocks until you come to the flashing yellow light, and so forth. Another example is how to cook an egg: get a skillet, put a little butter in it, heat it until the butter melts, get an egg, crack the shell, and drop the contents into the skillet. As you can see, although the word *algorithm* may bring up bad memories from math class or cause you to think of nerdy guys with horned-rimmed glasses and pocket protectors, the term as used in programming is quite simple.

There are many algorithms commonly used in programming languages that work well for tasks such as sorting and searching. Although there are algorithms designed for very particular types of problems, generally the term is used for something that is a standard solution to common problems in many situations. But besides being able to solve the problem at hand, an algorithm's worth is measured by its ability to do the task efficiently, meaning in the shortest amount of time or while using the least amount of storage space. The analysis of algorithms involves quantifying factors such as these to compare the efficiency of different algorithms doing the same task. Despite this, there is not one perfect algorithm for every task. The most efficient algorithm for a particular problem will vary depending on what you are trying to do and the nature of the programming language you are using.

An algorithm has the following characteristics:

- There are a finite number of steps that produce some result (even if that result is a message saying the desired outcome could not be achieved).
- Each step must be performed in order.
- Each step must be precisely defined.
- Steps can be repeated, but cannot continue being repeated forever.
- Some of the steps may involve making a choice about whether to continue going in one direction or skipping that series of steps entirely and doing something else.

Once you are able to take a problem and design an algorithm to solve it, the next step is to use a programming language to express the algorithm so that a computer can handle the problem.

Variables

A basic function of computers employed by all users in one way or another is their ability to store and manipulate data. If you think of some of the most common activities personal computers have been used for—balancing a checkbook, writing letters at home, and keeping track of customers and suppliers, employees, products, and inventory in business—all involve some form of data processing. Thus, when programming, a fundamental need is a place to put data. A **variable** is a place to put data in a program. The name comes from the fact that we expect this data to change or *vary* over time. A variable holds the data assigned to it until a new value is assigned or until the program is finished.

A programmer names variables in a brief, descriptive way so that it is clear what the data inside the variable is. `Total`, `my_scores`, and `BloodPressure` are all examples of descriptive names for variables. The underscore character (_) is used to separate words in variable names, as spaces are not acceptable.

Tech Tip

Elegant Algorithms
The study of frequently used algorithms is a good technique to advance your knowledge of a particular language. Algorithms are used a lot because they work well and are efficient. By analyzing existing ones, you can sharpen your ability to write better and more useful code.

Types of Variables

There are several possibilities for what kind of data can be entered in a variable. These can be categorized in terms of their *type*. There are two main types of information that can be entered: numbers and letters. Let's take a look at the numbers type first. Here are some examples of number data that can be entered in a variable:

- 39
- 10,072
- –670
- 1.5

The first three are examples of **integers.** For the purpose of our discussion, integers are numbers that don't include fractions. The numbers 39, 10,072, and –670 are all nonfractional numbers. The fourth number, 1.5, is a fraction and therefore not an integer. These numbers are called *real* numbers. Examples of real numbers are

- 33.3
- 5.7
- 10½

Thus, in the first category of **variable type,** the numbers, you have two possibilities: integer and noninteger, or real, number types.

The second category of variable type is letters. Here again there are two possibilities. The first is a single letter, or *character*. This character can be either a letter of the alphabet or a symbol, such as !, *, or #. Thus, the following are all examples of character variable types:

- E
- $
- q
- %

As you may have guessed, the second type in the letter category is a variable that contains more than one character. Examples are as follows:

- John Jones
- !^&%)
- leather
- dc

This character data type is known as a **string.** String data types allow words or phrases to be input as data. Any more than one letter classifies the data type as a string.

Thus, a variable type describes the kind of data entered in that variable. There are two main types: numbers and letters. Each of these in turn is divided into either integers or real numbers, or characters and strings.

A computer must know this information in order to work with a variable because it must allot a certain amount of memory to the variable, and it does so based on type.

Declarations and Statements

The first thing to do when writing a program is to identify to the computer what type of variables you will be using before you use them so that it can allocate the proper amount of memory. As you would think, real numbers and character strings take up more space than integers and single characters. This process of identifying a variable type is called *declaring* a variable. Most programs use multiple variables of different types. Once the variable type is defined in a **declaration,** you must conform to all the rules that have to do with that type of variable or an error message will ensue.

In addition to declaring the type, you also must declare the variable name upfront. The name of the variable is known as its identifier. Names should be brief and descriptive to enable others' and your own understanding of the code you've written. `Mother's_maiden`, `order_number`, and `last_deposit` are examples of good identifiers for variables. You often will be using more than one value of the same type, so a good name is crucial in order to avoid confusion.

A **statement** is a descriptive phrase that produces machine language instructions. In terms of the grammar, or syntax, of programming languages and spoken languages, statements are analogous to sentences. Statements represent a discrete chunk of information used to construct the overall program. A program could be said to be made up of statements, just as an essay could be said to be made up of sentences.

There are many different kinds of statements. A common one is an **if-then-else** statement. *If* something is true, *then* do this; if not, do something *else* (this is an example of a concept discussed earlier, of a choice between two routes being made in a step of an algorithm). An example of this type of statement in code could look like this:

```
IF answer = "John Jones" THEN
   PRINT "Yes"
ELSE
   PRINT "No"
END IF
```

This is also an example of another type of statement, a `PRINT` statement.

Finally, the above example also demonstrates that a single statement need not be only on one line. Because of the nature of what is written, the above statement is clearer and easier to understand because it is on two lines.

Assigning Values to Variables

Yet another statement is what's called an **assignment** statement. What this does is give the variable a **value.** First, you declare the types and names of your variables, and then you assign your variables a value. Before assigning your variables, the variable is empty. An assignment statement must be executed in order to fill it.

An assignment statement typically has the following syntax:

```
VARIABLE = Value
```

As can be seen from this structure, the variable name is followed by a symbol that indicates that a value is being assigned to that variable. You must enter a value that conforms to the type of variable you declared. An integer must be assigned to an integer type variable, a character into a character type variable, and so on, as demonstrated in the following examples:

```
first_name = "John" (string type variable assigned a
   string value).
salary =30500.25 (real number type variable assigned a
   real number value).
```

Often the *user* of the program, rather than the programmer, is the one that inputs the value of the variable. In this scenario, the program will prompt the user to insert a value, many times just by placing a flashing cursor in an empty text box. The user then fills the empty box by typing the appropriate response on his or her keyboard. This will be familiar to anyone who's ever filled out an online form, such as the kind you need to register with a Web site or to place an order.

Operators

We have progressed to the point where we have declared the types and names of our variables and assigned values to them. Now it is time to do something with these values. If you think of it, many tasks that programs do involve taking a value and doing something with it, for example, coming up with the sum of a series of numbers in a budget spreadsheet, comparing a possible medication to prescribe a patient to another list of the same patient's allergies (you want to make sure that program works right), or extending a series of values from previous weather patterns to predict future trends. All of these tasks involve computing values of some kind.

An **operator** is a symbol used to perform a computation on a value. Simple operators that we use every day are the mathematical + (addition), – (subtraction), / (division), and * (multiplication) operators on a calculator or keyboard numeric pad. Examples are

- 699 / 3 = = 233
- 51 * 7 = = 357
- 27,898.48 – 12,375.97 = =15,522.51

Note that the double equal sign "= =" means *equivalent to* (what we normally think of when we see a single equal sign). The reason for this is to distinguish *equivalent to* from the action of assigning a value to a variable, which uses the assignment operator "=", as discussed in the previous section.

Other operators provide either a "true" or a "false" result, for example:

```
member_name "John Jones" = = entered_name "Sam Jones"
```

returns an answer of False and

```
"60,000" > "35,000"
```

returns an answer of True.

This last example demonstrates the common operators > (greater than), >= (greater than or equal to), < (less than), and <= (less than or equal to), which provide results that are not numbers, but rather "true" or "false."

There are many other types of operators, but these should serve to demonstrate what an operator does.

Branching and Looping

There are two important logical structures that most programs have: branching and looping. Branching is when you reach a point in a program where a condition must be evaluated, and from that evaluation the program proceeds down one of two or more paths. The simplest branch is usually something called an immediate IF statement: IF(condition=true), "do this"; "else do that"). Some programs modify these IF statements to allow yet a third action if something is neither true nor false, and IF statements can be nested to allow for more than one branch. Since each IF statement must be processed, you want to structure an IF so that the direction that is most often chosen or quickest to execute is the true part of the statement. A better construct than nested IFs is to use a CASE structure if the language you are using allows for this. A CASE statement is similar to an IF but evaluates a set of conditions, one at a time, and when a statement is encountered that is true, it executes that statement and exits the CASE statement. For example, consider the following:

```
CASE (
    condition1, do this
    condition2, do this
    condition3, do this

    ...
    OTHERWISE, do that)
```

In the CASE structure above, the first clause is evaluated and if true its action is the next step in the program. If condition1 isn't true, the CASE function continues to evaluate condition2, then condition3, and so forth, executing the first true statement it finds. Again, you want to populate condition1 with the situation that is the most common or the fastest (hopefully both) in order to get the best performance. Not all languages have CASE statements, and not all support an OTHERWISE clause. When you put a CASE statement into an event like a button's MouseUp() event, that logic is only applied when you click on a button and release the mouse button.

Have you ever been on the phone with a phone messaging system, for example, calling the customer service department of a company? If so, you probably have first-hand experience of what a loop is. The voice prompt of the messaging system asks you to enter your account number. If you don't enter anything, it asks you again. It keeps on asking until you enter something, or until it disconnects you.

A **loop** is a repetition within a program. Certain steps are repeated a particular number of times or until some result is obtained. Here is an example of a loop statement:

```
INPUT "Please enter your password"; Password$
DO WHILE Password$ <> "open"
   PRINT "I'm sorry, I don't recognize your password.
      Please try again."
   INPUT "Please enter your password"; Password$
LOOP
PRINT "Thank you. Welcome to the main vault of Fort Knox!
   How may I serve you?"
```

The above program continues to loop back and repeat the "enter your password" prompt until it gets what it is asking for.

Functions

A **function** is a separate piece of code that performs some task for the program. The function performs the operation and then returns the result of the task back to the program. The task can be large and require a significant amount of processing or it can be as simple as adding two numbers. Functions exist outside of the main part of the program and only do their particular task when they are instructed to. This request by the program to have the function perform its task is named a **function call.** When the function completes its task, the compiler will go back to the next line of code following the call.

To give an analogy, think of a breakfast buffet in a restaurant. Often, there is an omelet chef who stands ready in case someone wants an omelet. Customers pick out whatever they want from the rest of the buffet, but the omelet chef only swings into action if someone wants an omelet. At that point, the customer tells the chef what ingredients he wants—the chef takes this input and performs his task. When he is done, he returns the result.

In the same way, a program calls a function to perform a task. Let's say the function's job is to sort a series of numbers from low to high. Like the omelet chef who is told by the customer what ingredients to use, the function is told by the program what numbers to sort. The unsorted numbers are the input. The function returns the sorted list of numbers as the output.

Programs may make millions of function calls while they are running. The function can exist as a separate chunk of code within a program or be in another program entirely. It also may be part of an external file directory that is combined with the program when it is being compiled.

In the following example, the function is designed to return the gross sales of a particular item:

```
function calculateTotal (quantityOrdered, itemPrice) {
   var result = quantityOrdered * itemPrice
   return result
}
```

By inserting the values corresponding to the number of items ordered (quantityOrdered) and the cost of each item (itemPrice), this function multiplies the two and returns a result corresponding to the total, or gross sales amount, of the item.

Notice in this same example the importance of using descriptive names. If instead you had named the values a (instead of quantityOrdered) and b (instead of itemPrice), the code would have worked and your end result would have been the same. The problem is, however, that it would be much more difficult to figure out what it was that you were doing here. If you did not remember that a stands for the quantity ordered and b stands for the price of the item, you would be lost. Anyone else coming along and trying to understand what you've done would be equally confounded. Thus, although the name you use is irrelevant in terms of the ability of the function to return the desired result, it is very relevant in terms of reading and maintaining your program.

Data Structures

When you write a program, a fundamental need is a way to store the data that is inputted into the program. Of course, the new data, like anything that is newly inputted, is stored in the computer's memory. But this information cannot be put just anywhere; it must be entered in an organized way. Programs store newly inputted information in what is called a **data structure.** A data structure is a physical layout of data so that it is organized and easily accessible.

A good data structure not only serves as a place to store information; it also allows for more efficient algorithms to be used, thereby improving the overall performance of the program. The choice of the type of data structure is a major design consideration when programs are being written. Difficulties in implementation and maintenance can result in large systems if the best data structure is not used.

This has given rise to object-oriented programming languages (such as Java) where the data structures, rather than algorithms, are the key organizing principles.

Arrays

An **array** is one of the simplest types of data structures. It is used to hold variables of the same type, but of different values. As an example, take a list of employee names. Let's say there are 100 employees. The employee names are the variables. They would all be of the same type, a character string, but each name would be different. In an array, each variable has to go into its own container, or *member*. Thus you will need 100 members of the array to hold the list of names.

An array must be declared, just like a variable, before it is used. The reason for this is the same as why variables must be declared: the compiler must know how much space to allocate for the array. Since arrays hold a fixed number of equal-sized data elements in a contiguous block of memory, to properly set aside space the compiler needs to know the number of members and the data type that will be stored in each one.

Most programming languages have arrays built into them.

QuickCheck Questions

5. What is an object?
6. Explain an event handler.
7. What is meant by the term **algorithm**?
8. Why do we need to declare variables in a program?
9. What is an operator?
10. Explain the term **function**. What is it, and what does it do?
11. What is an array? How does it relate to the term **data structure**?

Where You Go from Here

This section focused on providing a general theoretical base that applies to all types of programming, regardless of the language. Although you will need to delve far further into individual programming concepts in order to execute them with confidence in your language of choice, the ideas introduced here will serve as a foundation for the process.

The general state of programming is one of constant change. Many of the languages that are popular today were unknown just a few years ago. New technologies are constantly springing up, linking computers in everything from phones to TVs to refrigerators. As a result, the arrival of new languages and programs to manipulate computers in a distributed environment is inevitable. The knowledge contained in this chapter will be viable regardless of what the latest innovation is because of its universality.

To continue your investigation of programming concepts, which space did not allow, the next areas to consider would be things such as lists, stacks, and queues in the general category of data structures; array functions and different examples of arrays; and the ins and outs of debugging program errors.

Summary

Programming is a logical enterprise that has a few basic rules regardless of the particular computer language you use. This chapter introduces some of the principles of programming, particularly from a Web programmer's perspective. The key idea of programming is that binary logic works like a switch. The action flows along the logical path that is true, just like electricity flows through a closed switch. Programs take input, do processing, and produce output. When you are building programs, think about modularity and reusability. It may help to consider a top-down design approach; that is, consider what the program must accomplish and work backward from there.

An object is something that you can name, that has a set of properties and methods, and that responds to events. Objects needn't be something physical like a page; they can be a concept like a timer. But most often there will be a physical representation to an object.

This chapter introduced the concepts of algorithms and functions, as well as variables and data types. Variables need to be instantiated or declared in a program, using a declaration. Variables that must contain more than one value are represented by arrays, which are named objects in which each position in the array has an address. Arrays have their own set of functions.

Programs are a set of statements in which functions are called, variables are assigned or reassigned, and their values are modified. Functions often use operators, which are built-in routines for providing output based on your input.

Logic is an important part of the structure of a program. Logic is most often found in branching or looping statements.

This chapter sets the stage for the next chapter, in which you will learn about object programming.

Key Terms

algorithm	high-level language	operator
array	if-then-else	programmer
assignment	integer	property
compiler	interpreter	source code
data structure	loop	statement
declaration	low-level languages	string
event	machine language	translator
event handler	method	value
function	object	variable
function call	object code	variable types

Review Questions

1. What are a low-level language and source code?
2. Describe what top-down design is, and what problem it solves.
3. What are the three most important features of an object?
4. How is an algorithm different from a function?
5. What is an operator?
6. Describe some of the different data types that a variable can have. Do data types differ from language to language?
7. Enumerate some of the classes of functions that are common to most programming languages.
8. What two things do you have to do in order to use a variable in your program?
9. How do CASE statements work?
10. What is an array?

Exercises

1. Addition is a common function to all programming languages. Consider the different kinds of variables, data types, and objects that an addition operation might apply to and show how addition would operate on them. Indicate when additions offer more than one course of action, one that requires the programming language to make a choice.
2. Using a graphical programming language like Visual Basic, describe two different objects (preferably one with physical representation and one without) and show what properties, events, and methods they have.
3. Sketch a simple diagram describing how an elevator might be programmed.

Object Programming

OBJECTIVES

1. To learn why object programming offers efficiencies.

2. To understand what an object is, and how it uses properties and methods.

3. To examine some basic examples in code on how objects, classes, and other OOP structures are expressed.

4. To get an introduction to the construction of object programs.

5. To learn about object relationships and models.

INTRODUCTION

All programmers want to be able to develop code that can be reused later in their future work, and to be able to reuse the work of other programmers as well. In addition to **portability,** which is the need to have a program run on different computers or a **module** run in different applications, reusability is the key to efficient and practical programming. You might think that computers being a science would have developed the equivalent of Esperanto, the universal language that was supposed to unite the world. But it is not so. Computer programming is bedeviled by the same cacophony of languages that led those ancient Mesopotamians to build the Tower of Babel.

The very earliest computers required that their operating system and all routines and programs written for them be written from scratch. Work done in the 1960s in computer programming and in operating systems at AT&T (and in other places) established the concept of developing computer operating systems around a portable kernel, or core set of input/output routines that every operating system needs to support. With a standard kernel that could be licensed, computer manufacturers could write a translation layer that made their computers work with much less effort on their part. Eventually, their work led to the UNIX operating system and to the adoption of portable kernel architecture, which is now used in nearly all modern operating systems, a concept that has been referred to as platform-independent programming.

In order to make programming easier, language developers began to look at a scheme for organizing the code that programmers write into logical entities called **objects.** Further organization led to objects that have relationships to one another in a hierarchical structure, and in which a child object can inherit the properties of its parents—but still express differentiation. What came to be called object programming has had several notable languages written for it, including SmallTalk, Lingo, and others. Object programming is now a part of most of the higher level computer languages in use today.

Higher level languages differentiate languages like C, Java, or Basic from Assembly language, and require a compiler to transform their programming into a more compact and efficient code that can be more easily used by the computer. An interpreter then converts the code line by line into Assembly or some other machine language, a language that can communicate directly with a microprocessor. An executable file, or .EXE, is compiled code. Thus, you will find that programmers use languages today such as C++ to build applications and operating systems, and the "++" means that this language includes object support.

In an effort to make programming languages portable, in much the same way that operating system developers endeavored to make kernel code platform independent, recent work on programming languages also has endeavored to do the same. Perhaps the best example is the development of Java. Java was initially created to program set-top boxes and other networked devices at Sun Microsystems. Sun decided to release Java as an open-source program to make it broadly available. Under an open-source license, the users have free reign to use the language as they see fit, but are required to share advancements in the code they develop. Java applications were made primarily to run inside browsers, although their popularity quickly gave rise to full-blown applications. To have Java run on different platforms (e.g., Windows, Macintosh, Linux), each platform must have a Java Virtual Machine or JVM loaded, giving rise to the concept of "Write Once, Run Everywhere."

Hand in hand with the concept of objects is that of the **PEM** approach, which stands for properties, events, and methods. Objects have **properties,** which are attributes that describe the objects. A set of events can act on each object, and in an object-oriented environment, each event can be coded to program a certain action. Additionally, each object has a set of **methods,** or functions that it exposes that can be called on as a service by its reference in outside code. The PEM approach has often been described as **exception programming.** Objects are coded so that they express inherited or default properties. When you want to program some special or different behavior, you enter code into the associated event that overrides any default behavior. In this chapter, we will expand on these concepts so that you can see how they can save you time and streamline your code.

The development of object programming is now over 20 years old, and goes hand in hand with the idea of developing operating systems that use what is called the event-driven model. Most modern operating systems sit in a wait state awaiting events that will trigger specific operations. Ever since the pioneering work at Xerox PARC in the mid-1980s, the concept of event-driven programming has come to be associated with the graphical user interface, or GUI, the visual display we've come to expect as part of Macintosh, Windows, and all of the desktops that are used in UNIX and Linux these days. But an event-driven program doesn't require that a GUI be used; it can all be done programmatically.

The goal of Web programming is to quickly and efficiently create the effects your Web sites need. Thus, you will find yourself using languages such as C++, VB.NET, Java, C# (C Sharp), or, for more efficiency with a certain loss of power, Java Script or VBScript. All of these languages support the concept of objects. Each language has its own method for handling objects, organizing those objects into classes, and providing a means for communicating between those objects, but there are underlying concepts that apply to all of the object languages that will be discussed in this chapter. As application and operating system vendors make different capabilities available through standard modules, the need to be able to call on the services of those modules using standard program calls is required of all programming languages. The ability to manipulate an application programming interface, or API, for an intended purpose is among the first prerequisites of deciding which computer language to use.

Microsoft's development of Web services as part of their "Dot Net" initiative is nothing more than an attempt to create a standard set of universally used services such as client identification (e.g., Passport), security standards (public/private keys and Kerberos), robust messaging, and other capabilities. Nor is Microsoft alone in this regard, as all major vendors are focused on a distributed computer programming model. Many other companies are offering APIs that other programmers can use. You'll find published object-oriented APIs for major databases like Oracle, for network framework programs like Hewlett Packard's OpenView or Computer Associate's Unicenter TNG, for large intelligent storage arrays such as EMC's Symmetrix servers, for banking services, and an almost infinite number of other applications.

Objects

Fundamental to the concept of object programming is, of course, objects. An object is an entity or thing to which you can give a name, and about which you can assign a set of attributes or properties and to which you can assign actions or, as they are called programmatically, methods. Put another way, an object has two important features: *state* and *behavior*.

A beach ball is an object; it has colors, a certain size, and a material of construction; and one of its behaviors is a bounce. Similarly, in programming a visual display, screen, or report can be an object; and their properties can include size, resolution, color, whether to display or hide, and so on; and all have associated behaviors built into them. Both of these examples are concrete—that is, you can see and touch them—and so they are each straightforward to conceptualize.

Many programming languages offer a graphical interface that allows you to do drag and drop programming, the so-called **visual languages.** However, object programming makes no such requirement. In a strictly text-based coded language, you can still use objects. You declare the object, define its scope or where the object applies and how long it lives (and this may determine where the definition is located in the programming), define its properties and methods, and make any default assignments that are needed. If the object is derived from another object type, you can just add or subtract what is necessary in order for the object to do the job you need it to do.

So far you've been given two physical examples of objects, but there's no requirement that an object be concrete. Many objects represent ideas or actions. That is, objects can be verbs as well as nouns. For example, Visual Basic offers you the Timer object, something that you can drag from your palette of objects onto the Visual Basic design surface to make part of your program. A Timer doesn't offer a lot of properties, but the ones it does offer are often quite valuable. With a Timer you can add delays or an event initiator to your program.

Some objects, like Timers, more or less stand on their own. A Timer can be part of another object such as a program module, but a Timer doesn't offer the property of containment. Containment is one of the key concepts of object programming, because from containment flows the concept of inheritance. We'll consider inheritance in more detail a little later in this chapter. In addition, containers allow for logical collections of objects to be made and named. For example, an input screen or form is a container of numerous objects. When users go to a checkout screen for a shopping cart on a Web site, they see text fields, radio buttons, check boxes, POST and GET buttons (Submit and Update), and so forth. Each is an object. Additionally, the text labels, lines, and the screen itself are all objects.

From a programming standpoint then, perhaps the best definition of an object is that it is a software package of variables and methods. The point of having methods is to surround and hide an object from other objects, something called *encapsulation*. Access to an object's methods is controlled by a set of access rights or privileges.

Object programming really requires a different mind-set from more traditional programming methods. The goal of object programming is to create the appropriate set of objects necessary to perform the tasks you require and then program those objects to perform the actions required to do those tasks. Let's consider the simple example of an event log. The log needs to do the following things:

1. Store events of interest and their description.
2. Organize events into logical groups.
3. Provide a sorting function.
4. Provide a search function.
5. Provide a reporting function.
6. Create a print output.
7. Provide an export function.
8. Have the ability to clear the log or flush the log in some logical way (such as First In, Last Out, or FILO).

From the standpoint of the event log object, the object has several methods that it exposes that provide these functions as part of the object definition, as shown in Figure 6.1. It's the association of these different methods with an object that differentiates object programming from more linear programming methods where the function itself is the center of attention.

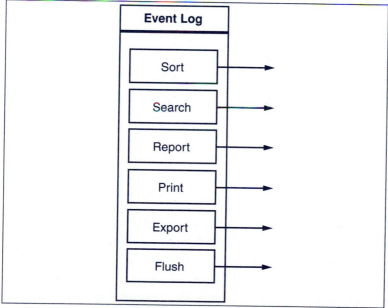

FIGURE 6.1   An Event Log Object with Its Associated Methods

To summarize then, object programming offers two very important properties: modularity and information hiding.

Properties

The first step in defining an object that will serve as the prototype of a class is to assign its properties or attributes. Properties (attributes) are a data structure or container that is considered part of the object's definition and has an assigned data type. Among the data types commonly used are INT, LONGINT, CHAR or TEXT, DOUBLE, NUM, and so on. A property can have only one data type, so if you need to store more than one data type, you need to define more than one property for that data.

If you were programming an object in code, then you might do so as follows:

```
// Log_entry
string name;
int event_type;
string description;
time timedate;
. . .
```

Here we've defined four different properties for a Log_entry object, along with three different data types. To use these properties programmatically, you would address them using the following method:

```
Event_Log.Log_entry.name = "Share Access"
```

Here you've specified that the *name* property be set to "Share Access", and you've differentiated the name property of the Log_entry object from other name properties that you might have by indicating which object it belongs to.

Objects can often have many properties, so even though you can code for them as part of your program, visual languages typically display the properties of an object using the concept of a **property sheet.** An example of a property sheet is shown in Figure 6.2. As you create objects in your program through coding, or using the visual approach by dragging and dropping an object to the design surface—a process called **instantiating** an object—the properties of that object as defined by the class follow along. To alter the property of an object's instance, you would declare what that property should have as its contents. Above we declared in code that the name property should be `Share Access`; in a visual interface you would simply type that name into the name text box.

The collection of variables is called instance variables, and they define a state for an object or an instance. One of the important properties of an object is its **scope.** As mentioned earlier, scope defines where an object exists in a program and how long it lives. You might instantiate a Timer object, and once that timer fires it is released from memory. Depending upon the object in question, you may or may not have to release or destroy the object in your code.

FIGURE 6.2   An Object's Properties Dialog Box in Visual Basic 6

QuickCheck Questions

1. What is meant by a "higher level language"?
2. What does PEM refer to?
3. What two features are central to the concept and definition of an object?
4. What are visual programming languages?

Instantiation

Objects **invoke** a function by initiating a call to that function. Any function that instantiates the object and makes a value assignment is called a **constructor** above. A constructor is a special function that has the same name as the class, and it does not return any value.

A *call* is a program statement that names that function and, if necessary, passes appropriate values or variables (called *parameters*) to that function. In nearly all instances, the object calls a function that works on or affects that object. Programming languages nearly all support the concept of functions, from simple arithmetic functions to custom and complex functions; but a call to a function associated with an object requires that the object be named as part of the function call. Thus, you might have the following program call for an object:

```
Object_name.function_name (parameter list),
```

which, for our example, might take the form

```
EventLog.Sort(Time,Date)
```

Notice the use of a period to separate the object's name from the name of the function. In an object hierarchy, you would add additional names separated by periods, as follows:

```
Grandparent_name.Parent_name.Child_name.Function_
    name(Parameter list)
```

It isn't always necessary to pass a parameter to a function; however, it is always necessary to include a set of parentheses after the function name. Normally you pass or input a value to a function; it processes that value and produces input. In the case where you want a function to process variable input, you use a parameter. Say, for instance, that you have a program that searches a database for a florist in a certain zip code. The LOOKUP function takes the parameter ZipCode and returns a list of florists. When a buyer comes to the Web page for the order, they enter the zip code into a text field, or perhaps enter the zip code into a pop-up dialog box. This value is then assigned to the ZipCode parameter, and when the Submit button is activated, the appropriate list is returned.

A class can have one or more constructors for an object, and the manner in which properties are assigned is not specified. In some instances, the constructor assigns a static value; in another, it might get a system variable such as your computer's internal time stamp; and in yet a third instance, the constructor might post a dialog box that allows a user to interactively enter a value that is assigned to the object the constructor creates. A simple example of a constructor is the one that copies one object onto another, often referred to as a *copy constructor.*

If you were using a constructor to instantiate a check box group, it might look something like this:

```
Eventtype_cbox ( )
{
title = "System Events"
box1 = "Input/Output" default;
box2 = "Memory access";
. . .
}
```

In instances where you want to use a parameter list for later assignment, the check box instantiation would look like this:

```
Eventtype_cbox (string ctitle, boolean bbox1, Boolean
    bbox2, . . .)
{
title = ctitle
box1 = bbox1
box2 = bbox2
. . .
}
```

You will often see what is called the **scope resolution operator** (::) used to relate a function to a particular class. There could be numerous instances where objects have a `sort( )` function. In order to know which object the `sort( )` function is being associated with, you scope it. An example is shown below:

```
integer event_log :: sort( )
```

Here the scope operator identifies the `sort( )` function as a member of the event_log object class, and assigns an integer value as the return type.

Classes and Inheritance

Similarly grouped objects and their functions in an **object-oriented programming (OOP)** language are organized into groups called **classes.** Each particular object type is a member of that class. Since classes contain similar objects, in nearly all cases the class defines most of the important characteristics of an object—otherwise, why put an object in that class? The identical property sheet you would see for newly instantiated objects is an expression of the class's characteristics. Indeed, probably the best way to think of an object is to think of a template. If you tear a page off a pad, then each page would be the object and the pad would be the class. Another way of describing a class is that it is a prototype or blueprint for an object.

In programming, each object has only one parent, unlike Gregor Mendel's bean sprouts. In a hierarchy with two parents, you would never be certain which **attribute** the offspring might get, but in programming you always need to and do know.

The purpose of **inheritance** is to reuse as much of a class's definition for each object as possible. Any property or method that is standard should be defined; and if you have a property or method that isn't standard, that property or method shouldn't be part of a class definition. Methods that are part of a class definition are called *class methods*; parameters or variables that are defined as part of a class are called *class variables*. When you alter a method or variable for an object, you are creating an instance method or instance variable, respectively. Class methods can be invoked directly using the class definition, but if you need to invoke an instance, you must do so using the particular instance.

In object-oriented parlance, a child object's class is called a **subclass** and the parent object's class is called the **superclass.** When you create a subclass, it inherits all of the superclass's properties and methods. However, subclasses not only can override the inherited methods and properties, but they can add additional properties and methods to suit their more specialized function. The purpose of an object hierarchy is to go from a general category to a specialized one. In Java, for example, the topmost object is called the Object class. Object expresses all of the necessary characteristics required for an object to run within the Java Virtual Machine.

Inheritance provides the ability to reuse code developed in a hierarchy in all of the objects that are descended from that class. Another useful feature is that there is no requirement that the high-level objects have a physical representation. You can define superclasses with default behaviors, but with many undefined or unimplemented properties and methods. Generic superclasses are referred to as *abstract* classes.

Messages

In order for OOP to work properly, objects must interact with other objects, and they communicate with each other by passing **messages.** One object typically sends a message to another to have the target object perform one of its functions. The message sometimes requires no information, but in instances where the function must act on a particular piece of data, parameters are sent as part of the message.

Suppose you have an object that performs a dump of your event log (`Dump ( )`), and its final action is to clear all events from the log. Suppose further that the action of clearing the log is a method of the Event_Log object, called the `Clear( )` method. To pass the message from `Dump( )` to the Event_Log, you need three pieces of information:

1. The target object (Event_Log).

2. The name of the method (Clear).

3. The value of any parameters that need to be passed to the method (System, Security, etc.).

A message might take the following form then:

```
Event_Log.Clear(Security);
```

The advantage of passing messages between objects is that all interactions between objects are supported by activating object methods. Also, both of these objects can be independent of each other; they need not be on the same system or even in the same process. Thus, messaging supports asynchronous processing, something of great value in the packet-passing world of the Internet.

QuickCheck Questions

5. How do you instantiate an object?

6. What is a class?

7. How does inheritance work?

8. Give an example of one object sending a message to another.

File Organization

Many languages use what are called **header files** to store object definition, along with the headings for the functions associated with those objects. Header files serve as a summary of the member functions that are part of the classes used in the program that the header file is associated with. A class definition is shown in a header file within a set of braces ({ . . . }), and, depending on the language, those definitions are often followed by a semicolon. Since the goal of object programming is reusability, you'll often find that the header for one program can serve as the header file for another. That's more often the case when the programming language is the same in both instances.

A second file that is often used is called the *implementation* file, and that file stores the details and code for the functions that are going to be used. The program file is where the code for your program is stored. A **client file** is then used to declare class objects and to access the functions that the class supports. Client files are separated from the code in order to make them readable, and are called client files because they require the class definitions in order to execute. It's a lot easier to see when the objects are used, and what actions they are asked to perform, when you don't have to slog through the code describing all of these things.

Consider a client file for the program that is used to create the Event Log described earlier. The file might look a little like this:

```
          .
          .
          .
<- log_event is the object ->

log_event.Add_entry( );
log_event.Input_data( );
log_event.Sort(TimeDate);
          .
          .
          .
```

The log_event object is calling on three functions: `Add_entry`, `Input_data`, and `Sort`. The code for implementing each of these functions is hidden, and it's obvious what is being accomplished in this part of your program, making this a much friendlier program to understand. Often a header file includes a public and a private section. The difference between the two is a question of scope. Anything in the **public** section of a header file can be accessed by the client file, whereas anything in the **private** section cannot be accessed directly by a client program. By using the private section, programmers can hide the inner workings of their code from other programs, which removes detail that the client program doesn't need to know about. Another reason for having a private section is that it allows you to store class functions so that they are only available to the class itself.

The entire set of component files described in this section works together to form a more easily understood and modifiable program. Compartmentalization or modularity is the key to the productivity gains that object-oriented programming offers. When you get a routine to work as a function, that routine can be stored away as a function; and when you get a group of functions successfully programmed that can define an object, those two can be stored. Should you need to make modifications or debug an error that comes up, your code is easier to debug because it is compartmentalized as part of your class definition.

A number of languages support a feature called **preprocessor directives,** which are most often called **include files.** They are called include files because they are text files in various languages like C++ that begin with an #include statement. A preprocessor directive lets you set up your programming environment prior to the running of the program, indeed prior to running the interpreter that would compile high-level code. There are several reasons why using include files is valuable. To begin with, many programs written for different computer platforms (different processor types or architectures, for example) require differently named variables, disabling or enabling specific features and so forth. Your include file performs those substitutions.

Putting this all together, an include file has the following structure:

```
#include <headerfile.h>
class Event_Log
{
public: // public functions listed
. . .
private: // private functions listed
);
```

If you don't specify that a set of functions and class members are public or private, then anything that you specify is considered to be private. For that reason, it's a good idea to always label a public and private section, even if you don't have any public functions at the time. Doing so makes it easier for programmers who come after you to understand your work.

Interfaces

An **interface** is a set of exposed controls that can be manipulated. In an object environment, an interface is a construct that lets unrelated objects interact with one another. In order for an interface to work properly, there needs to be a set of accepted conventions or protocols that let objects manipulate one another.

For an interface to work in an object environment, an interface requires that its protocols be available to any class regardless of that class's position in the object hierarchy. Programs use interfaces to be able to group similar behaviors in classes that are unrelated, and without requiring that there be a class relationship between those classes. An interface's protocols also let you declare standard methods for one or more classes. You also can use an interface to make an object's methods available without exposing the class, what is referred to as the object's programming interface.

A collection of methods exposed as part of an interface is called an **application programming interface,** or **API.** The purpose of an API is to provide the functionality of the objects it contains, while hiding the internal mechanisms or methods used to effect those functions. When a program publishes an API, there is the expectation that the program calls are going to remain constant or change little over time, even if the code that performs these tasks is under constant revision.

Many programs and systems have published APIs. For example, Microsoft Windows has a number of APIs that the company has published from which third-party developers have written all kinds of programs. One of those APIs is the GDI, or Graphics Display Interface. Programs use these routines to post windows and display things on a screen. If Microsoft changed the names of functions and parameters of the GDI at some point, then programs that used those particular functions might no longer work and those products would need to be reprogrammed.

As much as possible, vendors aim to keep an API unchanged over time. Sometimes change is required, for example, when a new processing type is required. As Microsoft went from 16-bit computing, to 32 bits, and now to 64-bit processing, changes were required. However, as much as possible, backward compatibility is maintained. In instances where it isn't possible to maintain backward compatibility, the approach has been to create an emulated environment to run programs using their program calls translated for the new environment.

Naming Conventions

As you can imagine, once you get beyond basic programs, the number of objects multiplies substantially. Often developers keep an object map handy to see how one object is related to another, and there are also development packages that allow you to see object hierarchies. Still, it is very useful to apply naming conventions to objects just as you would variables in a program.

Many people use a naming convention that puts the data type into the name of the object. Thus,

- cFirstName is a first-name field containing character data.
- iAge is an age field with integer values.
- bPicture is a BLOB, or binary large object, field that contains a picture file.
- tTime is a field with time data.

With a system like this, you don't have to remember the data type each time you encounter this object or a variable in your code. So you are less likely to make errors associated with data typing. Similarly, a system of object names also can be of great use when you are programming in an object-oriented language.

If you have a collection of screen objects—buttons, radio buttons, check boxes, text input fields, labels, and so forth—you could collect them into groups and assign them codes that make a particular object's assignment obvious. In some instances, you might want to use a single-letter code such as R for radio buttons and T for text boxes. Or perhaps you might use a two-letter code that groups similar objects together in their class and specifies the object type as well. Both radio buttons and check boxes are often put into a class of objects called option groups. Thus, you might want to name them ORiRadi_Button_Name, where O is the class, R is the object type, and i denotes that this object stores an integer value, which indeed is how radio buttons work.

With the addition of three letters to a name, you've managed to convey a great deal of valuable information that can help you not only avoid programming errors but speed up your work as well. Consider that you want to make changes to a particular type of object, but you don't want to do it universally as a class. With a naming convention like this, you could sort your objects in an object browser. An example of an object browser in the Visual Basic environment is shown in Figure 6.3. In Visual Basic, it is a common practice to name objects and controls (visual objects) with a three-letter prefix. Observe that all of the radio buttons in Figure 6.3 have been named accordingly.

The point is that nomenclature is very valuable to programmers, and deserves quite a lot of thought *before* you start programming. Once you've created the program, changing all of your code to conform to a naming system can be quite a chore.

Object Collections

If you have an object that is related to an unknown number of other objects, the link between them can serve as the definition of a collection. A **collection** can be named as a class (collection class), and this class exists to define a

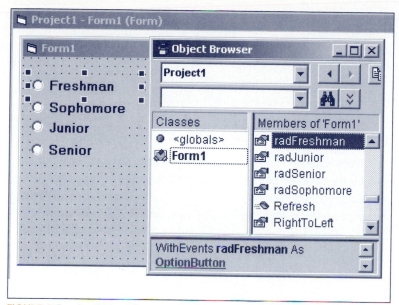

FIGURE 6.3   An Object Browser in the Visual Basic 6 Environment
All radio buttons have been named with the "rad" prefix.

group of objects in the related class of objects. The concept of related classes and collections gives rise naturally to a namespace, or universe of related object classes collected for a common purpose, commonly called an **object model.** Most models are hierarchical in structure, although this isn't strictly necessary. An object model is the scheme of connections, links, or relationships that classes of objects can have.

The purpose of developing a hierarchy of object collections is to create a model or **framework** for complex program development. There are a number of object models in use today, and the most useful ones are those that are the work of industrywide organizations with widespread backing. The **Common Object Request Broker Architecture,** or **CORBA,** is one such framework; and its value is that it allows different object models that conform to CORBA standards to talk to other object models that also comply.

One such object model is Microsoft's **Component Object Model,** or **COM** (see www.microsoft.com/com/default.asp). Using first COM, then COM+, followed by DCOM (D equals Distributed), Microsoft fostered the creation of component objects that were able to use services of the Windows operating system and Microsoft Office. **ActiveX** components are based on COM and offer both interfaces and programming tools. One expression of COM and its descendents is the Object Linking and Embedding services that provide for compound documents.

You will learn more about object models later in this book. From a Web programming standpoint, one very important object model is the W3C's **Document Object Model,** or **DOM**   (see www.w3.org/DOM/), something that is described in more detail in Chapter 9. Microsoft offers an object model for its Office suite for use by developers. You can find a brief introduction to object models at www.objs.com/survey/objmodel.htm.

QuickCheck Questions

9. What files might you find in an object-oriented program?
10. What is the purpose of a header file and preprocessor directives?
11. What does an interface do?
12. Describe how and why object models are used.

Summary

In this chapter, you learned about object-oriented programming, or OOP. The reason that OOP is used for higher level programming such as Web site design is that it enables the programmer to reuse more of the code that is developed, and it provides an organizational scheme for programming that enables programming to be modularized more easily than traditional languages. With modularization comes less debugging, more standardized routines, and an easier assignment of programming pieces of a project by individuals and groups.

Object programming requires a different mind-set over linear programming languages. You program objects that have certain properties, and can perform certain functions that you need to perform. Your program then consists of getting the objects you create to perform the sequence of actions or responses that are necessary. Object programming makes a good companion to the event-driven programming model in use today in many operating systems.

Although objects can be defined programmatically, many OOPs are visually oriented environments. Objects consist of properties or attributes and methods, and a visual environment can express these as part of a property sheet. Objects also can be grouped into classes of similar objects, and often programs define a hierarchy of objects so that descendant objects can inherit the properties of their parents.

Key Terms

ActiveX
application programming
 interface (API)
attribute
class
client file
collection
Common Object Request Broker
 Architecture (CORBA)
Component Object Model (COM)
constructor
Document Object Model (DOM)
exception programming
framework

header file
higher level language
include file
inheritance
instantiate
interface
invoke
localization
messages
method
module
object
object model

object-oriented programming
 (OOP)
PEM
portability
preprocessor directive
private
property
property sheet
public
scope
scope resolution operator
subclass
superclass
visual language

Review Questions

1. What is the definition of an object?
2. How do you create an object from its class?
3. What would be the headings of the constructors or functions that define a sphere object?
4. Give an example of the code that defines a class?
5. How would you label the file myfile.txt as a header file or as an implementation file?
6. How do you initialize an object for use programmatically?
7. What is meant by an object's scope and how is it different from or relate to the scope resolution operator?
8. Why does an interface require a set of protocols?
9. Why does OOP support the concept of an application programming interface, or API?
10. Why are naming conventions useful?

Exercises

1. Create a set of objects that define all of the important elements in this book's table of contents.
2. Draw an object hierarchy for the objects you created.
3. Create a property sheet for a Chapter object, then instantiate it and show the properties of Chapter 6.

8. Concerning naming conventions, JavaScript is case-_____.

9. Declaring a variable means that you inform the program in advance so that memory space can be assigned to the variable to store the variable. True or False?

10. Which of the following is *not* true of JavaScript?

    a. A JavaScript program is compiled before being sent to the browser.

    b. JavaScript is considered good for rapid program development.

    c. JavaScript is most commonly used on the client-side.

    d. You do not have to declare the types of variables in JavaScript.

11. The `dim` keyword is used by JavaScript to declare a variable. True or False?

12. The data type for a variable in JavaScript is `subscript`. True or False?

13. The assignment operator in JavaScript is:

    a.

    b.

    c.

    d.

14. Which variable type does JavaScript support?

    a. string

    b. variable

    c. numbers

    d. variant

15. Which of the following is the correct way to declare a variable in JavaScript?

    a. `dim Name`

    b. `new Name`

    c. `dim Name`

    d. `var Name`

16. Individual pieces of an array are called _____.

    a. collections

    b. variables

    c. elements

    d. variants

17. A _____ construct allows you to repeat blocks of code.

    a. looping structure

    b. repeating structure

    c. decision control

    d. variable control

Client-Side Scripting with JavaScript

JavaScript

OBJECTIVES

1. To adding JavaScript to HTML pages.

2. To working with JavaScript variables.

3. To working with objects.

4. To controlling JavaScript programs.

5. To make forms with JavaScript.

Introduction: Getting to Know JavaScript

JavaScript is Netscape's cross-platform, object-oriented scripting language. JavaScript is supported by all major browsers like Netscape and Internet Explorer. It is *not* a scaled-down version of Java. It is *not* Java. It is *not* related to Java.

Core JavaScript contains a core set of objects, such as `Array`, `Date`, and `Math`, and a core set of language elements such as operators, control structures, and statements. Core JavaScript can be extended for a variety of purposes by supplementing it with additional objects; for example: *client-side JavaScript* extends the core language by supplying objects to control a browser (Navigator or another Web browser) and its Document Object Model (DOM). For example, client-side extensions allow an application to place elements on an HTML form and respond to user events such as mouse clicks, form input, and page navigation.

Core JavaScript

Client-side and server-side JavaScript have the following elements in common:

*   Keywords.

- Statement syntax and grammar.
- Rules for expressions, variables, and literals.
- Underlying object model (although client-side and server-side JavaScript have different sets of predefined objects).
- Predefined objects and functions, such as `Array`, `Date`, and `Math`.

JavaScript gives HTML designers a programming tool. HTML authors are normally not programmers, but JavaScript is a very light programming language with a very simple syntax! Almost anyone can start putting small "snippets" of code into their HTML documents.

- JavaScript can put dynamic text into an HTML page.
- JavaScript can react to events.
- JavaScript can read and write HTML elements.
- JavaScript can be used to validate data.

A First Look at JavaScript

Scripting languages like JavaScript or VBScript are designed as an extension to HTML. The Web browser receives **scripts** along with the rest of the HTML document, then parses and processes the scripts. Look at the following script example:

```
<!- Welcome.htm ->
<html><head></head>
<body>
<script language="javascript">
   document.write("Welcome to JavaScript!")
</script>
</body>
</html>
```

Looking at the script line by line, you see the familiar HTML tags `<head>` and `</head>` indicating the beginning and ending of the head section. Next the `<body>` tag marks the beginning of the body section. Following it are the three lines of JavaScript and then the `</body>` tag denoting the end of the body section. Notice that the JavaScript is located within the body of the HTML code and those three lines of code produce the output, as shown in Figure 7.1.

If nothing else, you can tell that HTML and JavaScript go hand in hand. In the next section, you'll quickly learn how to get the two working together.

Adding JavaScript to Web Pages

A solid foundation in HTML is key to implementing JavaScript in a Web page. You're simply going to extend HTML using JavaScript, which allows you to mix its syntax with HTML tags. All you need to do to be proficient is to under-

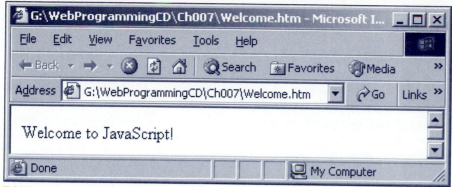

FIGURE 7.1   The Output Generated by the JavaScript Code in Welcome.htm

stand the mechanics of JavaScript. Take another look at the script above. You'll notice two new, but obvious, HTML tags: `<script>` and `</script>`. HTML was extended to include these `<script>` tags to incorporate scripts into HTML. Adding JavaScript into a Web page is as simple as placing valid JavaScript code between the `<script>` tags.

The `<script>` Tags

The `<script>` tag indicates the start of the script section, while `</script>` marks the end of the script. Look at the script below:

```
<!-alert.htm ->
<html><head>
<title>Client-Side Scripting with JavaScript</title>
<script language="JavaScript">
  alert("Welcome to Web Programming!")
</script>
</head></html>
```

The initial `<script>` tag includes a `language` attribute that indicates the scripting language used. The `language` attribute is used because, as you may know, there is more than one scripting language. Without the `language` attribute, the Web browser would not know if the text between the tags was JavaScript, VBScript, or one of the many other scripting languages.

Everything between the opening `<script>` tag and the closing `</script>` tag is called the body of the script and everything that is part of the body section belongs to the script.

JavaScript to Display Information

Take another look at the first script example (Welcome.htm). Notice the line that reads

```
document.write("Welcome to JavaScript!")
```

One of the most common uses for JavaScript is to display text. JavaScript accomplishes this using an object called `document`. The `document` object provides access to the elements in an HTML page from within your script. This includes the properties of every form, link, and anchor (and, where applicable, any subelements), as well as global `document` properties such as background and foreground colors. The method used is called `write`. The syntax of the `write` method of the `document` object is

```
document.write("String")
```

Where to Put the JavaScript

HTML pages are divided into sections, for example, a head and a body. You can place your JavaScript code anywhere in the HTML document. Your decision on where to place your script can be a matter of aesthetics or function. Good programming practice leans toward function.

Sometimes you might want to **execute** a script when a page loads; other times when a user triggers an event. If you place scripts in the body section, they are executed when the HTML page is loading. In other words, the scripts will execute immediately. In the case where you want a script to execute when a user triggers an event, such as clicking a button or rolling the mouse over an area, you will want the script to load before anyone triggers it. To assure that the script is available and ready to be executed when called or when an event is triggered, place the script in the head section. This is often referred to as an event-procedure script.

Usually we put all the "functions" in the head section. The reason for this is to be sure that the script is loaded before the function is called.

The following is an example of a script placed in the head section:

```
<html>
<head>
<script language ="JavaScript">
some statements go here
</script>
</head>
```

When you place a script in the body section, as shown below, it's called an immediate script and it executes immediately. Place an immediate script in the portion of a Web page where you want the results displayed.

```
<html>
<head>
</head>
<body>
<script language ="JavaScript">
some statements go here
</script>
</body>
```

You can place an unlimited number of scripts in your document, so you can have scripts in both the body and the head section.

```
<html>
<head>
<script language ="JavaScript">
some statements go here
</script>
</head>
<body>
<script language ="JavaScript">
some statements go here
</script>
</body>
```

QuickCheck Questions

1. What do you use to embed JavaScript code in HTML documents?
2. Where can you insert JavaScript code in an HTML document?

Working with Variables

Programs need content to work with. We supply that content, known as data, by defining it to the computer system and reserving space in the computer's memory for the computer to store the data for later recall. This reserved space is called a *variable*. A variable is a named location in computer memory that JavaScript can use for storage of data during the execution of a script. The where and how variables are stored is not important. For our purposes right now, what you use them for and knowing how to use them are the important issues. You can use variables to

- Store input from the user gathered via your Web page.
- Save data returned from functions.
- Hold results from calculations.

JavaScript has four basic data types for variables:

- Numeric: 12, 16.71
- String: "122 Green Street"
- Boolean: true|false
- Null: value undefined

The syntax is

```
var variableName = variableValue
```

where sample values for any of the supported data types could be

- A number: `10`
- A string: `"JavaScript Tutorial"`
- Boolean: `false`
- Another variable: `x` [where `x` has already been assigned]
- An object property: `navigator.appName`
- The result of an object method: `window.confirm("Is your name "+name+"?")`
- No value [yet]: `null`

Let's look at a simple JavaScript to see how you can use a variable.

```
<!- UsingVariables.htm ->
<html><head></head>
<body>
<script language="javascript">
  var name = "Color"
  document.write(name)
  document.write("<h1>"+name+"</h1>")
</script>
</body></html>
```

The first line of this script example declares a variable named `name`. This reserves a place in the computer's memory that can be easily identified and quickly found for recall. The same line provides content for that variable with the string `"Color"`. The next line of the script writes the "value" of the variable for display in a document. The last line displays the variable again, only now it's formatted as a heading.

Defining and using variables in JavaScript is very straightforward and not unlike using variables in other programming languages. However, there is more that you should know to be fluid and consistent in writing JavaScript.

Declaring Variables

What's in a Name?
Variables are more useful and your code more readable if you use descriptive names that have some association with their contents or purpose. For example, if you're dealing with product prices, use the word *price* as part of the variable name.

Before you can use a variable to store some data, you must define or declare it. Declaring a variable means specifying its name at the very least.

You can create a variable with the `var` statement:

```
var strname = some value
```

You can also create a variable without the `var` statement:

```
strname = some value
```

Storing Values in Variables

It's a good idea to assign a value to a variable when you create it. This is referred to as **initializing** a variable. You assign a value to a variable by using the following format:

```
var strname = "Color"
```

or like this:

```
strname = "Color"
```

Now the variable `strname` has the value `"Color"`. Note that the name of the variable is entered on the left side of the assignment operator and the value of the variable is entered on the right side of the operator. Remember that the equal sign is an assignment operator, not an arithmetic operator.

QuickCheck Question

3. Write a JavaScript code that declares four variables named `name`, `address`, `city`, and `state`.

Scope of Variables

The scope of a variable dictates where it can be used in your script. A variable's scope is determined by where it is declared. If it is declared within a procedure, it is referred to as a local or procedure-level variable and can be used only within that procedure. You can have local variables with the same name in different functions, because each is recognized only by the function in which it is declared.

If it is declared outside of any function, it is a script-level variable and all the functions on your page can access it.

The example below demonstrates both script-level and procedure-level variables:

```
<html><body>
<script language ="JavaScript">
  var counter = 1
  function cmdButton_onClick()
  { var temp = 5
  }
</script>
</body>
</html>
```

The variable `counter` is a *script-level* variable and can be utilized throughout the script. The variable `temp` exists only within the `cmdButton_onClick()` function.

Working with Arrays

Until now we've worked with variables that store single values. Many times you will want to work with more than one value, such as in a set. This is where arrays come into play. Objects are the heart of JavaScript and the array is one such object.

Like an array in non–object-based programming languages, an array in JavaScript is a set of values grouped together under a single variable name. The primary difference is that you use something called an Array object constructor to create an array in JavaScript. You can create an Array literal by specifying the name of the array and the values of all its elements. The following example creates an array of three elements:

```
colors = new Array("Red", "Yellow", "Blue")
```

The elements of an array are indexed according to their order, starting with 0. You could, therefore, refer to the second element in the above array ("Yellow") as `colors[1]`. You can specify the number of elements in a new array by using a single numeric parameter with the Array constructor.

For example, the following code creates an array of seven elements:

```
dish = new Array(5)
```

If you create an array with a single numeric parameter, that number is stored in the length property, and the array doesn't actually have any elements until some are specifically assigned to it. If, however, the parameter is not a number, an array of one element is created and that value assigned to it. You can easily increase the size of an array by assigning a value to an element higher than its current length.

Here's an example of a simple array construction:

```
<!- Array1.htm ->
<html><body>
<script language="javascript">
  var famname = new Array(6)
  famname[0] = "Valda"
  famname[1] = "Glenn"
  famname[2] = "Sidney"
  famname[3] = "Myrna"
  famname[4] = "Jett"
  famname[5] = "Moonie"
  for (i=0; i<6; i++)
  {
     document.write(famname[i] + "<br>")
  }
</script>
</body></html>
```

We also can write the code like this and produce the same output:

```
<!- Array2.htm ->
<html>
<body>
<script language="javascript">
  var famname =
```

```
      new Array("Valda","Glenn","Sidney","Myrna","Jett",
        "Moonie")
    for (i=0; i<famname.length; i++)
    {
      document.write(famname[i] + "<br>")
    }
  </script>
  </body></html>
```

Both of these code snippets use a for loop. We'll discuss looping later in the chapter.

QuickCheck Questions

4. What does it mean for a JavaScript variable to have a "scope"?
5. How does JavaScript support arrays?

JavaScript Functions

JavaScript supports several functions that can be executed by an event or called from any script. Unlike a subroutine, which is executed every time it's called, a function runs code and can also return a result to the script that called it.

In JavaScript a Function procedure is a series of statements enclosed by the `Function` and `End Function` statements. A Function can take arguments in the form of constants, variables, or expressions that are passed to it by a calling procedure. If a Function procedure has no arguments, its `Function` statement must include an empty set of parentheses. A Function returns a value, which is always a variant, by assigning a value to its name in one or more statements of the procedure.

Defining a Function

You define functions at the beginning of a file (in the head section), and call them later in the document. To create a function, you define its name, any values (arguments), and some statements like this:

```
function myfunction(argument1,argument2,etc.)
{
some statements
}
```

A function with no arguments must include the parentheses:

```
function myfunction()
{
some statements
}
```

Arguments are variables used in the function. The variable values are values passed on by the function call. By placing functions in the head section of the document, you make sure that all the code in the function has been loaded before the function is called.

Some functions return a value to the calling expression:

```
function result(a,b)
{
c=a+b
return c
}
```

Calling a Function

A function is not executed before it is called; to use it, you have to call it. You can call a function as follows:

```
myfunction(argument1,argument2,etc.)
```

or without arguments:

```
myfunction()
```

The script below shows a more complete code that calls a function without arguments. This code defines a function, creates an input button that, when pressed, calls the function, which in turn displays an alert box with the message "Welcome".

```
<!- Function1.htm ->
<html><head>
<script language="javascript">
   function firstfunction()
   {
      alert("Welcome")
   }
</script></head>
<body>
<form>
<input type="button" onclick="firstfunction()"
        value="Call function">
</form>
</body></html>
```

The `return` Statement

Sometimes you want to call a function that calculates or makes a decision and then returns that result to the script that made the call. Functions that return a result must use the `return` statement. What if you have a function that returns the sum of two numbers like the following?

```
function total(a,b)
```

```
{
result=a+b
return result
}
```

When you call this function, you must send two arguments with it:

```
sum=total(2,3)
```

The returned value from the function (5) will be stored in the variable called sum.

Now here's the completed script:

```
<!- Total.htm ->
<html><head>
<script language="javascript">
  function total(a,b)
  {
    return a + b
  }
</script></head>
<body>
<script language="javascript">
  document.write(total(2,3))
</script>
</body></html>
```

How does it work? The script in the body section calls a function with two arguments, 2 and 3. The function set in the head section of the page returns the sum of these two arguments.

Controlling Your JavaScript Routines

JavaScript allows you to control the order in which your scripts process data through the use of conditional and looping statements. By using conditional statements, you can develop scripts that make decisions by evaluating data and criteria to determine what tasks to perform. **Looping** statements allow you to repetitively execute a line or lines of a script until certain conditions or criteria are met. Each method offers benefits that enable you to create complex and highly functional Web pages.

Using Conditional Statements

At some point in your Web programming, you'll need to step beyond simple interactive Web pages in which all the page does is collect information from users. You may want to respond to a user depending on some piece of information entered by that user. Perhaps you're working on a Web page for an athletic store that specializes in hiking shoes for all types of terrain. You might

Tech Tip

Create before You Call
Remember that a function must be created before it's called. This is the reason that you place function code in the head of an HTML document.

Tech Tip

Use and Reuse
Save functions in separate files so that you can use and reuse them in scripts that need them. This makes things easy to update, too.

ask, "Do you hike in mountains or desert?" If the user answered desert, you might have the JavaScript respond, "High desert or low desert?" The user's response to that question could lead to another question or a recommendation for a certain shoe.

The programming required to create this kind of logic is implemented via conditional controls known as **branching**. In JavaScript we have three conditional statements:

- `if` statement: used to execute a set of code lines when a condition is true.
- `if . . . else` statement: executes one set of statements if a specified condition is true and another if it is false.
- `switch` statement: used to select one of many sets of lines to execute.

`if` and `if . . . else` **Statements**

You should use the `if` statement when you want to execute some code if a condition is true. The syntax looks like this:

```
if (condition)
{
   code to be executed if condition is true
}
```

Notice that there is no `. . . else . . .` in this syntax. You're simply telling the code to execute some code lines if the condition is true.

Now, when you want to execute certain code if a condition is true and some other code if a condition is false, use the `if . . . else` statement. The syntax is as follows:

```
if (condition)
{
   code to be executed if condition is true
}
else
{
   code to be executed if condition is false
}
```

`switch` **Statement**

The `switch` statement tests an expression against a number of case options and executes the statements associated with the first one to match. If no match is found, the program looks for a set of default statements to execute, and if these aren't found either, it carries on with the statement immediately following `switch`. An optional `break` statement with each case ensures that once a set of statements has been executed, the program exits `switch`.

You should use the `switch` statement when you want to select one of many blocks of code to be executed. The syntax is as follows:

```
switch (color)
{
case label1:
  code to be executed if color = label1
  break
case label2:
  code to be executed if color = label2
  break
default:
  code to be executed
  if color is different
  from both label1 and label2
}
```

Here's how it works. First we have a single variable, color, that is evaluated once. The value of the color is then compared with the values for each case in the structure. If there is a match, the block of code associated with that case is executed. Notice the `break` statement after the code for `case label2`. If I omitted the `break`, the lines following it would also be executed.

Here's another example:

```
<!- Switch1.htm ->
<script language="javascript">
//You will receive a different greeting based
//on what day it is. Note that Sunday=0,
//Monday=1, Tuesday=2, etc.
var d=new Date()
theDay=d.getDay()
switch (theDay)
{
case 5:
  document.write("Finally Friday")
  break
case 6:
  document.write("Super Saturday")
  break
case 0:
  document.write("Sleepy Sunday")
  break
default:
  document.write("I'm looking forward to this weekend!")
}
</script>
```

Tech Tip

Flag Your Errors
Even though it is not
required, you should
include a `case else`
when working with
`select case` state-
ments to process
conditions that you
may not have antici-
pated. For these con-
ditions, you can
display something as
simple as a message
dialog to inform you
that a branch was ex-
ecuted in error.

Conditional Operator

JavaScript also contains a conditional operator that assigns a value to a variable based on some condition. A comparison operator compares two operands and returns a Boolean value (true or false) as to the validity of the comparison. Operands can be of numeric or string type.

The `==` (equal) operator returns a Boolean true if both the operands are equal. JavaScript will attempt to convert different data types to the same type in order to make the comparison. Here's what the syntax looks like:

```
Variable name=(condition)?value1:value2
```

For example:

```
greeting=(visitor=="PRES")?"Dear President ":"Dear "
```

which says, if the variable `visitor` is equal to `PRES`, then put the string `"Dear President "` in the variable named `greeting`. If the variable `visitor` is not equal to `PRES`, then put the string `"Dear "` into the variable named `greeting`.

QuickCheck Questions

6. When do you use conditional statements?
7. When do you use the `select case` statement?

Using Looping Statements

Looping statements are just the tools you need to force a program do something again and again a specified number of times, until some condition is met or as long as some condition exists. In JavaScript we have the following looping statements:

- `while`: loops through a block of code while a condition is true.
- `do . . . while`: loops through a block of code once, and then repeats the loop while a condition is true.
- `for`: runs statements a specified number of times.

These three statements can be divided into two groups based on their usage: `for` statements are best used when you want to perform a loop a specific number of times; `do . . . while` and `while` statements are best used to perform a loop an undetermined number of times or while a certain condition exists.

`while` Statement

The `while` statement will execute a block of code while a condition is true.

```
while (condition)
{
  code to be executed
}
```

The following example simply counts 1 through 10 by incrementing a counter by 1 each time for as long as the counter is less than 11:

```
var i = 0
while(i<11)
{
   document.write(i + "<br/>")
   i++
}
```

do . . . while Statement

The do . . . while statement executes one or more statements at least once, checking that a certain condition is met each time before repeating. If that condition is not met, then control moves to the statement immediately after the loop.

```
do
{
   code to be executed
}
while (condition)
do statements while (condition)
```

The following example counts up in twos for as long as the number is less than 20:

```
var i = 0
do
{
   document.write(i + ".<br/>")
   i+=2
}
while(i<20)
```

for Statement

The for statement creates a loop consisting of three optional expressions enclosed in brackets and separated by semicolons, and a block of statements to be executed. The first expression is used to initialize a counter variable, the second (optional) provides a condition that is evaluated on each pass through the loop, and the third updates or increments the counter variable.

```
{
   code to be executed
}
for ([initial-expression]; [condition]; [increment-
   expression])
{statements}
```

This example simply counts up from zero for as long as the counter is less than 10:

```
for(i=0; i<10; i++)
  document.write(i + ".<br/>");
```

QuickCheck Questions

8.   When do you use `for` statements?

9.   When do you use `while` statements?

JavaScript in Action

Until now you've had a gentle introduction to JavaScript designed to familiarize you with language constructs as well as get you acclimated to recognizing, analyzing, and creating basic scripts. Now, let's wade in a little deeper and look at more sophisticated JavaScript code.

JavaScript Syntax

Before we go any further, we should discuss some JavaScript syntax essentials. You've probably noticed some strange yet consistent characters and punctuation in the scripts you've seen to this point. The following list points out the essentials:

- `//` indicates that what follows is a comment and not code to be executed, so the interpreter doesn't try to convert it to machine code and run it. Comments are a handy way of putting notes in the code to remind us what the code is intended to do, or to help anyone else reading the code to see what's going on.

- `/*` indicates the beginning of a comment that covers more than one line.

- `*/` indicates the end of a comment that covers more than one line. Multiline comments are also useful if you want to stop a certain section of code from being executed but don't want to delete it permanently. If you were having problems with a chunk of code, for example, and you weren't sure which lines were causing the problem, you could comment a chunk at a time in order to isolate the problem.

- Curly braces (`{` and `}`) are used to indicate a block of code. They ensure that all the lines inside the braces are treated as one block.

- A semicolon defines the end of a statement, and a statement is a single command. Semicolons are, in fact, optional, but it's still a good idea to use them to make clear where statements end, because doing so makes your code easier to read and debug. (Although you can put many statements on one line, it's best to put them on separate lines in order to make the code easier to read.) You don't need to use semicolons after curly braces.

All About Forms

Remember that JavaScript is object based. Forms are an object. Forms allow us to prompt a user for input using elements such as radio buttons, check boxes, and selection lists. Data gathered in this manner can then be posted to a server for processing. A form is created by enclosing HTML controls and other elements within `<form> . . . </form>` tags. A page can contain as many forms as required, but they cannot be overlapping or nested (the closing `</form>` tag of a form must precede the opening tag of any subsequent form).

```
<form>
Some code goes here, HTML tags for example
</form>
```

Everything between the `<form>` and `</form>` tags belong to the form and is called the body of the form. Almost anything can go in the body of the form. You can design it using any HTML tag and make it as attractive as you wish.

Although the `<form>` and `</form>` tags are enough to create a form, such a form can hardly communicate with a script. One of the most important attributes you should set for a form is its name. The name allows a script to refer to the form and it can be used by files on the server level. To set the name of a form, assign an appropriate string to its name attribute.

You can use the `document.formname` syntax to refer to a form in a script. Suppose you create a form named frmReaderSurvey. If you want to refer to it from a script, you would use `document.frmReaderSurvey`. Alternatively, you also may refer to a form as `document.forms[n]`. In this case, `n` is the ordinal position of the form in the `document.forms` collection. Thus, if there are two forms in a Web page, you may refer to the second form as `document.forms[1]`. Often, a form contains many visual objects such as textboxes, check boxes, radio buttons, and list boxes. In a script, we can refer to them as `document.formname.objectname`. For example, if a form named `frmReaderSurvey` contains a textbox named `txtCity`, we can refer to its content as `document.frmReaderSurvey.txtCity.value`. In JavaScript and DOM (Document Object Model), there are many other ways to address and manipulate the form's objects. Two examples follow.

Check Box Example

```
<!- CheckBox.htm ->
<html><head>
<script language="javascript">
  function check()
  {
```

```
          var coffee=document.frmCoffee.chkCoffee
          var txt=""
          for (i = 0; i<coffee.length; ++ i)
          {
            if (coffee[i].checked)
            {
              txt=txt + coffee[i].value + " "
            }
          }
          document.frmCoffee.txtAnswer.value
            ="You ordered a coffee with " + txt
        }
    </script>
    </head><body>
    <form name="frmCoffee">
    How would you like your coffee?<br>
    <input type="checkbox"
    name="chkCoffee" value="cream">With cream<br>
    <input type="checkbox"
    name="chkCoffee" value="sugar">With sugar<br>
    <input type="text" name="txtAnswer" readonly="true"
      size="40">
    <input type="button" name="test" onclick="check()"
      value="Order">
    </form></body></html>
```

Drop-Down Box Example

```
<!- Dropdown.htm ->
<html><head>
<script type="text/javascript">
function put()
{
var option=
document.forms[0].dropdown.options[document.forms[0].
  dropdown.selectedIndex].text
var txt=option
document.forms[0].favorite.value=txt
}
</script></head><body><form><p>
Select your favorite browser:
<select name="dropdown" onchange="put()">
<option>Internet Explorer
<option>Netscape Navigator
</select>
</p><p>Your favorite browser is:
<input type="text"
```

```
name="favorite" value="Internet Explorer">
</p></form></body></html>
```

A Quick Form

First we have to set up the form where the user will enter the info. There are several types of form elements to use, but we will use the three most common: text field, drop-down box, and text area. Here's a form for collecting information about readers of this book:

```
<!- QuickForm.htm ->
<html><body><form>
Your Name: <input type="text" name="name"><br/>
your email: <input type="text" name="email"><br/>
Your programming skills are:
<select name="skills" size="1">
   <option value="non existent">Zip</option>
   <option value="pretty bad">Pretty bad</option>
   <option value="so so">so so</option>
   <option value="Good">Good</option>
   <option value="Excellent">Excellent</option>
   <option value="I should be teaching you!">
      I should be teaching you!</option>
</select><br/>
<input type="submit" value="submit">
</form></body></html>
```

There's nothing magical here. Once the form collects the information, a script can send the collected data to a file for validation. We'll get to that in Chapter 10, covering ASP coding.

Creating Mouseovers

Where would the Web be today without those sensational-looking menu effects? You can create them with both text and image hyperlinks using JavaScript. It's as simple as giving the hyperlink an ID or name and deploying a hyperlink event such as onMouseMove, onMouseOut, onMouseOver, and onClick. Using these event handlers, you can load a new image for the hyperlink or display text in the status bar of the browser in place of the hyperlink's URL.

Here's a rollover script that comes in two parts. The first bit goes in the <head> section of your HTML page, traditionally just before the </head> closing tag.

```
<script language="JavaScript">
   function showImage(imgName, imgSrc)
   {
      document.all[imgName].src=imgSrc
```

```
  }
</script>
```

And here's the second part of the code, the trigger, which goes inside the main <body> of your page at the exact place where you want the rollover to appear.

```html
<a href="the_page_you_want_to_move_to.html"
onmouseover="showImage('imgSomeImage','someImage.gif')"
onmouseout="showImage('imgSomeImage','someOtherImage.gif')">
<img name="someImage" src="FirstImage.gif"></a>
```

This script needs a little modification before it will work. The main change you need to make is to replace `"the_page_you_want_to_move_to.html"` with the address of the real HTML file you're linking to. If you save your rollover images in the same directory as the HTML file, this script will now work without further adjustment. Alternatively, you can change the filenames of the images within the script so they match the filenames and filepaths of the images you're using. Here is an implementation of a simple mouseover:

```html
<!- Mouseover.htm ->
<html><head>
<script language="JavaScript">
  function showImage(imgName, imgSrc)
  {
    document.all[imgName].src=imgSrc
  }
</script></head>
<body>
<h3>Here is a Mouseover example</h3>
<a HREF="http://www.mcgraw-hill.com/markets/mcgrawhill_
  education.html"
onmouseover="showImage('imgSomeImage',
  'McGrawHillEducation.gif')"
onmouseout="showImage('imgSomeImage',
  'McGrawHillCommunity.jpg')"
</a>
<img name="imgSomeImage" src='McGrawHillHome.gif'
  width="200" height="100"/>
</body></html>
```

When you open the Mouseover.htm code in a browser, it will first display the McGraw-Hill.gif image. When you roll the mouse pointer over the image, the system will automatically display the McGrawHillEducation.gif. You will be able to click on the image to display the McGrawHill_education page. When you move the mouse pointer away from the image, the system will display the McGrawHillCommunity.jpg.

You'll notice that the script in the `<head>` section of Mouseover.htm is a generalized script. You can make any changes in the body section and include any image and `<img>` tag without affecting the script itself. Most scripts operate this way—especially if they're well written.

File referencing and filepaths work in exactly the same way inside a script as they do outside it, in regular lines of HTML. There's no difference. So you can use http://www.mySitename.com/images/myImg1.gif or /images/myImg1.gif or ../images/myImg1.gif or whatever filepath protocol you generally use.

Opening a New Browser Window

When one window isn't enough, pop open another one using the `Window.open` method. This method takes four optional parameters:

- *Location* specifies the URL of the document to show within the new window. If it's left blank, the `"about:blank"` document (a blank document) is displayed.
- *Name* specifies the name of the new window.
- *Options* is a single string containing a series of comma-delimited parameters that specify how the new window will look.
- *Replace history item*, if set to true, won't add a new history item to the browser's history list as a result of the window opening.

The `Window.open` method returns a reference to the newly created window, and it's a good idea to store this object reference in a local variable so you can easily reference the window again (for example, to close it). Because you are dealing with object references, you should use the `Set` statement to assign the reference:

```
Set oNavWin = window.open("nav.html")
```

You also should assign a reference to the parent window within the new window, using the new window's Opener property.

The following code example shows how you can open a navigation window from an HTML page:

```
<!- OpenWindow.htm ->
<html><head>
<script type="text/javascript">
  function openwindow()
  {
    window.open("http://www.w3schools.com","my_new_
      window","toolbar=yes,location=yes,directories=no,
      status=no,menubar=yes,scrollbars=yes,resizable=no,
      copyhistory=yes,width=400,height=400")
  }
</script></head><body><form>
```

```
<input type="button" value="Open Window" onclick=
   "openwindow()"/>
</form></body></html>
```

As a Web programming tool, JavaScript gives you the ability to create Web pages that are more attractive, versatile, and interactive than with HTML alone. All that's needed to write JavaScript code is an ASCII text editor, such as Microsoft Notepad. To run JavaScript code, you need a host environment such as a Web browser that can interpret JavaScript (Microsoft Internet Explorer 3.0 and higher). Netscape browsers can be used with the addition of plug-ins.

QuickCheck Questions

10. What tags do you use to create a form?

11. How do you refer to a form in a script?

12. What can you use the `window.open` method for?

A Quick JavaScript Reference

JavaScript statements consist of keywords used with the appropriate syntax. A single statement may span multiple lines. Multiple statements may occur on a single line if each statement is separated by a semicolon.

Syntax conventions　All keywords in syntax statements are in `bold`. Words in *italics* represent user-defined names or statements. Any portions enclosed in square brackets, `[　]`, are optional. `{statements}` indicates a block of statements, which can consist of a single statement or multiple statements delimited by curly braces `{ }`.

break **Statement**

A `break` statement terminates the current `while` or `for` loop and transfers program control to the statement following the terminated loop.

Syntax

```
break
```

Example　The following function has a `break` statement that terminates the `while` loop when `i` is 3, and then returns the value `3 * x`.

```
function testBreak(x) {
  var i = 0
  while (i < 6) {
    if (i == 3)
      break
    i++
  }
  return i * x
}
```

Comments

Comments are notations by the author to explain what a script does. Comments are ignored by the interpreter. JavaScript supports Java-style comments:

- Comments on a single line are preceded by a double-slash (//).
- Comments that span multiple lines are preceded by a /* and followed by a */.

Syntax

1. `// comment text`

2. `/* multiple line comment text */`

Examples

```
// This is a single-line comment.
/* This is a multiple-line comment. It can be of any
   length, and
you can put whatever you want here. */
```

continue Statement A `continue` statement terminates execution of the block of statements in a `while` or `for` loop, and continues execution of the loop with the next iteration. In contrast to the `break` statement, `continue` does not terminate the execution of the loop entirely; instead,

- In a `while` loop, it jumps back to the *condition*.
- In a `for` loop, it jumps to the *update* expression.

Syntax

```
continue
```

Example

The following example shows a `while` loop that has a `continue` statement that executes when the value of `i` is 3. Thus, `n` takes on the values 1, 3, 7, and 12.

```
i = 0
n = 0
while (i < 5) {
   i++
   if (i == 3)
     continue
   n += i
}
```

for Statement

A `for` statement creates a loop that consists of three optional expressions enclosed in parentheses and separated by semicolons, followed by a block of statements executed in the loop.

Syntax

```
for ([initial-expression;] [condition;] [increment-
  expression]) {
  statements
}
```

Arguments

- *initial-expression* is a statement or variable declaration. It is typically used to initialize a counter variable. This expression may optionally declare new variables with the `var` keyword.
- *condition* is evaluated on each pass through the loop. If this condition evaluates to true, the statements in `statements` are performed. This conditional test is optional. If omitted, the condition always evaluates to true.
- *increment-expression* is generally used to update or increment the counter variable.
- `statements` is a block of statements that are executed as long as *condition* evaluates to true. This can be a single statement or multiple statements. Although not required, it is good practice to indent these statements from the beginning of the `for` statement.

Example   The following `for` statement starts by declaring the variable `i` and initializing it to zero. It checks that `i` is less than nine, performs the two succeeding statements, and increments `i` by one after each pass through the loop.

```
for (var i = 0; i < 9; i++) {
  n += i
  myfunc(n)
}
```

for . . . in **Statement**
A `for . . . in` statement iterates a specified variable over all the properties of an object. For each distinct property, JavaScript executes the specified statements.

Syntax

```
for (variable in object) {
  statements }
```

Arguments

- *variable* is the variable to iterate over every property.
- *object* is the object for which the properties are iterated.
- `statements` specifies the statements to execute for each property.

Example   The following function takes as its argument an object and the object's name. It then iterates over all the object's properties and returns a string that lists the property names and their values.

```
function dump_props(obj, obj_name) {
  var result = ""
  for (var i in obj) {
    result += obj_name + "." + i + " = " + obj[i] +
      "<br>"
  }
  result += "<hr>"
  return result
}
```

`function` **Statement**

A `function` statement declares a JavaScript function *name* with the specified parameters *param*. Acceptable parameters include strings, numbers, and objects.

To return a value, the `function` must have a `return` statement that specifies the value to return. You cannot nest a `function` statement in another statement or in itself.

All parameters are passed to functions by value. In other words, the value is passed to the function, but if the function changes the value of the parameter, this change is not reflected globally or in the calling function.

In addition to defining functions as described here, you also can define Function objects, as described earlier in the section "Defining a Function."

Syntax

```
function name([param] [, param] [. . ., param]) {
  statements }
```

Arguments

*   *name* is the function name.
*   *param* is the name of an argument to be passed to the function. A function can have up to 255 arguments.

Example

```
//This function returns the total dollar amount of sales,
  when
//given the number of units sold of products a, b, and c.
function calc_sales(units_a, units_b, units_c) {
  return units_a*79 + units_b*129 + units_c*699
}
```

`if . . .else` **Statement**

An `if . . .else` statement executes a set of statements if a specified condition is true. If the condition is false, another set of statements can be executed.

Syntax

```
if (condition) {
   statements1 }
[else {
   statements2}]
```

Arguments

- *condition*   can be any JavaScript expression that evaluates to true or false. Parentheses are required around the condition. If *condition* evaluates to true, the statements in `statements1` are executed.

- `statements1` and `statements2` can be any JavaScript statements, including further nested `if` statements. Multiple statements must be enclosed in braces.

Example

```
if ( cipher_char == from_char ) {
   result = result + to_char
   x++ }
else
   result = result + clear_char
```

new **Statement**

A `new` statement is an operator that lets you create an instance of a user-defined object type or of one of the built-in object types, such as `Array`, `Boolean`, `Date`, `Function`, `Math`, `Number`, or `String`.

Creating a user-defined object type requires two steps:

1. Define the object type by writing a function.

2. Create an instance of the object with `new`.

To define an object type, create a function for the object type that specifies its name, properties, and methods. An object can have a property that is itself another object.

You can always add a property to a previously defined object. For example, the statement `car.color = "red"` adds a property color to `car1` and assigns it a value of `"red"`. However, this does not affect any other objects. To add the new property to all objects of the same type, you must add the property to the definition of the `car` object type.

You can add a property to a previously defined object type by using the `prototype` property. This defines a property that is shared by all objects of the specified type, rather than by just one instance of the object. The following code adds a `color` property to all objects of type `car` and then assigns a value to the `color` property of the object `car1`.

```
Car.prototype.color=null
car1.color="black"
birthday.description="The day you were born"
```

Syntax

```
objectName = new objectType (param1 [,param2] ...
   [,paramN])
```

Arguments

- *objectName* is the name of the new object instance.
- *objectType* is the object type. It must be a function that defines an object type.
- *param1 . . . paramN* are the property values for the object. These properties are parameters defined for the *objectType* function.

Examples

1. **Object type and object instance.** Suppose you want to create an object type for cars. You want this type of object to be called `car` and you want it to have properties for `make`, `model`, and `year`. To do this, you would write the following function:

```
function car(make, model, year) {
   this.make = make
   this.model = model
   this.year = year
}
```

Now you can create an object called `mycar` as follows:

```
mycar = new car("BMW", "Z4", 2003)
```

This statement creates `mycar` and assigns it the specified values for its properties. Then the value of `mycar.make` is the string `"BMW"`, `mycar.year` is the integer 2003, and so on.

You can create any number of `car` objects by calls to `new`. For example,

```
valscar = new car("Chevy", "Corvette", 1972)
```

2. **Object property that is itself another object.** Suppose you define an object called `person` as follows:

```
function person(name, age, sex) {
   this.name = name
   this.age = age
   this.sex = sex
}
```

and then instantiate two new `person` objects as follows:

```
glenn = new person("Glenn Hilley", 40, "M")
val = new person("Val Hilley", 39, "F")
```

Then you can rewrite the definition of `car` to include an `owner` property that takes a `person` object, as follows:

```
function car(make, model, year, owner) {
   this.make = make;
   this.model = model;
   this.year = year;
   this.owner = owner;
}
```

To instantiate the new objects, you then use the following:

```
car1 = new car("BMW", "Z4", 2003, glenn);
car2 = new car("Chevy", "Corvette", 1972, val)
```

Instead of passing a literal string or integer value when creating the new objects, the above statements pass the objects `glenn` and `val` as the parameters for the owners. To find out the name of the owner of `car2`, you can access the following property:

```
car2.owner.name
```

`return` Statement

A `return` statement specifies the value to be returned by a function.

Syntax

```
return expression
```

Examples The following function returns the square of its argument, `x`, where `x` is a number.

```
function square( x ) {
   return x * x
}
```

`this` Statement

`this` is a keyword that you can use to refer to the current object. In general, in a method, `this` refers to the calling object.

Syntax

```
this[.propertyName]
```

Examples Suppose a function called `validate` validates an object's `value` property, given the object and the high and low values:

```
function validate(obj, lowval, hival) {
  if ((obj.value < lowval) || (obj.value > hival))
    alert("Invalid Value!")
}
```

You could call `validate` in each form element's onChange event handler, using `this` to pass it to the form element, as in the following example:

```
<b>Enter a number between 18 and 99:</b>
<input type = "text" name = "age" size = 3
  onChange="validate(this, 18, 99)">
```

var Statement

A `var` statement declares a variable, optionally initializing it to a value. The scope of a variable is the current function or, for variables declared outside a function, the current application.

Using `var` outside a function is optional; you can declare a variable by simply assigning it a value. However, it is good style to use `var`, and it is necessary in functions if a global variable of the same name exists.

Syntax

```
var varname [= value] [. . ., varname [= value] ]
```

Arguments

- *varname* is the variable name. It can be any legal identifier.
- *value* is the initial value of the variable and can be any legal expression.

Example

```
var num_hits = 0, cust_no = 0
```

while Statement

A `while` statement creates a loop that evaluates an expression, and, if it is true, executes a block of statements. The loop then repeats, as long as the specified condition is true.

Syntax

```
while (condition) {
   statements
}
```

Arguments

- *condition* is evaluated before each pass through the loop. If *condition* evaluates to true, the statements in the succeeding block are performed. When *condition* evaluates to false, execution continues with the statement following `statements`.

- `statements` is a block of statements that are executed as long as *condition* evaluates to true. Although not required, it is good practice to indent these statements from the beginning of the `while` statement.

Example The following `while` loop iterates as long as n is less than three.

```
n = 0
x = 0
while( n < 3 ) {
    n ++
    x += n
}
```

In each iteration, the loop increments n and adds it to x. Therefore, x and n take on the following values:

- After the first pass: n = 1 and x = 1.
- After the second pass: n = 2 and x = 3.
- After the third pass: n = 3 and x = 6.

After completing the third pass, the condition n < 3 is no longer true, so the loop terminates.

`with` **Statement**

A `with` statement establishes the default object for a set of statements. Within the set of statements, any property references that do not specify an object are assumed to be for the default object.

Syntax

```
with (object){
    statements
}
```

Arguments

- *object* specifies the default object to use for the `statements`. The parentheses around *object* are required.
- `statements` is any block of statements.

Example The following `with` statement specifies that the `Math` object is the default object. The statements following the `with` statement refer to the `PI` property and the `cos` and `sin` methods, without specifying an object. JavaScript assumes the `Math` object for these references.

```
var a, x, y
var r=10
with (Math) {
    a = PI * r * r
    x = r * cos(PI)
    y = r * sin(PI/2)
}
```

We have presented an overview of JavaScript in this chapter. Although JavaScript was initially introduced by Netscape, currently almost all browsers have extended their software to include the JavaScript interpreters. An HTML page is usually static in nature, and it does not provide much interaction with the user. We can use JavaScript codes in an HTML document to make it dynamic so that it can respond and react to various events (like on the click event of the mouse, or on the load event of a document, etc.).

Like most other computer programming languages, JavaScript offers programming structures such as if-then-else, iteration, and functions. It also offers data structures like arrays. JavaScript codes can be easily included in an HTML document using the <script language = "JavaScript"> tag.

We can employ the document Object Model's specifications to manipulate the contents of an HTML document dynamically using JavaScript codes. In JavaScript an HTML **document** can be treated as an object with many built-in methods and properties. For example, if needed, we can use the **document.write()** method to write text or HTML tags on an HTML document using JavaScript.

JavaScript codes can be effectively used to process a user's given data in an HTML form. An HTML form is created by enclosing HTML controls (like textbox, check box, radio buttons, command buttons) and other elements within the <form> </form> tags. We can manipulate the contents of these data-entry elements in the form using JavaScript. For example, if an HTML form named "frmPayroll" contains a textbox named "txtHours", the value of the textbox can be addressed as **document.frmPayroll.txtHours.value** in JavaScript. JavaScript plays a major role in real-world business Web applications. It is undoubtedly worthwhile to spend more time and effort to learn its basic features.

branching   initializing   script
execute   looping   scripting language

1. JavaScript is a compiled language often used to customize applications. True or False?
2. To run JavaScript, you need _____.
3. Two advantages of scripts over compiled programs are _____ and _____.
4. JavaScript can only run client-side. True or False?
5. The _____ method writes the specified text to the current HTML document.
6. HTML formatting tags can be added to the `document.write` statement. True or False?
7. a. The assignment operator for all data types is _____.
   b. _____ is the default JavaScript data type.

8. Concerning naming conventions, JavaScript is case-_____.

9. Declaring a variable means that you inform the program in advance so that memory space can be assigned to the variable to store the variable. True or False?

10. Which of the following is *not* true of JavaScript?

   a.   A JavaScript program is compiled before being sent to the browser.

   b.   JavaScript is considered good for rapid program development.

   c.   JavaScript is most commonly used on the client-side.

   d.   You do not have to declare the types of variables in JavaScript.

11. The `dim` keyword is used by JavaScript to declare a variable. True or False?

12. The data type for a variable in JavaScript is `subscript`. True or False?

13. The assignment operator in JavaScript is:

   +

   \

   =

   #

14. Which variable type does JavaScript support?

   a.   string

   b.   variable

   c.   numbers

   d.   variant

15. Which of the following is the correct way to declare a variable in JavaScript?

   a.   `dim:Name`

   b.   `new Name`

   c.   `dim Name`

   d.   `var Name`

16. Individual pieces of an array are called _____.

   a.   collections

   b.   variables

   c.   elements

   d.   variants

17. A _____ construct allows you to repeat blocks of code.

   a.   looping structure

   b.   repeating structure

   c.   decision control

   d.   variable control

1. **Hello World.** Write a script that displays **Hello World** on the HTML page.
2. **Hello World again . . . and again.** Add a `for` loop to the page to display **Hello World** 100 times.
3. **A thinking page.** Write a script that will display **Good morning, Good afternoon,** and **Good night** according to the time of the day.

Exercises

8

Client-Side Scripting with VBScript

OBJECTIVES

1. To add VBScript to HTML pages.

2. To work with variables.

3. To work with objects.

4. To control VBScript programs.

5. To design forms with VBScript.

Introduction: Getting to Know VBScript

In the world of Microsoft Internet Explorer, beginning with Internet Explorer version 3.0, VBScript is the default scripting language used to link and automate the wide variety of objects contained in a Web page. It can perform countless tasks such as validating HTML forms, controlling animation effects, and interacting with users via pop-up dialogs and message boxes. In fact, you encounter many of these kinds of tasks daily as you click through the Web. Anytime you stop on a page that does more than sit, there's a script in the midst and it could very well be a VBScript. Note: Only Internet Explorer 3.0 and above support VBScript.

JavaScript versus VBScript

Many people wonder whether or not it makes sense to learn VBScript. We covered JavaScript in Chapter 7, and we're using the same techniques to present VBScript in this chapter. Both languages can do a lot of the same things, and in similar manners. People look at JavaScript and say, hey, JavaScript works on all browsers; why use anything else? But . . .

197

VBScript is identical, syntactically and grammatically, to Visual Basic and Visual Basic for Applications, making it easy to move on to other types of programming projects. And because Visual Basic is so easy, anyone can learn it. And because VBScript is so easy to learn, you'll be able to master things such as HTML, Dynamic HTML, Cascading Style Sheets (CSS), and other Web technologies quickly.

As a final note, while JavaScript is supported on all major browsers, you should consider the environment you're programming for. If you're building applications for an intranet where Microsoft technology reigns, use VBScript. Even if you're building pages for the rest of the world, VBScript is a safe bet since Internet Explorer is the dominant browser on today's desktops.

A First Look at VBScript

Scripting languages, like JavaScript and VBScript, are designed as an extension to HTML. The Web browser receives scripts along with the rest of the HTML document, then parses and processes the scripts. Look at the following script example:

```
<!- VbWelcome.htm ->
<html><head></head><body>
<script language="vbscript">
   Document.Write("Welcome to VBScript!")
</script>
</body></html>
```

Without knowing a bit of VBScript, you should be able to decipher this **script** based on what you know of HTML. Looking at the script line by line, you see the familiar HTML tags <head> and </head> indicating the beginning and ending of the head section. Next, the <body> tag marks the beginning of the body section. Following it are the three lines of VBScript and then the </body> tag denoting the end of the body section. Notice that the VBScript is located within the body of the HTML code and those three lines of code will produce the output as shown in Figure 8.1.

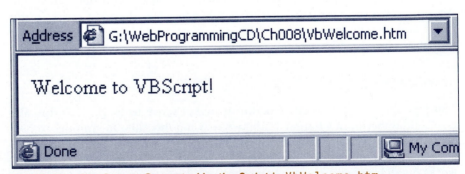

FIGURE 8.1   **The Output Generated by the Script in** VbWelcome.htm

If nothing else, you can tell that HTML and VBScript go hand in hand. In the next section, you'll quickly learn how to get the two working together.

Adding VBScript to Web Pages

Everything you've learned about HTML is applicable to VBScript. You're simply going to extend HTML using VBScript, which allows you to mix its syntax with HTML tags. All you need to do to be proficient is to understand the mechanics of VBScript. If you take a long look at the script above, you'll notice two new, but obvious HTML tags: `<script>` and `</script>`. HTML was extended to include these `<script>` tags to incorporate scripts into HTML. Adding a VBScript into a Web page is as simple as placing valid VBScript code between the `<script>` tags.

The `<script>` Tag

The `<script>` tag indicates the start of the script section, while `</script>` marks the end of the script. Look at the script below:

```
<!- MsgBox.htm ->
<html><head><title>Client-Side Scripting with VBScript
  </title>
<script language="VBScript">
  MsgBox "Welcome to Web Programming!"
</script>
</head><html>
```

The initial `<script>` tag includes a language attribute that indicates the scripting language used. The language attribute is used because there is more than one scripting language. Without the language attribute, the Web browser would not know if the text between the tags was JavaScript, VBScript, or one of the many other scripting languages.

Everything between the opening `<script>` tag and the closing `</script>` tag is called the body of the script and everything that is part of the body section belongs to the script. Like HTML, VBScript is not **case-sensitive**. This means that script, SCRIPT, and Script are the same.

VBScript to Display Information

Take another look at the first script sample. Notice the line that reads:

```
Document.Write("Welcome to VBScript!")
```

One of the most common uses for VBScript is to display text. VBScript accomplishes this using an object called `Document`. The `Document` object manages many of the instructions that VBScript can handle for HTML. One of the functions of that object is to display a string or text on the screen. The function used is called `Write`. The syntax of the `Write` function of the `Document` object is

```
Document.Write(String)
```

Where to Put the VBScript

Most HTML pages are divided into two sections: a head and a body. You can place your VBScript code anywhere in the HTML document. Your decision on where to place your script can be a matter of aesthetics or function. Good programming practice leans toward function.

Sometimes you might want to execute a script when a page loads, other times when a user triggers an event. If you place scripts in the body section, they are executed when the HTML page is loading. In other words, the scripts in the body will execute immediately. In the case where you want a script to execute when a user triggers an event, such as clicking a button or rolling the mouse over an area, you will want the script to load before anyone triggers it. To assure that the script is available and ready to be executed when called or when an event is triggered, place the script in the head section. This is often referred to as an event procedure script.

Usually we put all the "functions" in the head section. The reason for this is to be sure that the script is loaded before the function is called.

The following is an example of a script placed in the head section:

```
<html>
<head>
<script language ="vbscript">
some statements go here
</script>
</head>
```

When you place a script in the body section, as shown below, it's called an immediate script and it executes immediately. Place an immediate script in the portion of a Web page where you want the results displayed.

```
<html>
<head>
</head>
<body>
<script language ="vbscript">
some statements go here
</script>
</body>
```

You can place an unlimited number of scripts in your document, so you can have scripts in both the body and the head section.

```
<html>
<head>
<script language ="vbscript">
some statements go here
</script>
</head>
<body>
<script language ="vbscript">
some statements
</script>
</body>
```

QuickCheck Questions

1. What do you use to embed script code in HTML documents?
2. Where can you insert VBScript code in an HTML document?

Working with Variables

Programs need content to work with. We supply that content, known as data, by defining it to the computer system and reserving space in the computer's memory for the computer to store the data for later recall. This reserved space is called a *variable*. A variable is a named location in computer memory that VBScript can use for storage of data during the execution of scripts. Where and how variables are stored is not important. For our purposes right now, what you use them for and knowing how to use them are the important issues. You can use variables to

- Store input from the user gathered via your Web page.
- Save data returned from functions.
- Hold results from calculations.

Let's look at a simple VBScript to see how you can use a variable:

```
<!- DisplayName.htm ->
<html><head></head>
<body>
<script language ="vbscript">
   Dim name
   name="Valda Hilley"
   Document.Write(name)
</script>
</body></html>
```

The first line of this script example defines a variable named name. This reserves a place in the computer's memory that can be easily identified and quickly found for recall. The next line provides content for that variable with the string `"Valda Hilley"`. The last line of the script writes the "content" for display in a document.

Defining and using variables in VBScript is very straightforward and not unlike using variables in other programming languages. However, there is more that you should know to be fluid and consistent in writing VBScripts.

Declaring Variables

Before you can use a variable to store some data, you must define or declare it. Declaring a variable means to specify its name at the very least. There are two methods for declaring variables in VBScript: **explicitly** and **implicitly**. You usually declare variables explicitly with the `Dim` statement:

    Dim Name

This statement declares the variable `Name`. You also can declare multiple variables on one line, as shown below, although it is preferable to declare each variable separately:

    Dim Name, Address, City, State

While you can declare variables implicitly by simply using the variable name within your script, this can invite errors in your code and make it more difficult to debug.

Until your programming prowess grows, you can force yourself into a good habit by instructing VBScript to require all variables to be explicitly declared by including the statement `Option Explicit` at the start of every script. Any variable that is not explicitly declared will then generate an error.

VBScript's Only Data Type

We've already discussed the first component of a variable, its name. All variables need some kind of content, value, or data. That leads us to the second variable component, a data type. The data type specifies the kind of data the variable can store. Once a variable is initialized with a specific data type, that data type becomes the standard for that variable.

In VBScript there is only one data type, called a *variant*. This can be a little misleading or tricky to understand because this one data type can store several different types of data, hence the term *variant*. The types of data that a variant can store are referred to as subtypes. Table 8.1 describes the subtypes supported by VBScript.

Professional Visual Basic developers typically use a three-character prefix to name a variable. For example, the name of a string variable is prefixed with "str", and the name of an integer variable is prefixed with "int". Table 8.2 shows the standard three-character prefixes for some common VBScript subtypes.

TABLE 8.1   **Variant Subtypes**

Subtype	Description
Byte	Integer numbers between 0 and 255
Boolean	True and false
Currency	Monetary values
Date	Date and time
Double	Extremely large numbers with decimal points
Empty	The value that a variant holds before being used
Error	An error number
Integer	Large integers between −32,768 and 32,767
Long	Extremely large integers (between −2,147,483,648 and 2,147,483,647)
Object	Objects
Null	No valid data
Single	Large numbers with decimal points
String	Character strings

TABLE 8.2   **Naming Conventions in VBScript**

Subtype	Prefix
Boolean	bln
Byte	byt
Date	dtm
Double	dbl
Error	err
Integer	int
Long	lng
Object	obj
Single	sng
String	str

Since VBScript has only one data type, you don't need to identify the variable type when you declare the variable. The advantage of using a variant data type is that you can place any type of data in the variable and the variable will

> [!NOTE]
> **Tech Tip**
>
> **SCRIPT Means script**
> VBScript variables are case-insensitive. That means that if you type script, SCRIPT, or Script, it interprets all three variations as the tag `SCRIPT`. Just remember to include the tag brackets < >.

behave according to the type of data it stores. Once you grasp the idea of the variant, you'll find that it's easy to manipulate variables in VBScript.

How to Name a Variable

Every VBScript variable requires a name and each variable must have a unique name so that VBScript can identify it and locate it. You can exercise creativity when naming variables as long as you follow these rules:

- Begin the name with an alphabetic character.
- Do not use embedded periods in the name.
- Use no more than 255 characters.
- Maintain unique names within the same scope. (Scope will be discussed later in this chapter.)

Storing Values in Variables

> [!NOTE]
> **Tech Tip**
>
> **What's in a Name?**
> Variables are more useful and your code more readable if you use descriptive names that have some association with its contents or purpose. For example, if you're dealing with product prices, use the word *price* as part of the variable name.

It's a good idea to assign a value to a variable when you create it. This is referred to as **initializing** a variable. You assign a value to a variable by using the following format:

```
Variable_name = value
```

For example:

```
Name = "Valda Hilley"
ChapterNo = 8
MoreToDo = True
```

Note that the name of the variable is entered on the left side of the assignment operator and the value of the variable is entered on the right side of the operator. Remember that the equal sign is an assignment operator, not an arithmetic operator.

> **QuickCheck Question**
>
> 3. Write a VBScript code that declares four variables named `name`, `address`, `city`, and `state`.

Scope of Variables

The scope of a variable dictates where it can be used in your script. A variable's scope is determined by where it is declared. If it is declared within a procedure, it is referred to as a procedure-level variable and can be used only within that procedure. If it is declared outside of any procedure, it is a script-level variable and can be used throughout the script.

The example below demonstrates both script-level and procedure-level variables:

```
<html>
<body>
```

```
<script language ="vbscript">
Dim counter
Sub cmdButton_onClick
   Dim temp
End Sub
</script>
</body>
</html>
```

The variable `counter` is a script-level variable and can be utilized throughout the script. The variable `temp` exists only within the cmdButton_onClick sub-procedure.

Working with Arrays

Until now we've worked with variables that store single values. Many times you will want to work with more than one value such as in a set. This is where arrays come into play. In VBScript you declare an array using the `Dim` statement, just as with single variables:

```
<!- VbScriptArray.htm ->
<html><body>
<script language ="vbscript">
   Dim famname(5)
   famname(0)="Hilley"
   famname(1)="Ellis"
   famname(2)="Embry"
   famname(3)="Copeland"
   famname(4)="Tripp"
   famname(5)="Wilkins"
   For i=0 to 5
      Document.Write(famname(i) & "<br />")
   Next
</script></body></html>
```

VBScript also provides support for arrays whose size may need to change as the script is executing. These arrays are referred to as dynamic arrays. A dynamic array is declared without specifying the number of elements it will contain:

```
Dim Family()
```

What if you need to change the size of the array while the script is running? Use the `ReDim` statement to change the size of the array from within the script:

```
ReDim Family(20)
```

There is no limit to the number of times an array can be redimensioned during the execution of a script.

Procedures and Functions

A procedure is a piece of code that you ask VBScript to perform in addition to, or to complete, the normal program flow. It is designed to work in conjunction with the control's events of a script. There are two kinds of procedures in VBScript: a sub procedure and a function. They behave differently and their use depends on your program goals.

A sub procedure is a section of code that carries an assignment but doesn't give back a result. To create a sub procedure, start the section of code with the Sub keyword followed by a name for the sub procedure. To differentiate the name of the sub procedure from any other regular name, it must be followed by opening and closing parentheses. The Sub keyword and the name of the procedure (including its parentheses) are written on one line (by default). The section of the sub procedure code closes with End Sub as follows:

```
Sub ShowMeTheDough()
End Sub
```

The name of a sub procedure should follow the same rules we learned to name the variables, omitting the prefix. If the sub procedure performs an action that can be represented with a verb, you can use that verb to name it. Here are some examples: show, display, computeWage, FindTax, and so forth. You should use explicit names that identify the purpose of the sub procedure. If a procedure would be used as a result of another procedure or a control's event, reflect it on the name of the sub procedure. Examples would be afterupdate and longbefore. If the name of a procedure is a combination of words, start each word in uppercase. Examples are AfterUpdate and SayItLoud.

In the following example, a sub procedure named DisplayFullName is created. It retrieves fields of two text boxes (first name and last name) on a form and displays a full name as a result of combining them:

```
Sub DisplayFullName()
   txtFullName = txtFirstName + " " + txtLastName
End Sub
```

Calling a Procedure

After creating a procedure, you can call it from another procedure, function, or control event. To call a simple procedure such as the above DisplayFullName, you can just write the name of the sub procedure.

In the following example, the `DisplayFullName` sub procedure is called when the user clicks the Detail section of the form:

```
Sub Detailer()
    DisplayFullName
End Sub
```

Arguments

To carry an assignment, sometimes a procedure needs one or more variables to work on. If a procedure needs a variable, such a variable is called an *argument*. A procedure can use more than one argument if required. The number and types of arguments used in a procedure again depend on program goals.

If you are writing your own procedure, then you will decide how many arguments your procedure would need. You also decide on the type of the argument(s). For a procedure that is taking one argument, in the parentheses of the procedure, write a name for the argument. Here is an example:

```
Sub CalculateArea(Radius)
    Dim dblPI
    Dim dblArea

    dblPI = 3.14159
    dblArea = Radius * Radius * dblPI
End Sub
```

As you can see, an argument is provided to the procedure so the procedure can use it to carry out its assignment. A procedure can take more than one argument. If you are creating such a procedure, between the parentheses of the procedure, write the name of the first argument followed by a comma; add the second argument and subsequent arguments and close the parentheses. There is no relationship between the arguments; for example, they can be of the same type:

```
Sub CalculatePerimeter(Length, Height)
    Dim dblPerimeter

    dblPerimeter = 2 * (Length + Height)
End Sub
```

The arguments of your procedure can also be as varied as you need them to be. Here is an example:

```
Sub DisplayGreetings(strFullName, intAge)
    Dim Sentence
    Sentence = "Hi, " & strFullName & ". You are " & intAge
        & " years old."
End Sub
```

We saw already how to call a procedure that doesn't take any argument. Actually, there are various ways you can call a sub procedure. As we saw already, if a sub procedure doesn't take an argument, to call it, you can just write its name. If a sub procedure is taking an argument, to call it, type the name of the sub procedure followed by the name of the argument. If the sub procedure is taking more than one argument, to call it, type the name of the procedure followed by the names of the arguments in the exact order they are passed to the sub procedure, separated by a comma. Here is an example:

```
Sub Result()
   Dim dblHours, dblSalary

   CalcAndShowSalary dblHours, dblSalary
End Sub
Sub CalcAndShowSalary(Hours, Salary)
   Dim dblResult

   dblResult = Hours * Salary
   txtResult = dblResult
End Sub
```

Alternatively, you can use the keyword `Call` to call a sub procedure. In this case, when calling a procedure using `Call`, you must include the argument(s) between the parentheses. Using `Call`, the above procedure could call the `CalcAndShowSalary` as follows:

```
Sub Result()
   Dim dblHours As Double
   Dim dblSalary As Double

   dblHours = txtHours
   dblSalary = txtSalary

   Call CalcAndShowSalary(dblHours, dblSalary)
End Sub
```

VBScript Functions

VBScript supports a wide range of functions that can be called from any script. Unlike a subroutine, which is **executed** every time it's called, a function runs code and also returns a result to the script that called it.

In VBScript a Function procedure is a series of statements enclosed by the `Function` and `End Function` statements. A `Function` can take arguments in the form of constants, variables, or expressions that are passed to it by a calling procedure. If a Function procedure has no arguments, its `Function` statement must include an empty set of parentheses. A `Function` returns a value, which is always a variant, by assigning a value to its name in one or more statements of the procedure.

A `Function` statement in VBScript looks like this:

```
nameFunction(argument1, argument2, . . . argumentN)
```

The example below shows a simple argument-less function.

```
<!- SimpleFunction.htm ->
<html><head>
<script language ="vbscript">
  Function SimpleAddition(x,y)
    Dim Result
    Result = x + y
    SimpleAddition = Result
  End Function
</script>
</head>
<body><h3>
<script language="vbscript">
  Dim sum, a, b
  a=2
  b=4
  sum = SimpleAddition(a,b)
  Document.Write("The Sum is " & sum)
</script></h3>
</body></html>
```

As you can see, we have two scripts in `SimpleFunction.htm`. The first script in the `<head>` section defines a function named `SimpleAddition(x,y)`. Obviously, the function, when called, will receive two arguments. It will then add the values of the arguments and return the result. In the second script, three variables have been defined. This script then passes the values of two variables to the function. The returned result is received in the variable named `sum`. Finally, we have used the `Document.Write` statement to display the sum of the numbers. Observe that we are using the VBScript concatenation operator (`&`) to display the result preceded by `"The Sum is "` string. When you open `SimpleFunction.htm` in a browser, the system will display a screen as shown in Figure 8.2.

Controlling Your VBScript Routines

VBScript allows you to control the order in which your scripts process data through the use of conditional and looping statements. By using conditional statements, you can develop scripts that make decisions by evaluating data and criteria to determine what tasks to perform. **Looping** statements allow you to repetitively execute a line or lines of a script until certain conditions or criteria are met. Each method offers benefits that enable you to create complex and highly functional Web pages.

Tech Tip

Create before You Call
Remember that a function must be created before it's called. This is the reason that you place function code in the head of an HTML document.

Tech Tip

Use and Reuse
Save functions in separate files so that you can use and reuse them in scripts that need them. This makes things easy to update, too.

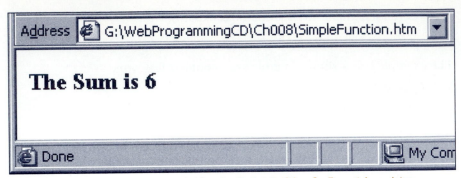

FIGURE 8.2   The Output Generated by the Script in `SimpleFunction.htm`

Using Conditional Statements

At some point in your Web programming, you'll need to step beyond simple interactive Web pages in which all the page does is collect information from users. You may want to respond to a user depending on some piece of information entered by that user. Perhaps you're working on a Web page for an athletic store that specializes in hiking shoes for all types of terrain. You might ask, "Do you hike in mountains or desert?" If the user answered desert, you might have the VBScript respond, "High desert or low desert?" The user's response to that question could lead to another question or a recommendation for a certain shoe.

The programming required to create this kind of logic is implemented via conditional controls known as **branching**. VBScript provides two forms of conditional statements:

- `If...Then...Else`
- `Select Case`

Both forms allow VBScript to test some condition. If the condition is true, the program does one thing; if the condition is false, the program does another.

If...Then...Else
The `If...Then...Else` statement is used first to evaluate a condition to see if it is true or false and, second, depending upon the condition, to execute a statement or set of statements. The simplest version of an `If` statement is one that contains only one condition:

```
<!- VBIfThenElse.htm ->
<html><head>
<script language="vbscript">
Function mygreeting()
   i=hour(time)
   If i < 10 then
```

```
       Document.Write("Good morning all!")
     Else
       Document.Write("Have a great day!")
     End if
  End Function
  </script>
  </head>
  <body onload="mygreeting()">
  </body></html>
```

In this example, the script tests to determine if the time of day is before 10 A.M. The condition is true, so the script writes "Good morning all!". If the condition is not met, the script does not execute the "Good morning all!" line and processes the Else statement leading to "Have a great day!". Using the If statement in this manner means that one of the lines of code will be processed, but not both.

With this form of the If statement in VBScript, one or more statements can be executed when the condition is true, by placing them between the If statement on top and the End If statement on the bottom. This is referred to as a *compound conditional statement*. In plain English it looks like this:

If some condition is true

    Execute this first block of statements

Else another condition is true

    Execute this second block of statements

Else yet another condition is true

    Execute this third block of statements

And so on . . .

Until it reaches the end if statement.

VBScript accepts another form of the If statement that uses the If . . . Then . . . Else format to allow a script to perform one set of statements if the condition is true and another set when the condition is false. Here is an example:

```
<!- VBIfThenElse2.htm ->
<html><head>
<script language="vbscript">
Function mygreeting()
  i=hour(time)
  If i < 10 then
    Document.Write("Good morning all! <br/>")
    Document.Write("Let us start our meeting")
  Else
    Document.Write("We had a grand meeting! <br/>")
    Document.Write("Thanks to all of you. <br/>")
    Document.Write("See you at the Dinner")
  End if
```

```
End Function
</script>
</head>
<body onload="mygreeting()">
</body></html>
```

The last form of the VBScript If statement that we will look at is the If . . . Then . . . ElseIf. This If statement causes the script to test conditions until it finds either one that is true or an Else statement. Here's an example:

```
<!- VBIfThenElse3.htm ->
<html><head>
<script language="vbscript">
Function mygreeting()
  Dim i
  i=hour(time)
  MsgBox(i)
  If i = 10 Then
    Document.Write("Just getting the day started!")
  Elseif i = 11 Then
    Document.Write("Can't wait for lunch!")
  Elseif i = 12 Then
    Document.Write("Finally lunchtime!")
  Elseif i = 16 Then
    Document.Write("Time to go home!")
  Else
    Document.Write("Unknown")
  End If
End Function
</script></head>
<body onload="mygreeting()">
</body></html>
```

As you see, VBScript offers you plenty of options when it comes to If statements. Mastering their usage will enable you to build more intelligence and sophistication into your scripts.

Altering Paths with Select Case

VBScript has a Select Case statement that provides additional processing control compared to the If . . . Then . . . Else statement. It is designed for complex situations where there are a number of possible conditions for the value being checked. Like the If statement, the Select Case statement checks a condition, and, based on that condition being true, it executes a series of statements. The following is an example of the Select Case statement in VBScript:

```
<!- SelectCase.htm ->
<html><body>
```

```
<script language ="vbscript">
   Dim d
   d=weekday(date)
Select Case d
   Case 1
      Document.Write("Easy Sunday")
   Case 2
      Document.Write("Blue Monday")
   Case 3
      Document.Write("Only Tuesday!")
   Case 4
      Document.Write("Wednesday!")
   Case 5
      Document.Write("Thursday...")
   Case 6
      Document.Write("TGI Friday!")
   Case Else
      Document.Write("Super Saturday!!!!")
End Select
</script></body></html>
```

In this example of the Select Case statement, the user receives a different greeting based on the day of the week. We have assigned the case values as follows: Sunday=1, Monday=2, Tuesday=3, Wednesday=4, Thursday=5, Friday=6, and anything else must be Saturday.

The Select Case statement checks each of the Case statements until it finds one that will result in the condition being true. If none are found to be true, it executes the statements within the Case Else.

QuickCheck Questions

6. When do you use conditional statements?
7. When do you use the Select Case statement?

Using Looping Statements

Looping statements are just the tools you need to force a program do something again and again a specified number of times, until some condition is met or as long as some condition exists. VBScript provides four forms of looping statements:

- For . . . Next
- For Each . . . Next
- Do loop
- While . . . Wend

Tech Tip

Flag Your Errors
Even though it is not required, you should include a Case Else when working with Select Case statements to process conditions that you may not have anticipated. For these conditions, you can display something as simple as a message dialog to inform you that a branch was executed in error.

These four statements can be divided into two groups based on their usage. For statements are best used when you want to perform a loop a specific number of times. The Do...While and While...Wend statements are best used to perform a loop an undetermined number of times or while a certain condition exists.

For...Next **Statement**

The For...Next statement uses a counter variable that is incremented or decremented with each repetition of the loop. The following example demonstrates a simple For loop:

```
For counter = 1 To 10
   result = 5 * counter
   MsgBox counter & " times 5 is " & result
Next counter
```

In this example, the variable counter is incremented by 1 with each repetition of the loop. In the first line, the number 1 indicates the start of the loop and 10 indicates the end of the loop. Each time the loop executes, it displays a dialog box message containing the product of multiplying five times the counter as it runs from 1 to 10. Note that in a decrementing loop, the starting number is greater than the ending number.

For Each...Next **Statement**

The For Each...Next is similar to the For...Next loop but instead of repeating a loop for a certain number of times, it repeats the loop for each member of a specified collection.

Do...Loop **Statement**

The Do...Loop statement repeats a block of statements until a specified condition is met. Normally, when using a Do...Loop, the condition being checked is the result of some operation being performed within the body of the loop. Two versions of this statement are provided: Do While and Do Until.

Do While **Statement**

A Do...Loop that contains the While keyword will execute as long as the condition being tested is true. You have the option of checking the condition at the start of the loop, as follows:

```
Do While condition
   statement
   statement
   ...
Loop
```

or at the end of the loop, as shown in the following example:

```
Do
   statement
   statement
   . . .
   Loop While condition
```

The difference between these two formats is that the first example may never perform the statements included within its structure while the second example will always perform its statements at least once.

Do Until Statement

In the following example, the user enters a password before the script performs the conditional part of the Do . . . Loop the first time. If he or she enters the correct password the first time, the statements within the loop's structure will never execute. If the user were to enter an invalid password, then the statements within the Do . . . Loop structure would execute, and a message displays prompting the user to reenter his or her password.

```
<!- password.htm ->
<html><body>
<script language ="vbscript">
   Dim pwd
   pwd = InputBox("Enter your password:")
   Do Until pwd = "codeblue"
      Msgbox "Invalid password - please try again."
      pwd = InputBox("Enter your password:")
   Loop
</script></body></html>
```

While . . . Wend Statement

The While . . . Wend structure loops as long as the condition being checked is true. If the condition is true, the While . . . Wend statement operates similar to the Do . . . Loop structure but without its flexibility. The structure for the While . . . Wend statement is

```
While condition
   statement
   statement
   . . .
   Wend
```

QuickCheck Questions

8. When do you use For statements?
9. When do you use While statements?

VBScript in Action

Until now you've had a gentle introduction to VBScript designed to familiarize you with language constructs as well as get you acclimated to recognizing, analyzing, and creating basic scripts. Before moving on to higher level client-side scripting such as Dynamic HTML and the like, let's wade in a little deeper and look at more sophisticated VBScript code.

All About Forms

A form is the central control that manages the other controls. Although the controls can send their data to a script, a form can be used to collect the values typed or selected on the controls, gather them as if they constituted one control, and make these values available to a validating file on a server.

To create a form, you use the `<form>` tag. Because a form is a collection of controls and their values, the form must have an end that lets the browser know where the form closes. This is done with the `</form>` closing tag:

```
<form>
Some code goes here, HTML tags, for example
</form>
```

Everything between the `<form>` and the `</form>` tags belongs to the form and is called the body of the form. Almost anything can go in the body of the form. You can design it using any HTML tag and make it as attractive as you wish.

Although the `<form>` and the `</form>` tags are enough to create a form, such a form can hardly communicate with a script. One of the most important properties you should set for a form is its name. The name allows a script to refer to the form and it can be used by files on the server level. To set the name of a form, assign an appropriate string the `Name` attribute of the `<form>` tag. To refer to a form in a script, type the `Document` keyword, followed by a period (the period is an operator), followed by the name of the form. Suppose you create a form called `ReaderSurvey`. If you want to call it from a script, you would use

```
Document.ReaderSurvey
```

A Quick Form

First we have to set up the form where the user will enter the info. There are several types of form elements to use, but we will use the three most common: text field, drop-down box, and text area. Here's a form for collecting information about readers of this book:

```
<!- VbQuickForm.htm ->
<html><body><form>
Your Name: <input type="text" name="name"><br/>
Your email: <input type="text" name="email"><br/>
Your programming skills are:
<select name="skills" size="1">
  <option value="non existent">Zip</option>
  <option value="pretty bad">Pretty bad</option>
  <option value="so so">so so</option>
  <option value="Good">Good</option>
  <option value="Excellent">Excellent</option>
  <option value="Can teach">Can Teach</option>
</select><br/>
<input type="Submit" value="Submit">
</form></body></html>
```

There's nothing magical here. Once the form collects the information, a script can send the collected data to a file for validation. We'll get to that in Chapter 10 on Active Server Pages.

Creating Mouseovers

Where would the Web be today without those sensational-looking menu effects? You can create them with both text and image hyperlinks using VBScript. It's as simple as giving the hyperlink an ID or name and deploying a hyperlink event such as onMouseMove, onMouseOut, onMouseOver, and onClick. Using these event handlers, you can load a new image for the hyperlink or display text in the status bar of the browser in place of the hyperlink's URL.

In the following example, we'll use the onMouseOver and onMouseOut events of a button object to display a message in the status bar. We also will change the color of a hyperlink text as the mouse passes over it. Here's the complete code:

```
<!- VBMouseover.htm ->
<html><head>
<script language="vbscript">
Sub Link1_OnMouseOver()
  Link1.style.color = "red"
End Sub
Sub Link1_OnMouseOut()
  Link1.style.color = "green"
End Sub
Sub btnChangeStatus_OnMouseOver()
  Window.Status = "See, I changed the status bar"
End Sub
```

```vbscript
Sub btnChangeStatus_OnMouseOut()
  Window.Status = ""
End Sub
</script></head><body>
<a href=" " id="Link1" >Link1</a><br/><br/>
<input type="button" id= "btnChangeStatus" value="Change
  Status Bar" />
</body></html>
```

Opening a New Browser Window

When one window isn't enough, pop open another one using the `Window.Open` method. This method takes four optional parameters:

- *Location* specifies the URL of the document to show within the new window. If it's left blank, the `"about:blank"` document (a blank document) is displayed.
- *Name* specifies the name of the new window.
- *Options* is a single string containing a series of comma-delimited parameters that specify how the new window will look.
- *Replace history item*, if set to true, won't add a new history item to the browser's history list as a result of the window opening.

The `Window.Open` method returns a reference to the newly created window, and it's a good idea to store this object reference in a local variable so you can easily reference the window again (for example, to close it). Because you are dealing with object references, you should use the `Set` statement to assign the reference:

```vbscript
Set oNavWin = Window.Open("nav.html")
```

You also should assign a reference to the parent window within the new window, using the new window's Opener property. The following code example shows how you can both open and close a navigation window from an HTML page:

```vbscript
<!- OpenCloseWindow.htm ->
<html><head><script language="vbscript">
' Dim a local variable to hold a reference to the new
  window.
Private oNavWin
Function OpenNavWindow()
' Call the open method and assign the resultant window
  reference
```

```
   ' to your local variable.
      Set oNavWin = Window.Open("http://www.mcgraw-hill.com/", _
         "McGrawHill", "height=400, width=400, status=yes, _
         toolbar=no, menubar=no")
      ' Pass a reference to this window to the new window.
      Set oNavWin.opener = self
   End Function
   Function CloseNavWindow()
      ' Handle an error, just in case the window has already
         ' been closed!
      On Error Resume Next
         ' Close the window.
      oNavWin.Close()
         ' Release the object reference.
      Set oNavWin = Nothing
   End Function
   </script></head>
   <body><center>
   <h2>Main window</h2><br/><br/>
   <input type="button" name="cmdClose" onClick=
      "CloseNavWindow" value="Close navigation
      window"><br/><br/>
   <input type="button" name="cmdOpen" onClick=
      "OpenNavWindow" value="Open navigation
      window"></center>
   </body></html>
```

QuickCheck Questions

10. What tags do you use to create a form?
11. How do you refer to a form in a script?
12. What can you use the `window.open` method for?

As a Web programming tool, VBScript gives you the ability to create Web pages that are more attractive, versatile, and interactive than with HTML alone. All that's needed to write VBScript code is an ASCII text editor such as Microsoft Notepad. To run VBScript code, you need a host environment such as a Web browser that can interpret VBScript (Microsoft Internet Explorer 3.0 and higher). Netscape browsers can be used with the addition of plug-ins.

Table 8.3 summarizes the statements, functions, and operators used in VBScript.

TABLE 8.3   **VBScript Statements, Functions, and Operators**

Keyword	Type	Usage	Expression
Arithmetic			
`Atn`	Function	Returns the arctangent of a number	`Atn(number)`
`Cos`	Function	Returns the cosine of an angle	`Cos(number)`
`Exp`	Function	Returns a number raised to a power	`Exp(number)`
`Log`	Function	Returns the logarithm of a number	`Log(number)`
`Randomize`	Statement	Primes the internal random number generator	`Randomize`
`Rnd`	Function	Returns a random number	`Rnd`
`Sin`	Function	Returns the sine of an angle	`Sin(number)`
`Sqr`	Function	Returns the square root of a number	`Sqr(number)`
`Tan`	Function	Returns the tangent of an angle	`Tan(number)`
Array Handling			
`Dim`	Statement	Declares an array	`Dim arrayname([subscripts])`
`Erase`	Statement	Clears the contents of an array	`Erase arrayname`
`IsArray`	Function	Returns `True` if `var` is an array and `False` if not	`IsArray(var)`
`Lbound`	Function	In VBScript, always returns `0`	`Lbound(arrayname)`
`Preserve`	Statement	Copies the contents of a dynamic array to a resized dynamic array	`ReDim Preserve arrayname(subscripts)`
`ReDim`	Statement	Declares a dynamic array or redimensions a dynamic array (see `Preserve`)	`ReDim arrayname()` or `ReDim arrayname([subscripts])`
`UBound`	Statement	Returns the largest subscript of an array	`Ubound(arrayname)`
Assignment			
`=`	Operator	Assigns a value to a variable or property	`variable = value`
`Set`	Statement	Assigns an object reference to a variable	`Set variable = object`

Continued

TABLE 8.3   VBScript Statements, Functions, and Operators (continued)

Keyword	Type	Usage	Expression
Comment			
Rem	Statement	Declares the following line as a comment to be ignored by the language engine	Rem *comment_text*
Constants/Literals			
Empty	Literal	Declares a special uninitialized variable	value *variable* = Empty
False	Constant	A Boolean value representing 0	*variable* = False
Nothing	Literal	Used to disassociate an object reference from a variable; used in conjunction with Set	Set *variable* = Nothing
Null	Literal	Represents no valid data	*variable* = Null
True	Constant	Boolean value representing -1	*variable* = True
Conversions			
Abs	Function	Returns the unsigned (absolute) value of a number	Abs(*number*)
Asc	Function	Returns the ANSI/ASCII code of a character	Asc(*string*)
CBool	Function	Returns a Boolean subtype Variant value from any valid expression	CBool(*expression*)
CByte	Function	Returns a Byte subtype Variant value from any valid expression	Cbyte(*expression*)
CDate	Function	Returns a Date subtype Variant value from any valid date expression	CDate(*expression*)
CDbl	Function	Returns a Double Precision subtype Variant value from any valid numeric expression	CDbl(*expression*)
Chr	Function	Returns the character corresponding to the ANSI or ASCII code	Chr(*number*)
CInt	Function	Returns an Integer subtype Variant value from any valid numeric expression	CInt(*expression*)

Continued

TABLE 8.3   VBScript Statements, Functions, and Operators (continued)

Keyword	Type	Usage	Expression
CLng	Function	Returns a Long Integer subtype Variant value from any valid numeric expression	CLng(*expression*)
CSng	Function	Returns a Single Precision subtype Variant value from any valid numeric expression	CSng(*expression*)
CStr	Function	Returns a String subtype Variant value from any valid expression	CStr(*expression*)
DateSerial	Function	Returns a Date subtype Variant from valid year, month, and day values	DateSerial(*year,month, day*)
DateValue	Function	Returns a Date subtype Variant value from any valid date expression	DateValue(*expression*)
Hex	Function	Returns a String subtype Variant representing the hexadecimal value of a number	Hex(*number*)
Int	Function	Returns an Integer subtype Variant rounded down from the number supplied	Int(*number*)
Fix	Function	Returns an Integer subtype Variant rounded up from the number supplied	Fix(*number*)
Oct	Function	Returns a String subtype Variant representing the octal value of a number	Oct(*number*)
Sgn	Function	Returns an Integer subtype Variant representing the sign of a number	Sgn(*number*) values > 0 return 1 values = 0 return 0 values < 0 return -1
TimeSerial	Function	Returns a Date subtype Variant from valid hour, minute, and second values	TimeSerial(*hour,minute, second*)
TimeValue	Function	Returns a Date subtype Variant value from any valid time expression	TimeValue(*expression*)

Continued

TABLE 8.3 VBScript Statements, Functions, and Operators (continued)

Keyword	Type	Usage	Expression
Dates and Times			
Date	Function	Returns the current system date	Date()
DateSerial	Function	Returns a Date subtype Variant from valid year, month, and day values	DateSerial(year,month, day)
DateValue	Function	Returns a Date subtype Variant value from any valid date expression	DateValue(expression)
Day	Function	Returns an Integer subtype Variant representing the day (1–31) from a valid date expression	Day(dateexpression)
Hour	Function	Returns an Integer subtype Variant representing the hour (0–23) from a valid time expression	Hour(timeexpression)
Minute	Function	Returns an Integer subtype Variant representing the minute (0–60) from a valid time expression	Minute(timeexpression)
Month	Function	Returns an Integer subtype Variant representing the month (1–12) from a valid date expression	Month(dateexpression)
Now	Function	Returns the current date and time of the system	Now()
Second	Function	Returns an Integer subtype Variant representing the second (0–60) from a valid time expression	Second(timeexpression)
Time	Function	Returns the current system time	Time()
TimeSerial	Function	Returns a Date subtype Variant from valid hour, minute, and second values	TimeSerial(hour,minute, second)
TimeValue	Function	Returns a Date subtype Variant value from any valid time expression	TimeValue(expression)
Weekday	Function	Returns an Integer subtype Variant between 1 and 7 representing the day of the week, starting at Sunday, from a date expression	Weekday(dateexpression)
Year	Function	Returns an Integer subtype Variant representing the year from a valid date expression	Year(dateexpression)

Continued

TABLE 8.3   VBScript Statements, Functions, and Operators (continued)

Keyword	Type	Usage	Expression
Declarations			
Dim	Statement	Declares a variable	Dim *variable*
End	Statement	Declares the end of a Sub procedure or function	End Sub End Function
Exit	Statement	Use with Do, For, Function, or Sub to prematurely exit the routine	Exit Do/For/Function/Sub
Function	Statement	Declares a function and the argument list passed into the function, and declares the end of a function; also used with Exit to prematurely end a function	Function *functionname* (*[argumentlist]*) Exit Function End Function
Public	Statement		Public *variable*
Sub	Statement	Declares a custom procedure or event handler and the argument list, if any, and declares the end of a custom procedure or event handler; also used with Exit to prematurely end a custom procedure or event handler	Sub *subroutinename* (*[argumentlist]*) Exit Sub End Sub
Error Handling			
Clear	Method	A method of the Err object to reset the Err.Number property to 0	Err.Clear
Description	Property	A property of the Err object that contains a description of the last error as specified in the Err.Number property	Err.Description
Err	Object	An object containing information about the last error	Err.*property*|*method*
On Error	Statement	Used in conjunction with Resume Next to continue execution with the line directly following the line in which the error occurred	On Error Resume Next
Raise	Method	A method of the Err object used to simulate the occurrence of an error specified by number	Err.Raise(*errornumber*)

Continued

TABLE 8.3   VBScript Statements, Functions, and Operators (continued)

Keyword	Type	Usage	Expression
Number	Property	A property of the Err object that contains the error code for the last error, or 0 if no error has occurred	Err.Number
Source	Property	Returns the name of the object or application that raised the error	Err.Source
Input/Output			
InputBox	Function	Displays a dialog box to allow user input	InputBox(*caption*[,*title*][,*value*][,*x*][,*y*])
MsgBox	Function	Displays a dialog box	MsgBox(*prompt*[,*definition*][, *title*])
Operators			
+	Operator	Addition of two numerical expressions	*result = expression1 + expression2*
And	Operator	Logical conjunction operator	If *expression1* AND *expression2* Then
/	Operator	Division operator	*result = expression1 / expression2*
=	Operator	Equality operator	If *expression1 = expression2* Then
Eqv	Operator	Logical equivalence operator	If *expression1* Eqv *expression2* Then
^	Operator	Exponentiation operator	*result = expression1 ^ expression2*
>	Operator	Greater than comparison	If *expression1 > expression2* Then
>=	Operator	Greater than or equal to comparison	If *expression1 >= expression2* Then
Imp	Operator	Logical implication	If *expression1* Imp *expression2* Then
<>	Operator	Inequality comparison	If *expression1 <> expression2* Then
\	Operator	Integer division operator	*result = expression1 \ expression2*
<	Operator	Less than comparison	If *expression1 < expression2* Then

Continued

TABLE 8.3   VBScript Statements, Functions, and Operators (continued)

Keyword	Type	Usage	Expression
`<=`	Operator	Less than or equal to comparison	`If expression1 <= expression2 Then`
`Mod`	Operator	Modulus arithmetic; returns only the remainder of a division of two numbers	`result = expression1 mod expression2`
`*`	Operator	Multiplication	`result = expression1 * expression2`
`-`	Operator	Subtraction	`result = expression1 - expression2`
`Or`	Operator	Logical disjunction	`If expression1 Or expression2 Then`
`&`	Operator	Concatenation of two string values	`result = string1 & string2`
`Xor`	Operator	Logical exclusion	`If expression1 Xor expression2 Then`
Options			
`Option`	Statement	Forces a compile-time error if an `Explicit` undeclared variable is found	`Option Explicit`
Program Flow			
`Call`	Statement	Passes execution to a subroutine or event handler; also can be used to replicate the actions of the user	`Call myroutine()` `Call cmdbutton_OnClick()`

`Do...Loop`	Statement	Repeats code while a condition is met or until a condition is met	`Do While condition`
			`...`
			`Loop`
			or
			`Do Until condition`
			`...`
			`Loop`
			or
			`Do`
			`...`
			`Loop While condition`
			or
			`Do`
			`...`
			`Loop Until condition`

Continued

TABLE 8.3   VBScript Statements, Functions, and Operators (continued)

Keyword	Type	Usage	Expression

`For . . . Next`	Statement	Repeats a block of code until the counter reaches a given number	`For counter = lower To upper [step]`
			`. . .`
			`Next`

`If . . . Then . . . Else`	Statement	Conditional execution of code	`If condition Then`
			`. . .` (condition met)
			`Else`
			`. . .` (condition not met)
			End If

`Select Case`	Statement	Selective execution of code, where `testexpression` must match `expression`	`Select Case`
			`testexpression`
			`Case expression`
			`. . .`
			`Case expression`
			`. . .`
			`Case Else`
			`End Select`

`While . . . Wend`	Statement	Execution of a code block while a condition is met	`While expression`
			`. . .`
			`Wend`

Strings			
`InStr`	Function	Returns the starting point of one string within another string, or `0` if not found	`result = InStr(start, searched, sought)`
`Lcase`	Function	Converts a string to lowercase	`result = LCase(string)`
`Left`	Function	Returns the n leftmost characters of a string	`result = Left(string)`
`Len`	Function	Returns the length of a string	`result = Len(string)`
`Ltrim`	Function	Removes all leading spaces	`result = LTrim(string)`
`Mid`	Function	Returns a string of length L, starting at S within `string`	`result = Mid(string, S, L)`
`Right`	Function	Returns the rightmost n characters	`result = Right(string, n)`
`RTrim`	Function	Removes all trailing spaces from a string	`result = RTrim(string)`
`Space`	Function	Returns a string consisting of n spaces	`result = Space(n)`

Continued

TABLE 8.3   VBScript Statements, Functions, and Operators (continued)

Keyword	Type	Usage	Expression
StrComp	Function	Returns an Integer subtype Variant representing the result of a comparison of two strings	result = StrComp(*string1*, *string2*) *string1* < *string2* returns -1 *string1* = *string2* returns 0 *string1* > *string2* returns 1
String	Function	Returns a string consisting of character C, of length L	result = String(L, C)
Trim	Function	Removes both leading and trailing spaces	result = Trim(*string*)
UCase	Function	Returns a string as uppercase alphabetical characters	result = UCase(*string*)
Variants			
IsArray	Function	Returns True (-1) if *expression* is an array and False (0) if not	result = IsArray(*expression*)
IsDate	Function	Returns True (-1) if *expression* is a valid date and False (0) if not	result = IsDate(*expression*)
IsEmpty	Function	Returns True (-1) if *expression* equates to an Empty subtype and False (0) if not	result = IsEmpty(*expression*)
IsNull	Function	Returns True (-1) if *expression* equates to a Null subtype and False (0) if not	result = IsNull(*expression*)
IsNumeric	Function	Returns True (-1) if *expression* is a valid numeric expression and False (0) if not	result = IsNumeric(*expression*)
VarType	Function	Returns an integer representing the sub data type of a Variant	result = VarType(*expression*)

VBScript can be used to develop client-side code. It is only compatible with Internet Explorer because no other browsers have included the VBScript interpreter. Nevertheless, it is worth learning because it is a relatively easy language to learn and it is very similar to Visual Basic and Visual Basic for Application. Furthermore, the Internet Explorer is one of the most popular browsers that are currently in use. In this chapter, we have provided an overview of the client-side VBScript.

VBScript codes are inserted in an HTML page using the `<script language="vbscript">` tag. VBScript has access to the Document Object Model, and as such we can use the Document object's properties and methods to insert or change the contents of HTML elements dynamically. For example, we can issue code for a statement like **Document.Write**("Hello World") to write the text "Hello World" in a HTML document.

VBScript variables are usually declared as **Dim variable _name**. For example, a variable named city can be declared as **Dim city**. VBScript offers only one data type for its variables. This data type is known as a variant. The variant data type can accommodate many subtypes such as Byte, Currency, Date, Double, Integer, String, and so on. You can build data structures like arrays using VBScript. VBScript codes can be composed of subprocedures or functions. A subprocedrue is a section of code that performs certain tasks but does not return a result to the calling routine. On the other hand, a function contains a set of codes that performs certain tasks. Like most other programming language, VBScript offers If-Then-Else, and a variety of looping structures. You can use **For . . . Next, Do . . . Loop, Do While . . . Loop**, or **Do Until . . . Loop** structures to build loops.

Although most browsers have not included the VBScript interpreter, it would not be wise to ignore VBScript as a programming language. The server-side VBScript is extensively used in Active Server Side technology. Server-side VBScript is identical to client-side VBScript, except that it has access to server objects. You will learn server-side VBScript in Chapter 10.

Summary

branching

case-sensitive

execute

explicit

implicit

initializing

looping

scripting language

Key Terms

1. VBScript is a compiled language often used to customize applications. True or False?
2. To run VBScript, you need _____.
3. Two advantages of scripts over compiled programs are _____ and _____.
4. VBScript can only run client-side. True or False?
5. The _____ method writes the specified text to the current HTML document.
6. HTML formatting tags can be added to the `Document.write` statement. True or False?
7. a. The assignment operator for all data types is _____.
   b. _____ is the default VBScript data type.
8. Concerning naming conventions, VBScript is case-_____.
9. Declaring a variable means that you inform the program in advance so that memory space can be assigned to the variable to store the variable. True or False?
10. The `dim` keyword is used by VBScript to declare a variable. True or False?
11. The data type for a variable in VBScript is subscript. True or False?
12. The assignment operator in VBScript is:

    +

    \

    =

    #

13. Which variable type does VBScript support?
    a. string
    b. variable
    c. numbers
    d. variant
14. Which of the following is the correct way to declare a variable in VBScript?
    a. `dim:Name`
    b. `new Name`
    c. `dim Name`
    d. `var Name`
15. Individual pieces of an array are called _____.
    a. collections
    b. variables
    c. elements
    d. variants
16. A _____ construct allows you to repeat blocks of code.
    a. looping structure
    b. repeating structure
    c. decision control
    d. variable control

1. **Hello World.** Write a script that displays **Hello World** on the HTML page.
2 **Hello World again . . . and again.** Add a `For` loop to the page to display **Hello World** 100 times.
3. **Time and Hello World.** Use the `Time` function to post the time on your last **Hello World** page.
4. **A thinking page.** Write a script that will display **Good morning**, **Good afternoon**, and **Good night** according to the time of day.

Understanding Dynamic HTML

OBJECTIVES

1. To work with CSS.

2. To use the DOM.

3. To write JavaScript to handle events.

4. To learn basic DHTML techniques.

INTRODUCTION

Dynamic HTML (DHTML) is not a single entity but rather the interaction of several technologies used to enable Web pages to react to events and thereby become dynamic Web pages. These events, generally initiated by the end user through a mouse click and/or a keyboard action, also can be triggered by scripts embedded in the page. No matter what triggers the event, the end result is that the layout, design, and/or contents of the page change.

Creating dynamic HTML pages requires you to be familiar with four technologies. First, you need HTML. By manipulating HTML tags, you initiate changes in the browser. Second, you need Cascading Style Sheets (CSS) to alter style specifications. Third, you need a Document Object Model (DOM) as implemented by a browser. The DOM provides the interface to page objects, property settings, and methods belonging to the associated page elements. Finally, you need a scripting language to speak to and program the page elements you want to change. For this you'll use JavaScript.

QuickCheck Questions

1. What technologies are required to create DHTML?
2. Is DHTML considered server-side or client-side processing?
3. What is a DOM?

Tech Tip

Note
While there are DOM standards (W3.org) to provide common approaches to using DHTML, not all browsers follow these standards. Over the years there have been significant differences between the DOM implementations in the big two browsers, Netscape Navigator and Microsoft Internet Explorer. This has caused nightmares in cross-browser compatibility because programmers needed to know the different DOMs. Netscape has made the leap to conform more closely to these standards with the release of Netscape Navigator 6; however, for this introduction, we're going to work with Microsoft Internet Explorer 6.

The CSS Factor

Combining Cascading Style Sheet methodology with HTML enables Web designers to redefine the way existing HTML tags work. The power of CSS is in its ability to use different rules from different sources to weave a Web page to your exact specification.

To achieve "dynamic effects" on your Web page, you use techniques that show or hide elements, move, resize, change color, change style, and change content. CSS provides the controls you need to create these effects.

Between the HTML Tags

HTML tags hold the information contents of a Web page. In this respect, we think of HTML tags as containers and to use DHTML you need to be familiar with the common container tags and their various properties and methods. In this section, we'll review the Paragraph, Division, and Span containers.

`<p>` Paragraphs `<\p>`

The most common container is the paragraph. The opening and closing `<p>` . . . `</p>` tags enclose text blocks, offsetting them from surrounding page elements. In addition, `<p>` tags can include style attributes to apply various styles to the enclosed text.

```
<p style="font-family:arial; font-size:12pt">
This is a styled paragraph.
</p>
```

`<div>` Divisions

The `<div>` (division) tag is a block-level container used to enclose text and HTML tags in order to treat the collection as a unit. By default, the `<div>` tag causes a line break to appear before and after the opening and closing tags.

```
<div>
holds text and HTML tags as a unit
</div>
```

`<span>`

The `<span>` tag, in contrast with the `<div>` tag, is an in-line container enclosing a string of text in order to apply style or positional settings to it.

```
<span> . . .text string . . .</span>
```

There are no blank lines appearing before and after the opening and closing tags; therefore, `<span>` tags can appear within sentences and paragraphs in order to control styles.

Laying Out with Styles

When you code HTML, elements appear on the Web page according to the order in which you code their tags. To override this behavior, you apply stylesheets to the tags that allow you to position the elements exactly where you want them. These positioning style properties as set by the stylesheets are the keys to controlling a Web page's structure. In fact, it's the position styles that also provide the ability to change an element's position dynamically, as we'll show later in this chapter. Table 9.1 lists the stylesheet settings used to position elements on the page. We'll discuss these settings in the following sections.

TABLE 9.1 Stylesheet Settings

CSS Reference	Effects
position:*type*	Specifies the manner of positioning a page element; *type* can be relative—to retain its normal position in the flow of page elements—or absolute—to position it at exact pixel coordinates on the page.
left:*distance*	Specifies, for a positioned element, its distance from the left edge of its container element. Measurement is normally in pixels (px).
top:*distance*	Specifies, for a positioned element, its distance from the top edge of its container element. Measurement is normally in pixels (px).
z-index:*layer*	Specifies, for a positioned element, its layer; higher values position the element on top of elements with lower values; *layer* is an integer value.
width:*size*	Specifies a width for a page element; *size* is measured in pixels or percentages.
height:*size*	Specifies a height for a page element; *size* is measured in pixels or percentages.

Positioning Elements

How do you know the exact position of an element within a Web page? We measure an element's position relative to its container element. Generally, the primary container element is the Web page itself, and any element position within the page is measured relative to the top-left corner of the page. The top-left corner is represented by the coordinates 0,0, meaning that its position is 0 horizontal pixels from the left edge of the page and 0 vertical pixels from the top edge of the page.

Within the Web page, HTML tags serve as containers so that the position of an element located within these tags is measured relative to this container. Just as with the page container, the top-left corner of the tag container is represented by the coordinates 0,0, and top-left settings for the enclosed element are measured relative to the tag container's location.

Every element has a natural location within the flow of a Web page. Controlling an element's flow and the effect of other positional settings on the element is done using two **positioning** methods called relative and absolute positioning. **Relative** positioning refers to moving an element with respect to its original location and **absolute** positioning means to specify an element's precise position with respect to its container.

Relative Positioning   The `position:relative` style places the element at its natural location within the flow of other elements on the page. Any accompanying left or top settings adjust the element relative to this location.

```
<img src="somepicture.gif" style="position:relative">
```

This code causes the image to appear at the location at which the `<img>` tag appears in the code. If the page contained any other elements that were not explicitly positioned, those elements would simply flow relative to the image's location according to the order in which they were coded. Therefore, you do not need to adjust the position of the other elements to make room for the image. When an element is positioned relative, any left or top settings are applied relative to its current position on the page. For example, the following code causes the image, which has left and top properties specified, to offset from its coded position:

```
<img src="McGrawHillCommunity2.jpg" style="position:
    relative; left:50px; top:-50px"/>
```

Figure 9.1 shows two Web pages. In the first one, we have displayed an image at its natural position. In the second one, we have used `position:relative` to offset the image by 50 pixels from the left and –50 (negative 50) pixels from the top of its natural position.

Here is another example of relative positioning, this time using `<span>` tags to enclose text in order to position words on the page. The following tags declare relative positioning. Without further specifications, the words appear in their natural locations:

These words are relative:

```
<!- RelativePositioning2.htm ->
<span style="position:relative">These</span>
<span style="position:relative">words</span>
<span style="position:relative">are</span>
<span style="position:relative">relative.</span>
```

FIGURE 9.1   Offsetting an Image from Its Natural Position

These relative settings can be modified so that the words are adjusted relative to their normal positions. These words are adjusted:

```
<!—RelativePositioning3.htm —>
<span style="position:relative">These</span>
<span style="position:relative; left:+20px;
   top:+10px">words</span>
<span style="position:relative; left:+50px;
   top:+20px">are</span>
<span style="position:relative; top:-10px;
   left:+100px">adjusted.</span>
```

The plus and minus pixel values for the left and top properties place the words to the left and right and above and below their normal positions across the line.

Absolute Positioning   The absolute property setting places the element at an exact location in the document. This absolute position can be its natural location in the flow of page elements, or it can be relative to its container element. Unlike relative positioning, the absolute positioning style not only affects the location of the positioned element; it also affects the location of surrounding elements. When an element is positioned absolute, subsequent elements are positioned relative to other, nonpositioned elements. The positioned element is taken out of the flow of nonpositioned elements. This effect is seen in the following graphic and text paragraph:

```
<!—AbsolutePositioning1.htm —>
.............................................Here
   is a nonpositioned text paragraph.
<img src="McGrawHillCommunity2.jpg"
   style="position:absolute">
```

```
<p>........................................Here
    is a nonpositioned text paragraph.</p>
```

In this example, the `position:absolute` style defines the `<img>` tag as a positioned element. Its location is established at the exact position where it is coded on the page, and, importantly, it is taken out of the flow of other nonpositioned elements. Therefore, the accompanying paragraph appears behind the image. As a nonpositioned element, the paragraph's location is relative to the flow of other nonpositioned elements, namely, the preceding paragraph. The two paragraphs flow relative to each other; the image remains at its absolute location.

When a positioned element appears within the flow of nonpositioned elements, it may be necessary to adjust subsequent elements around the positioned element. One way to do this is with a `<br/>` tag to manage the subsequent flow of a nonpositioned element:

```
<!--AbsolutePositioning2.htm -->
.............................................Here
    is a nonpositioned text paragraph.
<img src="McGrawHillCommunity2.jpg"
    style="position:absolute">
<br/><br/><br/>
<p>.............................................Here
    is a nonpositioned text paragraph.</p>
```

The three `<br>` tags push the paragraph down the page relative to the preceding paragraph to make room for the absolutely positioned graphic. The reason for absolutely positioning an element is normally to adjust its left and top coordinates for exact positioning within its container. The following graphic, for example, has a `left:50px` property setting to position it exactly 50 pixels from the left edge of the page:

```
<!-- AbsolutePositioning3.htm -->
<img src="McGrawHillCommunity2.jpg"
    style="position:absolute; left:50px">
<br/><br/><br/>
```

Again, the graphic is followed by `<br/>` tags to move subsequent nonpositioned elements below the absolutely positioned image. When specifying a top coordinate for an absolutely positioned element, remember that the setting is relative to the top of the container element, in this case, the top of the Web page. The following image, therefore, has a `top:2030px` setting to place it exactly 2,030 pixels from the top of the page:

```
<!-- AbsolutePositioning4.htm -->
<img src="McGrawHillCommunity2.jpg"
    style="position:absolute; left:400px; top:2030px">
<br/><br/><br/>
```

As you can imagine, positioning an element absolutely on a page can be frustrating in finding its exact pixel position from the top of the page, especially if it appears well down a scrolling page. Also, you must deal with the positioning of surrounding nonpositioned elements. For these reasons, absolute positioning only works well in these instances: on a nonscrolling page, when positioning the element horizontally, or when positioning the element inside another container object.

Positioning Elements in 3-D

If you're familiar with a drawing or paint program, you've probably encountered that third dimension called a *layer*. Elements on a Web page can be positioned above or below other elements and, after moving elements around on the page, you may find that one overlaps another.

The value of `z-index` is a positive or negative integer to indicate a layer above or below other positioned elements. Elements with higher `z-index` values appear on top of elements with lower values. The text layer has a `z-index` value of 0. Positioned elements coded subsequently on the page appear on top of positioned elements coded previously; `z-index` settings change these original layers.

Hiding and Showing Elements

Hiding and showing elements is one way to customize a visitor's viewing experience. For example, you might want certain elements to hide or show depending on the visitor's language, browser type, interests, and some other criteria. The `visibility` style setting makes it possible to specify whether an element can be seen or is hidden. In the following example, we're creating a drop-down menu where items stay hidden until a user moves the mouse on the menu header and the hidden menu items appear.

```
<!- DropdownMenu.htm ->
<html><head></head><body>
<div id="MENU"
   style="position:relative; width:80px; text-align:center;
   background-color:#DC6000; color:#0000FF"
   onMouseOver="document.all.ITEMS.style.visibility=
     'visible';
       this.style.cursor='hand';"
   onMouseOut="document.all.ITEMS.style.visibility=
     'hidden'">
   <b>Menu</b>
</div>
<div id="ITEMS"
   style="position:relative; width:100px; text-align:
     center;
```

```
background-color:#DEB887; color:#0000FF; visibility:
  hidden"
onMouseOver="this.style.visibility='visible';
  this.style.cursor='hand';"
onMouseOut="this.style.visibility='hidden'">
<div style="background-color:#DEB887"
  onMouseOver="this.style.backgroundColor='#9D4602'"
  onMouseOut="this.style.backgroundColor='#DEB887'"
  onClick="location='http://www.mcgraw-hill.com'">
  <b>McGraw-Hill</b>
</div>
<div style="background-color:#DEB887"
  onMouseOver="this.style.backgroundColor='#9D4602'"
  onMouseOut="this.style.backgroundColor='#DEB887'"
  onClick="location='http://www.google.com/'">
  <b>Google Search</b>
</div>
<div style="background-color:#DEB887"
  onMouseOver="this.style.backgroundColor='#9D4602'"
  onMouseOut="this.style.backgroundColor='#DEB887'"
  onClick="location='http://www.dell.com/'">
  <b>Dell</b>
</div>
</div></body><html>
```

Figure 9.2 shows what this looks like when the page is opened in Internet Explorer.

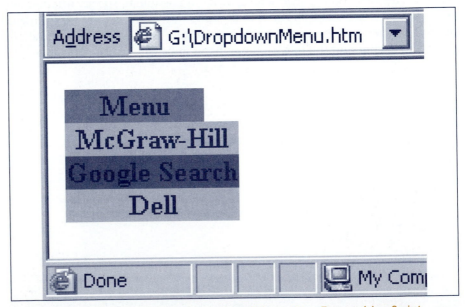

FIGURE 9.2   Implementing Drop-Down Menu Using `<div>` Tags and JavaScript

A closer look at the code reveals the following: We defined both the MENU header and the menu ITEMS as divisions and used the position:relative setting to align the two main divisions one after the other. Within the ITEMS division are three stacked divisions containing the individual menu items that are hidden initially by using the visibility:hidden setting. We used the visibility= 'visible' setting to reveal the menu ITEMS when the mouse is over the MENU division. The ITEMS division is also made visible with visibility='visible' on a mouseover event to keep it visible when the mouse is moved off the MENU division. When the mouse is moved off either division, visibility of the ITEMS division is hidden.

Even though the menu ITEMS division is initially hidden, it takes up space on the page by virtue of the fact that the division is positioned relative. Below is a recoding of the menu to overlay subsequent page elements rather than reserving space between them by setting the ITEMS division to use absolute positioning. Looking at Figure 9.3, you can see that the ITEMS division still appears after the relatively positioned MENU division, but it does not take up space on the page.

```
<!- DropdownMenu2.htm ->
. . .
<div id="MENU"
style="position:relative; width:80px; text-align:center;
background-color:#DC6000; color:#FFFFFF"
. . .
</div>
```

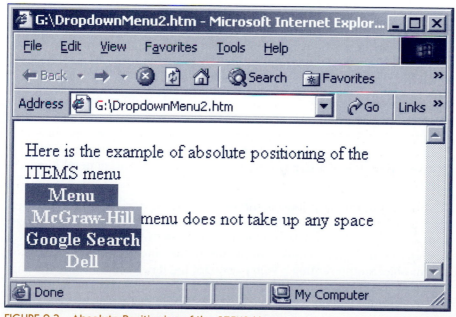

FIGURE 9.3   Absolute Positioning of the ITEMS Menu

```
<div id="ITEMS"
style="position:absolute; width:80px; text-align:center;
background-color:#DEB887; color:#FFFFFF; visibility:hidden"
. . .
</div>
```

QuickCheck Questions

4. What does CSS stand for?
5. CSS can be used to
    a. Show and hide HTML element's contents dynamicaily.
    b. Move images dynamically.
    c. Change font styles dynamically.
    d. To accomplish all of the above, if necessary.
    e. None of the above can be accomplished using CSS.
6. The `<span>` is a block-level container tag. True or False?
7. Suppose that you would like to display an image named "puppy.jpg" using relative positioning with 20 pixels left (offset) and 40 pixels top (offset) from its natural position in the document. Show the code using the sytle attribute.

The DOM: A Roadmap to a Web Page

You liven up HTML by applying scripts that alter the elements on a Web page. Remember that HTML tags are scriptable because they themselves are software **objects** with properties and methods that you can program. Also remember that **properties** are characteristics of the **element**, generally specified by the style settings associated with the tag, and **methods** are actions the tag can perform. HTML tags, then, can activate scripts that in turn set properties and initiate methods. Suddenly, the page comes alive.

The **Document Object Model (DOM)** is the scripting interface to the HTML objects appearing on a Web page. It describes and relates the structure of components that comprise a Web page. It also provides the means for identifying objects and manipulating their properties and methods. Simply put, the DOM represents a hierarchy of browser components. This general hierarchy is shown in Figure 9.4.

Starting at the top-most level is the browser (navigator) object. At the next level is the window object, the main browser window in which Web pages appear. The window object might contain frame objects, if the window is divided into frames, and both window and frame objects can contain the document objects representing a Web page. Drilling down even further, the page itself contains other objects, such as HTML tags and any forms, and the forms contain various field objects.

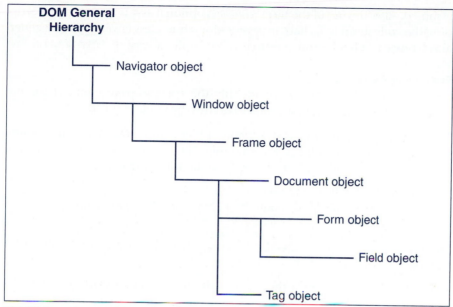

FIGURE 9.4   General Hierarchy of Objects in the DOM

Just what can you do with the DOM? You can

- Change the CSS properties of an element on the screen.
- Hide or show elements on the screen.
- Control the position of elements.
- Move elements on the screen.

These are just a few of the things you can alter and control via the Document Object Model.

Weaving through the DOM

The scripting language is the tool you use to speak to or command page elements that are defined within the DOM. In order to act on a specific page element, you have to point it out or identify it to the script. Following paths through the Document Object Model, you compose references, which can be thought of as addresses much like conventional postal addresses, based on the element's hierarchical path. We call this procedure "referencing objects" and we use dotted notation to identify objects on a Web page and to reference them in scripts. For example:

```
window.frame.document.form.field
```

The code example above draws a path from the browser window down to a field in a form. The window is followed by a frame name (if there are any frames), then by document, next by the form name, and finally by the name of the form field. Notice that the navigator object is not used in path references; it is assumed. Also, the use of the term *window* is optional as it is also assumed. Stripping the code down to its bare necessities for a frameless environment, a general reference to a field within a form can be simply `document.form.field`.

Specifying Elements

As mentioned above, you must identify the specific page element for the script to act on. There are two ways to do this: by name or by **ID**.

HTML forms support the `name` **attribute**, which allows you to use an assigned name to reference an object. For example, HTML forms and their fields use `name` attributes for identification. Observe the following example:

```
<form name="MyFirstForm">
Text Field: <input name="MyFirstField" type="text">
</form>
```

In this example, the DOM reference to the text field object is `document.MyFirstForm.MyFirstField`.

Only HTML forms support the `name` attribute, so you must use ID values to identify all other HTML tags. To assign ID values, simply include `ID="value"` within the tag. Make sure that each element's ID value is unique within the page and that you follow JavaScript naming conventions when assigning a name. When using ID values, DOM references to page elements are in the `document.all.id` format, where `document.all` refers to the collection of all HTML elements on the page in which the identified element is a member.

For example, the paragraph `<p>` tag does not support the `name` attribute, so to identify it within the DOM, we give it an ID value as follows:

```
<p id="MyFirstParagraph">
     This paragraph has an ID value. </p>
```

The DOM reference to this paragraph object is

```
document.all.MyFirstParagraph
```

Referencing Properties and Methods

With proper reference to a page object, you can change an element's attributes on the fly. This is how you put the "D" in HTML; change property settings and call processing methods and HTML becomes dynamic. You reference the properties and methods associated with particular objects by appending the property name or the method name to the end of the object reference. For example, to identify and change a property setting, the syntax looks like this:

```
document.form.field.property
```

or

```
document.all.id.property
```

And, to activate a processing method associated with a page element:

```
document.form.field.method()
```

or

```
document.all.id.method()
```

You've learned how to reference or point to a specific page object or element. In the next section, you'll learn how to make things happen by changing properties and activating methods.

Table 9.2 lists selected objects, used in this chapter, that comprise the browser Document Object Model. The associated properties, methods, and **event handlers** are listed.

TABLE 9.2   DOM Object Reference

DOM Object	Properties	Methods	Event Handler
BODY	alink background bgColor id innerHTML innerText leftMargin link outerHTML outerText parentElement rightMargin style tabIndex tagName text title topMargin vLink	click() getAttribute(*attributeName*) insertAdjacentHTML(*where, string*) insertAdjacentText(*where, value*) removeAttribute(*attributeName*) scrollIntoView([showAtTop]) setAttribute(*attributeName, value*)	onChange onClick onDblClick onDragStart onMouseDown onMouseMove onMouseOut onMouseOver onMouseUp
button	disabled form id innerHTML innerText name outerHTML outerText parentElement tabIndex tagName title type value	blur() click() focus() getAttribute(*attributeName*) insertAdjacentHTML(*where, string*) insertAdjacentText(*where, value*) removeAttribute(*attributeName*) scrollIntoView([showAtTop]) setAttribute(*attributeName, value*)	onBlur onClick onDblClick onDragStart onFocus onMouseDown onMouseMove onMouseOut onMouseOver onMouseUp

Continued

TABLE 9.2   DOM Object Reference (continued)

DOM Object	Properties	Methods	Event Handler
DIV	align id innerHTML innerText outerHTML outerText parentElement style tagName title	blur() click() focus() getAttribute(*attributeName*) insertAdjacentHTML(*where, string*) insertAdjacentText(*where, value*) removeAttribute(*attributeName*) scrollIntoView([showAtTop]) setAttribute(*attributeName, value*)	onBlur onChange onClick onDblClick onDragStart onFocus onMouseDown onMouseMove onMouseOut onMouseOver onMouseUp
document	activeElement alinkColor bgColor fgColor lastModified linkColor location parentWindow referrer title URL vlinkColor	clear() close() elementFromPoint(*x,y*) open() write() writeln()	onClick onDblClick onMouseDown onMouseMove onMouseOut onMouseOver onMouseUp
event	altKey button clientX clientY ctrlKey layerX layerY offsetX offsetY pageX pageY screenX screenY shiftKey type which x y		

Continued

TABLE 9.2   DOM Object Reference (continued)

DOM Object	Properties	Methods	Event Handler
FORM	action id innerHTML innerText length method name outerHTML outerText parentElement style tagName target title	click() getAttribute(*attributeName*) handleEvent() insertAdjacentHTML(*where*, *string*) insertAdjacentText(*where*, *value*) removeAttribute(*attributeName*) reset() scrollIntoView([showAtTop]) setAttribute(*attributeName*, *value*) submit()	onClick onDblClick onMouseDown onMouseMove onMouseOut onMouseOver onMouseUp onReset onSubmit
P	align id innerHTML innerText outerHTML outerText parentElement style tagName title	click() getAttribute(*attributeName*) insertAdjacentHTML(*where*, *string*) insertAdjacentText(*where*, *value*) removeAttribute(*attributeName*) scrollIntoView([showAtTop]) setAttribute(*attributeName*, *value*)	onClick onDblClick onDragStart onLoad onMouseDown onMouseMove onMouseOut onMouseOver onMouseUp
SPAN	id innerHTML innerText outerHTML outerText parentElement style tagName title	blur() click() focus() getAttribute(*attributeName*) insertAdjacentHTML(*where*, *string*) insertAdjacentText(*where*, *value*) removeAttribute(*attributeName*) scrollIntoView([showAtTop]) setAttribute(*attributeName*, *value*)	onBlur onClick onDblClick onDragStart onFocus onMouseDown onMouseMove onMouseOut onMouseOver onMouseUp onSelectStart
text	disabled form id maxlength name outerHTML	blur() click() focus() getAttribute(*attributeName*) insertAdjacentHTML(*where*, *string*) insertAdjacentText(*where*, *value*)	onBlur() onChange() onClick onDblClick onFocus() onMouseDown

Continued

TABLE 9.2   DOM Object Reference (continued)

DOM Object	Properties	Methods	Event Handler
	outerText	removeAttribute(*attributeName*)	onMouseMove
	parentElement	scrollIntoView([showAtTop])	onMouseOut
	readOnly	setAttribute(*attributeName*, *value*)	onMouseOver
	size	select()	onMouseUp
	style		onSelect
	tabIndex		
	tagName		
	title		
	type		
	value		

Changing a property setting is a matter of placing an appropriate event handler within the desired object to trigger the change. The event handler then activates a script that identifies the property through its DOM reference and then assigns it a new value. The following code sample illustrates this:

```
<!- ChangeColorAndText.htm ->
<html><head>
<script language="JavaScript">
function ChangeHeading()
{  if (document.all.MyFirstHeading.style.color == "blue")
    {  document.all.MyFirstHeading.style.color = "red";
       document.all.MyFirstHeading.innerText = "First
          Heading";
    }
    else
    {  document.all.MyFirstHeading.style.color = "blue";
       document.all.MyFirstHeading.innerText = "Second
          Heading";
    }
}
</script></head><body>
<h2 id="MyFirstHeading" style="color:blue"
onclick="ChangeHeading()">
Click Me </h2>
<body></body></html>
```

Here's how this works:

1. An onClick event handler attached to the `<h2>` tag captures mouse clicks when a user clicks on the content of the tag.

2. The event handler script calls a function named `ChangeHeading()`. Notice the tag `id` value, `MyFirstHeading`, is used to identify this object and to refer to it within the script.

3. The `ChangeHeading()` function does the following:
- Changes selected properties associated with the heading.
- Changes the content of the heading through the object's `innerText` property.
- Changes its color through the `color` property.

The script uses an `if . . .else` control structure to change the property settings back and forth.

The object's properties are changed by assigning them different values using JavaScript assignment statements. These properties are referenced through DOM path notation, using the `id` value to point to the heading object:

```
document.all.MyHeading.style.color = "red"
document.all.MyHeading.innerText = "New Heading"
```

Given HTML, CSS, and a DOM, change can't happen without a script. It's JavaScript that drives the style and content changes by manipulating the tags with their attached scripts.

QuickCheck Questions

8. What does DOM stand for?

9. The browser (navigator) object node is at the top most level of the DOM hierarchy. True or false?

10. Show the DOM hierarchy starting from the Navigator to the Field.

11. Suppose that you have a field in a form. Further, suppose that the form is being displayed in a frame. Show the DOM dotted notation syntax to refer to the field.

12. Consider the following paragraph in an HTML document.

```
<p id= "Para5"> This is the story of my life. </p>
```

How will you refer to this paragraph's text contents in a script?

JavaScript: The Event Connection

There are two kinds of scripts: those that execute when a page loads and those that execute in reaction to something a visitor has done. The latter lends an air of interactivity. This is what engages visitors and holds them to the page. In this chapter, we're concerned with using JavaScript to respond to user actions to make the Web page both dynamic and interactive. The relationships between a user's initiated event and its subsequent action on the document object is illustrated in Figure 9.5.

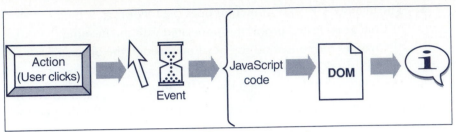

FIGURE 9.5   User's Initiated Event and Its Subsequent Actions

Understanding User Events

Referring to Figure 9.5, you see that changes to a Web page can be initiated by user actions or other events that take place after the page is loaded in the browser window. For example:

• The user points the mouse cursor to a block of text or to a graphic image appearing on the page.
• The user clicks the mouse button on top of the element.
• The user moves the mouse across the element.
• The user releases the mouse button while hovering over the element.
• A keystroke is detected.

In any case, the user-initiated event is a trigger to run a script that changes the layout, style, or content of the page.

Coding Event Handlers

There is another piece to the scripting puzzle called the *event handler*. All HTML tags are sensitive to particular events and provide event handlers to react to those events. The event handler connects an action in the browser window to a JavaScript, which in turn issues commands. Internet Explorer 6 can generate events from any element in the browser window. All you need to do is place the event handlers inside the HTML tags for which you want to capture events. Table 9.3 describes some common event handlers associated with mouse actions and their corresponding events.

In the following code example, you can see that the script employs four event handlers: onMouseOver, onMouseDown, onMouseUp, and onMouseOut.

```
<!- MouseEvents.htm ->
<html><body><form>
<input type="button" value="A Button"
onMouseOver="this.value='Mouse is over'"
onMouseDown="this.value='Mouse is down'"
onMouseUp="this.value='Mouse is up'"
onMouseOut="this.value='Mouse is out'">
</form></body></html>
```

TABLE 9.3 Mouse Action Event Handlers and Events

Event Handler	Event
onMouseOver	The user points to (moves the mouse over) a page element.
onMouseDown	The user presses the mouse button while positioned over a page element.
onClick	
onMouseUp	The mouse button is released while the cursor is positioned over a page element.
onDblClick	The mouse button is double-clicked while the cursor is positioned over a page element.
onMouseOut	The user moves the mouse off a page element.
onMouseMove	The user moves the mouse cursor across the screen.

Each event handler activates a script to change the text label (the `value` property) of the button. Event handlers are coded inside the tags to which they apply, that is, between the opening < and closing > symbols. In this example, the event handlers are coded on separate lines, although this is not required; it just makes them easier to read.

Coding Event Handler Scripts

There are two general methods for activating scripts within an event handler:

- `eventHandler = "statement [; statement]..."`
- `eventHandler = "functionName()"`

The name of the event handler is followed by an equal sign and either of two types of quoted strings. The event handler can execute one or more JavaScript statements, or commands, separated by semicolons; or the event handler can call a JavaScript function to perform the processing. The format used depends on the number and complexity of statements to be executed and on whether a generalized function exists to service the same event for multiple HTML tags. You will probably develop your own style of coding event handlers since there is no particular rule on when to use one or the other format. In our previous example (`MouseEvents.htm`), a single JavaScript statement was coded within each individual event handler; function calls were not used. The following code (`MultipleStatements1.htm`), though, demonstrates the call to a function containing multiple statements in response to a mouse click.

```
<!-MultipleStatements1.htm ->
<html><head>
```

```
<script language="Javascript">
function ChangeButton(ThisButton)
{
  ThisButton.value = "Changed Button"
  ThisButton.style.backgroundColor = "red"
  ThisButton.style.color = "white"
  ThisButton.style.fontFamily = "impact"
  ThisButton.style.fontSize = "14pt"
}
</script>
<head><body><form>
<input type="button" value="Original Button"
  onClick="ChangeButton(this)">
</form></body></html>
```

In this case, the function named `ChangeButton()` is called from within the onClick event handler. The function is passed a reference to the clicked button (`this`) and manipulates the button's properties through the internal variable `ThisButton`. Calling a function is a matter of convenience. We loaded five statements inside the function instead of coding them as separate statements within the event handler. However, the script works just the same if we code the statements inside the event handler as follows:

```
<!- MultipleStatements2.htm ->
<input type="button" value="Original Button"
onClick="this.value='Changed Button';
  this.style.backgroundColor='red';
  this.style.color='white';
  this.style.fontFamily='impact';
  this.style.fontSize='14pt' ">
```

QuickCheck Questions

13. What type of actions can trigger an event?
14. Name three types of event handlers.
15. How many ways can you activate scripts within an event handler?

Making It Dynamic

HTML elements that have been positioned as relative or absolute can be repositioned through scripting. Repositioning involves changing the element's left and top style settings. There are four properties that can be scripted to effect this change (see Table 9.4).

TABLE 9.4 Dynamic Positioning Properties

CSS and DOM Reference	Effects
`left:value` `object.style.left="value"`	Sets the left edge of the element relative to its container element; `value` is a string measurement unit; e.g., `left="100px"`
`top:value` `object.style.top="value"`	Sets the top edge of the element relative to its container element; `value` is a string measurement unit; e.g., `top="100px"`
`object.style.pixelLeft=value`	Sets the left edge of the element relative to its container element; `value` is numeric for use in calculations
`object.style.pixelTop=value`	Sets the top edge of the element relative to its container element; `value` is numeric for use in calculations

The `left` and `top` properties provide replacement values for those initially coded in a stylesheet. The following image, for example, is initially positioned on the page with a style specification declaring a left location of 50 pixels relative to the container document:

```
<img src="Somepicture.gif" style="position:relative;
   left:50px"
onMouseOver="this.style.cursor='hand'"
onClick="this.style.left='300'">
```

When the icon is clicked, it is moved to the right by resetting the `left` property from 50 pixels to 300 pixels. This change takes place through an onClick event handler that dynamically changes this property setting.

The `left` and `top` properties are treated as string values. The stored value is in the form `"50px"`. Thus, this pair of property settings can only be used when replacing a current positional value with a different string value. You cannot use `left` or `top` if you need to perform calculations to derive these settings.

Where you need to calculate a positional setting, the `pixelLeft` and `pixelTop` properties are provided. These two properties treat positions as numbers rather than as strings—as the numeric value `50` rather than the string value `"50px"`. Below is the image scripted to change its left setting, this time incrementally in response to mouseover events, moving 50 pixels to the right until it reaches the right edge of the page.

```
<!- MovingImage.htm ->
<html><head>
<script>
function MoveImage(TheImage)
{    if (TheImage.style.pixelLeft < 400)
     {   TheImage.style.pixelLeft += 50 }
}
</script></head><body>
<img src="McGrawHillCommunity2.jpg" style="position:
  relative; left:10px"
onMouseOver="this.style.cursor='hand'; MoveImage(this)">
</body></head>
```

The onMouseOver event handler in the <img> tag passes a self-reference to the MoveImage() function, where it is received as argument TheImage. As long as the left edge of the image is less than 400 (pixels) from the left edge of the page, 50 (pixels) is added to the current setting for the left edge of the image. The pixelLeft property is used in the calculation since it represents the numeric equivalent (50) of the string value ("50px") of the setting and can be used to calculate (not just replace) the property value.

There are many other ways to apply JavaScript codes to manipulate images and other objects. Here are some sample codes to illustrate alternative techniques to perform these types of tasks.

Change Text Position

```
<!- ChangeTextPosition.htm ->
<html><head>
<script type="text/javascript">
function moveleft()
{    header.style.position="absolute"
   header.style.left="0"
}
function moveback()
{    header.style.position="relative"
}
</script></head>
<body><h1 id="header" onMouseOver="moveleft()"
  onMouseOut="moveback()">
Mouse over this text</h1>
</body></html>
```

Change Image Position

```
<!- ChangeImagePosition.htm ->
<html><head>
```

```
<script type="text/javascript">
function moveleft()
{    image.style.position="absolute"
     image.style.left="0"
}
function moveback()
{    image.style.position="relative"
}
</script></head><body>
<img id="image" src="McGrawHillCommunity2.jpg"
    onMouseOver="moveleft()"
onMouseOut="moveback()" width="100" height="80" />
</body></html>
```

Moving an Image

```
<!- MovingImage.htm ->
<html><head>
<script>
function MoveImage(TheImage)
{      if (TheImage.style.pixelLeft < 400)
    {    TheImage.style.pixelLeft += 50 }
}
</script></head><body>
<img src="McGrawHillCommunity2.jpg" style="position:
    relative; left:10px"
onMouseOver="this.style.cursor='hand'; MoveImage(this)">
</body></head>
```

QuickCheck Questions

16. Suppose that you want to change the mouse pointer to a hard icon when the user brings the mouse over an image. Show the necessary code for the `<img>` tag. Assume that the image is saved in a file named "anImage.jpg".

17. On the click event of an image, we want to adjust its width to 200 pixels. Show the `<img>` tag that will accomplish this.

18. HTML elements that have been positioned as relative or absolute can be repositioned through scripting. True or False?

Summary

HTML pages are usually static, which means that an HTML page does not provide interactions with the user, and its contents does not change with time. Nevertheless, we can use four related technologies to make an HTML page dynamic. These technologies are Cascading Style Sheets, Document Object Model, scripting languages (like JavaScript or VbScript), and browsers that have implemented these technologies. We can combine these technologies in an HTML page to make it a Dynamic HTML (DHTML) page. In a dynamic HTML page, we can show, hide, move, resize, or change the contents of HTML elements dynamically.

In this chapter, we have shown how to use CSS and JavaScript event handlers to develop DHTML pages that are responsive to certain events. An event is usually triggered by an action taken by the user such as a mouse click, or it may be triggered by the system when the browser loads a document. The CSS technology provides us with the capability to position an HTML element in a desired location. Thus, we can use a JavaScript event handler to change the position of an HTML element.

The <div> tag has a CSS property named "visibility." Its value can be set to "visible" or "hidden." Like most other CSS properties of HTML elements, we can set the visibility property of a <div> tag to show or hide its contents. This is accomplished through JavaScript codes. We have presented a number of examples on how to move and resize various elements. Using the techniques illustrated in these examples, you will be able to provide special visual effects to your DHTML pages. A comprehensive list of DOM objects, properties, methods, and event handlers is tabulated in Table 9.2. When you venture into developing your own DHTML pages, you will find this table useful.

Key Terms

absolute	event handler	positioning
attribute	ID	property
Document Object Model (DOM)	method	relative
element	object	

Review Questions

1. What is Dynamic HTML?
2. What is the purpose of a Document Object Model?
3. What is at the top level of the Document Object Model?
4. What does it mean to reference an object?
5. What HTML object supports the `name` attribute?

1. All HTML objects support the `name` attribute.
2. The `ID` value only works with the FORM object.
3. The `<DIV>` tag is the most common HTML tag.
4. onMouseOut is used to signal that the mouse pointer had been moved out of the browser window.
5. You must code event handlers on separate lines within a script.

1. Write a simple script to change the layer of an element.
2. Write a simple script to position an element using the `position:relative` style setting.
3. Write a simple script to position an element using the `position:absolute` style setting.
4. Write a simple script to position an element using the onMouseMove event handler.
5. Write a simple script to position an element using the onMouseOver event handler.

TABLE 8.3 VBScript Statements, Functions, and Operators (continued)

	Type	Use	Example
<=	Operator	Less than or equal to comparison	If expression1 <= expression2 Then
Mod	Operator	Modulus arithmetic; returns only the remainder of a division of two numbers	result = expression1 Mod expression2
*	Operator	Multiplication	result = expression1 * expression2
-	Operator	Subtraction	result = expression1 - expression2
Or	Operator	Logical disjunction	If expression1 Or expression2 Then
&	Operator	Concatenation of two string values	result = string1 & string2
Xor	Operator	Logical exclusion	If expression1 Xor expression2 Then
Options			
Option	Statement	Forces a compile-time error if an explicitly undeclared variable is found	Option Explicit
Program Flow			
Call	Statement	Passes execution to a subroutine or event handler; also can be used to replicate the actions of the user	[Call] myroutine() [Call] onbutton_click()
Do	Statement	Repeats code while a condition is met or until a condition is met	Do While condition ... Loop Do ... Loop Until condition Do ... Loop While condition ...

Beginning Active Server Pages

OBJECTIVES

1. To get familiar with the ASP environment and ASP syntax.
2. To use Active Server Page objects for Web applications.
3. To collect information in forms.
4. To work with cookies.
5. To learn how to set up server-side include files.

INTRODUCTION

According to Microsoft's Web site, "Active Server Pages is an open, compile-free application environment in which you can combine HTML, scripts, and reusable ActiveX server components to create dynamic and powerful Web-based business solutions." The translation: Microsoft's Active Server Pages (ASP) technology is a server-side scripting environment designed for use in creating server-side script to automatically perform difficult or repetitious Web management tasks on dynamic Web pages.

Using only a standard text editor such as Notepad, you can write powerful Active Server scripts to

- Edit, change, or add content to a Web page on the fly.
- Customize a Web page to make it more useful for individual users.
- Respond to user queries or data submitted through HTML forms.
- Access any data or databases and return the results to a browser.

Since ASP scripts are server-side scripts that run exclusively on the Web server, they modify Web pages before they are delivered to the browser. You can think of server-side scripts as affecting how the Web server "assembles" a Web page before it's sent to the browser. Understanding and using Active Server Pages builds on everything you've learned to this point in this book; from the World

Wide Web, to the basics of building Web pages, to scripting language like JavaScript and VBScript. An ASP file is simply an HTML file that can contain text, HTML, XML, and scripts. The core of an ASP file is the script.

While a script is its core, ASP uses HTML to display information on a Web browser. An Active Server Page differs from an HTML page in that when a browser requests an ASP page, it is the Web server that processes the request and returns the results to the Web browser as plain HTML. Here's how it works. An ASP file can contain any combination of HTML, script, or commands. The script can assign values to variables, request information from the server, or combine any set of commands into procedures. It works like this:

1. A browser requests an ASP file from your Web server.

2. The **Internet Information Server** passes the request to the ASP engine.

3. The ASP engine reads the ASP file, line by line, and executes any commands in the file.

4. Finally, the ASP file is returned to the browser as plain HTML, which is displayed on the page.

To run ASP, you need Microsoft's Internet Information Server, which runs under Windows NT 4 and Windows 2000, or the **Personal Web Server (PWS)**, which is a scaled-down version of IIS that can run on Windows 95 or Windows 98. Mix up some HTML and/or XML with a little VBScript or JavaScript and attach the ASP file extension to the file and you've got an Active Server Page.

Before You Begin . . .

An ASP page is a server-side application. When a user requests an ASP page, the page is processed at the server side before it is sent to the client. That means, unlike HTML pages, you cannot view Active Server Pages without running a Web server. To test your own pages, you should save your pages in a directory mapped as a virtual directory and then use your Web browser to view the page. A virtual directory is nothing but an "alias" of a physical directory.

We typically save all related pages and other resources for an application in a given virtual directory. For example, you may create a virtual directory named "TermProject". This virtual directory may actually point to a physical directory like `d:\MyASP\MyProject`. In this case, you should save all of your term project–related pages in this folder. You also may create subfolders like `d:\MyASP\MyProject\Images` and save all relevant images in this folder. Before you begin developing and testing your own ASP pages, you must create a virtual directory using the Virtual Directory Creation wizard. In Appendix A, we have provided a step-by-step procedure on how to create a virtual directory.

A virtual directory is actually a logical name given to a particular physical folder where you save your Web files. Suppose that you have saved a file named `Welcome.asp` in the `d:\MyASP\MyProject` folder. Also suppose that you have created a virtual directory named `MyWeb` that points to the `d:\MyAsp\MyProject` folder. To test an ASP file named `Welcome.asp`, you should first save it in the `d:\MyAsp\MyProject` folder and then open this file in Internet Explorer using http://Your_Server_Name/MyWeb/Welcome.asp or http://localhost/MyWeb/Welcome.asp in the URL.

Speaking the Language of ASP

Active Server Page (ASP) technology is language-independent. VBScript® and JScript scripting languages are supported right out of the box. However, you can use any scripting language for which the appropriate scripting engine is installed on your Web server. A **scripting engine** is a program that processes commands written in a particular language. In fact, several scripting languages can be used within a single .asp file. In addition, because scripts are read and processed on the server-side, the browser that requests the .asp file does not need to support scripting.

VBScript is the default scripting language for ASP, so if you omit the language directive, the server simply assumes it's VBScript. You can set the **primary scripting language** on a page-by-page basis, or for all pages in an ASP application. You also can use JavaScript as the scripting language for a particular page by inserting it into the language directive at the top of the page:

```
<%@ language="javascript"%>
```

Using VBScript on the server in an ASP page isn't very different from using it in applications or on ordinary Web pages. Nearly all of the VBScript commands are available for use on the server. VBScript commands that interact with the user, however, are not available. For example, imagine a command that opens a dialog box on the server. No one is around to dismiss it, and the system can do nothing until someone dismisses it!

If you choose to use JavaScript, just remember that, unlike VBScript, JavaScript is case-sensitive, requiring you to write ASP code with uppercase letters and lowercase letters as dictated by the language's syntax. Whatever scripting language you use, you can simply enclose script statements in special delimiters for ASP. The starting delimiter is `<%` and the closing delimiter is `%>`.

QuickCheck Questions

1. What is the default scripting language for ASP?
2. Can you use other scripting languages to create ASP files?
3. Does the browser see ASP code during processing?

ASP Syntax

An ASP file normally contains HTML tags, just like an HTML file. One way to think about ASP pages is that they are really just HTML pages with extra stuff added. You can develop your basic pages the way you always have—as Web pages—and add the appropriate scripting.

However, it's the scripts that put the "Active" in the page. It couldn't be easier to convert an existing HTML page to an ASP page—just change the extension from .htm/.html to .asp. Of course, it won't be a meaningful ASP page until you add some scripting commands. The .asp filename extension enables IIS to parse and execute the scripts in your files.

You may recall from the earlier chapters on scripting languages that the syntax for a script uses the delimiters <% and %>. These scripts, referred to as **server-side scripts,** are executed on the Web server and can contain any expressions, statements, procedures, or operators valid for the scripting language used. After executing the scripts, the server sends the results to clients or browsers. As such, the browser never sees the actual ASP source code. The following example shows the syntax for a simple Active Server Page:

```
<!– MyFirstAsp.asp –>
<%@ Language=VBScript %>
<% Response.Buffer = True %>
<html><head><title>Welcome to My First ASP Page</title>
</head><body><h2>Welcome</h2>
<h2><% Response.Write ("This is My First ASP Page")
  %></h2>
<h3>The time is now<%= Now %></h3>
</body></html>
```

You should recognize the first line as the language directive, which specifies the scripting language being used. The delimiters, <% . . . %>, tell the Web server that it must run the enclosed script code before the server transmits to the browser. This script, albeit a simple example, uses two **ASP objects.** We'll look at these objects and others in later sections of this chapter. For now we will simply describe their function as used here.

The next line, `<% Response.Buffer = True %>`, tells the Web server to create the entire Web page in memory before sending it to the client. By default, a Web page is sent to the browser line by line as it is generated. Finally, the `<% Response.Write %>` sends the text to the browser.

ASP Variables

A variable is a variable is a variable. In typical programming constructs, it's used to store information, and so it is in ASP. Two caveats are

1. If the variable is declared outside a procedure, it can be changed by any script in the ASP file.

2. If the variable is declared inside a procedure, it is created and destroyed every time the procedure is executed.

To declare variables accessible to more than one ASP file, declare them as session variables or application variables. Session variables are used to store information about a single user and are available to all pages in one application, where an application is a collection of ASP pages. For example, you would store information like a user' name, id, and preferences in session variables. Application variables are also available to all pages in one application. Application variables are used to store information about *all* users in a specific application.

ASP Procedures

ASP source code can contain procedures and functions with a good deal of flexibility. For example, you can use both JavaScript and VBScript functions (or procedures) in the same ASP page. However, in this case, you need to use the `<script language= "language" runat="server">` statement before you insert the necessary code. The following ASP page (`VbMultiplyTwo Numbers.asp`) defaults to VBScript:

```
<!- VbMultiplyTwoNumbers.asp ->
<html><head>
<%
Sub vbproc(num1,num2)
  Dim result
  result = num1 * num2
  Response.Write(result)
End sub
%>
</head><body>
```

```
<p>3 multiplied by 4 is: <%call vbproc(3,4)%></p>
</body></html>
```

Now, suppose that we would like to add two numbers using a JavaScript function. The following code (`JSAddTwoNumbers.asp`) can be used to accomplish this task:

```
<!- JSAddTwoNumbers.asp->
<html><head>
<script language="JavaScript" runat="server">
function jsproc(num1,num2)
{ var sum;
  sum = num1 + num2;
  Response.Write(sum);
}
</script>
</head><body>
<p>Sum of 3 and 4 is: <% call jsproc(3,4) %></p>
</body></html>
```

Finally, suppose that you would like to use a VBScript procedure and a JavaScript function in the same ASP document. In this case, simply use the `language` attribute of the `<script>` tag to specify the language used in the code. In the following code (`VbAndJavaScriptInOneASP.asp`), we have used a JavaScript function and a VBScript procedure to display the sum and product of two numbers:

```
<!- VbAndJavaScriptInOneASP.asp->
<html><head>
<script language="JavaScript" runat="server">
function jsproc(num1,num2)
{ var sum;
  sum = num1 + num2;
  Response.Write(sum);
}
</script>
<script language="VBScript" runat="server">
Sub vbproc(num1,num2)
  Response.Write(num1*num2)
End sub
</script></head><body>
Using JavaScript Function: 3 + 4 = <%call jsproc(3,4)%>
  <br/>
Using VBScript Sub: 3 * 4 = <% vbProc 3,4 %><br/>
</body></html>
```

When the `VbAndJavaScriptInOneASP.asp` page is opened using Internet Explorer, the system will display a screen as shown in Figure 10.1.

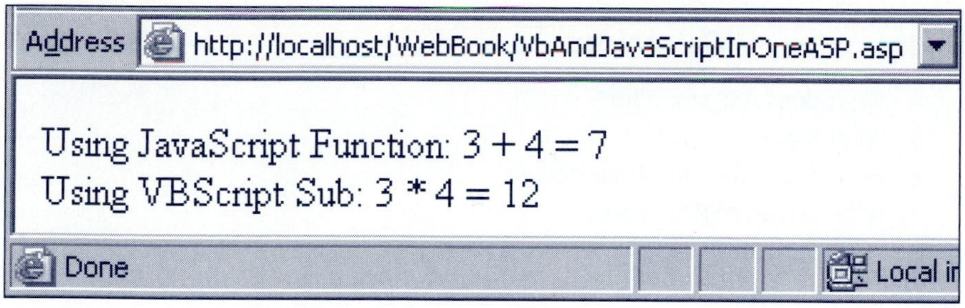

```
Address  http://localhost/WebBook/VbAndJavaScriptInOneASP.asp  ▼

Using JavaScript Function: 3 + 4 = 7
Using VBScript Sub: 3 * 4 = 12

  Done                                              Local in
```

FIGURE 10.1   Using JavaSript and VBScript Functions in One ASP Page

ASP Objects

Most of the functionality you can build into an ASP page comes from objects on the server. These objects enable your pages to communicate effectively with the server, the application, the current session, and the user.

An object in ASP is a software representation of a real-word object. A real-word object has various characteristics: what properties it has, what it can do, and how we can interact with it. In ASP, an object can have collections, properties, methods, and events. The Request and Response objects contain **collections** (bits of information that are accessed in the same way). Objects use methods to do some type of procedure (if you know any object-oriented programming language, you already know what a method is) and properties to store any of the object's attributes (such as color, font, or size).

Use the built-in objects just like any other object in a script—by accessing properties, methods, and events. For example, the general format for using the `Request` object looks like this:

```
Request[.Collection](variable)
```

In the following sections, we'll explore five of the built-in ASP objects commonly used for Web application development to handle chores such as

- Alerting users about relocated Web content by redirecting them using the ASP `Redirect` method to automatically redirect or route a browser to another Web page or Web site.
- Monitoring user preferences and behavior by using ASP to place **cookies,** small text files stored on the user's browser by the server, to determine which part of the Web site a user is looking at and how long that user lingers on certain Web pages.
- Obtaining user feedback by using the ASP Form and QueryString collections to gather user input from an HTML form. These collections simplify the creation of Web sites that process user feedback, such as a departmental bulletin board, an online survey, or a data retrieval system.

Request Object

When a browser asks for a page from a server, it is called a request. The ASP **Request object** is used to get information from the user. The `Request` object contains all of the data sent to the Web server when a browser makes a request. You can use the `Request` object to parse encoded URLs, access information from a form, and read cookies. We have tabulated various ASP collections, properties, and methods in Table 10.1.

TABLE 10.1   ASP Collections, Properties, and Methods

Collection, Property, or Method	Description
Collections	
ClientCertificate	Contains all the field values stored in the client certificate
Cookies	Contains all the cookie values sent in an HTTP request
Form	Contains all the form (input) values from a form that uses the `post` method
QueryString	Contains all the variable values in an HTTP query string
ServerVariables	Contains all the server variable values
Properties	
TotalBytes	Returns the total number of bytes the client sent in the body of the request
Methods	
BinaryRead	Retrieves the data sent to the server from the client as part of a `post` request and stores it in a safe array

User Input and Subsequent Processing

Typically, we include various data entry controls (like textboxes, check boxes, radio buttons, and many others) in an HTML form. We also provide a Submit button. The users are expected to enter the relevant data and click the Submit button. In this context, two attributes of the `<form>` tag are of major importance. These attributes are **method** and **action**. We can use the `method` attribute to specify exactly how the system will send the user-inputted data to the server. In this case, we have two alternatives: **get** and **post**. If we specify `method = "get"`, the data are submitted via the URL. On the other hand, if we specify `method= "post"`, the data are submitted inside the body section of an HTTP package.

Now let us discuss the `action` attribute of the `<form>` tag. When the user clicks the Submit button, the `action` attribute is used to request a desired document from the server. Consider the following `<form>` declaration:

```
<form name="frmCollectName" method="get" action=
   "Welcome.asp">
```

When the user enters data in the above form and clicks the Submit button, the browser will perform two important tasks:

1. It will request the document named `Welcome.asp` from the server.

2. It will pass the form's data (usually entered by the user) to the server via the URL.

Perhaps an example would be helpful to understand these concepts. Let us consider the `CollectName.htm` document as shown below:

```
<!- CollectName.htm ->
<html><head></head><body>
<form method="get" action="Welcome.asp">
First Name: <input type="text" name="txtName"><br/><br/>
<input type="submit" value="Welcome Me">
</form></html>
```

When you open the `CollectName.htm` file in a browser, it will display a textbox and a button as shown in Figure 10.2.

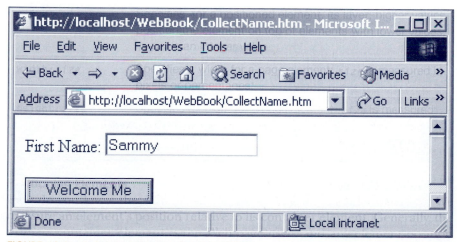

FIGURE 10.2   Collecting the Name of the User

If you enter your name in the textbox and click the Welcome Me button, your browser will construct the appropriate URL for the `Welcome.asp` page. It also will append the URL with your name (i.e., the content of the textbox named `txtName`). Finally, it will send the augmented URL to the server. The ASP engine at the server side will package the submitted data in the `Request` object and process the `Welcome.asp` to produce an output. These concepts will become more clear once you see the code for the `Welcome.asp` as shown below.

```
<!- Welcome.asp ->
<html><head></head>
<body>
Welcome
<%
  Response.Write(Request.QueryString("txtName"))
%>
</body></html>
```

Now let us refer back to Figure 10.2. Recall that once you enter your name in the textbox and click the Welcome Me button, your browser will request the `Welcome.asp` document from the server and pass the value of `txtName` as data. The server will locate the requested document and pass it to the ASP engine for processing. Essentially, the ASP engine will copy all nonscript codes from the ASP document to the `Response` object. However, when it comes to a sever-side script, it will fire the VBScript (or JavaScript) interpreter to execute the code. In the `Welcome.asp`, we have asked the ASP engine to place the passed value of `txtName` on the `Response` object using the `Response.Write(Request.QueryString("txtName"))` statement. Finally, the `Response` object will be sent to the client by the server. The result of this process is shown in Figure 10.3. Observe the URL in this figure carefully. The entire URL of http://localhost/WebBook/Welcome.asp?txtName=Sammy was actually constructed by the browser.

FIGURE 10.3   Output of `Welcome.asp`

Obviously, there are a number of other issues that need to be discussed before you understand the entire process. Let us proceed!

Request.Form **Collection**

User input can be retrieved in two ways: with Request.QueryString or Request.Form. You have seen an example of Request.QueryString in the Welcome.asp example. We will elaborate on it further in a later section. Let us focus on the Request.Form instead. The Request.Form collection is used to collect values in a form that are submitted via method="post". Information sent from a form with the post method is invisible to others and has no limits on the amount of information to send. To make it clear, let us revise the <form> tag in the CollectName.htm so that the browser sends the data via the post method. The revised code, named RevisedCollectName.htm, is shown below:

```
<!- RevisedCollectName.htm ->
<html><head></head><body>
<form method="post" action="RevisedWelcome.asp">
  First Name: <input type="text" name="txtName">
    <br/><br/>
<input type="submit" value="Welcome Me">
</form></html>
```

Observe that we have used method="post" in this document. We also have changed the value of the action attribute to RevisedWelcome.asp. In this particular case, when the user clicks on the Submit button, the browser will pass the form's data via the post method and will request the Revised Welcome.asp from the server. The result of this process will be displayed on the browser as shown in Figure 10.4.

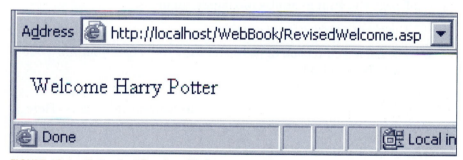

FIGURE 10.4   Output of RevisedWelcome.asp

When a client sends a request and sets the method attribute to post, the data sent with the form is stored in the Form collection of the Request object. To retrieve Form data sent by the post method, you use the Form collection of the Request object. For example, if you have created a form with two textboxes named txtFirstName and txtLastName, you can retrieve the data in this way:

```
<%=Request.Form ("txtFirstName")%>
<%=Request.Form ("txtLastName")%>
```

Using the `Request.QueryString` Collection

Another way to send information to the Web server is to use `QueryString`. In the case of the `get` method, `QueryString` appears in the URL. For example:

```
http://somepath/demo.asp?username=myid&email=
    myemail@server.com
```

Notice that the syntax of the `QueryString` uses a *name=value* pair separated by the `&`. In this example, the browser is sending a `QueryString` with two variables named `username` and `email` to the server. You can retrieve the contents of the `QueryString`s using the following codes:

```
<%= Request.QueryString ("username") %>
<%= Request.QueryString ("email") %>
```

The `Request.QueryString` command is used to collect values in a form with `method="get"`. Information sent from a form with the `get` method is visible to everyone (it will be displayed in the browser's address bar) and has limits on the amount of information to send. You have already seen the use of `method="get"` and `Request.QueryString` in `CollectName.htm` and `Welcome.asp`. Observe the browser-generated URL in Figure 10.3 to see a `QueryString` in action.

`ServerVariables` Collection

Another useful `Request` object collection is the `ServerVariables` collection. This collection includes information about many aspects of the server environment. It also contains information about the client's browser. Suppose that in an ASP page you want to display two important items:

1. The client's browser's environment.

2. The name and version of the server software (where your ASP code would be running).

You may use `Request.ServerVariables("HTTP_USER_AGENT")` and `Request.ServerVariables("SERVER_SOFTWARE")` to accomplish these tasks. Here is an example:

```
<!- ServerVariable1.asp ->
<html><head></head><body>
<b>The requestor's browser environment is:
<%
   Dim clientsEnv
   clientsEnv= Request.ServerVariables("HTTP_USER_AGENT")
   Response.Write(clientsEnv)
   Response.Write("<br/>")
%><br/>
The server software is
<% Dim serverEnv
   serverEnv=Request.ServerVariables("SERVER_SOFTWARE")
```

```
        Response.Write(serverEnv)
    %>
    </body></html>
```

The output of the `ServerVariable1.asp` code is shown in Figure 10.5.

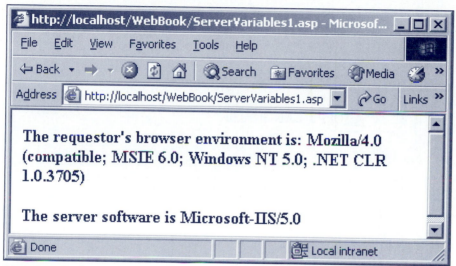

FIGURE 10.5 Extracting Client's and Server's Environments Using `Request.Server Variables`

Obviously, you would want to know the names of all of the members of the `ServerVariables` collection. Well, you do not have to search the Internet for those. You may simply run the following ASP page, named `Server Variables2.asp`, to get a list of all of these members:

```
    <!- ServerVariables2.asp ->
    <html><body><p>
    All possible server variables:</p>
    <%
      For Each Item in Request.ServerVariables
        Response.Write(Item & "<br />")
      Next
    %>
    </body></html>
```

In the `ServerVariables2.asp` code, as shown above, we have used a `For Each` construct to iterate through each member of the `ServerVariables` collection. A truncated version of the output of this program is shown in Figure 10.6.

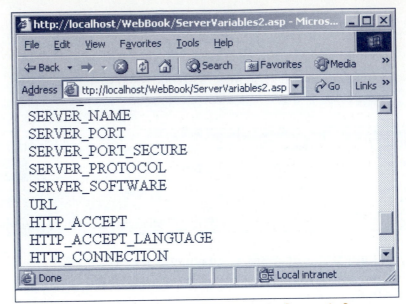

FIGURE 10.6   Displaying the List of Members in the `Request.Server Variables` Collection

Response Object

The ASP **Response object** is used to send output to the user from the server. When a user clicks a hyperlink or types an HTTP address into the Web browser, the browser sends a request to the Web server. The Web server processes the request and the server `Response` object transmits a response back to the browser. Table 10.2 lists the `Response` object's collections, properties, and methods.

`Response.Write` Method

The `Response.Write` method is used for writing information in the format that the browser understands so that it can be displayed by a Web browser. This information can be the contents of a server-side variable, the return value of a function, or a string constant inside double quotes.

```
<% Response.Write "This is a string of text" %>
```

In this example, the text `"This is a string of text"` will be displayed.

There is a shortcut version of the `Write` method using the `<%= . . . %>` syntax. The following two lines do exactly the same thing:

```
<%= Now %>
<% Response.Write Now %>
```

You also may include text formatting HTML codes in the `Write` method's argument. The example following Table 10.2 illustrates such techniques.

TABLE 10.2 Response **Object's Collections, Properties, and Methods**

Collection, Property, or Method	Description
Collections	
Cookies	Sets a cookie value; if the cookie does not exist, it will be created and take the value that is specified
Properties	
Buffer	Specifies whether to buffer the page output or not
CacheControl	Sets whether a proxy server can cache the output generated by ASP or not
Charset	Appends the name of a character set to the content-type header in the Response object
ContentType	Sets the HTTP content type for the Response object
Expires	Sets how long (in minutes) a page will be cached on a browser before it expires
ExpiresAbsolute	Sets a date and time when a page cached on a browser will expire
IsClientConnected	Indicates if the client has disconnected from the server
Pics	Appends a value to the PICS label response header
Status	Specifies the value of the status line returned by the server
Methods	
AddHeader	Adds a new HTTP header and a value to the HTTP response
AppendToLog	Adds a string to the end of the server log entry
BinaryWrite	Writes data directly to the output without any character conversion
Clear	Clears any buffered HTML output
End	Stops processing a script and returns the current result
Flush	Sends buffered HTML output immediately
Redirect	Redirects the user to a different URL
Write	Writes a specified string to the output

```
<!- FormattingText.asp ->
<html><body>
<%
  Response.Write("<h2>You can use HTML tags to format the
    text!</h2>")
  Response.Write("<p style='color:#0000ff'>This text is
    styled with the style attribute!</p>")
```

```
%>
</body></html>
```

Response.IsCientConnected Method

The `Response.IsClientConnected` method is useful when you want to detect if the client is still logged on. Here is an example of how to use this method:

```
<!- IsClientConnected.asp ->
<html><body>
Is client connected?
<%
   If Response.IsClientConnected=True Then
      Response.Write("Yes, the user is still connected!")
   Else
      Response.Write("Sorry, the user is not connected!")
   End If
%>
</body></html>
```

Response.Redirect Method

Often, we need to redirect the user from one ASP page to some other page. In these cases, the `Response.Redirect` method becomes handy. The following code illustrates the use of `Response.Redirect`:

```
<!- RedirectUser.asp ->
<html><head></head><body>
<%
If Request.Form("radSelect")<>"" Then
      Response.Redirect(Request.Form("radSelect"))
End If
%>
<form action="RedirectUser.asp" method="post">
<input type="radio" name="radSelect" value=
   "FormattingText.asp">
<b>Formatting Text<b><br/>
<input type="radio" name="radSelect" value=
   "ServerVariables1.asp">
<b>Client's and Server's Environments<b><br/><br/>
<input type="submit" value="Go!">
</form></body></html>
```

Response.Buffer Property

The `Buffer` property specifies whether the server output is stored in a buffer until the processing is complete. When the output is buffered, the server will hold back the response to the browser until all of the server scripts have been processed. The syntax for not buffering output is

```
<% Response.Buffer = False %>
```

In the example below, there will be no output sent to the browser before the loop is finished. If the buffer was set to False, then it would write a line to the browser every time it went through the loop.

```
For i=1 to 100
   Response.Write (i & "<br>")
Next
%>
```

The statement to set the Buffer property should be at the top of all pages that you want buffered. The Buffer property is set to True by default. If a page has a lot of processing to do, buffering the information may cause a period of inactivity on the client side. If the user hits the browser's Refresh button, the whole process is started again.

Controlling the Buffer If you decide to buffer your output, you do not necessarily have to wait to send some results until the buffer is full. At any instance of the code execution, you may decide to flush the buffer and send its contents to the client. In the following example, the system will flush the buffer when the value of intI is a multiple of 100:

```
<!- FlushBuffer.asp ->
<% Response.Buffer=True %>
<html><head></head><body>
<h2> Example of Response.Flush </h2>
<%
  Dim intI, intSum
  intI=1
  intSum=0
  For intI = 1 To 1000
    intSum = intI + intSum
    If intI Mod 100 = 0 Then
       Response.Write("<br/><b>Flushing</b><br/>")
       Response.Flush
    End If
    Response.Write("<br/> So far the sum is " & intSum)
  Next
  Response.Write("<br/> Final Total is " & intSum)
%>
<br/>We are done</body></html>
```

ASP Cookies

Everyone that surfs the Web has encountered a "cookie." A *cookie* is a small file that the Web server embeds or hides, depending on your point of view, on the user's computer usually to identify a user. Each time the same computer requests a page with a browser, it will send the cookie too. With ASP, you can both create and retrieve cookie values using the Response.Cookies collection.

You can use cookies, as well as session and application variables, to store and retrieve information. IIS makes cookie values available to you with the `Request` object's `Cookies` collection. You can set cookie values with the `Response` object.

Creating a Cookie

In order to be able to use a cookie, you must first set the cookie. You can use the **Response.Cookies** method to write the cookie. Because IIS sends all header information before the document content, you must set cookies before the `<html>` tag. Thus, the `Response.Cookies` statement must appear *before* the `<html>` tag. In the example below, we will create a cookie named `"firstname"` and assign the value `"Valda"` to it:

```
<%
   Response.Cookies("firstname")="Valda"
%>
```

It is also possible to assign properties to a cookie, like setting a date when the cookie should expire:

```
<%
   Response.Cookies("firstname")="Valda"
   Response.Cookies("firstname").Expires=#January 6,2003#
%>
```

Retrieving Cookie Values

The **Request.Cookies** command is used to retrieve a cookie value. In the example below, we retrieve the value of the cookie named `"firstname"` and display it on a page:

```
<%
   fname=Request.Cookies("firstname")
   Response.Write("Firstname=" & fname)
%>
```

A Simple Cookie Example

Let us illustrate the use of cookies with a simple example. Suppose that we want to write a cookie named `HobbyCookie` in the client computer's disk. Our objective is to retrieve and use this information when the user requests certain pages from our site in the future. We will use three Web pages in this illustration:

1. First, we will collect the hobby information from the user via an HTML form (`CollectHobby.htm`). The user will select a hobby from a list of hobbies and will click the Submit button. In the

`<form>` tag, we will use `action= "WriteHobbyCookie.asp"` so that the browser requests the `WriteHobbyCookie.asp` upon submission of the form. The code shown in `CollectHobby.htm` will accomplish these tasks. The browser will display this page as shown in Figure 10.7.

```
<!- CollectHobby.htm ->
<html><head></head><body>
<form action="WriteHobbyCookie.asp" method="post">
<h2>Please select a hobby</h2>
<input type="radio" name="radHobby" value="Fishing">
  <b>Fishing<br/>
<input type="radio" name="radHobby" value="Gardening">
  <b>Gardening<b/><br/><br/>
<input type="submit" value="Submit">
</form></body></html>
```

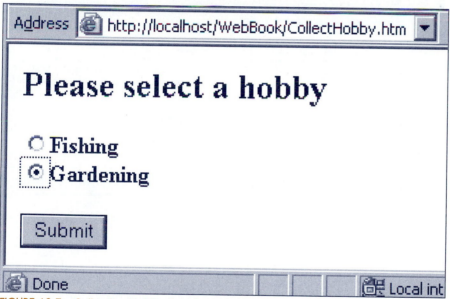

FIGURE 10.7   Collecting Hobby Data from the User

2.   Second, we will set the `HobbyCookie` in the `WriteHobbyCookie.asp` code. The output of this ASP page is shown in Figure 10.8.

```
<!- WriteHobbyCookie.asp ->
<%
  Dim strHobby
  Dim dteExpireDate
  strHobby= Request.Form("radHobby")
```

```
dteExpireDate=DateAdd("d", 30, Now) ' adds 30 days
  ' You can use DateAdd("n", 10, Now) to add
    10 minutes,
  ' or use DateAdd("m",1,Now) to add 1 month
' Write the cookie and set its expiration date
Response.Cookies("HobbyCookie")=strHobby
Response.Cookies("HobbyCookie").Expires =
  dteExpireDate
%>
<html><head></head><body><h2>
Thank you for providing the information</h2>
</body></html>
```

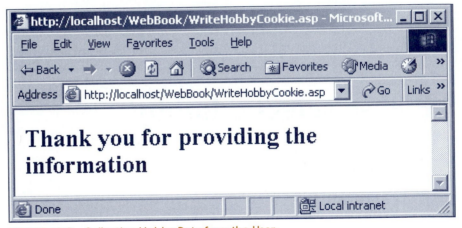

FIGURE 10.8   Collecting Hobby Data from the User

3. Third, we will develop a page named `Products.asp`, where we will retrieve the `HobbyCookie` and use its value to redirect the user to other appropriate pages. Figure 10.9 shows the output of the `Gardening.htm` page that was being redirected from the `Products.asp` page. *Note:* For illustration purposes, we kept the examples simple. In reality, the `Products.asp` page should first check if the cookie is available. If it is not available, it should redirect the user to `CollectHobby.htm`.

```
<!- Products.asp ->
<html><head></head><body>
<% Dim strHobby
```

```
    strHobby = Request.Cookies("HobbyCookie") ' Retrieve
      the cookie
    ' Redirect the user to appropriate page
    Select Case strHobby
      Case "Fishing"
        Response.Redirect("Fishing.htm")
      Case "Gardening"
        Response.Redirect("Gardening.htm")
      Case Else
        Response.Redirect("AllProducts.htm")
    End Select
%>
</form></body></html>
```

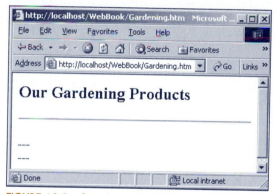

FIGURE 10.9 `Gardening.htm` Being Redirected
by the `Product.htm` Based on the Cookie Value

Multivalued Cookies

A cookie may contain more than one key-value pair. In this case, we say that
the cookie is multivalued and it has keys. In the example below, we have created a cookie named "user" that has four keys and values.

```
<!- WriteMultiValuedCookie.asp->
<%
  Response.Cookies("user")("firstname")="Valda"
  Response.Cookies("user")("lastname")="Hilley"
  Response.Cookies("user")("country")="US"
  Response.Cookies("user")("age")="22"
  Response.Write("<h3>Cookie Written</h3>")
%>
```

Read Multivalued Cookies

Assume that we have already written the multivalued cookie named "user" in a client's disk. When the user requests a page from our site, the user's browser will send all cookies to the server. Now we want to read all these cookies sent to the server. The RetrieveCookies.asp shown below illustrates how to do it (note that the code checks if a cookie has keys with the HasKeys property). The output of the code is shown in Figure 10.10.

```
<!- RetrieveCookies.asp ->
<html><body>
<%
   Dim x,y
   For each x in Request.Cookies
     If Request.Cookies(x).HasKeys Then
        Response.Write("Multiple values in the <b>" & x &
           "</b> cookie are: <br/>")
        For Each y in Request.Cookies(x)
           Response.Write("<li>"& y & "=" & Request.
              Cookies(x)(y) & "</li>")
        Next
     Else
        Response.Write(x & " = " & Request.Cookies(x))
     End If
     Response.Write "<br/>"
   Next
%>
</body></html>
```

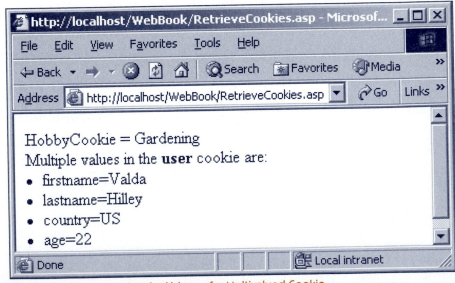

FIGURE 10.10   Retrieving the Values of a Multivalued Cookie

Server Object

The ASP **Server object** is used to access properties and methods on the server. Table 10.3 describes its properties and methods.

TABLE 10.3   Properties and Methods of the Server **Object**

Property or Method	Description
Properties	
ScriptTimeout	Sets or returns the maximum number of seconds a script can run before it is terminated
Methods	
CreateObject	Creates an instance of an object
Execute	Executes an ASP file from inside another ASP file
GetLastError()	Returns an ASPError object that describes the error condition that occurred
HTMLEncode	Applies HTML encoding to a specified string
MapPath	Maps a specified path to a physical path
Transfer	Sends (transfers) all the information created in one ASP file to a second ASP file
URLEncode	Applies URL encoding rules to a specified string

File Last Modified

```
<html>
<body>
<%
Set fs = Server.CreateObject("Scripting.FileSystemObject")
Set rs =
fs.GetFile(Server.MapPath("demo_lastmodified.asp"))
modified = rs.DateLastModified
%>
This file was last modified on: <%response.write(modified)
Set rs = Nothing
Set fs = Nothing
%>
</body>
</html>
```

Session Object

The **Session object** is used to remember information during a user's session. A session is the time a user spends at your site on a visit. It begins when a user opens any page and continues while the use is navigating from page to page in the site. Multiple pages may need to share certain variables. The `Session` object allows you to save these variables and retrieve or modify these in any page that is subsequently requested by the user (in the same session). Essentially, the `Session` variables can store information that will be available to every page in a session and are private to a particular user. They are commonly used to track things like the contents of a user's shopping basket, or a flag indicating that this user has been properly authenticated.

A session ends when the user closes his or her browser or when its timeout period expires. A session also can be terminated via code. Once a session ends, all of the `Session` variables are removed. The general syntax for the `Session` object is

```
<% Session("variableName") = someValue %>
```

The following shows how to create a `Session` variable when the user successfully logs in:

```
<% Session("validUser") = True %>
```

The `Session` variable may now be used throughout the site.

```
<%= Session("validUser") %>
```

The `Session` object has two events: OnStart and OnEnd. The Session_OnStart event is called every time a new user begins a session with the Web site and Session_onEnd is called whenever a session terminates. You can initialize a `Session` variable in Session_OnStart. These events are usually defined inside a file called `Global.asa`. Each application has only one **Global.asa** and it is always placed in the application's root directory. The `Session` object's collections, properties, methods, and events are described Table 10.4.

Example of Session ID and Timeout

When a session starts, the system allocates a Session ID to the session. Typically a session ends when the user closes his or her browser. However, we can set the session timeout via code. We also can use the `Session.Abandon` method to terminate a session. In the following example, we have illustrated how to display the Session ID and how to set its timeout.

```
<!- SessionTimeout.asp ->
<html><body>
Session ID:
<%
Response.Write(" " & Session.SessionID)
%>
```

TABLE 10.4 The `Session` **Object's Collections, Properties, Methods, and Events**

Collection, Property, Method, or Event	Description
Collections	
`Contents`	Contains all the items appended to the session through a script command
`StaticObjects`	Contains all the objects appended to the session with the HTML `<object>` tag
Properties	
`CodePage`	Specifies the character set that will be used when displaying dynamic content
`LCID`	Sets or returns an integer that specifies a location or region; contents like date, time, and currency will be displayed according to that location or region
SessionID	Returns a unique ID for each user that is generated by the server
`Timeout`	Sets or returns the timeout period (in minutes) for the `Session` object in this application
Methods	
Abandon	Destroys a user session
`Contents.Remove`	Deletes an item from the `Contents` collection
`Contents.RemoveAll()`	Deletes all items from the `Contents` collection
Events	
`Session_OnEnd`	Occurs when a session ends
`Session_OnStart`	Occurs when a session starts

```
<p><b>Timeout Information</b></p>
<%
  Response.Write("Default Timeout is: " & Session.Timeout
    & " minutes.")
  Session.Timeout=30
  Response.Write("<br/>Timeout is now: " & Session.Timeout
    & " minutes.")
%>
</body></html>
```

Application Object

A group of files that work together to perform some purpose is usually called an *application*. Microsoft has defined an ASP application as "all the files, pages, handlers, modules, and executable code that can be invoked from a virtual directory." The `Application` object in ASP is used to tie these files together. The ASP engine (`ASP.dll`) creates the `Application` object in response to the first request from the site. It remains available until the server is shut down.

The purpose of the `Application` object is to provide a repository to store variables and object references that are available to all pages opened by all users. The `Application` object is similar to the `Session` object except that it stores global information as opposed to information about an individual user's session. So the major difference is that *all* pages and *all* users share one `Application` object, while with sessions there is only one `Session` object for *each* user.

There is only one `Application` object for each application on the Web server. You can initialize application variables in the Application_OnStart event of the `global.asa` file. You also may include necessary code in the Application_OnEnd event, which will be executed whenever the application terminates. The `Application` object's collections, methods, and events are described in Table 10.5.

TABLE 10.5 The `Application` **Object's Collections, Methods, and Events**

Collection, Method, or Event	Description
Collections	
`Contents`	Contains all the items appended to the application through a script command
`StaticObjects`	Contains all the objects appended to the application with the HTML `<object>` tag
Methods	
`Contents.Remove`	Deletes an item from the `Contents` collection
`Contents.RemoveAll()`	Deletes all items from the `Contents` collection
Lock	Prevents other users from modifying the variables in the `Application` object
Unlock	Enables other users to modify the variables in the `Application` object (after it has been locked using the `Lock` method)
Events	
`Application_OnEnd`	Occurs when all user sessions are over and the application ends
`Application_OnStart`	Occurs before the first new session is created (when the `Application` object is first referenced)

QuickCheck Questions

8. What is an ASP application?
9. What kind of information does an application object hold?
10. Why use an application object?

Using the `Application` Object: An Example

Suppose that we would like to keep track of the number of visitors (hits) to our site. In the `global.asa` file, we can initialize a counter variable to 0 in the Application.OnStart() event. We also can increment the counter by 1 in the Session_OnStart() event. Thus, when the first visitor visits our site, the `Application` object will be created and the counter will be set to 0. Every time a new session starts (i.e., a new visitor visits our site), the Session_OnStart() event will be triggered and our counter will be incremented by 1. Here is the code for the `global.asa` file.

```
<!- global.asa ->
<!- Note: The global.asa file should be saved in the
    virtual directory, and not in any of its subfolders. ->
<script language="VBScript" runat="server">
  Sub Application_OnStart()
    Application("visitCount")=0
  End Sub
  Sub Session_OnStart()
    Application.Lock
    Application("visitCount") = Application("visitCount")
       + 1
    Application.Unlock
  End Sub
</script>
```

On a given instance, more than one session may be running on the system. Two or more sessions may collide with each other when updating a given application resource. Because of this, you will need to use the `Application.Lock` before you update an application variable. Obviously, you also would need to unlock the resource after you have updated it.

To illustrate the use of the above `global.asa` file, let us develop a simple ASP file that would display the number of visitors. A sample code is shown below:

```
<!- ShowVisitCount.asp ->
<html><body><h2>
Number of visits since the server was started =
<%
  Dim intCount
```

```
        intCount = Application("visitCount")
        Response.Write(" " & intCount)
    %>
    </body></html>
```

The output of `ShowVisitCount.asp` is shown in Figure 10.11.

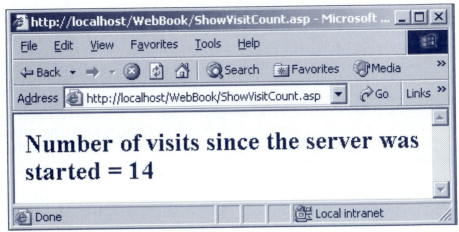

FIGURE 10.11   The Output of `ShowVisitCount.asp`

Server-Side Includes (SSI)

It is possible to insert the content of another file into an ASP page before the server executes it, with the `#include` directive. When ASP sees `#include`, the contents of the file are placed into the ASP file in place of the `#include` command. Thus, the contents of the SSI behave as though they were typed directly into the ASP file. The common use of SSI is to store functions, headers, footers, or elements that will be reused on multiple pages. For example, in your database-driven Web sites, most pages will need a connection string to access the database. You can use SSI to store the connection string. Since the SSI file is the only place to store the connection string, if the connection details change (for example, the location of the database), you do not need to edit every affected ASP file. Instead, you just change the contents of the SSI file. Therefore, SSI is a very useful way of making your site easier to manage.

To insert a file into an .asp file, use the following syntax:

```
<!- #include virtual | file ="filename" ->
```

The `virtual` and `file` keywords indicate the type of path you are using to include the file, and `filename` is the path and filename of the file you want to include.

Use the `virtual` keyword to indicate a path beginning with a virtual directory. For example, if a file named `Footer.inc` resides in a virtual directory named `/Myapp`, the following line would insert the contents of `Footer.inc` into the file containing the line:

```
<!- #include virtual ="/myapp/footer.inc" ->
```

Included files do not require a special filename extension; however, it is considered good programming practice to give included files an .inc extension to distinguish them from other types of files.

Use the `file` keyword to indicate a relative path. A relative path begins with the directory that contains the including file. For example, if you have a file in the directory `/Myapp`, and the file `Header1.inc` is in `/Myapp\Headers`, the following line would insert `Header1.inc` in your file:

```
<!- #include file ="headers\header1.inc" ->
```

Note that the path to the included file, `Headers\header1.inc`, is relative to the including file; if the script containing this **#include** statement is not in the directory `/Myapp`, the statement would not work.

You should provide the path of the file as well if the SSI file is not in the same directory as the ASP file. An SSI file is just a plain text file. You can save your SSI file with the extension .txt, .inc, or .asp. However, if your SSI file has an .inc or .txt extension and a user manages to browse to it directly, the contents of the SSI file will be displayed on the screen. For this reason, it is always safer to use the .asp extension for your SSI files since the source code of an ASP file will not be visible after the interpretation.

An included file can, in turn, include other files. An .asp file also can include the same file more than once, provided that the `#include` directives do not cause a loop. For example, if the file `First.asp` includes the file `Second.inc`, `Second.inc` must not in turn include `First.asp`. Nor can a file include itself. ASP detects such loop or nesting errors, generates an error message, and stops processing the requested .asp file.

ASP includes files before executing script commands. Therefore, you cannot use a script command to build the name of an included file. For example, the following script would not open the file `Header1.inc` because ASP attempts to execute the `#include` directive before it assigns a filename to the variable name.

```
<!- This script will fail ->
<% name=(header1 & ".inc") %>
<!- #include file="<%= name %>" ->
```

Script commands and procedures must be entirely contained within the script delimiters `<%` and `%>`, the HTML tags `<SCRIPT>` and `</SCRIPT>`, or the

HTML tags `<OBJECT>` and `</OBJECT>`. That is, you cannot open a script delimiter in an including .asp file, then close the delimiter in an included file; the script or script command must be a complete unit. For example, the following script would not work:

```
<!- This script will fail ->
<%
  For i = 1 To n
    statements in main file
    <!- #include file="header1.inc" ->
  Next
%>
```

The following script, however, would work:

```
<%
  For i = 1 to n
    statements in main file
%>
<!- #include file="header1.inc" ->
<% Next %>
```

QuickCheck Questions

11. Why use a server-side include?

12. What is the file format for an SSI file?

13. What components can an SSI file contain?

Summary

Active Server Page technology can be used to develop server-side Web applications. The term "server-side" refers to the occasion when a user requests for an ASP page and when the page is initially processed at the server before it is sent to the client. ASP also offers Common Gateway Interface (CGI) under the hood. However, you will learn about CGI in Chapter 12. To develop and test ASP pages, you will either need access to a server that has Web server software or you will need to install Microsoft's Internet Information Server (IIS) or Personal Web Server (PWS) on your machine.

ASP pages usually contain standard HTML codes and server-side scripts. It may also contain client-side scripts. The server side scripts are usually included in a <%@ Language= "VBScript"> tag, or simply in a pair of <% %> tags. When a user requests an ASP page, the server locates the page and activates the ASP scripting engine (ASP.dll) to process it. Upon which, the ASP scripting engine processes the server-side scripts and generates a fresh new document called the Response object. The response object is then sent to the client.

VBScript is the default scripting language for ASP. However, server-side JavaScript can also be used, if so desired. When we develop ASP code, we can take advantage of many of the ASP objects that are offered by the server. Some of the major ASP objects are: Request object, Response object, Server object, Application object, and Session object. These objects provide many properties and methods that can be used to develop ASP code. For example, we can use the statement **Response.Write("<h1>Hello World</h1>")** to write the string "<h1>Hello World</h1>" in the Response object. The Response object is nothing but an HTML document generated by the scripting engine.

One of the major benefits of ASP technology is that it can process the data submitted by the user (via the HTML <form> element) at the server. Depending on the data submission method (like "get" or "post"), the submitted data can be retrieved as **Request.QueryString("x")** or **Request.Form("x")**, where x is the name of a data entry element in the submitted form.

ASP also allows us to write and retrieve small amounts of named data in the client's disk. These data are known as cookies. We can write cookies using the **Response.Cookies** method. Subsequently, we can retrieve a cookie using the Request.Cookies method.

ASP has been a very popular technology offered by Microsoft. There are other similar technologies such as Java Server Pages (JSP) and CGI with Perl. Nevertheless, Microsoft has developed a better and much-improved version of ASP, which is ASP.NET. However, if you acquire a good solid background in ASP, you will find it relatively easy to develop JSP or Perl CGI pages. Obviously, you should learn Java (introduced in Chapter 11), or Perl (covered in Chapter 12) before you venture into any of these technologies.

Key Terms

action
Application Object
Application.Lock
Application.Unlock
Application-OnEnd
Application-OnStart
ASP object
BinaryRead
ClientCertificate
collections
cookie
CreateObject
Form
get

Global.asa
include files
Internet Information Server
method
Personal Web Server (PWS)
post
primary scripting language
QueryString
Request object
Request.Cookies
Response object
Response.Buffer
Response.Cookies
Response.IsClientConnected

Response.Redirect
Response.Write
scripting engine
Server object
Server.CreateObject
server-side scripts
ServerVariables
Session ID
Session Object
Session Abandon
Sesson-On Start
Session-OnEnd
TotalBytes

1. What does ASP stand for?

    a.   Action Server Page

    b.   Active Standard Pages

    c.   Active Server Pages

    d.   A Standard Page

2. ASP server scripts are surrounded by which delimiters?

    a.   `<%> . . . </%>`

    b.   `<script> . . .v</script>`

    c.   `<% . . . %>`

    d.   `<&> . . . </&>`

3. To write `"Hello World"` in ASP, use which of the following?

    a.   `Document.Write("Hello World")`

    b.   `Response.Write("Hello World")`

    c.   `"Hello World"`

4. Using `"<%="` is the same as:

    a.   `<%Write`

    b.   `<%Equal`

    c.   `<%Response.Write`

    d.   `<%Document.Write`

5. What is the default scripting language in ASP?

    a.   PERL

    b.   JavaScript

    c.   EmmaScript

    d.   VBScript

    e.   Java

6. How can you script your ASP code in JavaScript?

    a.   Start the document with `<%@ language="javascript" %>`

    b.   End the document with `<% language="javascript" %>`

    c.   Start the document with `<% language="javascript" %>`

    d.   JavaScript is the default scripting language.

7. How do you get information from a form that is submitted using the `get` method?

    a.   `Request.QueryString`

    b.   `Request.Form`

8. How do you get information from a form that is submitted using the `post` method?

    a.   `Request.QueryString`

    b.   `Request.Form`

9. Which ASP property is used to identify a user?

   a. An ASP `Cookie`

   b. The `Server` object

   c. The `Application` object

10. All users of the same application share *one* `Session` object. True or False?

11. All users of the same application share *one* `Application` object. True or False?

12. If a user has `Cookies` enabled, a session variable is available to all pages in one application. True or False?

13. Include files must have the file extension .inc. True or False?

14. What is the correct way to include the file `time.inc`?

   a. `<include file="time.inc">`

   b. `<!-#include file="time.inc"->`

   c. `<% #include file="time.inc" %>`

   d. `<% include file="time.inc" %>`

1. **Write text using ASP.** Write a script that demonstrates how to write text with ASP.

2. **Clear the buffer.** Write a script that demonstrates how you can clear the buffer.

3. **Set the type of content.** Write a script that demonstrates how to specify the type of content.

4. **Find a browser's type, IP address, etc.** Write a script that determines the type of browser and other server variables.

5. **Welcome cookie.** Write a script that displays this text on the page: **Welcome!** This is the first time you are visiting this Web page.

Exercises

11

Introduction to Java Applet Programming

OBJECTIVES

1. To learn what a Java applet is.

2. To learn the Java applet structure.

3. To create a Java applet.

4. To embed an applet in an HTML document.

5. To execute a Java applet.

Introduction: Getting to Know Java Technology

Java technology encompasses both a programming language and a platform. The Java programming language is a true object-oriented (OO) programming language that combines an elegant language design with powerful features that were previously available primarily in specialty languages. Java is not JavaScript nor is it related to JavaScript in any way. In addition to the core language components, Java programming language software distributions include many powerful, supporting software libraries for tasks such as database, network, and **graphical user interface (GUI)** programming.

Java as a Platform

A platform is the hardware or software environment in which a program runs. Some of the most popular platforms are Windows 2000, Windows XP, Linux, Solaris, and MacOS. Most platforms can be described as a combination of the operating system and hardware. The Java platform differs from most other platforms in that it's a software-only platform that runs on top of other hardware-based platforms.

The Java platform has two components:

- The **Java Virtual Machine** (Java VM or JVM) is "virtual" because it is generally implemented in software on top of a "real" hardware platform and operating system. All Java programs are compiled for the JVM. Therefore, the JVM must be implemented on a particular platform before compiled Java programs will run on that platform. The JVM plays a central role in making Java portable.

- The Java Application Programming Interface (Java API) is a large collection of ready-made software components that provide many useful capabilities, such as graphical user interface (GUI) widgets. The Java API is grouped into libraries of related classes and interfaces; these libraries are known as **packages**.

Java as a Programming Language

With most programming languages, you either compile or interpret a program so that you can run it on your computer. The Java programming language is unusual in that a program is both compiled and interpreted. With the compiler, first you translate a program into an intermediate language called Java **bytecodes**—the platform-independent codes interpreted by the interpreter on the Java platform. The interpreter parses and runs each Java bytecode instruction on the computer. Compilation happens just once; interpretation occurs each time the program is executed.

Think of Java bytecodes as the machine code instructions for the Java Virtual Machine. Every Java interpreter, whether it's a development tool or a Web browser that can run applets, is an implementation of the Java VM.

Java bytecodes help make "write once, run anywhere" possible. You can compile your program into bytecodes on any platform that has a Java compiler. The bytecodes can then be run on any implementation of the Java VM. That means that as long as a computer has a Java VM, the same program written in the Java programming language can run on Windows 2000, a Solaris workstation, or an iMac.

QuickCheck Questions

1. What are bytecodes?
2. Is Java a compiled or interpreted language?
3. Can Java programs run on more than one operating system?

What Can Java Technology Do?

The most common types of programs written in the Java programming language are applets and applications. As a veteran Web surfer, you're probably familiar with applets. An applet is not a standalone program. It is a program that adheres to certain conventions that allow it to run within a Java-enabled browser. Java applets are graphical mini-programs that run in the context of another program, meaning that they're windowed. They run in a restricted JVM often called a *sandbox* and have limited power so that file I/O and printing are impossible.

Since an applet depends on the browser to provide a context in which to run, the browser implements common applet functions and provides those functions to the applet by way of a **Java Application Program Interface (Java API)**. The browser also controls the execution of the applet. An applet is graphical by nature. Each applet occupies a rectangular panel in its viewer's window. Applets are meant to be embedded within a graphical document, such as an HTML document.

The Java programming language is not just for applets for the Web. Using the powerful API, you can write many types of programs including applications. An application is a stand-alone program that runs directly on the Java platform. It may be a simple console application or a windowed application and have the same capabilities of any other program on the system. For example, a programmer can create

- Applications that serve and support clients on a network such as Web servers, proxy servers, mail servers, and print servers.
- Specialized programs called *servlets*. A **servlet** can be an applet that runs on the server. In fact, Java servlets are popular for building interactive Web applications, often replacing CGI scripts. Servlets are similar to applets in that they are runtime extensions of applications. Instead of working in browsers, though, servlets run within Java Web servers.

Java API can support all these types of programs through its packages of software components that provide a wide range of functionality. Every full implementation of the Java platform gives you the following features:

- The essentials: Objects, strings, threads, numbers, input and output, data structures, system properties, date and time, and so on.
- Applets: The set of conventions used by applets.
- Networking: URLs, TCP (Transmission Control Protocol), UDP (User Datagram Protocol) sockets, and IP (Internet Protocol) addresses.
- Internationalization: Help for writing programs that can be localized for users worldwide. Programs can automatically adapt to specific locales and be displayed in the appropriate language.
- Security: Both low-level and high-level, including electronic signatures, public and private key management, access control, and certificates.
- Software components: Known as JavaBeans™, can be plugged into existing component architectures.
- Object serialization: Allows lightweight persistence and communication via **Remote Method Invocation (RMI)**.

- Java Database Connectivity (JDBC™): Provides uniform access to a wide range of relational databases.

Embedding an Applet into HTML

Unlike Java applications that typically are executed by a Java-compatible interpreter, applets are executed within a Java-enabled Web browser that includes an integrated bytecode interpreter. This means that the applet must be embedded or referenced in the HTML document. The <APPLET> tag is used to reference a Java applet, making it part of a Web page.

```
<html><body>
<applet code="HelloWorld.class" height="200" width="500">
</applet> </body> </html>
```

HTML Java-Specific Tags

When a user selects a page that contains an applet, the bytecode is downloaded from the Web server and executed by the browser's integrated bytecode interpreter. The following HTML code shows the use of the <APPLET> tag. This HTML document contains an embedded Java applet named "HelloWorld.class" that is 500 pixels wide and 200 pixels in height. The **<APPLET>** tag has the following syntax:

```
<APPLET
[CODEBASE = applet-URL]
CODE = applet-filename WIDTH = pixel-width HEIGHT =
    pixel-height [ALT = alternate-text] [NAME = applet-name]
[ALIGN = alignment(LEFT | RIGHT | TOP | TEXTTOP
| MIDDLE | ABSMIDDLE | BASELINE | BOTTOM |
ABSBOTTOM]
[VSPACE = vertical-pixel width] [HSPACE = horizontal-
    pixel-space]
>
[<PARAM NAME = parameter-name VALUE = parametervalue>]
[<PARAM NAME = parameter-name VALUE = parametervalue>]
[alternate-html]
</APPLET>
```

If a Web browser doesn't support Java applets, the `<APPLET>` tag is simply ignored and any HTML code included in the `alternate-html` section, if it exists, will be displayed instead. As the above brackets suggest, the only required applet attribute tags are `CODE`, `WIDTH`, and `HEIGHT`. Table 11.1 provides a summary of how each of these attributes can be used.

TABLE 11.1 Attributes of the `<APPLET>` Tag

Attribute Tag	Description
CODE	This required attribute is the name of the Java applet—the name of the .class file created by a Java-compatible compiler. The filename must be relative to the current URL of the HTML file containing the applet unless the `CODEBASE` attribute is used. In this case, the filename should be specified relative to the location specified by the `CODEBASE` attribute.
CODEBASE	This is an optional parameter that can be used to change the base URL. The default base URL is the directory specified in the URL of the referencing HTML document. This location can be specified absolute or relative and needs to be a directory, not a filename.
WIDTH	This attribute is required and is used to specify the initial width required by the applet in the Web browser. Use a number to indicate the number of pixels required.
HEIGHT	This attribute is also required and, like width, it is used to specify the initial height of the applet in pixels
ALT	This attribute is similar to the `alternate-html` section. Use this attribute to display HTML text in place of the applet in browsers that *do* understand the `<APPLET>` tag but *do not* support Java.
NAME	This attribute is used less often, but it is useful when you have two applets on the same page that need to communicate with each other. Applets that are running at the same time can look each other up with the `getApplet` method of the `AppletContext` class.
ALIGN	This attribute, also optional, is used to align applets relative to text in an HTML document. Text can either flow around an applet or be in line with the text. The values `LEFT` and `RIGHT` are used to wrap text around the applet. The rest of the values— `TOP`, `MIDDLE`, `TEXTTOP`, `ABSMIDDLE`, `BASELINE BOTTOM`, and `ABSBOTTOM`—are used to place applets in a line of text. These can be useful for smaller applets.
VSPACE	This optional attribute allows for space to be created above *and* below the applet. It is specified in pixels.
HSPACE	This optional attribute allows for space to be created to the left *and* to the right of an applet. It is also specified in pixels.
PARAM NAME	This optional attribute allows for passing named parameters from HTML documents to applets. You can pass multiple parameters to an applet. Parameters are passed as strings and can be retrieved with the `getParameter` method.

The Applet Class

Applets are embedded within an HTML document via the `<APPLET>` tag that references the Java applet's compiled `.class` file. Every applet is an extension of the `java.applet.Applet` class. The base `Applet` **class** provides methods that a derived Applet class may call to obtain information and services from the browser context. These include methods that do the following:

- Get applet parameters.
- Get the network location of the HTML file that contains the applet.
- Get the network location of the applet class directory.
- Print a status message in the browser.
- Fetch an image.
- Fetch an audio clip.
- Play an audio clip.
- Resize the applet.

Additionally, the `Applet` class provides an interface by which a browser obtains information about the applet and controls the applet's execution. The browser may

- Request information about the author, version, and copyright of the applet.
- Request a description of the parameters the applet recognizes.
- Initialize the applet.
- Destroy the applet.
- Start the applet's execution.
- Stop the applet's execution.

The `Applet` class provides default implementations of each of these methods. Those implementations may be overridden as necessary.

Writing Source Code

Writing source code for Java applications or applets is much like writing code for any other language: simply fire up an ASCII text editor and crank out code. Keep the following in mind:

- Java application source code is organized into classes.
- Every Java application must contain a method named. The `main` **method** marks the application's starting point.
- The file containing Java source code must have the filename *classname*`.java`, where *classname* is the name of the class in your Java source code.

A few common features of Java applets are discussed below:

- As in Java applications, Java applet source code is organized into classes.
- Unlike Java applications, Java applets must not contain a method named `main`. This is because a "behind-the-scenes" code already contains the `main` method.
- Most Java applets contain a method named `paint`. This method defines the actual appearance of the text and graphics that the Java applet will output.

Creating a Java Application

To develop and run a Java application, you will usually require the following steps:

1. **Prepare the source code**. Using any text editor, write the Java application source code. For example, enter the following source code and save it as `"HelloWorld.java"`:

```
// HelloWorld.java
class HelloWorld {
    public static void main (String args[]) {
        System.out.println("Hello World");
    }
}
```

2. **Compile the Java source code**. Open a Command Prompt Screen using the **Start > Run > cmd.** Set the path to the `bin` subfolder where you have saved your JDK software (downloaded from Sun). When this is done, the Java compiler creates a bytecode file. The `HelloWorld.java` file can be compiled as `javac`. This command will create a class file named `HelloWorld.class`.

3. **Run the class file**. Invoke the Java interpreter and run the class file using the `Java HelloWorld` command. It will run the bytecode file.

We have illustrated these steps in Figure 11.1.

If the source code file contains more than one class, the Java compiler will create a separate bytecode file for each class. For example, given a source code file containing three classes, the Java compiler will generate three bytecode files, named

- `class1-name.class`
- `class2-name.class`
- `class3-name.class`

Java applet source code is compiled the same way Java application source code is compiled.

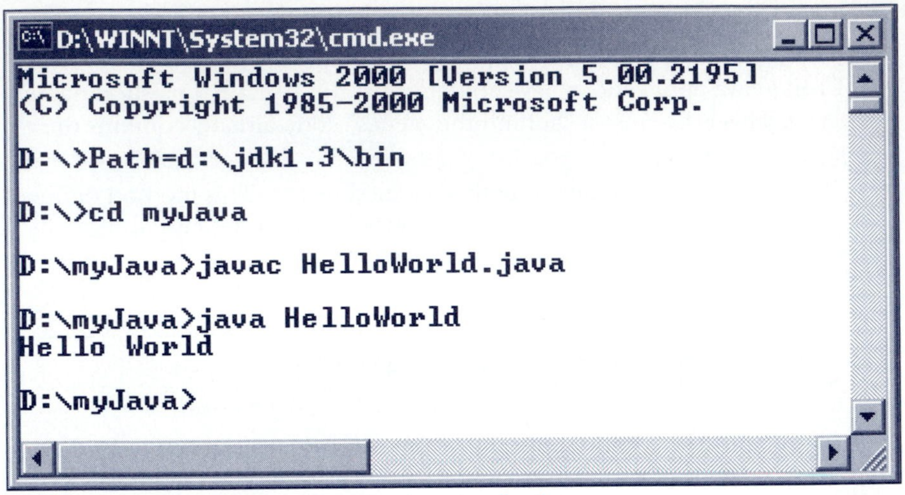

```
D:\WINNT\System32\cmd.exe                          _ □ ×

Microsoft Windows 2000 [Version 5.00.2195]
(C) Copyright 1985-2000 Microsoft Corp.

D:\>Path=d:\jdk1.3\bin

D:\>cd myJava

D:\myJava>javac HelloWorld.java

D:\myJava>java HelloWorld
Hello World

D:\myJava>
```

FIGURE 11.1   Compiling and Running Java Applications

Remember that one of the goals of Java is to create programs that can run on any platform. Therefore, the Java compiler generates platform-independent bytecode rather than platform-dependent machine code. Then, to run a program, the Java interpreter translates this bytecode into the machine code for whatever system the Java interpreter is on.

Because of the time the Java interpreter needs to translate bytecode into machine code, Java applications run somewhat slower than applications stored in native machine code. The programmer's path must contain the directory where the interpreter java is stored. The programmer also may need to add the directory containing his or her class files to the CLASSPATH environment variable.

Hello World

The place to start Java programming is a stand-alone console program as opposed to an applet. Tradition dictates that we begin our journey into Java by writing and analyzing the Hello World program. Here is the Hello World application again:

```java
// HelloWorld.java
class HelloWorld {
  public static void main (String args[]) {
    System.out.println("Hello World!");
  }
}
```

Despite its seemingly simplistic design, this five-line application has most of the features found in more complex Java programs as well as the features of an object-oriented program. Consider this:

- It is an object.
- It uses encapsulation and message passing.
- It defines a class.
- It uses inheritance.
- It uses access modifiers.

So you see, there's quite a lot going on in it. Now let's review it, line by line.

The first statement is the initial class statement that defines the program name, in this case `HelloWorld`. Actually, the initial class statement is more than just a line to give the program a name. It defines an "entity" that can be called not just from the command line but also by other parts of the same or different programs.

The `HelloWorld` class contains one method, the `main` method, which is defined in the second line of the program. The `main` method is where an application begins executing. We've declared this method as `public`, meaning that it can be called from anywhere. We've also declared it as `static`, meaning that all instances of this class share this one method. Next, we declared it as `void`, which means that this method does not return a value.

Finally, we pass any command line arguments to the method in an array of Strings called `args`. In this simple program, there aren't any command line arguments though. The last line says that when the `main` method is called, it does only one thing: print "Hello World" to the standard output, generally a terminal monitor or console window of some sort. This is accomplished by the `System.out.println` method.

Creating a Java Applet

Creating a Java applet requires the following steps:

1. Using any text editor, write Java applet source code.

2. Compile the Java applet source code. The compiler creates a byte-code file.

3. Create an HTML document to contain the applet.

4. Invoke the bytecode file by specifying it in an HTML document and then loading the HTML document.

5. Debug as necessary.

Running Java Applets

Java applets are not run the same way as Java applications are run. To run a Java applet, the programmer must first insert the HTML tag `<applet>` into an HTML document. The `<applet>` tag must have the following form:

```
<applet code="name of bytecode file" width="m"  height="n">
```

The `width` and `height` attributes designate the size of the applet window (in pixels). The `code`, `width`, and `height` attributes are required in every `<applet>` tag.

After creating the HTML document, the programmer needs to load it into a tool that can handle Java applets. The most common choice is a Java-enabled browser. The HTML document is loaded as one would load any HTML document from a browser:

1. Specify the full URL.

2. Specify the pathname on the local disk.

Note that users with Java-enabled browsers can disable Java, preventing applets from running on their machines. An applet may be invoked by embedding directives in an HTML file and viewing the file through an applet viewer or Java-enabled browser. The `<applet>` tag is the basis for embedding an applet in an HTML file.

The `code` attribute of the `<applet>` tag is required. It specifies the applet class to run. The `width` and `height` attributes are also required to specify the initial size of the panel in which an applet runs. Note that the size of the applet panel is determined in the document, not from within the applet. An applet may call its `resize()` method, but the browser is not guaranteed to update the display. The applet directive must be closed with an `</applet>` tag.

If an applet takes parameters, values may be passed for the parameters by adding `<param>` tags between `<applet>` and `</applet>`. The browser ignores text and other tags between the applet tags. Non-Java-enabled browsers do not process `<applet>` and `</applet>`. Therefore, anything that appears between the tags that is not related to the applet is visible in non-Java-enabled browsers. The programmer can take advantage of this feature to provide filler content for users with older browsers.

The browser looks for the compiled Java code at the location of the document. To specify otherwise, use the `codebase` attribute of the `<applet>` tag. Whether a `codebase` is specified or the default is used, it is important to keep in mind that the `codebase` is the root directory of the package tree. If the code is organized into packages, the Java class loader expects to find the class files in like-named subdirectories of the `codebase` directory. The `codebase` directory itself is the home of the default package. If an applet resides in a package other than the default, the holding package must be specified in the code attribute using the period character (.) to separate package/class components.

Hello World Applet: An Example

First, enter the following Java code and save it as `HelloWorldApplet.java`. Compile it to get the `HelloWorldApplet.class` file. If necessary, you may copy the class file and paste it in the folder where you usually save your HTM files.

```
// HelloWorldApplet.java
import java.applet.Applet;
import java.awt.Graphics;
public class HelloWorldApplet extends java.applet.Applet {
  public void paint(Graphics g) {
    g.drawString("Hello world!", 50, 25);
  }
}
```

Now you need to create an HTML file that will include your applet. The following simple HTML file will do:

```
<!- RunHelloWorldApplet.htm ->
<html><head><title> Hello World Applet</title>
</head><body>This is the applet:<p>
<applet code="HelloWorldApplet.class" width="150"
  height="70"/>
</p></body></html>
```

If you open the `RunHelloWorldApplet.htm` file using Internet Explorer, the system will display a page as shown in Figure 11.2.

In this example, the HTM file and the class file were both saved in the same folder. Alternatively, you could save the class file in the `classes` subfolder of your HTML folder. In that case the `<applet>` tag should be modified to `<applet codebase ="classes" code="HelloWorldApplet.class" width="150" height="70"/>`.

A Closer Look at the Hello World Applet

The Hello World applet adds several constructs to what we saw in the Hello World application. Moving from top to bottom, the first thing you notice is the two lines

```
import java.applet.Applet;
import java.awt.Graphics;
```

The **import** statement in Java pulls in the classes that are contained in a package elsewhere. A **package** is merely a collection of related classes. In this case, we're requesting access to the public classes contained in the basic release,

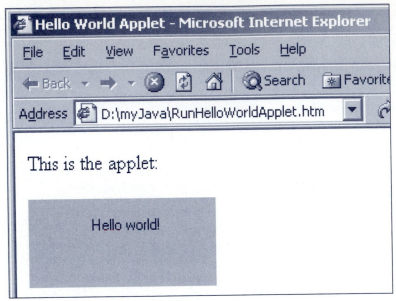

FIGURE 11.2 Displaying an Applet

`java.applet.Applet` and `java.awt.Graphics`. AWT stands for "abstract window toolkit."

The next change from the application is the class definition:

```
public class HelloWorldApplet extends Applet
```

The `extends` keyword indicates that this class is a subclass of the `Applet` class; or, to put it another way, `Applet` is a superclass of `HelloWorldApplet`. The `Applet` class is defined in the `java.applet.Applet` package that we just imported. Since `HelloWorldApplet` is a subclass of the `Applet` class, our `HelloWorldApplet` automatically inherits all the functionality of the generic `Applet` class. Anything an `Applet` can do, `HelloWorldApplet` can do too.

The next difference between the applet and the application is far less obvious. There's no `main` method! Applets don't need them. The `main` method is actually in the browser. Rather than starting at a specific place in the code, applets are event driven. An applet waits for one of a series of events such as a key press, the mouse pointer being moved over the applet's visible area, or a mouse click and then executes the appropriate event handler. Since this is our first program, we only have one event handler, `paint`. Most applets need to handle the `paint` event. This event occurs whenever a part of the applet's visible area is uncovered and needs to be drawn again.

The `paint` **method** is passed a `Graphics` object, which we've chosen to call g. The `Graphics` class is defined in the `java.awt.Graphics` package that we've imported. Within the `paint` method, we call g's `drawString` method to draw the string "Hello World!" at the coordinates (50,25). That's 50 pixels across and 25 pixels down from the upper-left-hand corner of the applet. This drawing takes place whenever a portion of the screen containing our applet is covered and then uncovered and needs to be refreshed.

Life Cycle of a Java Applet

Although Java applets are a form of a Java application, there is significant difference between their life cycles. Java applets do not require a `main()` method as Java applications do. When you run a Java application, you do so by invoking a Java-compatible interpreter that loads a `.class` file that contains the `main()` method. This is where a Java application's life cycle begins. Since applets are embedded in HTML documents, their life cycle is a bit more complex.

The `java.applet.Applet` class includes most of the methods you should be familiar with in order to control the life cycle of an applet. The first step in creating an applet is to subclass `java.applet.Applet` and override the appropriate methods. Review the sample code below. The first line of code is an `import` statement that can be used to import specific classes or entire packages. In this applet, we need to import the `java.applet` **package.** Next, we start our class definition by subclassing `java.applet.Applet`. Here is the beginning of our applet.

```
// HelloWorldApplet.java
import java.applet.Applet;
import java.awt.Graphics;
public class HelloWorld extends Applet {}
```

Since an applet is running inside a Web browser, the events in the Web browser need to be considered. For example, how do you deal with a user changing to and from different Web pages? Fortunately, methods exist for applets that are automatically invoked at various times, allowing for control over various stages in the life of the applet. To control the life cycle, you will override one or more of the following methods:

- `init()` method. The `init` **method** is called by the system when an applet is initially loaded. This is a good location for code that performs any activity that needs to be done once at the beginning of the applet's life cycle. This is a good place to create objects, set parameters, configure states, load images, and so forth.
- `start()` method. The `start` **method** is called by the system after the `init` method. It is also called each time a user returns to the Web page referencing the applet. Unlike the `init` method, the `start` method may be called many times during the life of an applet. If you

want code to be executed only once, put it in the `init` method. If you need code to be executed each time a user returns to a page, such as restarting a thread, the `start` method is the right place for this type of code.

- `stop()` method. The **stop method** is called each time the user leaves a Web page that references an applet. The `stop` method, similar to the `start` method, can be called a number of times during the life of an applet. It's important to note that the default behavior of an applet is to continue running even after the user has moved to another page; thus, the applet will continue to consume system resources. If you would like to halt the execution of an applet or part of its logic, override the `stop` method. Also, if you are doing animation, playing audio files, performing calculations in a thread, and so on, you may want to override the `stop` method. If not, you can likely ignore the `stop` method.

- `destroy()` method. The **destroy method** is called by the system when an applet shuts down normally. It is called only once. The `stop` method is called before the `destroy` method. This method also can be ignored for most applets; however, if your applet is consuming resources that should be returned, such as a window handle or a thread that your applet has created, this is good place for such code.

- `paint()` method. The **paint method** is perhaps the most commonly overridden applet method. Painting can occur many times in the life of an applet. The `paint` method is called once after `init` is called and again each time the Web browser is activated. For example, if a user selects another application window and then returns to the browser, the system will call the `paint` method.

The `paint` method takes an argument, unlike the other previously discussed methods. The argument is an instance of the class `Graphics` that is part of the package **java.awt**. The sample applet continued below will have a single method; it will override the `paint` method. Since the `paint` method requires an argument, we want to use another `import` statement at the beginning of our applet as follows:

```
import java.awt.Graphics
```

or

```
import java.awt.*
```

At the same time, we add the beginnings of the first member of our class, the method that overrides the `paint` method. The sample applet now looks as follows:

```
//import the java.applet package import java.applet.*;
//import the awt package import java.awt.*;
```

```
//subclass applet
public class HelloWorld extends Applet {
//override the paint method
public void paint(Graphics g) { }
}
```

Applet Security

Considering that Java is a powerful programming language designed to allow for loading code over the network, most of you probably have a very high degree of concern about security. What's to stop a malicious developer from creating a virus-like program? Because of this destructive harmful potential, various restrictions are placed on applets in order to minimize risk. Be aware that restrictions may vary from one browser to another.

In general, applets are restricted and cannot

- Read or write to the local file system.
- Remove or delete files from the local file system.
- Create or rename directories on the local file system.
- List directory contents or check for the existence of a file.
- Obtain file attribute information such as size, type, modification, time, and so forth.
- Create network connections to computers other than the source of the applet.
- Listen or connect via ports on the local system.
- Read from or modify various local system properties.
- Halt the execution of the Java interpreter.
- Load local libraries or invoke local executables.

Even with such restrictions, the power of the Java language can be abused, allowing for security holes. For example, malicious (or bad) code may inflict a denial of service attack. A denial of service attack is caused by code that stops or significantly degrades the performance of a critical resource.

Security is specific to the browser; some browsers are less constrained than others. Depending on the level of security implemented by the browser, other types of attacks could occur. Overall, the Java language and restrictions placed on applets are sufficient to provide a relatively safe computing environment.

Summary

Java applets are an ideal way to enhance the static world of HTML with a dynamic environment. This chapter provided an introduction to the anatomy of a Java applet. We described what an applet is and how it is a special case of a Java application. In the interest of space and time, we have not covered all the information related to the `java.applet` package and applets in general.

Key Terms

`<APPLET>`

`Applet` class

bytecodes

`CODEBASE`

`destroy` method

graphical user interface (GUI)

`import`

`init` method

Java API

java.awt

Java Virtual Machine

`java.applet` package

`main` method

`paint` method

package

Remote Method Invocation (RMI)

servlet

`start` method

`stop` method

Review Questions

1. A program written in the Java programming language can run on any platform because . . .
   a. Java programming is derived from C++.
   b. The Java Virtual Machine (JVM) interprets the program for the native operating system.
   c. The compiler is identical to a C++ compiler.
   d. The APIs do all the work.

2. An applet will run in almost any browser because . . .
   a. The server has a built-in JVM.
   b. The browser has a built-in JVM.
   c. The source code is interpreted by the browser.
   d. Applets don't need a JVM.

3. What is the purpose of the `main` method?
   a. To build a user interface.
   b. To hold the APIs of the application.
   c. To create buttons and scrollbars.
   d. To act as the entry point for the program.

4. The `Applet` class provides . . .
   a. A browser to run the applet.
   b. Methods to define the applet's behavior and appearance.
   c. A special HTML page.
   d. Permission to communicate with the server.

5. Which method will a Web browser call first on a new applet?

 a. `main` method

 b. `start` method

 c. `init` method

 d. `paint` method

6. Servlets are typically used for . . .

 a. Creating graphics.

 b. Extending a Web server by providing dynamic Web content.

 c. Storing information in applets.

 d. Loading buttons and menus.

7. Which of the following can an applet do?

 a. Write a file on the applet user's hard drive.

 b. Access any machine on the Internet.

 c. Find out the username and home directory of the user running an applet.

 d. Show a pop-up window without any warning messages.

 e. All of the above.

 f. None of the above.

8. What methods must be provided in a class that subclasses `Applet`?

 a. `init`, `start`, `stop`, `destroy`, and `paint`.

 b. `init`, `start`, `stop`, and `destroy`.

 c. `init`, `start`, and `paint`.

 d. `start` and `paint`.

 e. No methods.

1. Type the following Java program into a text editor, then compile and run it.

 Remember to save the file as a text file. You also must make sure that the filename is the same as the class name, so in this instance you must save the file as `Hello.java`. When you compile the program (`javac`), have a look for the Java bytecode in a file called `Hello.class`.

2. Modify the above application by adding an `if` statement that tests for command-line arguments:

3. Type the following Java program into a text editor and compile it. Once the program compiles successfully, write a very short HTML file to display the applet. Use a Web browser to view the HTML file.

4. Use the Java API documentation to find out about the `Font` class and experiment with the available fonts by modifying the above applet code.

 Modify the above applet so that the font type is changed, the font color is blue, and two further lines of text are neatly placed below the first.

CGI with Perl

OBJECTIVES

1. To get introduced to CGI.

2. To learn how CGI scripts work.

3. To choose a language for CGI.

4. To understand the basic principles of Perl.

5. To develop Data Collection Forms.

6. To use CGI scripts to process submitted data.

7. To work with CGI environmental variables.

8. To understand MIME and content type.

INTRODUCTION

The **Common Gateway Interface (CGI)** is a standard for interfacing external applications with information servers, such as HTTP or Web servers. Remember that a plain HTML document contains static information, which means it exists in a constant state: it doesn't change. A CGI program, on the other hand, is executed in real time so that it can output dynamic information.

Using CGI scripts benefits both you and your reader. The reader gets simplicity, automated responses to input, easy ways to make submissions, and fast ways to conduct searches. You get scripts that enable you to automatically process orders, queries, and much more. CGI programs are commonly used to do the following tasks:

- Process input, typically search strings, and output a document containing the results of the search.

- Validate user identification and password information and grant readers access to restricted areas of the Web site.
- Process input from image maps and direct the reader to associated documents.
- Add the reader's feedback or survey responses to a database or index.
- Track visitors to Web pages and post continually updated numbers to the Web page as it is accessed.
- Generate documents based on the type of browser the reader is using.
- Perform post-submission processing and possibly output results for the reader.

How CGI Scripts Work

CGI scripts are used to process input submitted by readers of your Web pages. Readers pass information to a CGI script by activating a link containing a reference to the script. The CGI script processes the input and formats the results as output that the Web server can use. The Web server takes the results and passes them back to the reader's browser. The browser displays the output for the reader.

Although readers see only the results of their submissions or queries, behind the scenes many things are happening. Transactions between a client and server have many parts. These parts can be broken down as follows:

1. The reader's browser passes the input to the Web server.

2. The server sets environment variables pertaining to input.

3. The server passes input as variables to the named CGI script.

4. The CGI script processes the input and passes it off to another application if necessary.

5. The server passes command line input or a standard input stream to the CGI script if one is present.

6. The server sets environment variables pertaining to output.

7. The Web server passes the output back to the reader's browser. The output from a CGI script can be anything from the results of a database search to a completely new document generated as a result of the reader's input.

8. The client processes input from the server.

The input usually consists of environment variables that the Web server passes to the CGI script. Environment variables describe the information being passed, such as the version of CGI used on the server, the type of data, the size of the data, and other important information.

QuickCheck Questions

1. What does CGI stand for?
2. List three tasks you can use CGI for.
3. Where is a CGI script executed?

Choosing a Language

You can write CGI scripts in almost any computer language that produces an executable file. For example, you could use any of the following languages:

- C/C++
- Perl
- Python
- Tcl
- Visual Basic
- Fortran
- Any Unix shell
- AppleScript

The best programming language to write your script in is one that works with your Web server and meets your needs. However, since most of the processing done by CGI scripts involves text manipulation, Perl has become the most widely used language for CGI scripts. It supports UNIX, DOS, Windows, Mac, and other operating systems. You can use Perl to do the following tasks:

- Easily manipulate files, text, and processes.
- Extract text strings and manipulate them in complex ways.
- Quickly and easily search files, databases, and indexes.
- Print advanced reports based on extracted data.

We'll use Perl in this chapter.

Basic Perl

Perl is an interpreted language. However, Perl does not have the limitations of most interpreted languages. You can use Perl to manipulate extremely large amounts of data, and Perl strings are not limited in size. The entire contents of a file can be used as a single string. Just as an HTML document has a certain structure, so does Perl. If you follow Perl's syntax rules, you can use Perl script as easily as HTML.

Perl is a very popular language because it is easy to learn, and it is available free of charge. If Perl is not loaded in your computer, you may download a free copy of Perl from www.perl.com or www.activestate.com. The download is available for Unix, Macintosh, and Windows. Please follow the installation instructions available in the download page and install Perl on your system accordingly.

Let's begin. Enter the following code in a text file and save it as `Hello World.pl` in any folder (for illustration purposes, we have saved our code in `g:\myPerl`):

```
#  HelloWorld.pl
print "Hello, World!\n";
```

In the above code, the first line is a comment (ignored by the Perl interpreter). The second line is obviously a Perl statement to display "Hello, World". Note, in some systems, the first statement should be a statement like `#!/usr/local/bin/perl`. The `#!/usr/local/bin/perl` tells the operating system that this is a Perl script and to use the program `#!/usr/bin/perl` to interpret it. However, if you have installed ActivePerl correctly on Windows systems using the defaults, this statement is not necessary. To run the `Hello World.pl`, use the following procedure:

1. Start a command prompt window using the **Start** > **Programs** > **Accessories** > **Command Prompt**.

2. Use DOS `cd` commands to navigate to the folder where you saved your Perl code.

3. Issue the `perl -c HelloWorld.pl` to check if there are any syntax errors. The `-c` is known as an option or switch, and it can be used to tell the interpreter to check for syntax errors. There are many such switches that can be used. In the command prompt, you may issue `perl -h` to display all possible switches.

4. If the code is free of errors, you may use the `perl -w Hello World.pl` or `perl HelloWorld.pl` to run your code.

These steps are illustrated in Figure 12.1. *Note:* If you have not used the default installation procedures when you installed Perl, you will need to set your path to `perl.exe` in the **Command Prompt screen** before you issue the `perl` command (**perl** `programName.pl` or **perl** `-c programName.pl`).

Hello World, from CGI

The next step is to modify your Hello World program so that it can be run from a Web browser, as opposed to running it directly from the Perl interpreter. We'll use CGI. A CGI program is still a Perl script, only it usually generates a Web page. Here's what it should look like:

```
#HelloFromCGI.pl
print "Content-type: text/html\n\n";
print "<body>\n";
```

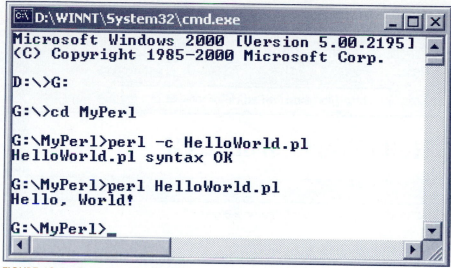

FIGURE 12.1   Execution of a Perl Program in Command Prompt

```
print "<h2>Hello World, from CGI<h2>\n";
print "</body></html>\n"
```

The `Content-type` describes the type of data that will be sent, expressed as a MIME type/subtype form. Since we want to generate an HTML page, we'll use text/html. To test the CGI application, use the following procedure:

1. First, test the code as a conventional Perl program using the procedures as illustrated in Figure 12.1.

2. Then copy the program to a virtual directory, unless the directory where you saved the code is already a virtual directory. (*Note:* If you do not know how to create a virtual directory in IIS environment, you may refer to Appendix A.)

3. Start Internet Explorer, and enter the URL as http://localhost/VirtualDirectoryAlias/HelloFromCGI.pl. The system will display the output as shown in Figure 12.2.

Hello World, in HTML

In the previous step, you generated CGI header lines and a single plain text "content" line. In this step, you will expand the content portion and embed HTML tags within it. As a result, when the data is displayed by a Web browser, it will be formatted as conventional HTML data. There's really nothing to generating the HTML data. You "write" it just like you normally do for a conventional HTML document, except that each line is placed inside a print statement and contains an explicit new-line (\n) character, if that is desired.

FIGURE 12.2   Output of a Perl Script on a Browser

Following is a Hello World, in HTML program, set up like a standard page:

```
#HelloWorldMoreHTML.pl
print "200 ok\n";
print "content-type: text/html\n\n";
print "<html>\n";
print "<head>\n";
print "<title>hello, world html </title>\n";
print "<h2>Hello, World, in HTML </h2>\n";
print "</head>\n";
print "<body>\n";
print "<hr/>\n";
print "Hello, World, in HTML\n";
print "</body>\n";
print "</html>";
```

It is a good practice to compile and debug most Perl codes using the procedures shown in Figure 12.1. Once you have removed most of the errors (bugs), you should copy the program in your virtual directory and open it using your browser.

Variables in Perl

Perl accommodates three intrinsic data types: `scalar`, `array`, and `hash`. A **scalar** variable can store only one value, whereas the `array` and **hash** variables can store lists of values. In this chapter, we will discuss only the `scalar` variables. Although Perl does not require us to explicitly declare variables, it is a good practice to declare all variables before we use them. To prevent Perl creating undeclared variables automatically, we may specify the **use strict;** statement at the top of the script.

The `scalar` variables are declared using the `my` keyword. All `scalar` variables must be named with a `$` prefix, such as `$name`, `$hours`, `$rate`, `$street`,

$city, $stateTax, and so forth. Perl does not have separate data types for integers, floating point numbers, and strings. Simply, use the my keyword to declare scalar variables as follows:

```
my ($variableName);
```

For example:

```
my ($name, $city, $zip);
my ($hours);
my ($rate, $grossWage);
```

As you can see from the above example, each Perl statement must be terminated by a semicolon. You may define one or more variables in one declare statement.

Conditional Statements in Perl

You can use the if keyword to build conditional structures in a Perl script. Like most other programming languages, Perl also accommodates the if . . . elsif . . . else structures. Since, these structures are very similar to the corresponding statements in many other languages like JavaScript, C, and Java, we will simply provide several examples without further discussions.

Conditional Statement Example 1: Using if in Perl

```
# if1.pl
print "content-type: text/html\n\n";
use strict;
my ($hours, $myMsg, $grossWage, $rate);
$hours= 30;
$rate = 10;
if ($hours < 40) {
  $myMsg="You have not done overtime";
  $grossWage= $hours * $rate;
}
```

Conditional Statement Example 2: Using if . . . else in Perl

```
# if2.pl
print "content-type: text/html\n\n";
use strict;
my ($hours, $myMsg, $grossWage, $rate);
$hours= 50;
$rate = 10;
if ($hours <= 40) {
  $myMsg="You have not done overtime";
  $grossWage= $hours * $rate;
}
else {
```

```
        $myMsg="You have done overtime";
        $grossWage = 40 * $rate + ($hours - 40) * 1.5 * $rate
    }
```

Conditional Statement Example 3: Using `if . . . elsif` **in Perl**

```
# if3.pl
print "content-type: text/html\n\n";
use strict;
my ($state, $scholarship);
$state= "KY";
if ($state eq "KY") {
    $scholarship= 2000;
} elsif ($state eq "IN") {
    $scholarship = 3000;
  } else {
      $scholarship = 0;
  }
```

Comparison Operators

Unlike Visual Basic or JavaScript, the comparison operators in Perl vary depending on numeric or text comparisons. For example, when we compare two strings, we need to use the eq **operator.** In the case where we compare two numeric values, we must use the == operator. Table 12.1 shows the respective operators for text and numeric comparisons.

TABLE 12.1   Perl Comparison Operators

Comparison	Numeric	String
Equals	==	eq
Does not equal	!=	ne
Greater than	>	gt
Less than	<	lt
Greater than or equal to	>=	ge
Less than or equal to	<=	le

Perl Logical Operators

Often you will need to combine two or more simple logical comparisons to build a compound logical statement. In this case, you will need to use the && **operator** for AND, the || **operator** for OR, and the ! operator for NOT. The following code excerpt will assign a scholarship of $2,000.00 to a student who is from Kentucky and has a GPA of more than 3.2.

```perl
# compound1.pl
--- ---
--- ---
if ($state eq "KY" && $gpa > 3.2) {
  $sch= 2000;
}
  else {
    $sch=0;
  }
```

Loops in Perl

Like most other programming languages, Perl also offers a wide variety of the **while** until, do . . . while, **for**, and **foreach** looping structures. We will simply provide selected examples without further discussion.

Loop Example 1: Using while

```perl
# while1.pl
# Add all integers from 1 to 10
print "content-type: text/html\n\n";
use strict;
my ($num, $sum);
$num= 1;
$sum = 0;
while ($num <= 10) {
  $sum=$sum + $num;
  $num = $num + 1;
}
print "<html>\n";
print "<head><title></title></head>\n";
print "<body>\n";
print "<h2> Using While </h2>\n";
print "<h3>";
print "Sum of all integers from 1 to 10 = $sum\n";
print "</body></html>";
```

Loop Example 2: Using for

```perl
# for1.pl
# Add all integers from 1 to 10 using "for"
print "content-type: text/html\n\n";
# Tell Perl not to create undeclared variables
use strict;
# declare variables
```

```perl
my ($num, $sum);

for ($num = 1; $num <= 10; $num++) {
   $sum=$sum + $num;
}
print "<html>\n";
print "<head><title></title></head>\n";
print "<body>\n";
print "<h2> Using For:   </h2>\n";
print "<h3>";
print "Sum of all integers from 1 to 10 = $sum\n";
print "</body></html>";
```

QuickCheck Questions

4. Why is Perl so popular?
5. What are the three intrinsic data types in Perl?
6. How do you declare a variable in Perl?
7. What command do you use to compile a Perl program?
8. How do you run a Perl script in a browser? (Recall that the script must reside in a virtual directory.)
9. Provide an example of a simple conditional statement in Perl.
10. Provide an example of a `while` loop in Perl.

CGI Forms

Forms are where CGI scripts have a foothold. They're everywhere, so this is a familiar place to begin getting acquainted with CGI scripts. It's easy enough to place form objects like radio buttons, checkboxes, and similar objects onto your Web page. Doing anything with them is a bit more involved. Creating a form generally involves two steps: creating a layout for the form and creating a CGI script on the server to process the information passed to the form.

Form Tags

The <form> **tag** is used to set apart a data input form and specifies the details about how the input from the form is handled.

* <form> begins a form.
* </form> ends a form.

You can insert any HTML tags you want to create a layout for the form (paragraphs, tables, etc.). However, you cannot nest form tags; that means no

`<form>...<form>...</form>...</form>` structure is allowed. The `action` **attribute** of a `<form>` tag is a URL that specifies where the results of the form should be sent. Usually this is the URL to some sort of CGI script.

```
<form action="URL">...</form>
,form method="".
```

The `method` **attribute** specifies the way in which the user's given data is sent to the `action` URL. The `method` attribute must be either `get` or `post`.

Data Collection Via Form

Inside the `<form>...</form>` tags, we usually provide the necessary HTML tags for displaying various data collection elements like textboxes, checkboxes, radio buttons, and many more. For example, the following code will display a textbox:

```
<form method="post" action="someURL">
<input type="text" name="txtUserName" />
</form>
```

The `<input>` **tag** is a simple form element. It has many attributes like `type`, `name`, `value`, `readonly`, and so on. We can use the `type` **attribute** to specify the type of the data collection element we want. For example `type="text"` will display a textbox, whereas `type="radio"` will display a radio button. Besides the `<input>` tag, we also may use several other tags such as `<select>`, `<option>`, and `<textarea>`. We have shown several such examples in Table 12.2.

Collecting Data from the User: An Example

The `<form>` tag plays a major role in Web development. At this stage, let us not worry about Perl. Let us focus our attention on how to construct a data entry form instead. We will illustrate the use of the HTML `<form>` tag's data collection elements via a simple example. Our objective is to develop an HTML form to collect tuition-related data from the user. The HTML document is displayed in a browser as shown in Figure 12.3.

As you can observe from Figure 12.3, we are using a textbox, two radio buttons, three checkboxes, a list box, and a `<textarea>` element to collect necessary data from the user. We have shown the Submit button for the purpose of showing how to develop a Submit button. At this stage, the Submit button would not be functional. The HTML source code for Figure 12.3 is shown in Figure 12.4.

TABLE 12.2 Selected Data Entry Elements (tags) in HTML

HTML Code	Description
`<input type="submit" value="Show Wage" />`	Displays a Submit button. If the user clicks on it, the browser sends the form's data to the server and requests the page as specified in the `action` attribute of the form.
`<input type="reset" value= "Clear Form"/>`	Displays a Reset button. On its click event, the browser clears all data entered by the user.
`<input type="text" name= "txtCity" size="5"/>`	Displays a textbox of size 5 pixels. The name is usually used to refer to it in scripts.
`<input type="radio" name= "radMajor" value="CSC"/> Computer Science  <input type="radio" name= "radMajor" value="IS"/> Information Systems`	Two radio buttons will be displayed. The user can select only one of the buttons. If the user selects **Computer Science**, the value of `radMajor` will be `CSC`. If the user selects **Information Systems**, the value of `radMajor` will be `IS`. Only one of the identically named radio buttons can be selected. If you want one of the buttons to be the default selection, use the `checked` attribute as shown in the example for checkboxes below.
`<input type="checkbox" name= "chkRecCenter" value="Y" checked/>Rec. Center  <input type="checkbox" name= "chkParking" value="Y"/> Parking  `	These statements will display two checkboxes. The first one will be checked by default. The user will be able to check none, one, or both of them. If a checkbox is checked, its value will be set to `Y` (in this example).
`<input type="password" name="txtPwd"/>`	Displays a textbox named `txtPwd` that will hide the text entered by the user.
`<input type="hidden" name= "hdnSum"/>`	Creates a hidden field, not viewable on the form. This type of field is usually used to preserve the states of certain variables.
`<select name="lstComputer" size="2"> <option selected value="PC">PC</option> <option value ="Mac">Macintosh </option></select>`	This is the way we populate and display a list box. You may specify `size="1"` to simulate a Visual Basic combo box. If the user selects Macintosh, the value of `lstComputer` will be set to `Mac`.
`<textarea name="txtAreaComments" rows="3" cols="30"> Enter your comments here</textarea>`	Will display a rectangular area where the user can enter more than one line of text.

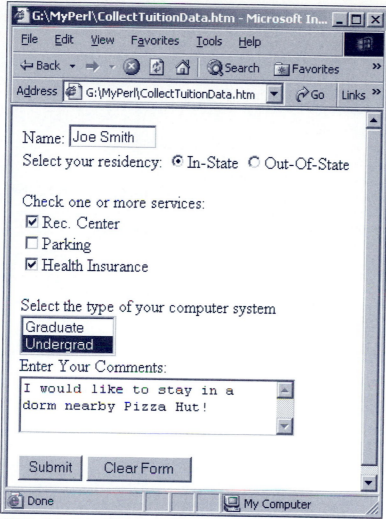

FIGURE 12.3   Using HTML Elements to Collect Data from the User

QuickCheck Questions

11. Why do we need the `<form>` tag in HTML?

12. What are the functions of the `method` and `action` parameters of a `<form>` tag?

13. How would you construct a list box in an HTML form?

14. How would you construct a drop-down box (Visual Basic combo box) in an HTML form?

15. Suppose that you want the user to enter some data in a textbox; however, you do not want to reveal the data on the screen. How would you accomplish this?

```
<!-CollectTuitionData.htm ->
<html><head></head><body>
<form>
  Name: <input type="text" name="txtUserName"
    size="10"/><br/>
  Select your residency:
  <input type="radio" name="radResidency" value="InState"
    checked/>In-State
  <input type="radio" name="radResidency" value=
    "OutOfState"/>Out-Of-State <br/><br/>
  Check one or more services:<br/>
  <input type="checkbox" name="chkRecCenter" value="Y"
    checked/>Rec. Center<br/>
  <input type="checkbox" name="chkParking" value= "Y"/>
    Parking<br/>
  <input type="checkbox" name="chkInsurance" value="Y"/>
    Health Insurance<br/><br/>
  Select the type of your computer system<br/>
  <select name="lstClass" size="2">
    <option selected value="Gr">Graduate</option>
    <option value ="Un">Undergrad</option>
  </select><br/>

  Enter Your Comments: <br/>
  <textarea name="txtAreaComments" rows="3" cols="30"
    wrap = "hard"></textarea> <br/>
  <input type="hidden" name="hdnRecipient" value=
    "something"/> <br/>
  <input type="submit" value="Submit"/> <input type=
    "reset" value="Clear Form"/> <br/>
</form></body></html>
```

FIGURE 12.4   The HTML Code for Collecting Tuition-Related Data

Using CGI Scripts to Process a Form's Data

The code shown in Figure 12.4 simply collects data from the user. Collecting data from the user is not an end by itself. The submitted data needs to be processed to accomplish a certain useful purpose. When the user provides the data and clicks the Submit button, the browser sends the form's data to the server. In most instances, we usually code the `<form>` as `<form method="post" action="somePerlScript.pl">`. In this case, when the user clicks the Submit button, his or her browser does two major activities: (1) it submits the form's data to the server and (2) it requests the *somePerlScript.pl* (or any such document that is specified in the action attribute). If the requested document is a CGI script, the server will first send the script to the CGI. In the CGI script, we can retrieve the submitted data using the param keyword (in the form **param("passedVariableName");**). An example is shown below:

```
$acNo = param("txtAcno");
```

In the above code, the CGI will extract the value of txtAcno from its param collection and store it in our variable named $acno. By the way, unlike ASP, the data retrieval in Perl is independent of the form submission methods get and post. That means we can use the param keyword irrespective of whether the data is submitted using post or get. In this context, we will provide two examples. First, we will illustrate the concept with a simple balance enquiry application. Later, we will provide a relatively comprehensive example on data handling from a variety of <input> elements (such as checkboxes, radio buttons, list boxes, etc.).

Balance Inquiry: Server-Side Processing Example 1

In this example, we will use an HTML document to collect the account number from the user. Once the user enters the account number and clicks the Submit button, we will use Perl script to display the appropriate balance. The HTML document named CollectAccountNumber.htm is shown in Figure 12.5. Its output is shown in Figure 12.6.

```
<! - CollectAccountNumber.htm ->
<html><head></head><body>
<form action="ShowBalance.pl" method="post"><h2>
Account Number: <input type ="text" name="txtAcno"
  size="10"/><br/></h2>
<input type="Submit" value="Show Balance"/>
</form></html>
```

FIGURE 12.5 CollectAccountNumber.htm Listing

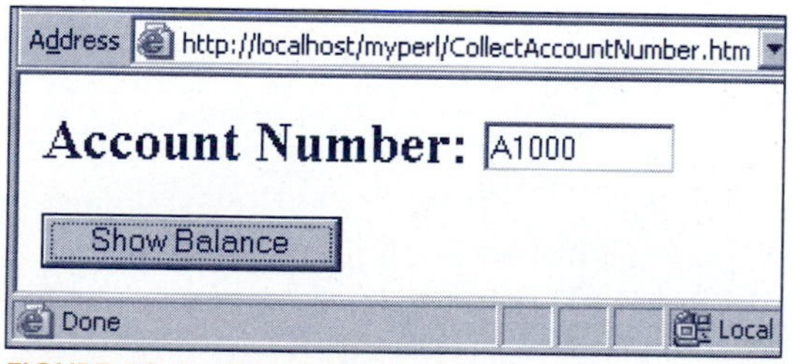

FIGURE 12.6 The Output of CollectAccountNumber.htm

On the click event of the Submit button (in Figure 12.6), the browser will submit the name and value of the textbox named txtAcno and will request the ShowBalance.pl. The code for the ShowBalance.pl and its output are shown in Figures 12.7 and 12.8, respectively. In a script, when we extract submitted data, we must specify the **use CGI qw(:standard -debug);** statement at the top or after the print "content-type" statement (as shown in the sixth line of Figure 12.7).

```perl
#showBalance.pl
# print "Content-type: text/html\n\n";
print "content-type: text/html\n\n";

# The following "use CGI" statement is mandatory when
# we retrieve submitted data
use CGI qw(:standard -debug);

# prevent Perl from creating undeclared variables
use strict;

#declare variables;
my ($acno, $balance, $myMsg);
# assign the passed data to variables
$acno= param("txtAcno");
# find balance: Here, in practice, the balance would have
    been
# found from a database. However, we are hard-coding the
balance in this example
if ($acno eq "A1000"){
   $balance = 134.56;
   $myMsg = "Thank you";
} elsif ($acno eq "B2000"){
   $balance = 222.22;
   $myMsg = "Thank you";
   }
   else {
      $balance = "Unknown";
      $myMsg="Bad Account Number"
   }
#create web page
print "<html><head><title></title></head>\n";
print "<body><h2>Balance Inquiry</h2>\n";
print "<h3>Your balance is $balance<br/>\n";
print "$myMsg</body></html>";
```

FIGURE 12.7 ShowBalance.pl Listing

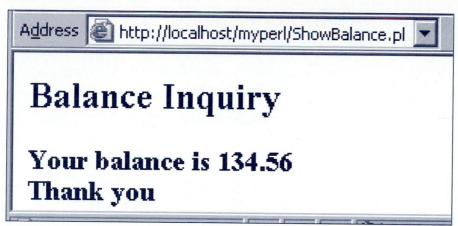

FIGURE 12.8   The Output of `ShowBalance.pl`

Computing Tuition and Fees: Server-Side Processing Example 2

Recall that in Figure 12.3, we illustrated how to collect tuition-related data from the user. However, the example illustrated in Figure 12.3 did not actually perform anything at the server side. In this example, we will enhance the application. After the data is submitted, we will employ a Perl script to compute and display the appropriate tuition and fees. The revised HTML code for data collection is shown in Figure 12.9 and its output is shown in Figure 12.10. The code is very similar to the code shown in Figure 12.4 with the exception that we have replaced the `<form>` specification with `<form method="get" action="AmountDue.pl">`. That means, on the click event of the Submit button, the browser will request the `AmountDue.pl` from the server.

On the click event of the Submit button (as shown in Figure 12.10), the client's browser will pass the form's data to the server and will request the `AmountDue.pl` script. The code for this script is shown in Figure 12.11 and its output is shown in Figure 12.12.

The results displayed in Figure 12.12 are not formatted nicely with the usual $ signs or with the usual comma separator and two digits after the decimal. Perl provides a number of other statements (functions), such as `printf` and `sprintf` to format and present data in a professional manner. Unfortunately, these functions are beyond the scope of this chapter.

```
<!- CollectTuitionDataFinal.htm ->
<html><head></head><body>
<form method="get" action="AmountDue.pl">
  Name: <input type="text" name="txtUserName" size=
    "10"/><br/>
  Select your residency:
  <input type="radio" name="radResidency"
      value="InState" checked/>In-State
  <input type="radio" name="radResidency"
      value="OutOfState"/>Out-Of-State <br/><br/>
  Check one or more services:<br/>
  <input type="checkbox" name="chkRecCenter" value="Y"
    checked/>Rec. Center<br/>
  <input type="checkbox" name="chkParking" value="Y"/>
    Parking<br/>
  <input type="checkbox" name="chkInsurance" value=
    "Y"/>Health Insurance<br/><br/>
  Select the type of your computer system<br/>
  <select name="lstClass" size="2">
    <option selected value="Gr">Graduate</option>
    <option value ="Un">Undergrad</option>
  </select><br/>

  Enter Your Comments: <br/>
  <textarea name="txtAreaComments" rows="3" cols="30"
    wrap = "hard"></textarea> <br/>
  <input type="submit" value="Submit"/> <input type=
    "reset" value="Clear Form"/> <br/>
</form></body></html>
```

FIGURE 12.9   Code Listing for `CollectTuitionDataFinal.htm`

QuickCheck Questions

16. Suppose that a form has submitted the data of an element named `txtCity`. In a Perl CGI program, how would you extract its value and save it in one of your `scalar` variables?

17. When would you need to insert the `use CGI qw(:standard -debug);` in your Perl code?

18. Explain how you will pass data contained in a number of radio buttons and checkboxes.

19. Explain how you will process the data submitted by a number of radio buttons and checkboxes.

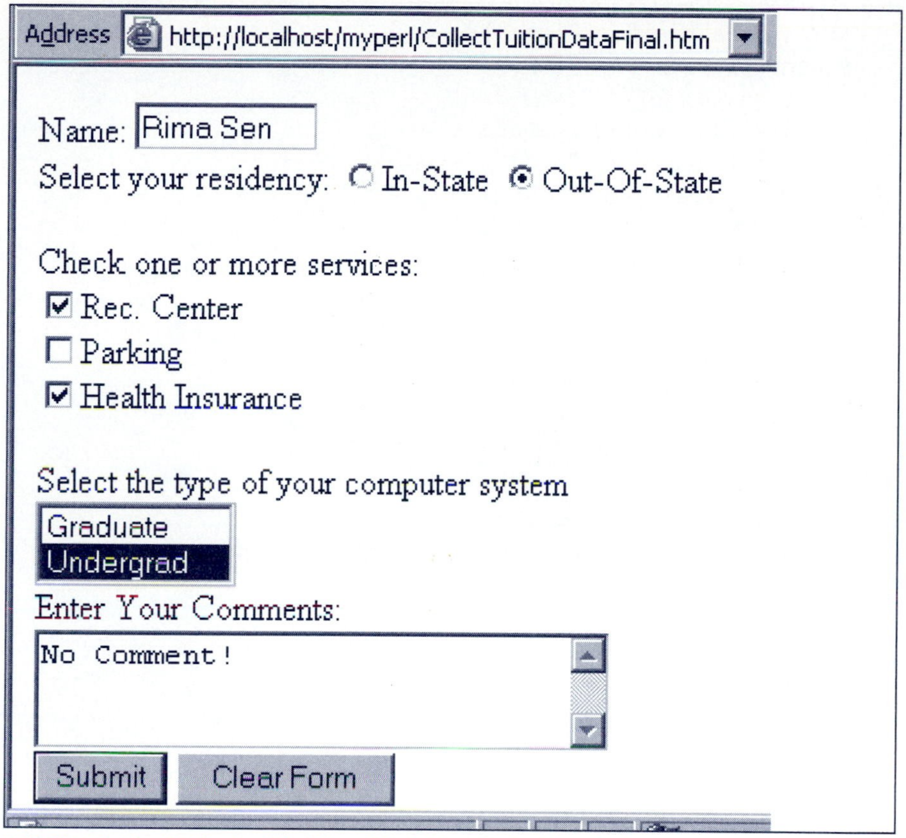

FIGURE 12.10 Output of `CollectTuitionDataFinal.htm`

```
# AmountDue.pl
print "content-type: text/html\n\n";
# The following "use CGI" statement is mandatory when
# we retrieve submitted data
use CGI qw(:standard -debug);

# Tell Perl not to create undeclared variables
use strict;

# declare variables
my ($name, $residency, $services, $class);
my ($tuition, $servFee, $amtDue);
# Store the submitted data into scalar variables
$name= param("txtUserName");
$residency= param("radResidency");
```

FIGURE 12.11 Code Listing for `Amount.pl` (continued)

```perl
$class = param("lstClass");
# compute tuition
$tuition= 0;
if ($residency eq "InState")
{    if ($class eq "Gr")
     {    $tuition = 1000; }
     else
     {  $tuition = 500; }
}
else
{  if ($class eq "Gr")
   {  $tuition = 2000; }
   else
   {  $tuition = 850; }
}
#compute service fees
$servFee = 0;
if (param("chkRecCenter") eq "Y")
{  $servFee = $servFee + 100;
}
if (param("chkParking") eq "Y")
{  $servFee = $servFee + 120;
}
if (param("chkInsurance") eq "Y")
{  $servFee = $servFee + 200;
}
# compute amount due
$amtDue = $tuition + $servFee;
#create the web page
print "<html>\n";
print "<head><title>Amount Due</title></head>\n";
print "<body>\n";
print "<h2> Tuition and Fees Computation </h2>\n";
print "<h3> Name : $name <br/>\n";
print "<br/>Tuition:  $tuition\n";
print "<br/>Service Fee: $servFee<br/>\n";
print "Amount Due: $amtDue</h3>";
print "</body></html>";
```

FIGURE 12.11   Code Listing for Amount.pl

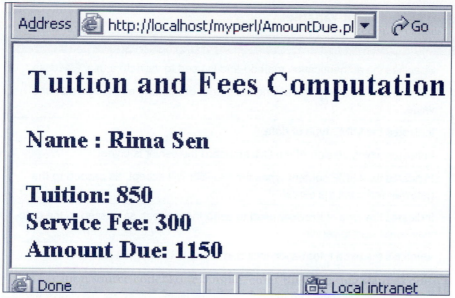

FIGURE 12.12   The Output of `Amount.pl`

Environment Variables

When a user activates a link to a CGI script, input is sent to the server. The server formats this data into environment variables and checks to see whether additional data was submitted via the standard input stream.

Input to CGI scripts is usually in the form of **environment variables,** which are pieces of information about the computer system such as IP address, operating system, and/or browser type. These values are hidden, but the Web server sends them to every CGI that's run. The environment variables passed to CGI scripts are associated with the browser requesting information from the server, the server processing the request, and the data passed in the request. Environment variables are case-sensitive and are normally used as described in this section. Although some environment variables are system-specific, many environment variables are standard. The standard variables are shown in Table 12.3.

As later examples show, environment variables are set automatically whenever reader input is passed to a server. The primary reason to learn about these variables is to better understand how input is passed to CGI scripts, but you also should learn about these variables so you know how to take advantage of them when necessary.

TABLE 12.3   Standard Environment Variables

Variable	Purpose
AUTH_TYPE	Specifies the authentication method and is used to validate a user's access.
CONTENT_LENGTH	Used to provide a way of tracking the length of the data string as a numeric value.
CONTENT_TYPE	Indicates the MIME type of data.
GATEWAY_INTERFACE	Indicates which version of the CGI standard the server is using.
HTTP_ACCEPT	Indicates the MIME content types the browser will accept, as passed to the gateway script via the server.
HTTP_USER_AGENT	Indicates the type of browser used to send the request, as passed to the gateway script via the server.
PATH_INFO	Identifies the extra information included in the URL after the identification of the CGI script.
PATH_TRANSLATED	Set by the server based on the PATH_INFO variable. The server translates the PATH_INFO variable into this variable.
QUERY_STRING	Set to the query string (if the URL contains a query string).
REMOTE_ADDR	Identifies the Internet Protocol address of the remote computer making the request.
REMOTE_HOST	Identifies the name of the machine making the request.
REMOTE_IDENT	Identifies the machine making the request.
REMOTE_USER	Identifies the user name as authenticated by the user.
REQUEST_METHOD	Indicates the method by which the request was made.
SCRIPT_NAME	Identifies the virtual path to the script being executed.
SERVER_NAME	Identifies the server by its host name, alias, or IP address.
SERVER_PORT	Identifies the port number the server received the request on.
SERVER_PROTOCOL	Indicates the protocol of the request sent to the server.
SERVER_SOFTWARE	Identifies the Web server software.

Extracting Visitor's Browser Information

We will illustrate the use of an environment variable with an example. In this example, we will develop a Perl CGI script that will extract the value of HTTP_USER_AGENT from the environment variables and display it on the browser. The following script will accomplish the objective, and its output is shown in Figure 12.13:

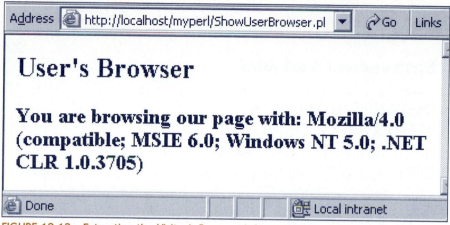

FIGURE 12.13   Extracting the Visitor's Browser Information

```
#showUserBrowser.pl
print "content-type: text/html\n\n";
my ($ubrowser);
$ubrowser = $ENV{"HTTP_USER_AGENT"};
print "<html><head><title></title></head>\n";
print "<body><h2>User's Browser</h2>\n";
print "<h3>You are browsing our page with: $ubrowser";
print "</body></html>";
```

Displaying All Environment Variables

Environment variables are stored in a hash called %ENV. Essentially, a hash structure is a collection of entries. It contains a "key and value" pair for each entry. You can use a foreach statement to retrieve the key and the values from a hash. The following code (#ShowAllEnvVariables.pl) will extract and display the name and values of each environmental variable.

```
#ShowAllEnvVariables.pl
print "content-type: text/html\n\n";
my ($k);
print "<html><head><title></title></head>\n";
print "<body><h3>Environment Variables</h3>\n";
foreach $k (keys(%ENV)) {
    print "$k = $ENV{$k}<br/>";
  }
print "</body></html>";
```

The output of the #ShowAllEnvVariables.pl code is shown in Figure 12.14.

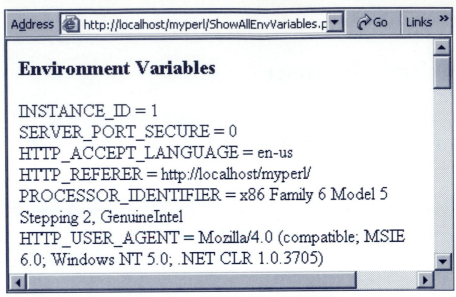

FIGURE 12.14   Displaying the Values of All Environment Variables

QuickCheck Questions

20. What are environment variables?

21. Name at least five environment variables.

22. How will you extract the value of the environment variable named `HTTP_REFERER`?

MIME Types

MIME stands for Multipurpose Internet Mail Extension. This is a protocol to send files via electronic mail (and now the Web) and have them interpreted in the correct manner. MIME types are important to CGI programmers since the scripts must conform to the MIME standards. What this means is your script must specify the type of file it is producing before it produces any other result.

We specify the output type by sending an ASCII message similar to

```
Content-type: text/html \n\n
```

(where `\n` is a new line). The second half of the message is the most important as it specifies the type of file. This example indicates that the data to come is a text file and, more precisely, an HTML text file. Other `Content-type:` examples include

- `image/jpeg`: jpeg graphical image.
- `audio/mpeg`: MP3 audio file.
- `application/pdf`: Portable Document Format (Adobe).
- `audio/x-pn-realaudio`: RealPlayer audio file.
- `text/plain`: ASCII text.
- `video/quicktime`: Quicktime video clip.

These MIME types can be used to specify the content of your CGIs, so they don't have to produce just HTML documents; they can produce images, audio files, just about anything! MIME types are broken down into basic type categories. Each data type category has a primary subtype associated with it. Table 12.4 shows the basic MIME types and their descriptions.

TABLE 12.4   Basic MIME Types

Type	Description
application	Binary data that can be executed or used with another application
audio	A sound file that requires an output device to preview
image	A picture that requires an output device to preview
message	An encapsulated mail message
multipart	Data consisting of multiple parts and possibly many data types
text	Textual data that can be represented in any character set or formatting language
video	A video file that requires an output device to preview
x-world	Experimental data type for world files

Some MIME content types can be used with additional parameters. These content types include `text/plain`, `text/html`, and all multipart message data.

CONTENT_TYPE

The `CONTENT_TYPE` variable indicates the data's MIME type. MIME typing is a feature of HTTP 1.0 and is not available on servers using HTTP 0.9. This variable is set only when attached data is passed using the standard input or output stream. The value assigned to the variable identifies the MIME type and subtype as follows:

```
CONTENT_TYPE = type/subtype
```

Summary

In this chapter, we have introduced you to the Common Gateway Interface (CGI). CGI scripts are executed at the server-side. When a user requests a CGI script, the server passes the requested script to the CGI. The CGI, in turn, produces the response object (document) from the script, which is then passed on to the user by the Web server.

CGI scripts can be developed using almost any programming language such as Perl, Python, Visual Basic, Java, JavaScript, and so forth. Since most CGI processing requires a significant amount of text manipulation, Web developers often use Perl for developing CGI scripts. Perl has certain powerful constructs for text manipulation, and it is also widely supported by Unix, Microsoft, and Macintosh.

It is relatively easy to learn the basic syntax of Perl. Like most other computer programming languages, Perl offers basic programming structures to build conditional statements and loops. However, Perl is a powerful language, and you will need to go beyond this textbook's materials to master it, if so desired. You also may find Perl somewhat similar to Java.

We usually employ the HTML <form> element to collect relevant data from an user. Once the data is submitted to the server, we can use Perl scripts to process the submitted data at the server-side and then take appropriate actions. Most of the server-side processing involves taking certain actions on databases, such as retrieving or updating the balance of a customer or storing the information about an order. Since the database technology is beyond the scope of this textbook, we have stayed away from such server-side processing. However, we have provided many examples on server-side processing that can be converted to database applications once you learn the database access technologies.

Key Terms

&& operator

|| operator

action attribute

Command Prompt screen

Common Gateway Interface (CGI)

environment variable

eq operator

for

foreach

<form> tag

hash

HTTP_REFERER

HTTP_USER_AGENT

if...elsif...else

<input> tag

method attribute

MIME

my ($variableName);

<option>

param("passedVariableName");

perl -c programName.pl

perl programName.pl

scalar

<select>

<textarea>

type attribute

use CGI qw(:standard -debug)

use strict;

while

1. Define a basic HTML document. Insert a text "Writing a Guestbook Form" as <h1>.

2. Define the beginning and end tags for the forms section. The form's data should be submitted using "post" and you should specify a script named firstform.cgi in the action attribute of the form.

3. Add 2 text boxes, 25 characters long for the "email" and "username" of the user.

4. Collect some Demographic Data. Ask the user "Where do you live?" and present them with 5 or 6 choices in a 2 line drop-down list box.

5. Provide a number of Check Boxes for response. Ask the user to check a number of remarks that would match their initial reaction to the homepage. You provide the remarks.

6. Provide a radio button rating choice. Offer the user a way to rate a page. Use a number of radio button 4 or 5 choices.

7. a. Collect comments. Set up a text area 50 to 60 columns wide by 8 to 10 rows deep where the user can enter comments.

   b. We are now just about finished with the form and ready to work on the cgi-script that will process the data. Be sure to put the following code at the end of the form so that we can have a button to submit the form:
   <input type="submit">

8. Develop the firstform.cgi. In this code, extract the submitted data and display them on the browser. .

Dreamweaver MX

OBJECTIVES

1. To introduce Dreamweaver and the Dreamweaver interface.

2. To create a basic Web page with Dreamweaver.

3. To understand the role of behaviors within Dreamweaver.

4. To understand how to create a Popup message with a Dreamweaver behavior.

5. To understand how to create a Popup window with a Dreamweaver behavior.

6. To understand how to create a rollover image with a Dreamweaver behavior.

An Overview of Dreamweaver

Throughout this text, you have been shown various methods for implementing HTTP techniques such as HTML, XML, and DHTML. In addition, you have worked with several programming and scripting languages such as JavaScript and CGI. At this point, you have been able to see the power of programming for the Web as well as the complexity of these languages. In this chapter, we will introduce you to Macromedia's Dreamweaver MX. Dreamweaver is part of the suite of tools known as **Studio MX** and is the primary tool for visually designing, programming, and managing websites and pages.

A **visual web editor** is simply a tool that enables the developer to create and edit Web pages while being able to see what they will look like as they are created. Macromedia has a rich tradition of creating software tools to help developers create media-rich content for their Web pages. Macromedia offers other products in Studio MX such as Flash, Fireworks, and Freehand. All of these products are geared toward high-end, professional Web page design.

From the beginning, Dreamweaver is somewhat different from many different visual editors in that it uses **roundtrip HTML editing.** This technique creates Web pages either by using visual HTML editing tools or through straight text files without creating a difference in the resulting output. That is, Dreamweaver does not create proprietary HTML code; therefore, editing the HTML source code is much easier. Dreamweaver will automatically update code that it recognizes as invalid (such as extra closing tags) when you switch back to it from another editor, but it leaves valid code as it is.

The primary emphasis of Dreamweaver is the management of websites as opposed to just merely Web page development. For many organizations (small, medium, or large), the website is a combination of various tools such as HTML, XML, PHP, sophisticated backend programs such as Java, ASP, and database connectivity languages such as ColdFusion. In most cases, a team of professionals with highly specified duties design and manage the website instead of a single person who does it all. However, they all have to have access to the same source code for modification and maintenance. Dreamweaver provides the tools and functionality to manage a website in a distributed environment. This is the primary reason why Dreamweaver is the tool of choice for professional website developers, designers, and administrators.

Some of the more important features of Dreamweaver include

- CSS or Cascading Style Sheet support.
- Support for data-driven website development with tools such as ASP.Net, ColdFusion, PHP, and other popular server-side technologies.
- Cross-browser validation.
- Code editing support.
- JavaScript functions for client-side interactivity.

In this chapter, we will focus on the ability to implement client-side interactivity. Specifically, we will use the behaviors tools of Dreamweaver to implement a Popup message, Popup window, and a rollover image. But first, let's take a quick tour of the Dreamweaver MX interface and how the user interacts with it.

QuickCheck Questions

1. What programs are included in the Macromedia Studio MX?
2. What is a visual web editor?
3. What is roundtrip HTML editing?
4. Why is Dreamweaver so popular with Web professionals?

Dreamweaver MX Interface

When Dreamweaver is first opened, you will get a screen similar to the one shown in Figure 13.1. There are several key features that are important to being able to use Dreamweaver for efficient design and implementation of Web pages. These tools include the menu bar, the standard toolbar, the Insert tabs, the Properties Inspector, and the panel groups.

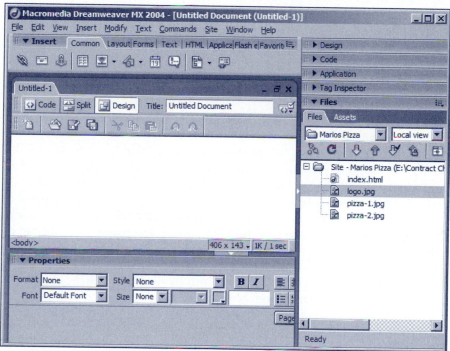

FIGURE 13.1   Dreamweaver Opening Screen

Menu Bar

The menu bar is where most of the commands that you will use through Dreamweaver are located. These include some of the more "standard issue" commands such as **File** > **Save** and **Edit** > **Copy**. In addition, all of the Dreamweaver tools and commands can be accessed though the menu bar.

Toolbar

The toolbar places many of the commands and functions that are located in the menu bar in the form of a button icon for quick access. The functions that are used most often include the Code View and Design View, Document Title,

Browser Check, and Preview in Browser. We will use some of these later in this chapter.

Insert Tabs

The **Insert tabs** contain eight categories of functions that are used for creating and inserting objects into the document window. By default, the object panel shows the Common tasks category of buttons. All of the functions of these buttons can be accessed from the various menus; however, the object panel is a quick way to access the various actions that will help you create your Web pages. The categories of functions include Common, Layout, Forms, Text, HTML, Application, Flash elements, and Favorites. Within the context of this text, we will not use the Insert tabs feature often; however, the importance of this feature cannot be understated. In the typical website and Web page design environment, this feature of Dreamweaver MX is used often within the context of daily use of Dreamweaver.

Properties Inspector

The **Properties Inspector** is where the primary formatting of the document occurs. This window provides a convenient way to apply properties to whatever you are working with in a document. What you see in the window will vary depending on what is selected in the document. For example, when a piece of text is selected, you can insert a hyperlink in the link field; apply a heading in the format field; change the font, font size, and color; make the text bold or italic; set the alignment; and format a bullet or numbered list. If an image is selected, then you can change the characteristics of the image such as the size, the alternative name, the image location, and so on. The Properties Inspector can be minimized or turned off completely in order to see more on the screen.

The Panel Groups

The **panel groups** are where the action is within Dreamweaver MX. These are groupings of commonly used features for both website design and management. The panel groups are also highly customizable. That is, you can group together various tools that you might use on a regular basis. For example, you can place the behaviors tools with the CSS tools. The categories of the panel groups include Files, Design, Code, Application, and Tag Inspector. The Files group is shown in Figure 13.1 and allows quick access to the files within the defined site or any other place on your computer or even within an FTP site on the network. The panel groups can be "put away" by clicking the arrow on the side of the panel groupings. This would allow you to see the entire screen while you are currently working within the document. In addition, a tool within the panel group can be undocked from the panel to be used as a floating tool window in your document.

Creating Your First Page in Dreamweaver

Figure 13.2 shows the Internet Explorer version of the Web page that we wish to create.

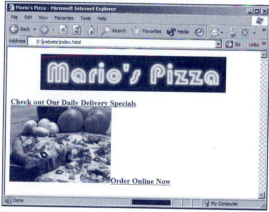

FIGURE 13.2   Mario's Pizza Web Page

There are several key features of this page that we will learn how to implement. First, the page shows two images and some basic text that have been inserted. In addition, we have two hyperlinks on the page. What is not seen is that the image of the pizza will include a rollover image. That is, when the user places his or her mouse over the image, the image will change. In this example, we will assume that it is an image that will tell the user about the pizza that is currently shown. The two links also have something that cannot be shown on a two-dimensional page. That is, the link that says "Check out Our Daily Delivery Specials" will actually trigger a Popup message while the "Order Online Now" link will create a Popup window in a new window. All three of these functions are implemented through the behaviors utility in Dreamweaver MX. Before we can get started with the behaviors, we must get a basic page started.

The Basics—Inserting Basic Text and Images

Let's get started by opening a new document in Dreamweaver MX. The steps in creating a new blank document are pretty simple. There are three ways you can accomplish this. First, you can simply click the **New File** icon on the toolbar under the **Code View** button. Second, you can select **File** > **New** from the menu bar. Third, you can press **Control+N** on your keyboard. All three methods will result in the same outcome: the New Document dialog window.

From this window, you can choose upfront what kind of document this will be. In previous chapters, we have shown you how to create an ASP file, a Java file, or a PHP file. From this dialog in Dreamweaver MX you can set what type of file you are trying to create. This also will designate how the page will behave in terms of panel groups and the Insert tab tools that can appear.

In this case, select **Basic Page** from the Category selector and then select **HTML page** from the Types menu. Finally, click **Create** on the dialog window and the new blank document will be created in your page.

Inserting an Image into the Blank Page

Through examination of Figure 13.2, we can see that the first task is to place the logo of our pizza company on the page. This actually is a pretty simple task within Dreamweaver and, as always, there are multiple ways to accomplish this task: Insert tab, menu bar, or keyboard.

Insert Tab

- First, make sure that your cursor is positioned at the top of the document.
- Select the **Insert Image** icon from the Common Insert tab. This will bring up the submenu shown in Figure 13.3.
- Move to **Image** and click. This will bring up the Select Image Source dialog window where you can search for and select the image name. In this case, we are looking for the file named logo.jpg.
- Finally, click **OK** to select the image and place it in the document at the cursor position.

Menu Bar

- Select **Insert** > **Image** from the menu bar.
- Select the image from the Select Image Source dialog window. You can search for and select the desired image.
- Click **OK** to select the image and place it in the document at the cursor position.

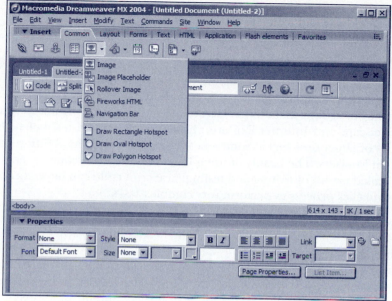

FIGURE 13.3   Insert Image Submenu

Keyboard

*   Select **Control+Alt+I** on your keyboard to open the Select Image Source dialog window.

The method by which you select an image is purely one of personal choice. Either of the three methods will result in the exact same outcome.

Behaviors

Dreamweaver uses a **behavior,** which is further defined by two terms: an event and an action. An **event** is simply something that the user does such as moving the mouse over a particular object or clicking a button. An **action** is the result of that event that performs some specific task. Dreamweaver comes prepackaged with about two dozen behaviors or you can create your own behavior to use throughout your website.

In Chapter 7, we introduced the concept of JavaScript code to process a form on the client side. In this chapter, we examine the use of predefined JavaScript code (behaviors) to perform specific tasks within Dreamweaver. The behavior actions included in Dreamweaver have been written to work in both Netscape and Internet Explorer; however, you should test behaviors in all types of target browsers as sometimes a behavior will behave differently in different browsers. The beauty of using behaviors within Dreamweaver is that the detailed nature of writing and testing JavaScript code can be reduced to a point-and-click process to perform very complex tasks.

Behaviors can create a more enjoyable user experience. A behavior can validate a form to ensure that when a user enters data into a particular text field that it is the type of data that you want. That is, for example, an e-mail field can be validated to ensure that the ampersand (@) character exists on the screen. A behavior can add interactivity to the site through the creation of the image swaps. The overall objective of any behavior should be to extend the functionality of the website through client-side actions. This will make your website more user friendly and intuitive to the end-user.

The basic procedure for attaching a behavior to a Dreamweaver element is as follows:

1. Select the element on the page to which you wish to attach the behavior. Note that you cannot attach a behavior to plain text. However, you can attach a behavior to the entire page through the `<body>` tag.

2. Choose **Window** > **Behaviors** from the menu bar to open the Behaviors panel in the panel groups.

3. Click the **Plus** button and choose an action from the Popup menu. The Popup menu will show the behaviors that are available for the current tag that is selected. In Figure 13.4, the current tag selected is the `<body>` tag. The behaviors that are shown will only be those that are relevant for this particular tag. In addition, the behaviors that are shown will only work for the selected browsers. You can change the selected browsers by choosing the **Show Events For** submenu on the **Plus** button menu.

4. Finally, select the behavior and enter the parameters for the action. These parameters will be different based on the event itself, the browser, and the tag for which you are applying the event.

The three types of behaviors that we will be implementing are: Popup window, Popup message, and rollover image. All three of these implement JavaScript into the page that Dreamweaver actually renders for you. Let's get started!

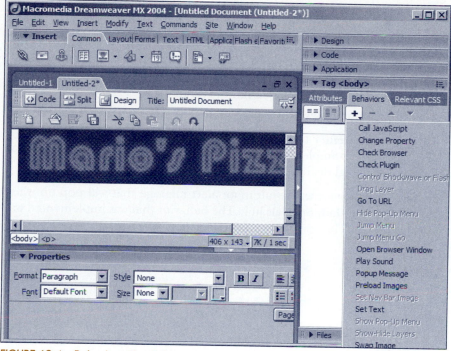

FIGURE 13.4   Behaviors Plus Submenu

QuickCheck Questions

11. What is a behavior?

12. What are the two basic parts of a behavior?

13. Describe the basic procedure for implementing a Dreamweaver behavior.

Popup Message

A Popup message or alert message is a quick and easy way to inform a user about an action that he or she is about to take or to inform the user about information that is pertinent to the user's experience. In our example, we will tell the user what the daily special is for Mario's Pizza. This entails clicking on a hyperlink and then having the alert message pop up to tell us what kind of pizza is currently on sale.

This is a little bit tricky, in that we will have to first type the text into the document window and then give it a fake URL for a hyperlink. We have to do this as the behavior we want to implement cannot be implemented simply on text; it has to be on a hyperlink. Therefore, follow these steps to implement this behavior.

- Enter the text that you wish to have a hyperlink associated with. In our example, we typed in **Check out Our Daily Delivery Specials**.
- Select the entire line of text.
- In the **Link Text** window on the Properties Inspector, type the **pound sign** (#). This will create a hyperlink that goes nowhere.
- Now, click the + **sign** in the Behaviors window.
- Go to **Popup message** and click.

In the dialog box, enter the text that you wish to show in the alert box, then click **OK**. In our example, I entered **The Large Supreme Pizza is only 10.99 delivered**. Not a bad deal!

The resulting behavior will result in an alert message that will pop up when the user clicks the **Daily Specials** link. The behavior that was implemented was simply JavaScript. The resulting code is shown below:

```
<html>
<head>
<title>Mario's Pizza</title>
<script language="JavaScript" type="text/JavaScript">
<!-
function MM_popupMsg(msg) {
    alert(msg);
}
</script>
</head>

<body>
<p><img src="logo.jpg" width="443" height="85"></p>
<p><a href="#" onClick="MM_popupMsg('The Large Supreme
    Pizza is only 10.99 delivered!')">Check out Our Daily
    Delivery Specials </a></p>
</body>
</html>
```

Look familiar? It should. It is very similar to the JavaScript that you implemented in the JavaScript chapter. However, you did not have to write a single line of script with the use of the Dreamweaver MX behavior.

Rollover Image

Now, let's insert a rollover image. The rollover image is one of the simpler behaviors to implement into a Dreamweaver MX page. When we examine Figure 13.2, we see the pizza photograph. This photograph can be changed when the user moves his or her mouse over the image. In Figure 13.5, we can see the image that will be shown when the image is rolled over.

FIGURE 13.5   Rollover Image: Mario's Pizza

To implement this behavior, follow these steps:

- Position your cursor at the place where you wish to insert the image.
- Click the **Insert Image** icon on the Insert tab menu.
- Move to **Rollover image** and click. This will bring up Insert Rollover Image dialog window (Figure 13.6), which asks for five pieces of information:

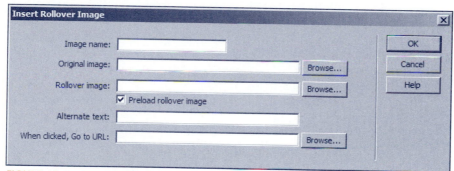

FIGURE 13.6   Insert Rollover Image Dialog Window

- Image name: This is the name of the image that will be used in the JavaScript that is created. In our case, let's name it **Pizza**.
- Original image: This is the name and path of the image file. You can use the **Browse** button to get to this image. We are looking for the file named **pizza-1.jpg**.
- Rollover image: This the name and path of the rollover image file. You also can use the **Browse** button to find this file name. We are looking for the file named **pizza-2.jpg**.
- Preload rollover image: You should click this checkbox. This will place the image in the user's cache so that there is no delay when the user rolls over the image.
- Alternate text: This is the text that will show up as a yellow tag when the user places his or her cursor on the image. It is polite

and good Web page design to include an alternate text tag. In this example, we should enter: **The Mario's Supreme Pizza**.

- When clicked, Go to URL: Finally, we can enter a URL to hyperlink the image. In our case, we can skip this area of the dialog.

- Now, click **OK** to set up the rollover image.

The resulting HTML code is as follows:

```html
<html>
<head>
<title>Untitled Document</title>
<meta http-equiv="Content-Type" content="text/html;
  charset=iso-8859-1">
<script language="JavaScript" type="text/JavaScript">
<!-
function MM_popupMsg(msg) { //v1.0
  alert(msg);
}

function MM_swapImgRestore() { //v3.0
  var i,x,a=document.MM_sr; for(i=0;
    a&&i<a.length&&(x=a[i])&&x.oSrc;i++) x.src=x.oSrc;
}

function MM_preloadImages() { //v3.0
  var d=document; if(d.images){ if(!d.MM_p) d.MM_p=new
    Array();
    var i,j=d.MM_p.length,a=MM_preloadImages.arguments;
      for(i=0; i<a.length; i++)
    if (a[i].indexOf("#")!=0){ d.MM_p[j]=new Image;
      d.MM_p[j++].src=a[i];}}
}
function MM_findObj(n, d) { //v4.01
  var p,i,x;  if(!d) d=document;
    if((p=n.indexOf("?"))>0&&parent.frames.length) {
    d=parent.frames[n.substring(p+1)].document;
      n=n.substring(0,p);}
  if(!(x=d[n])&&d.all) x=d.all[n]; for
    (i=0;!x&&i<d.forms.length;i++) x=d.forms[i][n];
  for(i=0;!x&&d.layers&&i<d.layers.length;i++)
    x=MM_findObj(n,d.layers[i].document);
  if(!x && d.getElementById) x=d.getElementById(n); return x;
}

function MM_swapImage() { //v3.0
  var i,j=0,x,a=MM_swapImage.arguments; document.MM_sr=new
    Array; for(i=0;i<(a.length-2);i+=3)
```

```
    if ((x=MM_findObj(a[i]))!=null){document.MM_sr[j++]=x;
      if(!x.oSrc) x.oSrc=x.src; x.src=a[i+2];}
}
//-->
</script>
</head>

<body onLoad="MM_preloadImages(pizza-2.jpg')">
<p><img src="logo.jpg" width="443" height="85"></p>
<p><a href="#" onClick="MM_popupMsg('The Large Supreme
  Pizza is only 10.99 delivered!')">Check out Our Daily
  Delivery Specials </a></p>
<p><a href="#" onMouseOut="MM_swapImgRestore()"
  onMouseOver="MM_swapImage('Image2','','pizza-2.jpg',1)">
  <img src="pizza-1.jpg" alt="Mario's Supreme Pizza" name=
  "Image2" width="240" height="180" border="0"></a></p>
</body>
</html>
```

That is a lot of JavaScript that Dreamweaver MX automatically implements into our website!

Popup Window

Our final example of using Dreamweaver MX to create high-quality interactions is to implement a Popup window when the user clicks a hyperlink. In this example, we want to give the user the ability to order this pizza online. We have prepared a form-based HTML page that has CGI script to process the order. This file is named order.htm. When the user clicks the link named **Order Online Now** (see Figure 13.2), we want a small window to pop up for the user to be able to order pizza. You will be pretty surprised to see how easy this behavior is to implement.

- First, type the text for your link at the desired cursor position. In our case, type **Click Here to Order Online** next to the pizza picture.
- Now, select the text for the link.
- Again, we will have to "trick" Dreamweaver into thinking that this is a hyperlink in order to implement the behavior. Therefore, type the **pound sign** into the Link box in the Properties Inspector.
- Select the + **sign** on the Behaviors panel group.
- Move to **Open Browser Window** and click. This will bring up the Open Browser Window dialog window (Figure 13.7). In this window we will need to provide five categories of information.

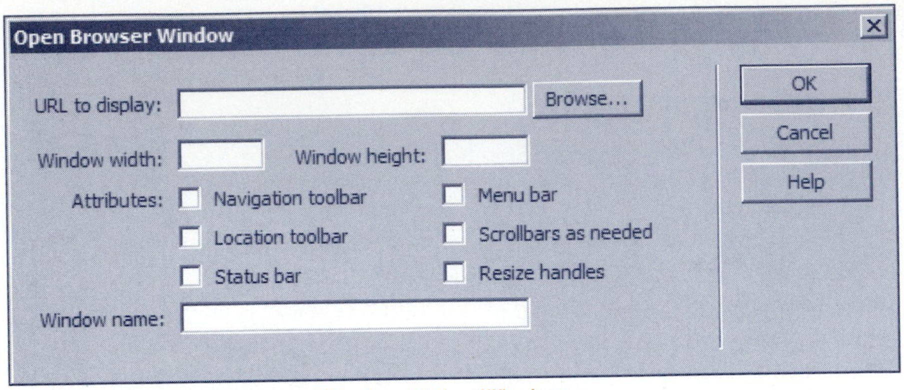

FIGURE 13.7   Open Browser Window Dialog Window

- URL to display: Enter the name of the file in this window. You can use the **Browse** button to indicate the file and file name. In our example, we want the **order.htm file**.

- Window width and Window height: These boxes enable us to set the size of the window in pixels. In this case, we want the window to be rather small. Therefore, enter **300** for both measurements.

- Attributes: This allows us to identify the various attributes of this Popup window. We can identify whether or not the window will have a navigation toolbar, a menu bar, a location toolbar, scrollbars, a status bar, and resize handles. These attributes will determine what the window will look like. You should experiment with these; however, for our example, do not click any of these attributes.

- Window name: Finally, give the window a target name of **order**.

- Now, click **OK** to implement the Popup window.

The JavaScript that was implemented in the <head> section is as follows:

```
function MM_openBrWindow(theURL,winName,features) { //v2.0
    window.open(theURL,winName,features);
}
```

The JavaScript that will implement the Popup at the hyperlink is defined as

```
<a href="#" onClick="MM_openBrWindow('order.htm','order',
    'width=300,height=300')">Order Online Now </a></p>
```

Again, the JavaScript that was implemented would have taken longer without Dreamweaver MX.

QuickCheck Questions

14. What is the basic procedure for implementing an alert or Popup message?

15. What is the basic procedure for implementing a rollover image?

16. What is the basic procedure for implementing a Popup window?

Dreamweaver MX makes for easy and quick implementation of some relatively advanced behaviors or JavaScript actions. The full functionality of this website management and Web page design tool cannot be adequately treated in this text. Therefore, you should become familiar with other tools that Dreamweaver MX implements such as CSS, HTML coding, site management, and many others. However, by understanding the concepts of this text, your ability to implement Dreamweaver MX will be significantly increased. That is, without a full understanding of what Dreamweaver is doing, you cannot edit the resulting code, which is something that a professional Web designer will have to do from time to time when working with any Web page design tool.

Summary

Key Terms

action
behavior
event

Insert tabs
panel groups
Properties Inspector

roundtrip HTML editing
Studio MX
visual web editor

Review Questions

1. How would you describe the primary purposes of Dreamweaver?
2. Describe the concept of roundtrip HTML. Why is it important for professional Web page design?
3. Describe the basic portions of the Dreamweaver interface.
4. What is the primary purpose of the panel groups?
5. Describe the two basic characteristics of a behavior.
6. What is the difference between attaching a behavior to an object on the Web page and attaching it to the `<body>` tag?
7. How does a behavior speed coding in the HTML environment?
8. Describe the process of implementing a Popup or alert message.
9. Describe the process of implementing a rollover image in Dreamweaver.
10. Describe the process of implementing a Popup window in Dreamweaver.

Exercises

1. Create your personal home page in Dreamweaver. Include on your page links to some of your favorite sites. These links should be in the form of opening a new window.
2. On your personal home page include a picture of yourself. Have an alternative image for rollover.
3. Place an alert message on a link on your page.

Creating Dynamic Web Pages with FrontPage

OBJECTIVES

1. To learn how to add dynamic effects to FrontPage.
2. To learn how to access the Script Editor and the Visual Basic Editor.
3. To explore some of FrontPage's Web components.
4. To learn when to use JavaScript and VBScript to add extra functionality to FrontPage.
5. To learn how to add multimedia effects in FrontPage.

INTRODUCTION

Microsoft FrontPage is the most widely used site design tool on the market today. It certainly is a strong and versatile tool, and one that has had critical acclaim, but its position in the market is largely a result of FrontPage's incorporation into the Microsoft Office suite of productivity applications. Although few programmers would argue that FrontPage is a programming tool, and veteran programmers might look down on the code FrontPage generates, there are few tools that will produce as good a result in as short a time. You may be called on as a Web programmer to work in FrontPage, and not only are there many ways in which programming skills can add value to FrontPage sites, but there are tricks to be learned in the manner in which FrontPage implements features and in the way it deploys its sites.

Integrated Development Environment (IDE)

FrontPage is what is known as an **Integrated Development Environment,** or **IDE**. The goal of an IDE is to create a program using a toolbox, usually with a graphical interface. Other examples of IDEs that you might be familiar with are

355

Microsoft's Visual Studio and Adobe Illustrator, and the more recent VB.NET. VB.NET allows you to build *programs* using Visual Basic and Web components and services through a click-and-drag procedure that moves program objects to a design surface. Among the many choices you might see in Visual Basic would be a timer object, graphical objects like field boxes on an input screen, a report or query object, a data source object, and so forth. It's obvious that Visual Basic is a programming environment because it forces you to be intimately involved in code. Although VB will write a lot of code for you, a programmer is constantly adding code for Properties, Events, and Methods (or the so-called PEM model of programming) for everything from modifying an object's action to creating an event handler. A lot of VB programming is what can be termed "exception" programming. You're modifying things that need to be different. There's also much in Visual Basic that is classic event-driven programming: error handling, I/O routines, calls to external programs of APIs, and so forth.

People don't generally think about Adobe Illustrator as an IDE, but it is. The language that Adobe Illustrator writes is the Adobe Postscript language, which is a text-based PDL, or page description language. If you opened an AI file, you would see it is text, and that there is a set of Postscript commands that tell the Postscript interpreter, either in your computer's operating system or in your printer, what to do. AI files contain header information that declares the contents to be an Illustrator file, but AI also can save out as a pure Postscript file, most typically saved as Encapsulated Postscript, or EPS. If you knew Postscript, you could edit an AI file and alter the page display that is output to your printer or screen (if you have Display Postscript installed). Editing a file is useful in that it allows you to create effects that aren't possible in Illustrator itself; in fact, many of those effects can be spectacular. Another reason you might want to edit Postscript is that it would allow you to correct any errors the file contained. If your output causes a memory overflow error that brought your printer to a stop, you could adjust the code to solve that problem. Few people program in PostScript these days, but the capability is there.

FrontPage is an IDE, and the results of a FrontPage Web design is HTML output. You look at a graphical design surface shown in Figure 14.1 and drag a textbox or Submit button to the screen, and FrontPage writes the necessary HTML POST code to add that feature to your output file. One FrontPage view is the HTML code that is written, as shown in Figure 14.2, and you can always switch to that view and edit the code. FrontPage offers a lot of features that you've already read about. You can add dynamic effects such as a "hover" button, which FrontPage will create using DHTML. FrontPage supports calls to external programs, JavaScript and VBScript, attachment to data sources, ASP code, ActiveX, and more. Some things such as hit counters, hover buttons, marquees, and many other things are FrontPage "components," elements internal in FrontPage that can be added without programming or external action. Other capabilities require the use of plug-in technology. Among FrontPage's many programming tools you will find a Script Editor for VBScript and JavaScript, a built-in Visual Basic Editor, and developing support for CSS, XML, and other leading-edge features.

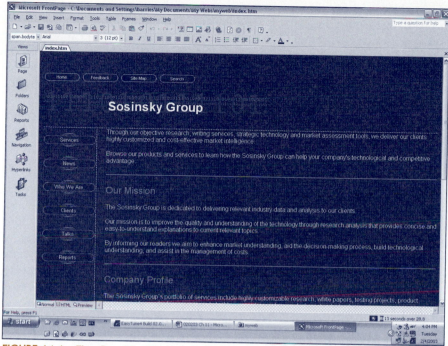

FIGURE 14.1   The Graphical Design Surface for a FrontPage Page

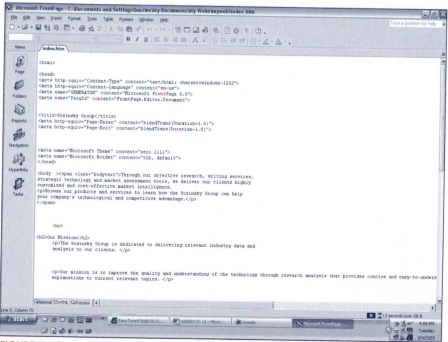

FIGURE 14.2   The HTML Code for the Page Shown in Figure 14.1

In this chapter, then, we are less concerned with how you perform basic tasks in FrontPage, something that is covered in a great many books that you can find in bookstores, and more concerned with the programming capabilities of this product. You've already seen many of these capabilities FrontPage offers done in straight code, but the friendliness of FrontPage can help you experiment with many of its more interesting features. Since HTML is the result, there's nothing stopping you from copying and pasting the appropriate code into your own programs and learning from the results. While many FrontPage features require client-side support in the form of the Windows Personal Web services or server-side support in the form of FrontPage extensions, many do not. You'll find a great many ISPs have servers that support FrontPage.

Unfortunately, FrontPage is a Windows-only product, and must be deployed on a Windows desktop or server. FrontPage Web sites can support browsers on any client, but Macintosh, Linux, and other operating systems require other design tools. In the previous chapter, you saw some of the capabilities of Macromedia Dreamweaver, which is noted for its use of animation. The comparison of the programming features of Dreamweaver to those you find in FrontPage should be instructive.

FrontPage Basics

FrontPage uses a multi-tabbed interface that has three main page views: Normal, HTML, and Preview. Normal is the graphical design surface, HTML is the code the program generates, and Preview is how the page would look in a browser. Using FrontPage you can include XML and ASP code in your pages, as well as XHTML. The only prerequisite for the data to be correctly displayed is that the markup conform to the appropriate rules required by an XML or XHTML parser.

Working with Source Code

You work with source code directly in the HTML view. FrontPage has a color-coding scheme for different coded elements. You'll find that black, which is the default color, is used for any text you type. HTML tags are in blue. Whenever you edit on the HTML tab, this color-coding scheme is observed. You can set Custom Coding from the `Tools` menu using the Color Coding tab of the Page Options dialog box (Figure 14.3), with the following options:

- Normal text. Text that is seen in a browser.
- Tags. The color of the tags.
- Attribute Names. Any attributes in a tag can be differentiated using color.
- Attribute Values. Similarly, color can be applied to a value.
- Comments. Comments are embedded text that is not displayed on the page.
- Scripts. Any script code, be it VBScript or JavaScript, can be color coded.

Tech Tip

Debugging with Colors These visual indicators can be quite useful, particularly in lengthy or complex code. Setting a color can be a good way to search for specific occurrences of code.

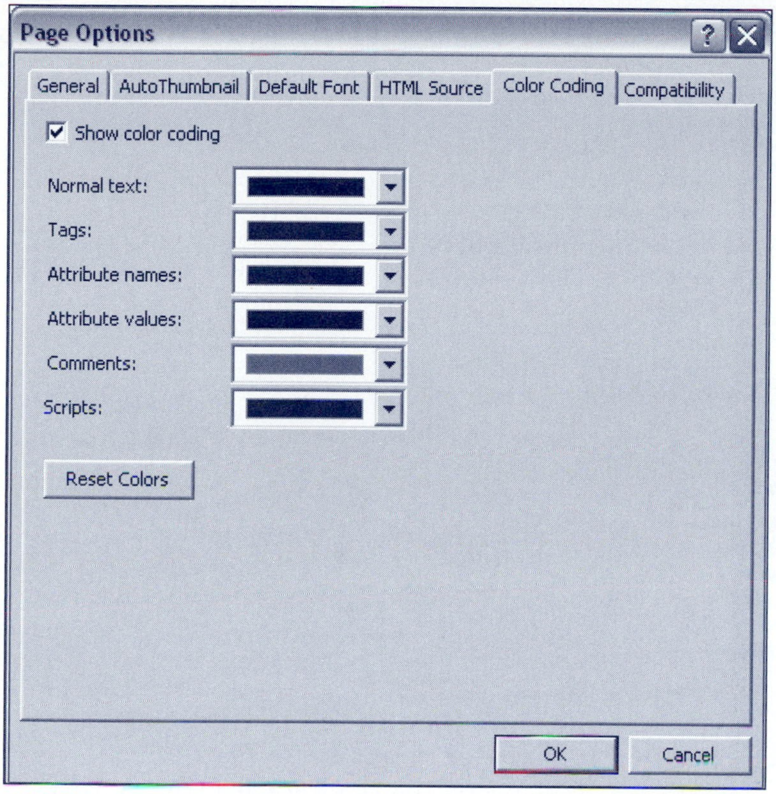

FIGURE 14.3   The Page Options Dialog Box
The Color Coding tab of the Page Options dialog box is used to make the HTML view easier to read and work with.

Another modification you might want to consider for your FrontPage code—be it generated by the program or code you enter into the HTML view yourself—is FrontPage's automatic reformatting option. This feature changes the way your code looks by adjusting the letter case of various elements, providing for indenting of nested code and setting line breaks and margins, among other things. The HTML Source tab of the Page Options dialog box shows these capabilities (see Figure 14.4). Most importantly, you have an option to format all of your current code using the Preserve Existing HTML radio button. Any selections that you make in the Source tab are applied to any pages you create or open from then on. Among the options you can set are line breaks; omitting of either the starting or ending tag; and indenting of contents. (As you learned previously in the Chapter 4 on XML, it isn't a good idea to leave tags unpaired in case you want future compatibility with XHTML.) **Indented code** is particularly useful in that it lets you visually identify blocks of code quickly. Figure 14.5 shows a sample of indented code.

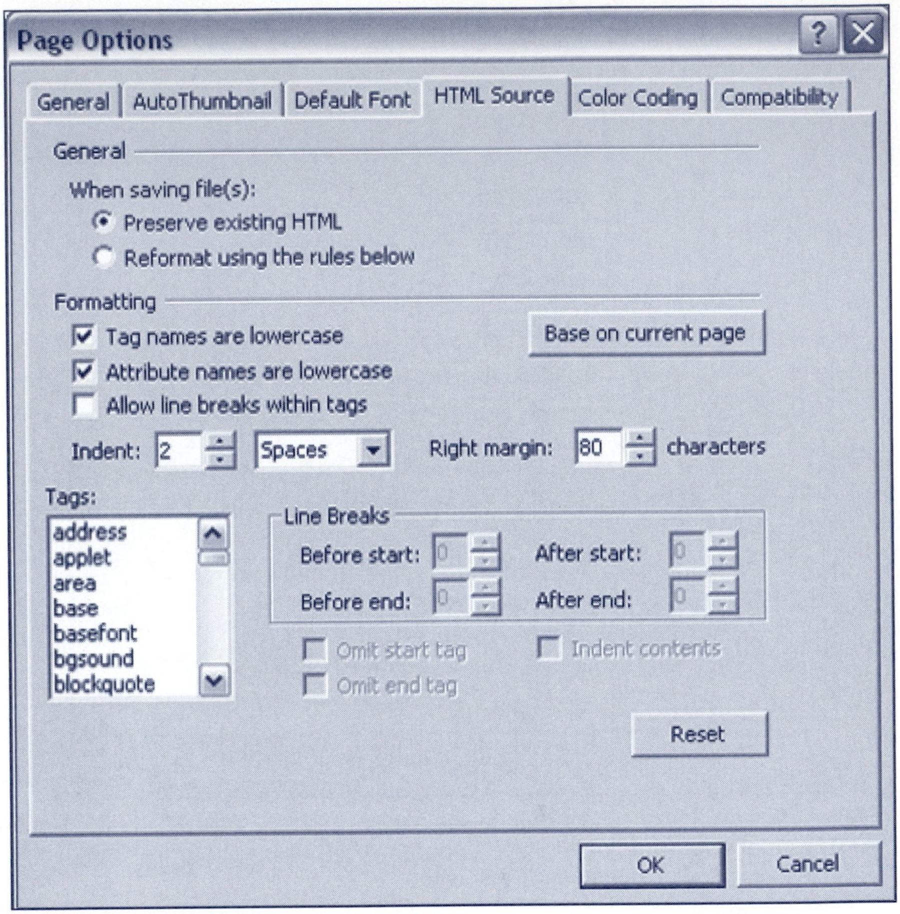

FIGURE 14.4   The Page Options Dialog Box
The HTML Source tab allows you to change the look of your FrontPage source code.

If you include XML code on your page, and you had previously set the formatting so that it didn't conform to XML, FrontPage overrides your settings and fixes the problem. Thus, if you fail to close your tags, FrontPage will do so in any portion of your page where an XML declaration was active.

QuickCheck Questions

1. What are the three different views in FrontPage?
2. Why would you choose to use FrontPage instead of programming your site in an HTML editor?
3. What two methods are there for making your source code easier to read?
4. Why isn't FrontPage available on the Macintosh?
5. What clients can FrontPage Web sites support?

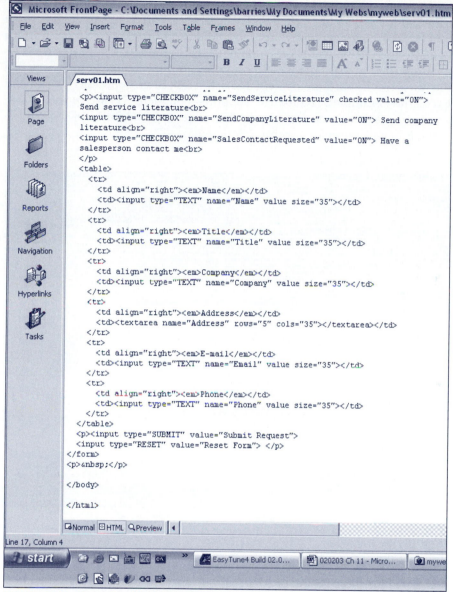

FIGURE 14.5   Example of Indented Code

Indented code is particularly useful in finding sections of code and making sure that your tags are paired.

The Script Editor

FrontPage comes with the Microsoft **Script Editor,** which lets you edit HTML tags and ASP files. This editor is useful to you when you need to work with VBScript or JavaScript that you add to your pages. Figure 14.6 shows some sample code in the Script Editor window. The Script Editor is a better environment for debugging code than FrontPage's HTML view, and it gives you a tool that works cooperatively with other Microsoft programming applications that also use the Microsoft Development Environment. You'll find Script Editor supported in many Microsoft programs, not only language programs like the Microsoft Visual Development Tools, but also Microsoft Office (Word and Excel, for example). FrontPage supports complete HTML preservation, which means that the Script Editor, while once required for careful programming, is mainly there for easier development.

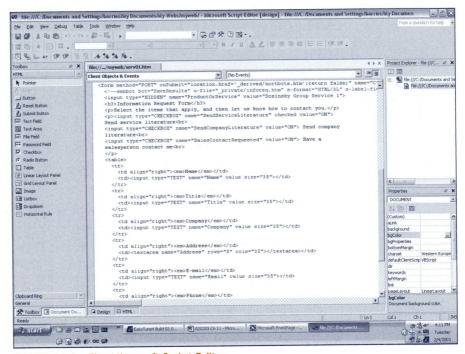

FIGURE 14.6 The Microsoft Script Editor

To open the Script Editor:

- Select the `Microsoft Script Editor` command from the `Macro` submenu on the `Tools` menu.
- Or press the Shift+Alt+F11 keystroke.

By default, the Script Editor opens with your current page's HTML in view. You can add and edit code into this window, and when you do so that code also will be displayed in the HTML view of the program. There are more tools in the Script Editor and no constraint on what you enter. If you make a mistake coding in the Script Editor, the error is retained and expressed until you fix it. Scripts are a lot more particular than HTML code. When you complete your script in the Script Editor, you can run your script from that program.

When you do so, the Script Editor will open Internet Explorer and then run the script. If a problem is detected, you will see an error dialog box that offers to open the **debugger** for you. Undoubtedly you've seen many of these alerts before for scripts on Web sites that don't run properly.

You'll most likely want to use the Script Editor for its debugging feature. For Microsoft Office, the debugger requires specific installation. It isn't part of the standard install. The debugger has four windows:

1. The *Immediate window,* which lets you alter a variable and immediately test your script.

2. The *Watch window,* which lets you watch the results of the watch expressions as the script runs.

3. The *Locals window,* which displays the value of local variables used in the script.

4. The *Autos window,* which automatically identifies variables used in the current and previous statements.

Adding Special Effects

FrontPage makes it easy to add special effects to your pages. You can use the built-in special effects such as page transitions, animation, and many other capabilities, or you can roll your own effects and add the code to FrontPage.

Hover buttons are an example of a built-in effect that you can use as is or create your own. First, let's look at the built-in effect. FrontPage supplies a Java applet that creates a hover button effect. The applet displays a button, and when the button experiences a MouseOver event, it triggers the hover effect. There are seven different effects you can choose from: color fill, color average, bevel out, bevel in, reverse gray, glow, and light glow. To create a hover button, you would do the following:

1. In Normal view, select the `Web Component` command from the `Insert` menu; the Web Components dialog box shown in Figure 14.7 appears.

2. Select `Dynamic Effects` in the Component Types list box, then select `Hover Button` in the Choose an effect list box.

3. Click Finish.

4. FrontPage puts the button on your layout, and opens the Hover Button Properties dialog box shown in Figure 14.8.

5. Select the properties you desire, then click the OK button.

6. Select the `Preview in Browser` command on the `File` menu to view your button's action.

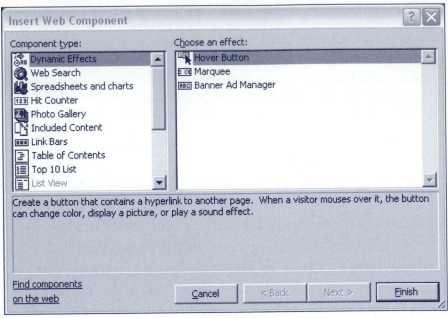

FIGURE 14.7   The Web Components Dialog Box

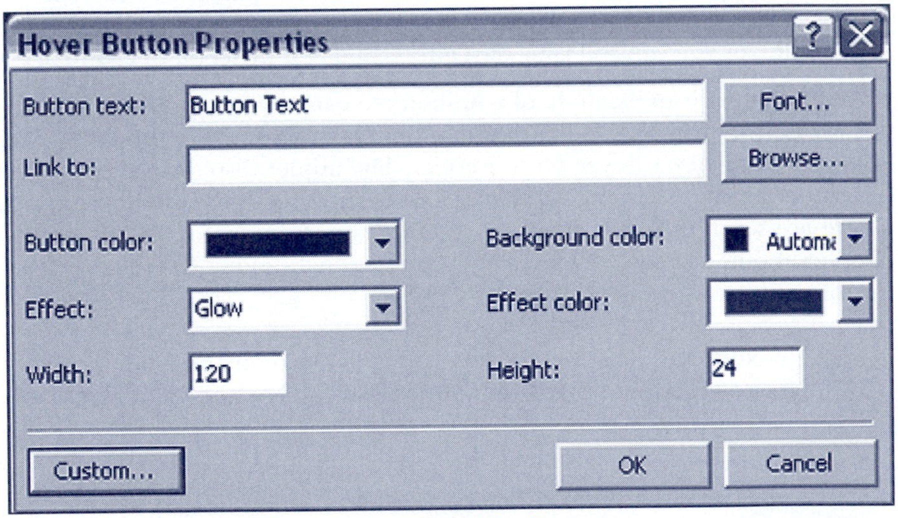

FIGURE 14.8   The Hover Button Properties Dialog Box

Banner ads and **marquees** are inserted similarly. A banner ad is a graphic that changed over time to display two or more ads in the same space. Marquees are moving lines of text.

Many special effects used on the Web are the result of JavaScript programs. A common example is what is known as a hover or a rollover effect. You see this type of special effect most often on buttons. As your mouse moves over the button, it changes its look in some way to indicate that it is the thing that will be activated with a click.

To build a *custom* hover button, you need to have a set of links that reference the location of individual images that represent different states of the button. Those images can be stored in a list, in a table, or wherever you wish. For example, suppose you have a Power button on your screen. There are four states to this button: On and Off without the MouseOver event, and On and Off with the mouse position over the button. Your image references take the form:

```
<img name="Power_On" src="c:/My Webs/images/PowerOn.jpg">
<img name="Power_On_Selected" src="c:/My Webs/images/
   PowerOnSelected.jpg">
```

Go to the Web page that contains the Power button and enter a script into the head section that will load the button images into memory. They are loaded as Image() objects, and the script sets the src properties for each image so that it points to the appropriate image files. An example script would follow this form:

```
<script type="text/javascript">
<!-

if (document.images) {
Power_On = new Image();
Power_On.src =":/My Webs/images/PowerOn.jpg";

Power_On-Selected = new Image();
Power_On_Selected.src =":/My Webs/images/
   PowerOnSelected.jpg";
. . .
}
// ->
</script>
```

In the script above, the if statement is used to differentiate browsers that can preload an Image object from those that can't. When a browser doesn't support this object, the statement is ignored.

Once the Image objects are loaded, the next step is to create the functions that determine the MouseOver event. These functions, which we'll call Selected() and Unselected(), are placed in the script section and determine if the position of the cursor falls in the area that the button occupies. A ButtonState method compares the string that results from the combination of the selection with the src when the name is composed that creates the Image object.

```
function Selected(ButtonState)
{
  If (document.images)
    {
    document[ButtonName].src=ButtonState(ButtonName +
      "PowerOn.src"};
    }
  }

function Unselected(ButtonState)
{
  If (document.images)
    {
    document[ButtonName].src=ButtonState(ButtonName +
      "PowerOn.src"};
    }
  }
```

Finally, you'll need to have the onMouseOver and onMouseOut events in your code. The onMouseOut event will call the `Out()` function, which should be stored with your image-loading references, as follows:

```
<a href="screenname.htm" onMouseOver="Over('Power')"
  onMouseOut="Off('Power')">
<img name="Power" src=" c:/My Webs/images/PowerOff.jpg">
```

Controlling the Presentation of a Document with Style Sheets

Style sheets, as you learned in Chapter 4, let you add colors, fonts, and position objects, and perform many other formatting tasks in a consistent and easily managed way. There are two specifications for style sheets in common use:

- CSS-1, which is the formatting version of Cascaded Style Sheets.
- CSS-2 (see http://www.w3.org/TR/REC-CSS2/), which is the positioning version of CSS.

FrontPage allows you to work with both versions and is one of the leading applications for applying the most recent advances in this technology. FrontPage lets you define your style parameters locally or in a separate template file. To set up an external style sheet, use the `Style Sheet Links` command from the `Format` menu to make the assignment. Figure 14.9 shows the Link Style Sheet dialog box.

FrontPage has an import feature that lets you add a style sheet to one or more pages. You also can add style parameters to page objects, with inline tags for paragraph text styles when you want control over individual pages. Keep in mind that style sheets have heredity, with styles based on another style retaining its properties. You can override any inherited style element in the child style. Also, inline styles will take precedence over any other type of style assignment.

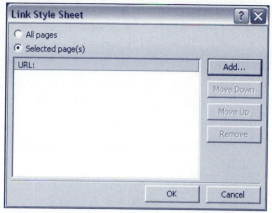

FIGURE 14.9   The Link Style Sheet Dialog Box

Style sheets are supported by Microsoft Internet Explorer 3.0 and above and Netscape Navigator 4.0 and above, with decent support not appearing until versions 5.5 and 6.01 of those two programs respectively. Failure to comply is handled, as many things are in HTML, by simply ignoring the assignment.

Modifying the Rendering of HTML Tags with Style Properties

If you select the `Style` command from the `Format` menu in FrontPage, you open the central Style dialog box, shown in Figure 14.10, where you can assign a style to selected elements on your Web page. It's easier to do this when you select objects in the Normal view than when you try and modify your code.

To create a style, you would click the New button in the Style dialog box, add your desired attributes, and name and save the style; while nested, a dialog box will lead you to the New Style dialog box and its Format section. FrontPage offers a number of canned styles or selectors that you can use, including header, headings, lists, tables, applet, address, and block quotes, among others. One valuable style that lends itself to dynamic interactivity is the `A` style for a hypertext link. There are three defined styles: `A:active` for an active hypertext link, `A:link` for a link that hasn't been used, and `A:visited` for a link that has already been visited. Typically, the colors of each are different, but you can create modifications and save them as user-defined styles.

Client-Side Programming

Much of the early automation associated with Web pages involved programs or scripts that ran on the Web server and required server-side processing. CGI, Perl, and other scripting technologies are primarily server based. While that

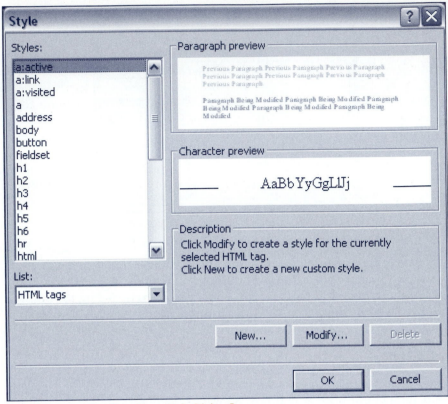

FIGURE 14.10 The FrontPage Style Dialog Box

sort of processing is useful in providing a standard set of results, there are two significant disadvantages of server-side processing over client-side processing. In server-side processing, you are creating significant server loading, which lowers the number of clients that a Web server can serve. The purchase of a more powerful server or, as is more often the case, multiple servers to distribute the load is a significant cost penalty. Additionally, server-side processing forces a uniformity of interaction with the user that runs counter to the desire to create an individual Web site experience.

This is where client-side processing comes in. When you create programs or scripts using something that can be processed inside a browser, you are off-loading the processing required. This lessens your server's requirements, as well as lowering your network loading. You also have the opportunity to create a more custom program based on user interaction. Browsers can support several different types of programming languages. We'll take a brief look at two of them: JavaScript and VBScript. Most browsers support JavaScript, and all operating systems either come with a Java Virtual Machine, or JVM, or can add one. For Microsoft Windows, there's strong support for Visual Basic, and specifically for VBScript in Internet Explorer and the Microsoft Office family of products.

However, this **client-side programming** comes at a cost, and that cost is compatibility. You'll find that many times when you program something in JavaScript that works in Netscape Navigator, it won't work properly or will be ignored in Internet Explorer. It's even more the case that programmed features that you create for Internet Explorer don't work properly or are ignored on Navigator. VBScript won't run at all on Navigator, and there are numerous style issues. Still, these are very popular techniques and developers put up with these incompatibilities to have their sites use special functions—even to the extent of creating or coding separate pages for the two different browsers.

QuickCheck Questions

6. What is a Web component?
7. What advantages does programming in the Script Editor offer?
8. What kinds of style sheets does FrontPage use?
9. Why is client-side programming sometimes preferable to server-side programming?

Enhancing Web Pages Using VBScript

VBScript is essentially a subset of Microsoft's Visual Basic language. You can incorporate VBScript on your FrontPage Web pages. The only significant downside to using VBScript is that it is not supported on Netscape and will not run on that browser. VBScript rendered on Internet Explorer is ignored by Netscape, which is why many developers put an IE logo on their sites or include a phrase something like "This site best viewed with Internet Explorer." For this reason, it is better to develop VBScripts for client-side execution when you know that your clients are going to be using Internet Explorer. If your Web site runs on Microsoft Internet Information Server (IIS), VBScript is a valuable addition to server-side scripting on Active Server Pages.

The main way that VBScripts are added to a FrontPage Web page is to either

- Insert the script directly into your code using the HTML view; or
- Open the Microsoft Script Editor to create the script and insert it using that tool; or
- Use the Visual Basic Editor to create and modify code (see Figure 14.11).

VBScript can be used to create interactive forms and is especially useful for client-side processing tasks. Given local execution, these scripts are typically much faster than those that run server-side, but you lose some of the capabilities of server-side computing such as access to a primary data source (in some cases). Developers also use VBScript for interactive buttons and menus on a page. When a selection is made, the VBScript can alter the page based on a

Tech Tip

VBScript's Range
The range of uses of VBScript in building dynamic Web pages is almost limitless; however, the range of browsers that can successfully process VBScript is not. Only Internet Explorer (3.0 and later) will process these scripts, provided that the VBScript Technology option is selected on the Compatibility tab of the Page Options dialog box. Other browsers don't normally include a VBScript interpreter. Keep in mind also that many Web sites consider VBScript routines to be active content and will disable them due to security issues. Therefore, you will always want to check with your webmaster to find out if VBScripts are allowed.

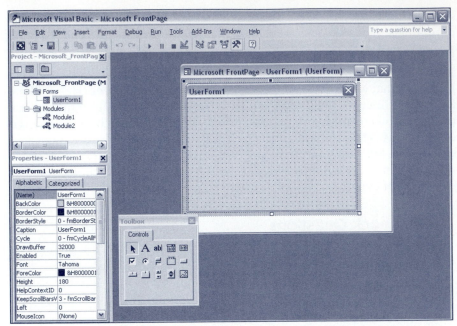

FIGURE 14.11   The Visual Basic Editor

response, again based on client-side processing. You have a wide range of possibilities in how you construct your code, drawing a value from an input field or from a dialog box that the VBScript posts as part of its routine.

VBScript is also useful in supplementing HTML's very modest calculation abilities, as it comes with a much wider range of functions. You'll find VBScript useful not only in applying simple mathematical functions, but in creating custom functions specific to your need at hand. VBScript also can be useful in report preparation. Since VBScript uses client-side processing, it has a speed advantage over CGI. With CGI you suffer the latency of submitting and receiving data to and from the server, as well as the time it takes for the server to process your data. CGI most often presents the data in a spawned window as a results page, something that isn't helpful in creating dynamic page effects. VBScript, on the other hand, requires local processing but can use the results to update or alter the same page.

As an example of how you would use VBScript to update an invoice totals field when the InvoiceTotUpdate button is clicked, you would do the following:

```
<script type="text/vbscript">
...
Sub InvoiceTotUpdate_OnClick()
InvoiceTotal=Subtotal.value + Tax.value + Shipping.value
End Sub
```

```
...(more subs)
</script>
```

For more complex custom VBScripts, you would declare your variables with a set of `Dim` statements, set those variables equal to some value, and perform your calculations on those variables to obtain a result.

If you are using Microsoft Server technologies, IIS, SQL Server, and others, then VBScript is an attractive **server-side programming** language. As you probably recall, with the Active Server Pages files (.ASP pages), you see a recipe for server-side processing that creates dynamic pages on Microsoft Internet Information Server (IIS) that are returned to your browser for viewing. ASP is a favored method of Web database processing and often shows up in reports that you view. The advantage of server-side processing is that since it only returns HTML as its output, any browser can view the results of an .ASP page.

An .ASP page is a text file saved with an .ASP extension. To run a script on the server, you will need to define the script and instead of using the `<script>` `...</script>` tags, you use the `<%` and `%>` delimiters to indicate server-side scripting. For example, you might do the following:

```
Current time <%=Time%>
```

which pulls the current time off of your server. Then, to put the time on your Web page, you would add

```
<HTML>
<HEAD><TITLE>Current time</TITLE></HEAD>
<BODY>
Current time 3/30/2004
</BODY>
</HTML>
```

Notice that your browser doesn't need to know anything about HTML because the scripting is being executed on the Web server.

The Capabilities of XML and XHTML

FrontPage is compatible with both XML and XHTML. As long as your tags are well formed and you maintain appropriate syntax, you can add XML to FrontPage pages, just as you would any other HTML page. The current version of FrontPage (2002) doesn't specifically offer automated features for adding this code, but you can create the code and put that code into your page as you would any other HTML page. FrontPage does have an XML formatting checker. To check your syntax, right-click on the source and select `Apply XML Formatting Rules`. FrontPage will search your code to see that it conforms to XML requirements.

The formatting tool is also useful to convert your code to a form that conforms to XHTML requirements. The only additional requirement for XHTML is that you must add the `<!DOCTYPE>` declaration to your code at the start of your page.

Using Dynamic HTML (DHTML) for Special Effects

Dynamic HTML lets you create special effects, animation, and even live data feeds to liven up your page. Developers use these effects to point out special features, liven up a Web site, and a host of other reasons. What's nice about DHTML is that it is client-side processing and doesn't depend on your server, access to data sources, or complex code. Your page undergoes a live update, generally triggered by a MouseOver or Click event, and once the page is modified, your browser displays the changes.

DHTML support began with Microsoft Internet Explorer and Netscape Navigator in version 4 of both of those products. Microsoft DHTML is implemented using the Internet Explorer object model, which is the model used for browser display, and not the model used for scripting, or for working with Java or ActiveX objects. Usually DHTML is scripted into a FrontPage page. Netscape's version of DHTML is implemented differently than Microsoft's.

A number of DHTML events are included in FrontPage, and you can quickly apply them using the DHTML Effects toolbar, shown in Figure 14.12. In FrontPage 2002, DHTML leverages style sheets, and most animation effects use the JavaScript `animate.js` module.

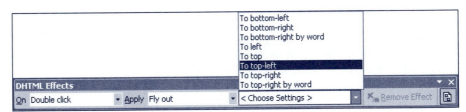

FIGURE 14.12   The DHTML Effects Toolbar

To open the DHTML Effects toolbar:

1. Move the cursor over the object you want to animate. You can animate words, paragraphs, textboxes, table cells, images, and other objects. When you animate an image, you can often substitute alternate images creating an animation effect.

2. Select the `DHTML Effects` command from the `Format` menu.

3. From the `On` drop-down menu, select an event that will start the animation.

4. From the `Apply` drop-down menu, select the effect you want to achieve.

5. Finally, use the `Effects settings` drop-down menu to select the properties associated.

You edit any object that has a DHTML effect applied to it by selecting that object again in the Normal view (which is FrontPage's design surface) and making new selections in the DHTML Effects toolbar. To remove an effect, click on the Remove Effects button on that toolbar.

The following code is generated by a DHTML effect applied to a paragraph. The effect chosen was blinking text triggered by a MouseOver event.

```
<p dynamicanimation="fpAnimformatRolloverFP1"
   fprolloverstyle="text-decoration: blink" onMouseOver=
   "rollIn(this)" onMouseOut="rollOut(this)" language=
   "Javascript1.2"><font face="Arial"><b>Gateway
   Destination 36&quot; TV Monitor w/ Tuner Switch</b>
   </font></p>
```

Notice that the scripts necessary to trigger blinking text are already coded for you using the `fpAnimformatRolloverFP1` JavaScript program (the name of the FrontPage component program module for this effect). You can determine this by examining the `language` attribute. Thus, you can't just copy and paste this code to another program, but you could copy and paste this code to another FrontPage page or Web page.

Commonly used DHTML effects in FrontPage are page transitions. A **page transition** is an effect that is applied to your page whenever you either open or close that page. Among the several effects are **wipes, fades, blinds,** and others. To create a page transition:

1. View the page you wish to apply the effect to.

2. Select the `Page Transition` command from the `Format` menu to view the Page Transitions dialog box, as shown in Figure 14.13.

3. Select the event that will trigger the transition from the `Event` drop-down menu; you can select the Page Enter, Page Exit, Site Enter, or Site Exit event.

4. Select the particular effect from the Transition Effect list box; or select the Random effect to switch between all of the listed effects.

5. Set the duration of the effect by entering the number of seconds in the Duration textbox.

6. Click OK to apply the effect.

Page effects can be applied to a single page, a set of pages, a site, or a style.

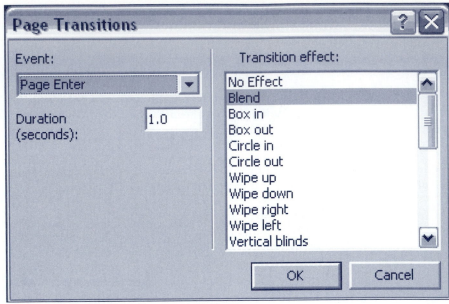

FIGURE 14.13   The Page Transitions Dialog Box

Using JavaScript in FrontPage

JavaScript is a scripting language based on Java, but it is not a subset of Java. Microsoft uses a version of JavaScript that is called JScript, and there have been efforts to standardize between the two by the EMCA. Unlike VBScript, JavaScript enjoys wider browser support and this makes it more suitable for both client-side and server-side scripting; and FrontPage 2002 fully supports JavaScript. One common use of JavaScript is to validate FrontPage forms.

Creating DHTML That Works across Multiple Browsers

Unfortunately, DHTML is still a work in progress. Although it enjoys support from the two major browsers—Internet Explorer and Netscape Navigator (versions 4.0 and above)—even those two browsers don't implement DHTML in a way that makes feature implementation compatible. Netscape's initial additions to DHTML include JavaScript Style Sheets and Layers, but Netscape has moved recently to make their browser more compatible with Internet Explorer. JSS is similar in effect to CSS but uses JavaScript in place of HTML. Since CSS is endorsed by the W3C, JSS is unlikely to achieve widespread support. Using layers, you can achieve positioning of objects, just like CSS-2 or CSS-P does. Microsoft's use of DHTML uses Microsoft's ActiveX technology. Since this is a proprietary technology, many Microsoft effects don't work cross-browser. Microsoft's DHTML centers around visual effects or filter for graphics and text, as well as Dynamic CSS.

Adding Multimedia to Your Web Site

FrontPage allows you to add both audio and video content to your Web pages. Through the use of plug-ins, it is also possible to call external programs such as QuickTime, Shockwave, or Flash that enable you to add animation and many additional special effects and capabilities, as well as draw from an expanding vast library of previous outside work.

Streaming Audio and Video

You can have FrontPage play a background sound whenever a viewer views that page, and the program is also capable of playing MIDI files. This feature is part of the Page Properties dialog box. Most of the time, you will want to add audio files to your pages directly by inserting that file directly on your page. You can insert the following files:

- *WAV files.* WAV files are commonly used on the PC, but not widely supported elsewhere.
- *AU.* Unix supports the AU format, as do most browsers.
- *ASF files.* This is the native format for Windows Media files.
- *RA.* Real Audio files are supported, and require the RealAudio player. You can obtain the free or commercial RealAudio player from www.real.com.

Inserting video clips into your page isn't any different than inserting a picture. You can add video files to your FrontPage Web pages in any one of three different ways:

- *Display the Video as a Picture File.* Internet Explorer will display the video as a picture, but without video (VCR-type) controls. This style creates a link that Netscape can't open.
- *Display the Video Using an ActiveX Control.* You can use a control to display the video. You need to specify which control, or it is the Windows Media Player by default.
- *Display the Video Using a Plug-In.* If this option is selected, the viewer must configure his or her browser so that the plug-in chosen can play this content.

FrontPage and your Web server can deliver that video to a client, but it is up to the browser on the client side to play the video that is sent to it. Among a wide range of formats that FrontPage supports are

- *Audio Visual Interleaved, or AVI, files.* This is a predominantly Microsoft format, but it enjoys wide industry support.
- *QuickTime.* Apple's QuickTime files, which were once called MOV or ActiveMovie files, can be incorporated into pages. To get a QuickTime Player, go to http://www.apple.com/quicktime/.

MPEG files can be played, although you will need an MPEG-capable player to do so. Although FrontPage can display animated GIFs, these files are considered to be rotating pictures, not video files.

Improving Browser Functionality with Plug-ins: Shockwave, Flash

You can add to your browser's capabilities by adding small programs called **plug-ins** that third-party vendors offer. These plug-ins are often called for when you try and download, open, or play a file incorporated into a Front-Page Web page. Thus, if you click on a PDF link, you would be prompted to download Adobe Acrobat's Web component for rendering Portable Document Format files on your screen. Many of these plug-ins are related to multimedia file types. We mentioned QuickTime in the previous section, but you may encounter a number of other useful plug-ins, particularly ones for Shockwave and Flash animation programs. The required plug-ins aren't downloaded, and must be installed first for their content to play correctly. So it's considered good form to include a link or a button containing a link to the location of the plug-in where the reader can download that component.

Microsoft lists downloadable content for its Internet Explorer at the following location: http://www.microsoft.com/windows/ie/download/default.asp. For Netscape, its browser plug-in jump page may be found at http://www.netscape.com/plugins/index.html.

QuickCheck Questions

10. When would you choose to write a script in VBScript?
11. When would you choose to write a script in JavaScript?
12. What types of DHTML effects are available in FrontPage?
13. How do you use some of the functionality in FrontPage in other Web sites?
14. How do you add an MPEG video file to your FrontPage site?

Summary

In this chapter, you learned about some of the capabilities and limitations of Microsoft FrontPage to be customized using programming methods. FrontPage is a member of the Microsoft Office suite of products, and it is meant for users who want to create a full-featured site quickly. Many of the advanced features that you might want to add to a site are preprogrammed for you in FrontPage. Still, it's possible to add very specific and customized features to FrontPage Web sites. In addition to supporting standard HTML as output, FrontPage can support XML, XHTML, ASP, and various combinations of these standards.

Scripting in FrontPage is most often done using either VBScript or JavaScript. Since VBScript is only supported on Windows, if your clients are using other browsers, you might want to avoid it. JavaScript is widely supported and can be used on all major browser platforms. However, there are different ways that programs written in JavaScript are expressed, so there are compatibility issues whatever you use.

You'll find advanced dynamic effects possible using DHTML, and FrontPage offers strong multimedia support for both audio and video content.

Key Terms

banners
blinds
client-side programming
debugger
fades

hover button
indented code
Integrated Development
  Environment (IDE)
marquees
page transition

plug-ins
Script Editor
server-side programming
streaming audio and video
wipes

Review Questions

1. Why did Microsoft include a Web site editor and management tool in Microsoft Office?
2. How do you view the code in a FrontPage Web site?
3. If you want to have the same feature appear on more than one page, what different methods could you use with this program?
4. What support does FrontPage have for styles and style sheets?
5. What advantages does the Microsoft Script Editor offer you over FrontPage's native tools?
6. Describe the advantages of client-side processing, and when it is best used.
7. When does it make sense to use VBScript to automate features?
8. When does it make sense to use JavaScript to automate features?
9. What concerns do you have to attend to in order to ensure compatibility between different leading browsers?
10. Give some examples of good DHTML applications.

Exercises

1. Create a Web site using one of FrontPage's built-in wizards. Describe the special functions that were added by the wizard, and why.
2. On your Web site, apply different dynamic effects to buttons or text on the main page.
3. Using a sound file, apply that sound to the home page as a sound that plays whenever the viewer is on that page. Add that sound as a file to another page on your Web site. Explain how you did all of this, and why you chose the file type, player, or other capabilities you employed.
4. Write a VBScript that closes your application when you click a button. Then create an Exit button that executes this script on your home page.
5. Open the page www.cnn.com in FrontPage. What things do you see in the code that tell you how that site was constructed?

Creating a Virtual Directory

In this appendix, we have presented a step-by-step procedure on how to create a virtual directory. We assume that you would either install Web server software like IIS or PWS in your system or have access to a server that has IIS installed. You can use the Virtual Directory Creation wizard to create a virtual directory. Our illustration is based on Windows 2000 and IIS. In other Microsoft software environments such as Windows 98 and PWS, the screen shots shown below may vary to some degree.

Step 1. Create a directory named `MyASP` in any of your hard drives (for example, the D: drive).

Step 2. Use `Start > Settings > Control Panel` to display the Control Panel screen.

Step 3. Click on the `Administrative Tools`, and select `Internet Services Manager` (as shown in Figure A1.1).

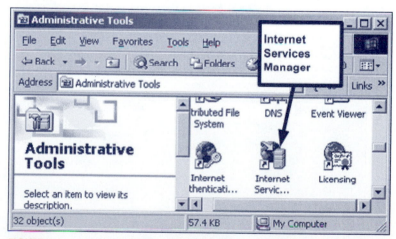

FIGURE A1.1   Internet Service Manager Icon in the Administrative Tools Screen

Step 4. The system will display the Internet Information Services dialog box as shown in Figure A1.2. You will see a Windows Explorer–like tree structure at the left; you also will see a second-level node with your server's name. Expand the server's node and select `Default Web Site`.

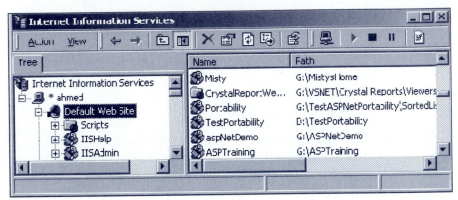

FIGURE A1.2   Internet Information Services Screen

Step 5. Click on `Action > New > Virtual Directory`. The Virtual Directory Creation wizard will display the Welcome screen. Click **Next**.

Step 6. The system will display the Virtual Directory Alias screen as shown in Figure A1.3. Enter an appropriate name like `MyWeb` and click **Next**.

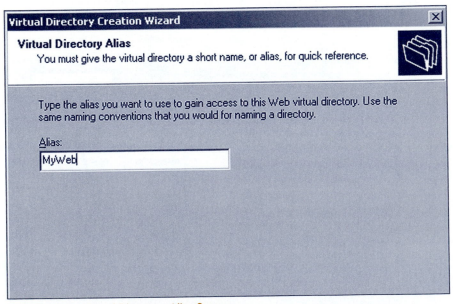

FIGURE A1.3   Virtual Directory Alias Screen

Step 7. The system will display the Web Site Content Directory screen as shown in Figure A1.4. In this screen, you may either enter `D:\MyAsp` or use the Browse button and locate the physical directory that you created in Step 1. Finally, click **Next**.

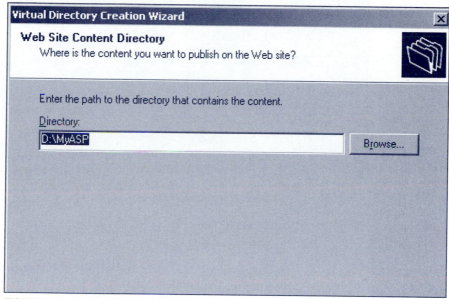

FIGURE A1.4   Web Site Content Directory Screen

Step 8. The system will display the Access Permissions screen as shown in Figure A1.5. Be sure that the Read and Run scripts check boxes are checked, and click **Next**.

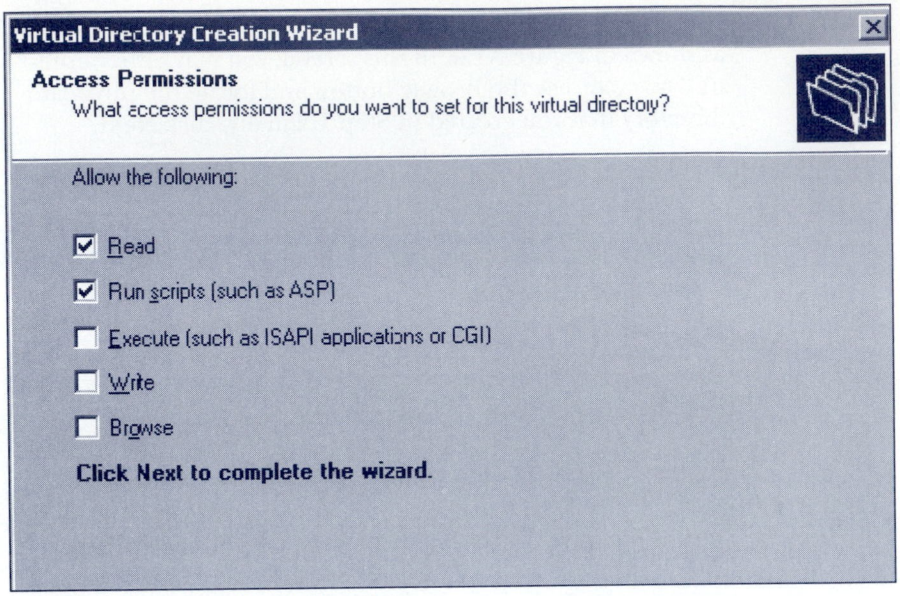

FIGURE A1.5   Access Permissions Screen

Step 9.   The system will display "You have successfully completed the Virtual Directory Creation Wizard". On this screen, click the Finish button. You are done.

Index

Symbols

<![CDATA[...]]> tag, 81

</dl> tag, creating definition lists, 40

<a> tag, targeting frames and, 58–60

<APPLET> tag, 296–297

<area> tag, and client–side image maps, 52–54

<div> tag, 234

<form> tag, 216, 266

  Common Gateway Interface (CGI) forms, 320–323

<h2> tag, 73

<img> tag, working with image attributes, 47–48

<input> tag, data collection with forms, 321–323

<map> tag, and client-side image maps, 52–54

<ol> tag, changing style of numbers, 39

<p> tag, 234

<script> tag, 165, 199

<span> tag, 234

<style> tag, 118

<ul> tag, creating bulleted lists, 39–40

3D, positioning elements and, 239

A

absolute positioning, 237–239

  and HTML commands, 120

Access Permissions Screen, virtual directories and, 381–382

action attributes, 266–268

Active Server Pages (ASP), 259

  vs. HTML pages, 260

  introduction to, 259–260

  procedures and, 263–265

  and Request Object, 266

  Response objects, 272–275

  server-side includes (SSI), 286–288

  syntax of, 262–263

  variables and, 263

ActiveX components, 159

addressing

  Domain Naming Services and, 12–13

  Dynamic Host Configuration Protocol (DHCP) and, 14

  firewalls and, 12

  Internet and, 11–15

  network interface cards (NIC), 12

  and network types, 14

  Uniform Resource Locators (URL), 12–13

algorithms, program design and, 134–135

ALIGN attribute, 297

alignment, character styles and, 123

ALT attribute, 297

Amount.pl, Code listing for, 329–330

anchors, defining relative and absolute anchors, 36–37

Andressen, Marc, 17

animated images, Dancing Baby web site, 53

APACHE, web servers and, 8

Applet class, Java Applet programming, 298

applet security, 307

applets

creating Java applets, 301–305

  embedding an applet into HTML, 296–297

  Hello World program, 303–305

  and Java technology, 294–296

  and life cycle of Java applets, 305–307

  security and, 307

Application objects

  collections, 284

  events, 284

  examples of, 285–286

  methods, 284

application programming interface (API), 157

arguments, and VBScript, 207–208

arithmetic, and VBScript functions, 220

array handling, and VBScript statements, 220

arrays

  and Dim statement, 205

  and program design, 142

  and working with, 169–171

ASCII text format, building web pages, 30

ASF files, 375

ASP objects, 262, 265–286

  Application objects and, 283–286

  and Buffer property, 275

  cookies and, 265, 275–280

  Response objects, 272–275

  Server objects, 281

  Session objects and, 281–283

assignments, and VBScript statements, 220

attributes

  <APPLET> tag and, 297

  action attribute, 266–268

  ALIGN attribute, 297

  ALT attribute, 297

  and border attributes, 120

  CODE attribute, 297

  CODEBASE attribute, 297

  colspan, 65

  creating

    default text style using base font attribute, 45

    frames with cols attribute, 55–56

    frames with rows attribute, 56–57

  elements and attributes in DTDs, 87–88

  Font Size Attribute, 42

  frameborder, 57

  HEIGHT attribute, 297